PROMOTING SOLIDARITY IN THE EUROPEAN UNION

Promoting Solidarity in the European Union

Edited by

MALCOLM ROSS

and

YURI BORGMANN-PREBIL

OXFORD
UNIVERSITY PRESS

OXFORD
UNIVERSITY PRESS

Great Clarendon Street, Oxford OX2 6DP

Oxford University Press is a department of the University of Oxford.
It furthers the University's objective of excellence in research, scholarship,
and education by publishing worldwide in

Oxford New York

Auckland Cape Town Dar es Salaam Hong Kong Karachi
Kuala Lumpur Madrid Melbourne Mexico City Nairobi
New Delhi Shanghai Taipei Toronto

With offices in

Argentina Austria Brazil Chile Czech Republic France Greece
Guatemala Hungary Italy Japan Poland Portugal Singapore
South Korea Switzerland Thailand Turkey Ukraine Vietnam

Oxford is a registered trade mark of Oxford University Press
in the UK and in certain other countries

Published in the United States
by Oxford University Press Inc., New York

First published 2010

British Library Cataloguing in Publication Data

Data available

Library of Congress Cataloging in Publication Data

Data available

Typeset by Newgen Imaging Systems (P) Ltd., Chennai, India
Printed in Great Britain
on acid-free paper by the
MPG Books Group, Bodmin and King's Lynn

ISBN 978–0–19–958318–8

1 3 5 7 9 10 8 6 4 2

Acknowledgements

This book is based on a one-day seminar held at Sussex Law School in May 2008 entitled 'Seeking Solidarity in the European Union—Towards Social Citizenship and a European Welfare State?' We gratefully acknowledge the financial support provided by the Modern Law Review for that event. In addition to the papers included in this volume, the day's proceedings were greatly enriched by the contributions of other participants, in particular Nina Boeger, Michael Dougan, Tammy Hervey, Eleanor Spaventa and Angela Williams. We are also extremely grateful to our Sussex colleague, Sue Millns, for her considerable involvement in planning and organizing the seminar.

Malcolm Ross
Yuri Borgmann-Prebil

Summary Contents

Detailed Contents

List of Abbreviations

BEPA	Bureau of European Policy Advisers
CEE	Central and Eastern Europe
CEPL	Centre for Environmental Policy and Law
CML Rev	Common Market Law Review
CMLR	Common Market Law Reports
CYELS	Cambridge Yearbook of European Legal Studies
DB	Defined Benefit
DC	Defined Contribution
DG EAC	Directorate General for Education and Culture
DG Empl	Directorate General for Employment, Social Affairs and Equal Opportunities
DWP	Department of Work and Pensions
EC	European Community
ECHR	The European Convention on Human Rights
ECJ	European Court of Justice
ECSC Treaty	European Coal and Steel Community
EEA	European Environment Agency
EGF	European Globalization Adjustment Fund
ELR	European Law Review
EMU	European Economic and Monetary Union
ENEA	European Network of Environmental Authorities
EP	European Parliament
ESC	European Social Charter
ESDP	European Spatial Development Perspective
ESM	European Social Model
ESPON	The European Spatial Planning Observatory Network
ETF	European Training Foundation
EU	European Union
EUI	European University Institute
Eur LJ	European Law Journal
FETD	Framework Equal Treatment Directive
GDP	Gross Domestic Product
German LJ	German Law Journal
IGC	Inter-Governmental Conference
ILJ	Industrial Law Journal
ILO	International Labour Organization
IORPs	Institutions for Occupational Retirement Provision
Med L Rev	Medical Law Review
MLR	Modern Law Review
NDC	Notional defined contribution
OECD	Organisation for Economic Co-operation and Development

OJ	Official Journal
OMC	Open Method of Coordination
OUP	Oxford University Press
PAYG	Pay as you go
PICUM	Platform for International Cooperation on Undocumented Workers
PLAs	Peer Learning Activities
QMV	Qualified Majority Voting
TEN-T	Trans-European transport network
TEU	Treaty on European Union
TFEU	Treaty on the functioning of the European Union

List of Contributors

Nafsika Alexiadou holds degrees from the Universities of Hull and Oxford. She is currently Senior Lecturer in the School of Public Policy and Professional Practice, University of Keele.

Karen Anderson holds degrees from the Universities of Virginia and Washington, USA. She is currently Associate Professor of Political Science at Radboud University, Nijmegen.

Catherine Barnard holds degrees from the University of Cambridge and the European University Institute, Florence. She is currently Professor of European Union Law at the University of Cambridge.

Mark Bell holds degrees from the University of Ulster and from the European University Institute, Florence, Italy. He is currently Professor of European and Labour Law at the University of Leicester.

Yuri Bormann-Prebil holds degrees from the Universities of Cologne, East Anglia, and Sussex. He is currently Lecturer in Law at the University of Sussex.

Gareth Davies holds degrees from the Universities of Cambridge, UCL, and Groningen. He is Professor of European Law at the VU University Amsterdam.

Stefano Giubboni holds degrees from the University of Perugia and the European University Institute, Florence. He is currently Professor of Labour Law at the University of Perugia.

Christopher Hilson holds degrees from the Universities of Cambridge and Sheffield. He is currently Professor of Law and Head of the School of Law at the University of Reading.

Jane Holder holds degrees from the University of Warwick. She is currently Reader in Environmental and European Community Law at University College London.

Wolfram Lamping holds degrees from the Universities of Darmstadt and Hannover. He is currently Professor of Politics at the University of Bremen.

Bettina Lange holds degrees from the University of Warwick. She is currently University Lecturer in Law and Regulation at the University of Oxford.

Antonia Layard holds degrees from the Universities of Oxford, Columbia, and the LSE. She is currently Lecturer in Law at Cardiff Law School.

Deborah Mabbett holds degrees from Victoria University of Wellington, New Zealand, and the University of Oxford. She is currently a Reader in Public Policy at the Department of Politics at Birkbeck, University of London.

Clemens Rieder holds degrees from the University of Innsbruck and the University of Notre Dame, USA. He is currently a PhD student and Teaching Fellow at the University of Reading.

Malcolm Ross holds degrees from the Universities of Warwick and Leicester. He is currently Professor of European Law at the University of Sussex.

1

Promoting European Solidarity: Between Rhetoric and Reality?

Yuri Borgmann-Prebil and Malcolm Ross

'Solidarity is part of how European society works and how Europe engages with the rest of the world.'[1] This bold claim, asserted by the European Commission in 2008, is hardly a self-evident truth but one which undoubtedly invites closer scrutiny. Solidarity as an idea, let alone in any distinctively European version, has proved notoriously difficult to pin down despite being a popular target for inquiry across many disciplines and a recurrent focus for the rhetoric of political struggle or ideology. Indeed, one study of solidarity a decade ago observed, 'it would be wrong to speak of an *embarras de richesse* with respect to theories on solidarity'.[2] All too often, according to a much more recent commentator, the result of having a tantalizing array of wide and narrow definitions of solidarity is that 'authors do not argue for a correct, but rather for a sound, use of the term'.[3] Today, in addition to the considerable intellectual challenges presented by such divergent and contested views, there is a further reason for exploration of solidarity as a timely concept. The numerous references to solidarity in the Lisbon Treaty[4] inexorably invite renewed political, judicial and scholarly interest.

Indeed, both the perceived necessity of the European Union (EU) constitutional debate as well as its failure, especially in the French Referendum of May 2005, have been linked, respectively, to either a need for[5] or the absence of,[6]

[1] Commission (EC), 'Renewed Social Agenda: Opportunities, Access and Solidarity in 21st Century Europe' (Communication) COM (2008) 412, 6.

[2] K. Bayertz, 'Four Uses of Solidarity' in K. Bayertz (ed) *Solidarity* (Berlin: Springer, 1999) 3.

[3] S. Derpmann, 'Solidarity and Cosmopolitanism' (2009) 12 Ethical Theory and Moral Practice 303, 305.

[4] Notably, but not only, in Arts 2–3 Consolidated Version of the Treaty on European Union, OJ [2008] C115/13.

[5] J. Fischer, 'From Confederacy to Federation: Thoughts on the Finality of European Integration', speech delivered at the Humboldt University Berlin, 12 May 2000, available at <http://www.auswaertigesamt.de/diplo/en/Infoservice/Presse/Reden/Archiv/2000/000512-FromConfederacyto.html>also J. Habermas, 'Why Europe needs a Constitution' (2001) 11 Sep New Left Review 5, available at <http://www.newleftreview.org/?getpdf=NLR24501&pdflang=en>.

[6] For an interesting perspective on the reasons of the failure of the referenda see A. Philippopulous-Mihalopoulos, 'When "No" means "Yes": A Constitution for Europe and the

(European) solidarity. Either way, the increased invocation of solidarity appears to reflect a 'crisis' mentality increasingly dominant across many levels of contemporary discourse. Such crises may be perceived in relation to a range of settings: for example, over what 'Europe' is for, or because of feelings of economic insecurity or loss of identity. Such attitudes may be determined by searches for counterpoints to the (malevolent) marches of neo-liberalism and globalization, sentiments likely to be exacerbated by collapsing financial systems and their consequences. In the particular context of the EU, liberalization of markets has deeply affected national systems of welfare provision and public services that were previously 'closed' without, it seems, replacing them with any coherent European-level facility. The relevant 'crisis' here usually consists of threats to solidarity itself (however that term is understood).

This volume accordingly engages with three broad questions that arise from this background: how solidarity can be meaningfully theorized for the modern EU context, the extent to which solidarity manifests itself (actually or potentially) in EU policies and relations between the EU and member states, and how far forms of solidarity might be translated into a lived experience through institutional practices and governance models. In addressing these questions, contributors consider the positioning of solidarity against more familiar or well-established building-blocks in the evolution of the EU, such as citizenship, free movement, equality and non-discrimination. These relationships, it will be noted, are not always in harmony. At the same time, the limitations of solidarity are highlighted by exploration of its ambivalences as a concept and the political forces to which it is inevitably subject when sitting at the intersection of market and social priorities on one hand and supranational and national competences on the other. Particular policy areas, such as healthcare, education, immigration and pensions, illustrate the tensions of solidarity-oriented approaches.

The chapters in this volume, all of which were presented as papers at a workshop held in May 2008 at Sussex Law School, bring together perspectives on these questions from law, political science and sociology. These interdisciplinary insights provide different interpretations of the scope for the institutionalization of solidarity, ranging from the dissection of the case law of the Court of Justice and policy initiatives of the European Commission to the analysis of how national systems of welfare, pensions funding and education respond to Europeanization through purported solidarity. In this sense the chapters point to the problems besetting the development of any distinctive thread of European social justice constructed on the basis of solidarity. However, solidarity is not just presented as a concept of intrinsic interest and importance in its own right but also as a fresh, illuminating tool with which to analyze contemporary challenges such as

Limits of Ignorance' in, H. Petersen, A. Kjaer, H. Krunke and M. Madsen (eds) *Paradoxes of European Legal Integration* (Aldershot: Ashgate, 2008) 29.

environmental protection and other nascent paradigms recognized by the Lisbon Treaty such as territorial cohesion.

As should perhaps be expected for productive scholarly exchange, the chapters provide contrasting outlooks concerning the value, viability and vitality of solidarity in political and legal contexts. These concerns about where solidarity sits along the spectrum from rhetoric to reality do not divide along disciplinary lines. Thus the considerable scepticism from political scientists about getting solidarity off the ground, as it were, is matched by at least one lawyer's reservations about the justiciability of solidarity as a legal concept. These positions may be set against the arguments for a reinvigorated or reworked concept of solidarity as a core constitutional value or pivotal foundation for notions of fairness and social justice presented by a number of authors in the brief summaries that follow.

Solidarity—A New Constitutional Paradigm for the EU?

The theoretical antecedents of solidarity are set out by Malcolm Ross, taking as his departure point Stjernø's seminal study on the history of solidarity as an idea[7] and drawing attention to the heightened contemporary interest in the conceptualization of solidarity among social theorists, philosophers, political scientists and other disciplines. Ross understands the motivation of these concerns often to be the quest for an antidote to current conditions characterized by individualism and consumerism. Trying to find a functioning theory of European solidarity is thus a reaction, and perhaps answer, to a (perceived) loss of social integration. Whilst acknowledging recurring commonalities amongst significant historical theorizations of solidarity, in particular the presence of some unifying characteristic defining (and bonding) the solidaristic group and a moral dimension in a commitment to act for the benefit or interests of that group as a whole, Ross rejects the suitability of any single 'essentialist' notion of solidarity as a helpful means to understand the modern, transnational and cosmopolitan-leaning, EU.

Instead, at its core, Ross' chapter conceptualizes European solidarity by portraying its multilayered character as a virtuous circle of reinforcement comprising creation, expression and sustainability. He sees value in this model on three levels: as a way of locating a distinctively European form of solidarity that gives shape to otherwise direction-less cosmopolitan tendencies; as recognition of the dynamic inter-relatedness of both theoretical and 'experienced' solidarity and, thirdly, as a rival to other discourses competing for

[7] S. Stjernø, *Solidarity in Europe: The History of an Idea* (Cambridge: Cambridge University Press, 2005).

political popularity and prevalence, especially security. These are ambitious claims, and Ross concedes that the actual working out of this virtual circle can only be tested empirically—a task for further interdisciplinary study—and in particular policy contexts (some of which are developed by other contributors to this volume).

What Ross does try to defend in more detail is that it is law which forms the key to the expression of solidarity in this virtuous circle, hence his claim that solidarity is a viable *constitutional* principle. To support the credibility of his arguments that solidarity already has a persistent but diverse presence in EU law, Ross draws upon evidence from the *acquis communautaire* provided by the Court of Justice and EU legislation, plus enumeration of the possibilities opened up by references to solidarity in the Lisbon Treaty. Whilst not making any claims that solidarity is a unique *deus ex machina* to solve the market-social tension at the heart of the EU's future direction, Ross insists that developing solidarity has the power to provide different answers from analyses that focus exclusively upon citizenship and/or fundamental rights. These two latter concepts could embrace somewhat divergent views of solidaristic bonds. On the one hand, citizenship may take a different view of what comprises 'us' vis-à-vis 'them' or the extent of what the duties and responsibilities of membership, or the treatment of non-members, might be.[8] Fundamental rights approaches, on the other hand, are likely to have some universalizing tendencies[9] and may envisage human qualities or minimum standards that might be too thinly spread to justify traditional descriptions of solidaristic groupings.

Ross' chapter may make uncomfortable reading for critics of the Court of Justice for part of his position relies upon the 'effectiveness' agenda and general creativeness of that institution as a reason for believing that solidarity is a constitutional paradigm waiting to be unveiled.[10] However, as Ross readily acknowledges, the Court's track record on weighing market and social priorities is hardly loaded (as yet) in favour of the latter.[11] Nor can the sustainability element of Ross' virtuous circle exist without solidarity being translated into political fact through legitimating processes. The later chapters in this volume that explore solidarity practices are thus particularly relevant to the development of this point.

[8] For a recent valuable addition to a wide literature, see J. Ciprut (ed) *The Future of Citizenship* (Cambridge MA: MIT Press, 2008).

[9] See M. Dembour, *Who Believes in Human Rights?* (Cambridge: Cambridge University Press, 2006), especially ch 6.

[10] cf the 'fundamental status' of citizenship revealed in Case C-184/99 *Grzelczyk* [2001] ECR I-6193, para 31.

[11] See the approach of the Court towards balancing fundamental rights and the single market rights of establishment and services in Case C-438/05 *Viking* [2007] ECR I-10779 and Case C-341/05 *Laval* [2007] ECR I-11767.

Mission Impossible? Limits and Perils of Institutionalizing Post-National Social Policy

By way of a sharp contrast from Ross' perception of solidarity as a legal bombshell waiting to be detonated, Wolfram Lamping provides an introduction to the potency of the concept of solidarity from a distinctly sceptical political science perspective. He does so by critically engaging with (the realisms of) a rights-based pan European solidarity identified by Habermas as a significant characteristic and instrument of a European identity.[12]

For Lamping, solidarity means primarily the establishment of redistribution and non-discriminatory public services to achieve specific social policy ends (more social justice, equity, equality). However, he adopts Vollaard's position that such solidarity 'can only be sustained in closed communities'.[13] Lamping's chapter accordingly starts from the premise that national welfare systems are still the fundamental mechanism of social closure. The reasons for this, Lamping identifies, are that social rights are traditionally associated with a common history, homogeneity, and a common identity which goes hand in hand with a willingness to accept the redistribution of costs of social policies. This premise is, however increasingly being eroded by European integration which leads to the necessity to assess the political and social repercussions of the erosion of national sovereignty over the social, and, what is more, the need to theorize a possible conceptual restating of the welfare state at the supranational level. This is not least the case because member state social policy developments cannot be understood without taking EU policies into consideration.[14]

Lamping uses a number of 'boundary-shifting' processes and conceptualizations to advance his argument. These are a 'bi-directional regime enlargement', whereby the supranational level impacts upon national policy and vice versa; a process of 'de-nationalisation and de-territorialisation'; a redefinition of 'internal fraternity and external *un*fraternity' whereby solidarity will no longer be an exclusively national concept; a simultaneous process of 'supranational integration and national disintegration' and an ongoing power shifting, including and resulting from power struggles between the EU and the member states. According to Lamping the boundary shifting is at a 'critical juncture', with the European welfare states being in a state of transition which is characterized by a high degree of strategic uncertainty.

[12] J. Habermas, 'Das illusionäre "Nein der Linken"', Blätter für deutsche und internationale Politik (2005) 755–757; 'Europa: Vision und Votum', Blätter für deutsche und internationale Politik (2007) 517–520.

[13] H. Vollaard, 'Solidarity, Territoriality, and Healthcare: Cross-National Policy Learning in Europe' in D. Levi-Four, and E. Vigoda-Gadot (eds) *International Public Policy and Management* (New York: Marcel Dekker, 2004) 267.

[14] See the contributions from Anderson and Mabbett, also political scientists.

Moreover, for Lamping the notion of a European social policy may not just amount to 'mission impossible'; there could even be real dangers from holding out too high expectations as to the power of solidarity in relation to the furtherance of a 'Social Europe'.[15] Indeed, Lamping is careful to warn of the risks of confusing or conflating individual rights with solidarity. As he notes, citizens' attitudes to the EU appear so far to be more instrumental than emotional—in other words a lack of the need for commitment also identified by Ross' theorization of solidarity.

Solidarity and the Commission's 'Renewed Social Agenda'

Catherine Barnard's contribution provides a rather more detailed appraisal of the relationship between solidarity and the construction of 'Social Europe' than the more abstract analyses of Ross and Lamping. She focuses on the policy positions represented by the European Commission's use of solidarity in two recent documents: *Opportunities, Access and Solidarity: towards a new social vision for the 21st Century* (2007) and *The Renewed Social Agenda: Opportunities, Access and Solidarity* (2008). In her examination of how exactly solidarity connects with 'opportunities' and 'access', Barnard treats the Commission's policy orientation as strongly imbued with Third Way thinking.[16] Thus, rather than placing an emphasis upon greater equality through redistribution of wealth (equality of outcomes), such thinking stresses the goal of the eradication of social exclusion (equality of opportunities). Indeed, as Barnard recalls, the concept of a 'social market economy' that is central to the Lisbon Treaty comes from that particular mould.

In her own theorizing of solidarity, Barnard picks up and draws on some of the literature surveyed by Ross, eg especially Stjernø's *Solidarity in Europe*.[17] She argues that the concept of solidarity, as used by the Commission, does at least contribute to proffering some degree of social justice as a counterweight to the market orientation of the Lisbon Agenda.[18] Solidarity is identified as a guiding principle not only behind the cohesion policies—eg the cohesion, structural and solidarity funds are referred to by the Commission as instruments of solidarity—but also for legislation. Barnard's discussion of the Commission's Citizens' Agenda of 2006 confirms that Ross' supposition that the renewed interest in

[15] For early origins, see Commission (EC) 'White Paper on Social Policy' COM (94) 333 for an elaboration of the values underpinning the 'European Social Model'. Barnard's contribution details subsequent developments.

[16] A. Giddens, *The Third Way and its Critics* (New York: Wiley, 2000).

[17] n 7, above.

[18] See the Lisbon Presidency Conclusions, 23–24 March 2000. The Agenda, re-launched in 2005, made the somewhat extravagant claim to make the EU 'the world's most competitive and dynamic knowledge-based economy' by 2010.

solidarity can be ascribed to the (perceived) capacity of the concept to serve as an antidote to individualism and consumerism associated with globalization, is certainly accurate with regard to the Commission. The Commission refers in this document to solidarity as the 'most unifying and fundamental value'.

Yet, as Barnard points out, this commitment to solidarity may not be entirely convincing. The original drafts of the Commission's 2007 Social Vision Communication[19] omitted solidarity altogether and referred only to opportunities and access. This would be tantamount to a neoliberal[20] view of the Third Way—throwing in solidarity as well gives the combined trio of objectives a distinct European twist. Although the 2007 document and its successor in 2008 endorse and propound solidarity, Barnard remains somewhat sceptical as to the practical effect of its inclusion.

In a close analysis of the 2008 paper from the Commission, Barnard uncovers that solidarity is used as a goal or objective, as an interpretative or guiding tool, as a means, a process and finally as an instrument, perhaps echoing Ross' view of the pervasiveness of the concept in EU law already. Like Ross, Barnard flags up the need to address the linkages between solidarity and fundamental rights, in particular in the context of individual and collective rights. At the same time, Barnard clearly shares Lamping's reservations about the work solidarity can be realistically expected to do. As she argues, how can solidarity—in any of its guises—possibly combat poverty?

Barnard's position, in tone at least as well as in some substantive respects, occupies a middle ground between the two opening chapters. On the one hand she agrees that solidarity is an active work-in-progress and that, even with its amorphous and multifaceted nature, it does constitute a distinctive feature of the European social model(s). On the other, she is highly doubtful about the connection between policy documents such as those produced by the Commission and citizens' confidence in the EU. The institutionalization of solidarity and its translation into policies and practice in a variety of contexts provide the focus for subsequent chapters.

The Price of Letting Courts Value Solidarity: The Judicial Role in Liberalizing Welfare

Gareth Davies targets the Court of Justice in his contribution, boldly claiming that its approach to restrictions on market freedoms and competition demonstrates only that 'solidarity is the blanket under which... furtive communitarianism takes place'. For Davies, liberalizing formerly public services threatens solidarity and national finances less than it threatens subtle communitarian

[19] COM (2007) 726.

[20] See generally, D. Harvey, *A Brief History of Neoliberalism* (Oxford: OUP, 2007).

values embodied in shared institutions. Davies draws his examples mainly from the burgeoning case law on access to welfare services. In his view, the institutions of the welfare state offer the broadest and deepest form of shared experience. He contrasts 'functional' justifications of restrictions, which tally with accepted derogations in the free movement case law, from 'communitarian' justifications, which the Court does not explicitly address because they are 'too amorphous for judicial review and are often a euphemism for protectionism or even nationalism'. The result is that solidarity becomes a cipher for these communitarian reasons, a justification for different rules to apply. However, Davies argues, the Court of Justice covers its respect for, and deference to, national institutions under the cloak of less-than-convincing arguments about solidarity expressed in the language of financial concerns.

Far from being the constitutional adjudicatory principle suggested by Ross, therefore, Davies is effectively arguing that solidarity is not easily justiciable and that its value is restricted to a less than transparent function. There are many legitimate reasons for restricting competition and individual choice which can be expressed in 'narrowly functional terms to provide the highest-quality services at the lowest cost to all customers'. The reasons are rather communitarian in nature in that they are associated with building relations and cohesion in society. Davies borrows from Rothstein[21] and suggests these reasons can best be expressed as social capital. These issues are normally, ie in other jurisdictions, not conducive to judicial settlement but rather political questions.

In building his argument, Davies draws on Hirschman's insight, formulated in his seminal work *Exit, Voice and Loyalty*[22], that, in monopolistic markets, a limited exit option may actually suit the monopolist in that it provides an opportunity for the more demanding, critical, and resourceful consumers to leave. This prevents them from raising their voice and to demand change from the provider. In other words, losing the most expensive customers comes with certain advantages for the provider. This, Davies, submits, is applicable to the current state of EU law on access to health services in other member states allowing for limited exit options for a selected few. According to Hirschman's paradigm, such a development leads to a deterioration of the service provided, ie limited competition from a health system of another member state may therefore endow a national health system with a 'freedom to deteriorate'. This is the more troubling as those customers who may benefit from this limited competition are not only those who are best suited to look after their own interests but also those most competent to exert political power. Thus, their loss of voice is significant in that those exiting customers would have been those best placed to demand improvement of the system.

[21] B. Rothstein, 'Social capital in the social democratic welfare state' (2001) 29 Politics and Society 207.

[22] A. Hirschman, *Exit, Voice and Loyalty—Responses to Decline in Firms, Organisations and States* (Cambridge, MA: Harvard University Press, 1970).

In his concluding remarks, Davies briefly points to alternative interpretations of the meaning of European solidarity. One is to regard the liberalization of the welfare services as a sign (or marker) of Europe's maturity in the sense that member states no longer rely exclusively on closed institutions for the provision of welfare. The other alternative interpretation, and this tallies to some extent with the Commission's Third Way policy orientation identified by Barnard, is to construe welfare service liberalization as an expression of an emerging European welfare solidarity which renders members states part of a 'wider community of states committed to welfare and solidarity' on a larger scale. Or, to use the language of cohesion that Davies himself thinks difficult for courts to engage with, retaining an appropriate degree of *national* freedoms might itself forge the bonds and strength of cohesion—and solidarity.

When Patients Exit, What Happens to Solidarity?

Clemens Rieder's chapter also uses Hirschman's paradigm in order to elucidate the Court of Justice's healthcare case law. The object of Rieder's contribution is to explore whether or not the limited exit option for patients really imperils solidarity in the sense of the functioning of *national* healthcare systems. In other words, Rieder's concern is less with the possibilities of supranational solidarity but more with the potential inequalities or injustice that may result from national systems being allegedly undermined by the supranational entitlements acquired by individuals in terms of their free movement rights.

To test this, Rieder adopts Hirschman's theory but in perhaps a more upbeat fashion than Davies. For example, unlike the latter, Rieder points out that that those patients who exit retain, at least to the extent that they are also nationals of their home health system, the right to vote and might therefore raise their voice effectively in spite of having exited for treatment. At the same time, Rieder questions whether Hirschman's notion of loyalty explains the fact that the vast majority of Europeans are not leaving for treatment in another member state. He argues that this phenomenon has less to do with loyalty and more with coercion. Certain groups of society are coerced to stay because of linguistic, spatial and financial barriers as well as because of an information deficit. This is concerning because only a vocal minority benefits from mobility and, on top of this, diverts resources from the poorly represented groups of society.

However, in spite of potentially undermining solidarity within a national society, the exit of a limited vocal few could be justified if it generated benefits for society as a whole. The obvious benefit lies in the potential to reform a flawed health system. Rieder does attribute a potential, to at least start a debate and perhaps trigger reform, to the case law of the European Court of Justice on healthcare mobility. Although the exit option confers a right on individuals and relieves them from the onerous burden of having to lobby for change from within the system, the significance of the European Court of Justice's case law in this area is that it not only identifies the conditions of exit. What is more, the publicity surrounding often high profile cases such as *Watts*[23] is tantamount to an element of voice, which, Rieder argues, may sensitize the political elite to problems inherent in the system (eg long waiting lists in the UK). Thus, therein lies 'judicial opportunity' in the Court's case law, which is a form of exercising voice.

Rieder's application of Hirschman's theory seems to canvas the view that national solidarities themselves are not inevitably 'in crisis' because of the beginnings of a partial EU healthcare framework. This, of course, does not resolve the question of where this leaves transnational, European, solidarity. Rieder's conclusion, however, is not in itself opposed to the potential in supranational solidarity perceived by other authors—indeed, in so far as he believes that national solidarity systems are not corroded, Rieder implicitly perhaps acknowledges that some form of mixed (and mutually beneficial) forms of solidarity might be capable of emerging. In this sense, Rieder's conclusions resonate with Lamping's observations about 'bi-directional regime enlargement'.

EU Environmental Solidarity and the Ecological Consumer: Towards a Republican Citizenship

Chris Hilson's chapter makes a claim for ecological citizenship by exploring the link between European citizenship and environmental solidarity. He contrasts the collective nature of institutionalized environmental solidarity in the EU with individualistic, or rights based, market and social citizenship and solidarity which has emerged from the Court's case law. A number of recent policy initiatives by the Commission[24] and Presidency[25] as well as many references to solidarity in the Lisbon Treaty[26] are taken as evidence of an increasing collective EU environmental solidarity. Hilson suggests that these references to environmental solidarity could be understood as endeavours to engender or strengthen a European identity. This linkage is clearly intelligible in the light of the first of the traditions of solidarity identified by Stjernø, ie the macro phenomenon of 'binding society together', and which is also noted in the first chapter by Ross.

Hilson advances a claim for ecological citizenship in which the consumption choices of the 'ecological citizen consumer' figure as acts of solidarity, rather than 'merely self-interested activity'. Ecological citizens go beyond ethical

[23] Case C-372/04 *Watts* [2006] ECR I-4325.

[24] eg 'Europe 2010: A Partnership for European Renewal: Prosperity, Solidarity and Security' COM (2005) which refers to the EU's sustainable development objective in the context of solidarity.

[25] eg the Presidency conclusions of 8/9 March 2007 underpin 'the spirit of solidarity' between member states with regard to energy supply.

[26] eg Art 122(2) TFEU contains an explicit reference to solidarity in relation to energy.

to political consumerism, in that their purchasing choices are underpinned by justice-based duties. The ecological citizen is acting 'solidaristically out of concern for the potential environmental harm she may be causing to other current humans and also future generations.' For Hilson this is tantamount to political participation, albeit not to replace democratic institutions. This provides an interesting and novel perspective which is somewhat contrary to the positioning of solidarity as an antidote to individualism and consumerism as suggested in the contributions by Ross and, to some degree, Barnard. Instead, Hilson portrays consumerism and individualistic consumer choices as a *means and expression of* solidarity rather than as something that needs to be addressed, redressed, or even counteracted, through acts of solidarity.

In order to formulate his argument, Hilson relies on and further develops an understanding of environmental solidarity that is both different and broader than conventional conceptions. Instead of drawing on the redistribution of resources as traditionally associated with solidarity,[27] Hilson's notion of environmental solidarity comprises 'a just avoidance of bads such as pollution' (a proposition also endorsed by Holder in the concluding chapter to this volume). These broader solidarity type duties, though exercised in the private sphere of the market, tally, according to Hilson, with a republican model of ecological citizenship. In contrast with orthodox accounts of republicanism which associate the political with the public sphere, he argues that, for the ecological citizen, there is no rigid disjunction between the private and the public. Similarly, consumerism can act as a locus for practising and encouraging citizenship virtues, which is also a central tenet of republicanism. Hilson thus distances himself somewhat from Advocate General Fennelly's definition of solidarity, which is also referred to by Barnard, as an 'inherently uncommercial act of *involuntary* subsidisation of one social group by another'.[28] Hilson, not unlike Rieder in his chapter with regard to the application of Hirschman's notion of loyalty, regards obligated solidarity as a weaker variant of the term. A parallel argument is made concerning the question whether reciprocity is a necessary ingredient of solidarity of acts of the ecologically acting consumer. Hilson bases the unilateral duty not to pollute on causal responsibility instead.

Furthermore, he acknowledges that, like citizenship, solidarity is usually regarded as territorially bounded, the normal container being the nation state where there is congruence between cultural and historic identity and citizenship/solidarity. However, he argues that whilst this congruence might be a requirement with respect to solidarity-based (re)distribution of 'goods', this is not the case for the duty to avoid harm or 'bads' which oblige the ecological citizen. This duty, he contents, is not implicated with state-based territorial assumptions but

[27] Like Ross and Barnard, Hilson also refers to the seminal work by Stjernø, n 7 above, who defines solidarity as the preparedness or duty to share resources.

[28] Case C-70/95 *Sodemare v Rgione Lombardia* [1997] ECR I-3395, para 29 of Opinion, emphasis added, both here and in Hilson's citation.

requires a broader geographical compass. In this regard, Hilson's stipulation of solidarity tallies to some extent with that advocated by Habermas as elaborated by Lamping's earlier contribution.

For these reasons, from the perspective of the ecological consumer, there is less of a tension between solidarity and the market citizen than is frequently portrayed in the literature or as is often present in the case law before the Court of Justice. Indeed, Hilson concludes by suggesting that the ecological consumer is actually a 'market actor who is able to act perfectly in tune with solidarity'.

Irregular Migrants: Beyond the Limits of Solidarity?

Mark Bell's analysis of solidarity reflects recurrent issues in solidarity both generally and in the EU context. On the one hand, his focus on irregular migrants provides a further assessment of the relationship between solidarity and EU citizenship. At the same time, Bell's use of fundamental rights, especially human dignity, provides an opportunity to revisit the universal/particular debate and the extent to which solidarity can be meaningfully conceptualized in human terms rather than more narrowly defined groups. Moreover, in analysing the extent of solidarity duties owed to irregular migrants within the EU, Bell also questions the territorial confines of solidarity.

Bell addresses the link between solidarity and fundamental rights flagged up by both Ross and Barnard. However, Bell's utilization of fundamental rights as a source of solidarity contrasts with the point of departure of Lamping's chapter which argues against the possibility of a rights-based European solidarity, as advocated by Habermas. Interestingly though, Bell interprets the case law of the Court of Justice on the rights of citizens as a manifestation of a reciprocal solidarity principle within the EU which binds Union citizens together. While Ross pointed at the capacity of solidarity to provide different answers than citizenship and fundamental rights, Bell concentrates upon European solidarity from the vantage point of fundamental rights. By contrasting this 'linkage of social solidarity to Union citizenship' with the position of third country nationals, Bell implies the existence of this link within the EU, which Hilson appeared to associate with the nation state rather than with the EU and unnecessary for the solidarity exercised by the ecological citizen. Bell uses international human rights documents as a vantage point for the assessment of solidarity towards third country nationals. Given this perspective, he accordingly identifies the universal principle of human dignity, which underpins fundamental rights, as the basis of a degree of solidarity owed to everyone, ie a degree of solidarity is inherent in the notion of personhood. It is this link between solidarity and human dignity which,

Bell claims, requires some basic level of labour rights protection for the irregular migrants in the EU.

The chapter traces the limited aspirations to assimilate the rights of legally resident third country nationals to those of European citizens to the Tampere Agenda of the European Council, which called for a fairer treatment of those groups and a more vigorous integration policy. Bell explains that this is reflected in the Long-Term Residents Directive which includes wide-ranging rights to equal treatment in the labour market, with regard to education, recognition of diplomas, social protection, tax benefits and the like.[29] However, crucially, in line with the premises of the Tampere Agenda, irregular migrants remain outside the scope of the Directive.

Bell presents evidence which demonstrates, first, that irregular migrants represent a very sizable part of the population[30] who significantly, though clandestinely, contribute to the economy especially the service sector, and secondly, that the expectation that many of them will leave is unrealistic. Therefore, given third country nationals' vulnerability, their exclusion from social solidarity is untenable. It can, and should be redressed by recourse to international human rights instruments. The International Convention on the Protection of the Rights of All Migrant Workers and Member of their Families, the main international human rights instrument in this regard, provides for equal rights with national workers in respect of remuneration, conditions, and terms of work and the right to join and participate in trade unions. Following the premise of universality inherent in fundamental rights, it applies to legal residents and irregular migrants alike and therefore dissociates immigration law matters from labour law concerns, ie the employer-employee relationship is severed from the relationship between the migrant and the state with regard to immigration law. None of the EU member states has ratified the convention, which may, as Bell surmises, be attributed to the integration of EU immigration policy.

With regard to European human rights instruments, Bell not only points at evidence from the jurisprudence of the European Court of Human Rights which suggests that states have a duty to provide protection to illegal immigrants against extreme forms of exploitation, but also attributes this to the EU's own 2000 Charter of Fundamental Rights. Although Article 15(2) thereof, which relates to working conditions, implicitly restates the distinction between (protected) legal residents and (excluded) irregular migrants, Article 5(1) outlaws conditions of servitude and Article 31(1) extends 'the right to working conditions which respect... health, safety and dignity' to *every* worker. Bell reads this as guarantee

[29] Directive (EC) 2003/1009 [2004] OJ L16/44.
[30] With estimates ranging from 2–8 million within the EU.

of a minimum threshold of basic working conditions required by the notion of human dignity.

In an echo of Ross' earlier references to the burgeoning security agenda, Bell's analysis of EU documents and initiatives on irregular immigration reveals that their approach is predominantly repressive in nature, with an emphasis on combating illegal immigration inter alia through repatriation, including forced return, combined with a re-entry ban. A Directive proposed by the Commission in 2007 provides for sanctions addressed against employers of illegal immigrants and envisages the conferral of limited-duration residence permits on irregular migrants conditional on their cooperation with the law enforcement authorities as well as a right to unpaid arrears against their employer. However, Bell points out that these limited rights appear to instrumentalize the complicit irregular migrant. This runs, of course, diametrically counter to the concept of human dignity, which, as his coverage of international human rights instruments shows, implies a degree of solidarity which can be claimed by everyone.

A Certain Degree of Solidarity? Free Movement of Persons and Access to Social Protection in the Case Law of the European Court of Justice

The connections between citizenship and solidarity are also closely scrutinized by Stefano Giubboni, who takes a detailed look at the case law of the European Court of Justice on access to benefits. He questions the emergence of a European solidarity—describing it as an 'individualistic and quite paradoxical paradigm' lacking in any 'collective, political cement' in the case law. Giubboni's analysis concentrates on evaluating the extent of any solidarity developed through Articles 12 and 18 EC (now Articles 18 and 21 TFEU) as fundamental principles. These provisions do not only contain the legal base for claims to solidarity but are also, and increasingly, reconstructed as constitutional benchmarks against which not only national but also secondary community law is tested.

Giubboni identifies a number of tensions between the case law and legislation and demonstrates how the Court transformed seemingly general rule-like exceptions to access to social advantages, such as Article 10 of Regulation 1408/71 which, as it does not apply to unemployment benefits, indirectly condones residence requirements in national legislation as a condition for entitlement, and Article 24(2) of Directive 2004/38 which permits member states to deny maintenance assistance to students prior to them having acquired permanent residence status, into general derogation grounds which are read in the light of general free movement right enshrined in Article 18(1) and the general non-discrimination provision of Article 12 EC. Therefore, member state rules which appear to comply with measures of secondary EC legislation are not automatically saved from scrutiny; rather, they are subjected to a rule of reason (and) proportionality test[31] whereby the question of compatibility of national law with European citizenship is determined on a case by case basis.

Thus interpreted, the prohibition to export benefits by definition implies a potential restriction of citizens' free movement rights which requires a justification by the rule of reason. Giubboni draws similar conclusions from the case law up to *Bidar*[32] with regard to member states' refusal to grant maintenance assistance to students prior to their acquisition of the status as permanent residents pursuant to Article 16 of Directive 2004/38. One could conceivably question whether the Court may have backtracked on this front in the recent case of *Förster*,[33] where it held that a five year residence requirement for entitlement to a student grant stipulated in a provision of Dutch law, which was not only compatible with the letter of Articles 24(2) and 16(1) of Directive 2004/38 but appeared to have been adopted to implement (this aspect of) the Directive, was a justified restriction of Article 18(1) EC. Be this as it may, Giubboni's assessment remains accurate in that the Court did regard the measure as a restriction, albeit a justified one. What is more, the Advocate General's Opinion in *Förster*, who arrived at the conclusion that the applicant was entitled to the student grant on account of having formed a genuine link with the host society, lends full support to Giubboni's analysis. As he reminds us, the Court had already held in *Swaddling*[34] that the length of the period of residence should not be regarded as the only indicator of an individual's connection with the host state. Rather, personal circumstances have to be considered too. Advocate General Mazák's arguments in his Opinion in *Förster* buttress this line of reasoning. In common with Bell and Hilson, Giubboni also laments the closure of the European welfare system in that it virtually excludes third country nationals.

Although his focus is different, Giubboni's somewhat sceptical position on the political entrenchment of solidarity resonates with the reservations in the earlier chapters from Lamping and Barnard. Thus, Giubboni points to initiatives that have either stalled or been too controversial to contemplate at the European level—such as a minimum European income or European funding for social benefits. Giubboni's relative disappointment with the Court's performance is not so much akin to Davies' questioning of the justiciability of solidarity but more to do with the legitimacy of a Court intervening piecemeal in areas of re-modelling solidarity boundaries that really require legislative authority. His chapter accordingly concludes by calling for a more determined effort by the Community legislators to institutionalize 'a properly European form of social solidarity'.

31 See Y. Borgmann-Prebil, 'The Rule of Reason in European Citizenship' (2008) 14 Eur LJ 328.
32 Case C-209/03 *Bidar* [2005] ECR I-2119.
33 Case C-158/07 *Förster* [2008] ECR I-8507.
34 Case C-90/97 *Swaddling* [1999] ECR I-1075.

Age Discrimination in Law and Policy: How the Equal Treatment Directive Affects National Welfare States

The translation of any putative European solidarity into national welfare systems forms the object of Deborah Mabbett's contribution from a political science perspective. She explores the relationship between the expanding corpus of EU non-discrimination law and organization of social policy at national level, especially in relation to age discrimination. Mabbett considers the extent to which non-discrimination norms contained in EU legislation can conflict with decisions about redistribution made at member state level. In particular, she argues that supranational measures, such as the Framework Equal Treatment Directive,[35] are better understood as reform levers in national welfare state politics. In this sense, her argument is an interesting pointer to how the symbolic and rhetorical properties of European level norm-building may actually facilitate the adoption of otherwise unpopular national policies.

Mabbett's analysis contemplates a distinction between two different notions of non-discrimination law within social policy. The first, which she calls 'ordinary' law, is primarily concerned with economic actors in market relationships. The second, which Mabbett terms 'constitutional', targets legislatures and governments and is about broader judicial scrutiny of political power. For Mabbett, the lack of such a distinction in EU law creates considerable problems. In particular, should discrimination which is unacceptable if applied by an employer be subject to the same legal sanction if pursued by an elected government for social policy objectives? Whilst legal scholars, especially recently,[36] have tended to explore this question in relation to the horizontal direct effect of the single market rules, Mabbett instead asks whether applying the same tests to these situations would go against the idea that social policy is in some way a 'countervailing force' to the market and conducted on different principles. She contrasts the approaches to sex equality (where the political debate canvassed the same line for both social policy and the market) and age discrimination, an area which has been said to be not so much a 'suspect ground' as race or sex.[37]

In relation to the latter, Mabbett asks why there should have been unanimous agreement to include a prohibition in the FETD if it was not intended to be applied in domestic social policy questions. Here, drawing on Sunstein,[38] she

[35] Council Directive 2000/78 establishing a general framework for equal treatment in employment and occupation OJ [2000] L303/16.

[36] eg S. Prechal & S de Vries, 'Seamless web of judicial protection in the internal market?' (2009) 34 ELR 5.

[37] *per* AG Mazák in Case C-388/07 *The Incorporated Trustees of the National Council on Ageing (Age Concern England) v Secretary of State for Business, Enterprise and Regulatory Reform* (Opinion 23 September 2008), para 74.

[38] C. Sunstein 'On the expressive function of law' (1996) 144 U of Pennsylvania L Rev 2021.

offers a number of examples of member states using the 'expressive power of law' as a way of changing attitudes such as the opening up of debates about compulsory retirement age. Mabbett applies her political analysis to engage with the case law of the Court of Justice, especially from *Mangold*[39] onwards, and draws the interesting conclusion that whilst that jurisprudence might be seen as a failure[40] the directive itself could be seen as transformative for domestic politics.

Mabbett's contribution thus illustrates a political *process* at work which transforms social policy. Its inclusion in this volume poses questions about whether this causal relationship might have relevance, or replication, in the emergence of any European solidarity of the social justice type—especially as discussed by Giubboni or Barnard.

Promoting a Multi-Pillar Model? The EU and the Development of Funded Pension Schemes

Karen Anderson's chapter also explores how European integration impacts on national solidarity, this time in the context of the development of member state pension systems. Her contribution also moves this volume more explicitly in the direction of governance and solidarity. In particular, she looks at the constrictions and opportunities that EU legislation, the case law of the European Court of Justice and also the Open Method of Coordination (OMC) processes place on national pension systems. The chapter surveys the multiple solidarities built into the latter across Europe by reference to five dichotomies. These are, universalism v segmentalism (ie does the system include everyone or are there different systems for different occupational groups), individual v breadwinner entitlement (ie is every person entitled in their own right or is the provision for derived entitlements, eg for the surviving spouse), flat-rate v earnings related entitlement (usually it is a combination of the two, only the Netherlands and Denmark provide adequate flat-rate pensions for all), *inter* v *intra* generational solidarity (are the current pensions financed by current workers, or are they individual savings with no pooling of risks) and finally, private v public provision (public pension schemes or privately organized, but not necessarily the most important aspect of pension design for solidarity purposes). These conceptualizations allow Anderson to contrast Nordic and liberal (UK and Ireland) approaches, where there is emphasis on individual entitlements and weak derivative benefits, with a 'Bismarckian' continental model that favours intergenerational segmentalism. The inevitable

[39] Case C-144/04 *Mangold v Helm* [2005] ECR-I549.

[40] Lawyers in particular have been scathing about *Mangold* in relation to its contribution to perennial debates about the notion of direct effect and the impact of Directives in national legal systems. For a recent analysis see P. Craig, 'The legal effect of directives: policy, rules and exceptions' (2009) 34 ELR 349.

consequence, as Anderson points out, is that the emerging EU approach to pensions will play out differently in these systems.

EU developments are built around the application of OMC[41] and specific Community legal instruments on pensions. Although member states remain reluctant to surrender competencies in social policy, there is a spillover of market integration in general, and free-movement jurisprudence in particular, which impacts significantly on national social policies. Market integration has not only induced member states to pursue social policy initiatives at the supranational level through the Community method, but also the application of OMC mechanisms, such as benchmarking and mutual learning, have produced a drift away from intergenerational to intragenerational solidarity and the individual's obligation to work. As Anderson observes, this tendency will be familiar to Nordic countries where there is a clear reliance on portable, defined contribution benefits. However, as she notes in her conclusion, the 2008/2009 financial crisis may raise severe questions as to whether this switch to funded pension provision as a normative principle of EU reform is financially sustainable.

How to Govern for Solidarity? An Introduction to Policy Learning in the Context of Open Methods of Co-ordinating Education Policies in the European Union

Even more so than the contribution by Anderson, the chapter by Lange and Alexiadou places particular emphasis on the OMC procedures, this time by providing an empirical account of policy learning in the expanding area of EU educational policies through OMC. This policy area is situated within the framework of solidarity in that it portrays European education policies as one significant manifestation, or to use Ross' terminology, expression, of the European social model. In this regard Lange and Alexiadou furnish empirical evidence that demonstrates a correlation between welfare and educational achievement. It emerges clearly from the data that the Nordic and Continental states, where formal educational achievement (measured by the proportion of the adult population educated to upper secondary degree level) is significantly higher than in the Anglo-Saxon and Mediterranean states have correspondingly significantly lower general poverty levels. In this regard policy learning through OMC, which develops a European dimension to national educational policies, is significant in enhancing educational standards, and by implication, overall welfare, in the EU.

The chapter distinguishes between four policy learning styles, ie mutual, competitive, surface and imperialistic learning and suggests that policy learning contributes to the construction of a European social model. The central concern for

[41] For a broader discussion, see M. Dawson, 'The ambiguity of social Europe in the open method of co-ordination' (2009) 34 ELR 55.

Lange and Alexiadou is to analyze the governance processes through which the social dimension of the EU is instituted. In so doing, the chapter adds to the analysis of the expressive aspect of solidarity as identified by Ross when discussing his virtuous circle model. Rather than focusing on constitutional provisions such as those amended by the Lisbon Treaty or case law, Lange and Alexiadou explore the soft law character of solidarity building. These soft law instruments structure and engender peer learning activities that open spaces for democratic contestation of social policies, which, as Ross also argues, leads to the development of solidarity. Lange and Alexiadou further argue that policy learning in the field of education could assist the emergence of progressive and substantial conceptions of solidarity. However, as the authors themselves concede, if the only product of EU education policies is the creation of intense competition for jobs in highly flexible labour markets, then insecurity, not solidarity, may be the unintended consequence.

Relating Territorial Cohesion, Solidarity, and Spatial Justice

The volume concludes with a forward-looking contribution from Jane Holder and Antonia Layard that explores developments in the law and policy of territorial cohesion within the EU and positions territorial cohesion and territorial solidarity within the broader debate about the European social model. They chart in detail different meanings and definitions of the concept of territorial cohesion. These include incorporating a spatial planning perspective into decisions that hitherto were primarily made solely on economic and social grounds, the lessening of territorial concentrations of Gross Domestic Product (GDP) in the industrial heartland of Europe, and a potentially more radical concern with 'spatial justice'. Indeed, the authors main concern lies with extracting this justice content of territorial cohesion. Or, put another way, they see the linking of territorial cohesion and solidarity as the joining of spatial and social protection. With this in mind they scrutinize a number of action programmes and other policy documents containing territorial cohesion initiatives and priorities, not all of them consistent with each other.

Holder and Layard relate critically to the genesis of both the notion of territorial cohesion and territorial solidarity, arguing that the development of the former has largely been motivated by, and mainstreamed with, economic goals rather than informed by criteria of justice and fairness, while the latter concept has not (yet) gone beyond the concern of equal access to services and participation in business activities. Instead, the authors advocate a notion of territorial cohesion that should not primarily be concerned with the redistribution of economic opportunities in spatial terms but should refer to a fair distribution of the environmental harms, such as pollution, that result from them. Making use of solidarity—in the sense of including notions of interdependence, shared responsibilities and burdens—is the crucial step in re-framing the conceptualization of territorial cohesion. In this sense, too, Holder and Layard connect solidarity to how concepts of intergenerational and intragenerational justice are understood.

At the same time, the authors are at pains to emphasize that any such development cannot be restricted to a purely intergovernmental process. Moreover, following Faludi,[42] they argue that a sense of identity can be forged by the very process of being involved in the deliberations that develop the spatial vision of a territory as more than a place of production. In common with a number of other contributors, this chapter combines an excitement about the work that solidarity might do with a more muted view as to the receptiveness of political frameworks to bringing it about.

European Solidarity: Rhetoric or Reality?

It has not been the intention of this volume to provide a single, all-encompassing definition of solidarity. Rather, it has been concerned to reflect upon why variants upon solidarity are becoming so prevalent in discourses about the European Union and how dimensions and applications of solidarity might do useful theoretical or political work. Contributors not only adopt different usages of solidarity but also express considerable variations in confidence as to its value and likely impact. So, apart from reinforcing what was already supposed—that solidarity as a notion is both theoretically contested and politically sensitive—what can be drawn from this set of insights?

At the very least, it seems clear that to ask what solidarity is for is a cipher for posing the same question about the EU itself. After all, the elephant that always seems to be in the room in many chapters is whether the balance (and ultimately choice) between market and social should be redrawn, to what extent and how. Neatly captured by cases such as *Viking* and *Laval*,[43] part of the appeal (or threat) of solidarity is the search for a different explanation of how to conduct and position that balance. At their heart, claims for a meaningful solidarity are calls for a *moral* dimension to justify the existence of a EU beyond markets and free movement. Solidarity in this way can be both a value to be upheld and a means by which to pursue it.

It is this latter conundrum which lends particular importance to the contributions in this volume about the effective and legitimate construction of new, potentially European, solidarities out of the tensions between supranational policies and existing, possibly fragmenting, national solidarities. The suggestion of solidarity as an iterative process, or perhaps as even a learned experience, implies that the image of the EU as a threat to national welfare states may bear a more

[42] A. Faludi, 'Territorial cohesion policy and the European model of society' (2007) 15(4) Eur Planning Studies 567.

[43] n 11 above.

subtle interpretation and one that is not necessarily socially destructive. The challenge for this volume, and indeed further research to come, is to engage with what 'new' solidarities might mean and how they come to be practised.

It should also be very apparent from this collection that solidarity can usefully interrogate other, perhaps more currently prevalent or fashionable, concepts and institutions in the evolving governance of the EU. After all, it might be argued that citizenship and fundamental rights, singly or together, could theoretically deliver the kind of social justice that solidarity represents for some authors in this volume. Yet, as Ward has noted elsewhere, citizenship continues to disappoint in an EU context: 'rather than providing a means to unite Europe, to provide it with a mechanism for crafting Community "solidarity", the idea of Union citizenship merely opens up an absurd array of different categories of European "person" '.[44] Does a multi-faceted solidarity have to fall, or risk falling, into these gradated patterns? Similarly, can solidarity in practice amount to anything more tangibly identity-building in character than a floor of social rights that could be attributable to a universal human rights agenda? Indeed, authors such as Ward would claim that it is solidarity itself that is outmoded and that should be overtaken by other concepts in the quest for a public philosophy in Europe.[45]

Certainly, the ambivalence of solidarity remains problematic. Solidarity obligations, for it seems there must be some, apply to whom and between whom, exactly—states, citizens, individuals present and future, animals, the environment? Member states baling out the banks, indeed with European approval (or at least rubber-stamping), in the recent financial crisis could be construed as a manifestation of solidarity of sorts, but hardly a social justice model. This raises the pertinent question of how far solidarities at different levels and among different groups, interact with each other and (possibly) are causally connected in some developmental fashion. There may actually be no crisis *in* solidarity at all—but new solidarities may be emerging which are themselves loaded with as many problematic features as insights. Part of the importance of the policy-based or sector-specific contributions in this volume is to trigger further reflection on this potential evolution in solidarity.

Thus, to address the title of this introduction explicitly, there is no consensus in this volume that identifies a single point currently occupied by solidarity along the spectrum from rhetorical flourish to practised reality. As with many things, context is all—and contributions here identify particular EU policies where solidaristic tendencies are either in play or have explicatory value. Nevertheless, there is agreement that something is happening out there—whether a 'work in progress' as cautiously adumbrated by Barnard or travelling in the direction of the more ambitious claims made by Ross and Holder respectively about solidarity

[44] I. Ward, *A Critical Introduction to European Law* (Cambridge: Cambridge University Press, 2009) 220.

[45] ibid ch 8; Ward himself canvasses a notion of cosmopolitan humanism.

as a constitutional paradigm or core element in spatial justice. The scepticism about solidarity in this volume is from the same school that continues, rightly, to address the legitimacy and governance of the Union, the proper scope of the Court of Justice's role and the sustainability of the European 'project' in the face of often defensive member states and anxious citizens.[46] Readers are accordingly invited to draw their own conclusions from the contributions that follow as to whether solidarity offers a view of the EU's future that might be sustained by a deeper root than merely 'conflictual coexistence'.[47]

[46] See also A. Giddens, P. Diamond and R. Liddle (eds) *Global Europe Social Europe* (Cambridge: Polity, 2006).

[47] U. Beck, 'Living your own life in a runaway world: individualisation, globalisation and politics' in W. Hutton and A. Giddens (eds) *On the Edge: Living with Global Capitalism* (London: Jonathan Cape, 2000).

2

Solidarity—A New Constitutional Paradigm for the EU?

*Malcolm Ross**

1. Introduction

The idea of solidarity can be traced back for more than two centuries, the term being associated with notions of *fraternité* at the time of the French Revolution and explicitly occurring in the 1804 Code Civil.[1] As with any enduring notion, the scope, meaning and significance of solidarity seem permanently contested within and across a range of intellectual disciplines. It has been both declaimed and decried along a spectrum from being *the* problem of the twenty-first century[2] to 'a largely empty feel-good slogan'.[3] A tendency to use solidarity for rhetorical effect has obscured its theoretical content and capacity and forced it to play catch-up against more fashionable targets for research. In political theory, for example, solidarity has been neglected in favour of inquiries into democracy, nationalism, community, multiculturalism and human rights.[4] In similar vein, a leading sociologist has found it 'amazing' that so little attention has been paid to establishing a precise meaning for solidarity.[5]

* An earlier draft of this chapter has been published in Italian as 'Solidarietà: un nuovo paradigma costituzionale per l'Unione europea?' (2009) Rivista del Diritto della Sicurezza Sociale 239.

[1] S. Stjernø, *Solidarity in Europe: The History of an Idea* (Cambridge: Cambridge University Press, 2005). The first mention of solidarity in the Oxford English Dictionary only appears in the mid-nineteenth century. The Latin root, *solidare,* connotes the combination of parts to form a strong whole. For a closer look at semantic usages see S-E. Liedman, 'Solidarity', accessed from <http://www.eurozine.com> (last visited 5 July 2008).

[2] D. Hollinger 'From Identity to Solidarity' (2006) 135 (Fall) Daedalus 4, at 23.

[3] R. Vischer, 'Solidarity, Subsidiarity, and the Consumerist Impetus of American Law' University of St Thomas School of Law, Legal Studies Research Paper No 07–08 at <http://www.ssrn.com/link/st-thomas-legal-studies.html> (last visited 5 July 2008).

[4] L. Wilde,'The concept of solidarity: emerging from the theoretical shadows?' (2007) 9 British J of Politics and Intl Relations 171.

[5] A. Giddens, *Europe in the Global Age* (Cambridge: Polity Press, 2007) 112.

Nonetheless, solidarity remains an 'elusive but perennially attractive idea'.[6] Indeed, recent major monographs[7] have led to a resurgence of interest and theoretical scrutiny, especially in the realms of philosophy, social theory and sociology. Solidarity is invoked to reinvigorate, illuminate or challenge a broad range of other concepts, including identity, democracy, justice, consumerism and globalization.[8] Of course, there is nothing surprising in this diversity of theoretical aims and applications. As Rehg notes, sociologists seek models of solidarity that explain social order and change, whereas philosophers will tend to link solidarity with normative theories of legitimate government, the good society, and morality.[9] Legal scholars have been rather slower to respond, other than in the specific context of healthcare and other aspects of social provision in the European Union (EU) where the tensions between market and non-market paradigms have been the paramount focus.[10] Yet here too there is recognition that solidarity 'is more than a token with a lustrous aura'.[11]

Why should there be this revival of interest in an idea that at first sight seems perhaps at best quaint or at worst irrelevant in today's technological, individually-oriented and consumerist post-modern (western) world? One motivation, for some theorists, is precisely in order to find an antidote to these latter conditions, or at least what are diagnosed to be their most pernicious symptoms. Indeed, it has been claimed that solidarity is what keeps an entity from disintegrating.[12] Or, put more specifically, one line of social theory asserts that social exclusion follows from a loss of solidarity, as undemocratic social subsystems of

[6] L. Wilde, (2007) 6 Contemporary Political Theory 117 (book review of Stjernø, n 1 above).

[7] Particularly Stjernø, n 1 above; H. Brunkhorst, *Solidarity: From Civic Friendship to a Global Legal Community*, trans. Flynn (Cambridge MA: MIT Press, 2005); U. Beck, *The Cosmopolitan Vision* (Cambridge: Polity Press, 2006). Collected works include: N. Karagiannis (ed), *European Solidarity* (Liverpool: Liverpool UP, 2007) and L. Magnusson and B. Stråth (eds) *European Solidarities—Tensions and Contentions of a Concept* (Brussels/New York: Peter Lang, 2007). For an earlier collection, mainly from a non-legal perspective, see K. Bayertz (ed) *Solidarity* (Springer, 1999).

[8] A brief selection of titles makes the point: J. Bohman, 'Democracy, solidarity and global exclusion' (2006) 32 (7) Philosophy and Social Criticism 809; C. Calhoun, 'Constitutional Patriotism and the Public Sphere: Interests, Identity and Solidarity in the Integration of Europe' (2005) 18 Intl J of Politics, Culture and Society 257; D. Heyd, 'Justice and Solidarity: The Contractarian Case against Global Justice' (2007) 38 (1) J of Social Philosophy 112; M. Pensky, 'Solidarity as fact or norm?: Social integration between system and lifeworld' (2006) 32 (7) Philosophy and Social Criticism 819; N. Stevenson, 'European Cosmopolitan Solidarity: Questions of Citizenship, Difference and Post-materialism' (2006) 9(4) Eur J of Social Theory 485; M. Weber, 'The concept of solidarity in the study of world politics: towards a critical theoretic understanding' (2007) 33 (4) Rev of Intl Studies 693.

[9] W. Rehg, 'Solidarity and the Common Good: An analytic framework' (2007) 38 (1) J of Social Philosophy 7.

[10] Notably led by G. de Búrca (ed) *EU Law and the Welfare State—In Search of Solidarity* (Oxford: OUP, 2005). See also C. Barnard, 'Social Policy Revisited in the Light of the Constitutional Debate' in C. Barnard (ed) *The Fundamentals of EU Law Revisited* (Oxford: OUP, 2007) especially 121–130.

[11] A. Somek, 'Solidarity Decomposed: Being and Time in European Citizenship' (2007) 32 ELR 787.

[12] Heyd, n 8 above.

bureaucratic administration or market economies assume a disproportionate and eventually hegemonic role in the work of social integration.[13] However, it should be stressed that in the discussion that follows there is no assumption that solidarity (however eventually defined) is intrinsically desirable. Equally, whatever the conceptual attractions offered by reconfigured models of solidarity, there is no assumption that these could be translated into what sociologists sometimes term lifeworlds. Indeed, there are often pessimistic conclusions on this point even among apologists for the conceptual opportunities offered by a reconstructed solidarity. Stjernø, for example, concluded in 2004 that it was difficult to be optimistic about immediate developments regarding solidarity.[14] In the aftermath of the failed Constitutional Treaty, a noted European lawyer remarked that the post-2004 climate for constitutional reform in Europe amounted to one of the 'least favourable and least promising—to put it mildly—moments for optimistic outbursts regarding the future of European solidarity'.[15]

Nevertheless, the subsequent preoccupation with solidarity in the run-up to, and final form of, the Lisbon Treaty suggests that some degree of climate change in relation to solidarity might not only be possible but even expected. Even the ratification storms of 2008 reflect, even if not always explicitly, the central relevance of solidarity to the future direction and content of European integration.[16] Indeed, the European Commission in 2007 launched a 'life-chances' social vision for Europe in which well-being is advanced through opportunities, access and solidarity—the latter said 'to foster social cohesion and social sustainability, and make sure that no individual is left behind.'[17] The three strands of this document have since formed the basis of the renewed social agenda published by the Commission in July 2008.[18]

Accordingly, whilst excited by the latent potency of the concept, the aim of this chapter is to skim away the rhetorical froth[19] too easily associated with solidarity and to conduct a re-appraisal which considers its relevance and potential as a transformative concept in the evolution of EU constitutional discourse and development. This chapter engages with the theorization and constitutional significance of solidarity in three ways. First, it briefly recalls the classical expositions of solidarity stretching from the eighteenth to late twentieth centuries with a view

[13] Pensky, n 8 above, 819, summarizing social theory traditions stretching from Weber to Habermas and Luhmann.

[14] n 1 above, 352.

[15] S. Giubboni, 'Free movement of persons and European solidarity' (2007) 13 Eur LJ 360, 376.

[16] cf H-J. Trenz, 'Elements of a sociology of European integration' (ARENA working paper no 11, May 2008; <http://www.arena.uio.no>) for an argument that prefers Europeanization rather than integration to describe the processes discussed here.

[17] Commission (EC), 'Opportunities, access and solidarity: towards a new social vision for 21st century Europe' (Communication) COM (2007) 726. Discussed further by C. Barnard in this volume.

[18] Commission (EC), 'Renewed social agenda: Opportunities, access and solidarity in 21st century Europe' (Communication) COM (2008) 412.

[19] Wilde, n 6 above.

to identifying pervasive themes and tensions in its conceptualization. Secondly, it refines a contemporary notion of solidarity in an EU context by positioning it against conflicting, congruent or complementary concepts drawn from law and other disciplines. Notions of cosmopolitanism and security are identified as especially significant comparisons when addressing the challenges of transnational governance. However, this chapter does not pursue a single overarching definition of solidarity. Instead, it attempts to embrace and harness a number of interdisciplinary insights to model the creation, expression and sustainability of solidarity as a virtuous circle. This model is then used in the final section of the chapter to explain solidarity's pervasiveness and constitutional significance in EU law by reference to both existing usages (primarily developed in the case law of the Court of Justice) and the changes introduced by the Lisbon Treaty 2007. This chapter accordingly concerns itself with the *potency* and *distinctiveness* of solidarity—measured by the special work that it can do as a *legal* concept—rather than engaging with the detailed manifestations and limitations of solidarity in specific legal contexts, many of which are developed by other contributors to this volume.

2. The classical expositions of solidarity

Stjernø[20] has identified three broad traditions in the development of solidarity as an idea. First, it has been a key concept in classic social theory, especially as set out by Durkheim and Weber, the former concentrating on a social view of solidarity as a macro phenomenon binding society together whilst the latter adopted a more micro-oriented and politicized approach in construing solidarity as a special type of social relationship.[21] Secondly, solidarity has occupied a central place in political thought. In particular, Stjernø points to the approach to solidarity evident (even if not always explicitly by that name) from the socialist theories of Marx and Kautsky and their subsequent divergence into distinctive branches of social democracy and Leninism. The third tradition in Stjernø's typology is a religious strand in Christian democracy dominated by Catholic and Protestant doctrines.

Refining these traditions, Stjernø distinguishes seven[22] concepts of solidarity across social theory, socialist theory and Catholic social ethics. These are then located against specific considerations, namely their foundation, objective/function, degree of inclusiveness and extent of collective orientation.[23] As the

[20] n 1 above.

[21] Trenz, n 16 above, attempts to place Durkheim and Weber in current debates about the EU. Thus Durkheim is treated as a federal thinker who would see Europeanization as a process of differentiation in which ties of organic solidarity across national borders intensify, but ties of mechanic solidarity within national borders weaken (ibid 17). Weber, according to Trenz, would see European integration as an expression of scientific-technical civilisation and bureaucratic domination. (ibid 18).

[22] Deriving three subsets from classic social theory, two from politics and two from religion.

[23] n 1 above, Table 3.3. p 86.

following (reduced) matrix indicates, solidarities will vary in degrees of thinness or thickness according to the manifestation of these criteria:

Foundation	Recognition of sameness	Shared interests	Universal (altruism)
Objective/function	Sustain togetherness	Strengthen class feelings	Good society or world
Inclusiveness	All who are the same (race, nation)	Class or class alliance	All human beings
Collective orientation	Strong...	...	...Weak

Figure 1. Stjerno's conceptual matrix[24]

From this analysis, Stjernø observes that the historic traditions share 'two necessary values, that an individual should identify with others, to some degree, and that a feeling of community should exist between the individual and (at least some) others, and as a consequence it can be argued that all these ideas of solidarity imply some sort of inclusiveness.'[25] At the same time, Stjernø's detailed historical analysis points to the significant differences in conceptualizations of solidarity: some accounts are purely descriptive, others normative, some focus upon inclusion and/or exclusion whilst others exhibit utilitarian or altruistic attributes.

Yet Stjernø's own definition of solidarity in modern society remains fundamentally statist in character. He concludes:

For the majority, it is based not on personal interest, but on political altruism: it is founded on empathy and cognition, and the balance between the two may vary. Solidarity is developed through communicative action and the ability to take the role of 'the other(s)'. It means the preparedness to share resources with others, through personal contributions to those who are struggling and through taxation and redistribution organised by the state. Thus, solidarity means a readiness for collective action and a will to institutionalise it through the establishment of rights and citizenship. It is normally expressed through relating to others who are engaged in struggle...[26]

At first sight, this does not look an auspicious analysis for the purposes of today's transnational EU, which lacks the means to levy direct personal taxation, possesses only limited capacity (if increasingly large) as a supranational 'welfare space' for redistributive purposes and is generally believed to be significantly in deficit so far as 'communicative action' is concerned.

Moreover, it may be noted that the legal framework identified by Stjernø is also expressed in equally traditional terms by reference to rights and citizenship as the institutionalization of solidarity. Indeed, his approach consciously[27] 'does

[24] Modified version of table, n 1. [25] n 1 above, 88/89.
[26] ibid 326. [27] ibid 18, n 8.

not include in its characterization of solidarity any notion of responsibility or obligation—for the very good reason that it is not a consistently identifiable feature of the classic traditions. However, the legal (as distinct, for example, from sociological) applications of a contemporary explanation of solidarity can fruitfully explore the complex relationship between solidarity and (mutual) responsibilities, extending beyond the limits currently attached to a rights-oriented EU citizenship for particular groups.[28]

Of course, one response to the traditional varieties of solidarity set out by Stjernø would be to assert the different nature of the EU (an extension as it were of the Court of Justice's own familiar mantra about the *sui generis* character of the entity) and thus avoid having to conceptualize transnational or supranational solidarity by absorbing any of the above characteristics. However, just as technological innovations such as the internet do not necessarily render pre-existing laws on privacy or freedom of expression redundant, new polities and configurations of power question (and may usefully be examined through) earlier rules and concepts, and may end up redefining them. In other words, the particularities and novelties of the EU's legal, political and social shape provide a context in which to interrogate and, possibly, renew solidarity. This is not to assume or apply some 'essentialist' approach to solidarity as a concept—on the contrary, this chapter acknowledges the notion of solidarit*ies* in the EU—but to suggest that there is illumination to be found regarding both the scope of solidarity and the constitutional contours of the EU by postulating that there might be some dynamic, mutual relationship between them.

In any event, it should be stressed that not all the traditional themes picked out by Stjernø as underpinning solidarity have been abandoned in recent literature across disciplines. Heyd,[29] for example, reinforces the ideological element to solidarity—indeed, it is this degree of commitment to an idea or cause that marks solidarity out from other feelings of bonding such as love. Thus, for Heyd, solidarity still signifies a struggle implying an 'other' against which the group in question is positioned. In other words, solidarity implies exclusion, albeit (and crucially) not necessarily in a hostile sense. Mutuality, too, is still widely seen as indispensable to any conceptualization of solidarity. As Wilde puts it, the idea captures the feeling of reciprocal sympathy and responsibility among members of a group which promotes mutual support.[30] In similar vein, Rehg identifies solidarity as a quality of human association, specifically the cohesive social bond that holds a group of people together in an association they both understand

[28] cf A. Honneth, who explicitly treats solidarity as a moral orientation beyond and essentially different from any integration of rights and duties. Solidarity is part of a triptych along with love and rights; see *The Struggle for Recognition: The Moral Grammar of Social Conflicts* (Cambridge: Polity Press, 1996). cf C. Offe, 'Obligations versus costs: Types and Contexts of Solidary Action' in Karagiannis (ed), n 7 above, 113.

[29] n 8 above. Heyd's position as a social philosopher is very much in the tradition of John Rawls.

[30] n 4 above.

themselves to be part of and value.[31] The moral implications of some of these interpretations are made explicit by Derpmann, who understands solidarity to refer to the care and the moral responsibility for the rights or welfare of others.[32] Members of a group are, or at least they *feel*, obliged to promote the well-being of other members.[33] But, as Baurmann argues, solidarity does not require self-sacrifice as such, where solidarity actions produce no self benefit; rather, solidarity can be based on securing fairness for a group, including the possibility of self benefit for individual members.[34]

Finally, although not always located within the parameters of a state-centred polity, there remains an abiding consensus that solidarity is conducted in, or mediated by, a public sphere.[35] In this way, solidarity is distinguished from charitable sympathy and support.[36] Above all, perhaps, solidarity cannot be divorced from its political context and character. As Derpmann puts it, '[i]ndependent of its alleged intrinsic moral value, solidarity is ascribed instrumental value in the realization of vital political functions.'[37] Or, as Karagiannis observes, 'solidarity is the periodic specification of social bonds in a political perspective.'[38] This posits political and social dimensions of solidarity as intertwined and leads to the conclusion that different solidarities will predominate at different historical times—in turn giving rise to the possibility of several ties of solidarity co-existing or in conflict in the context of competing political projects. The shifting and hotly contested polity constituted by the EU accordingly offers both challenges and opportunities for reworking solidarity as both analytical tool and normative concept. The next section pursues these questions by focusing upon the relevance of solidarity by positioning it against other competitors as fruitful concepts for analysis and discourse about the perceived 'crises' faced by the EU.

[31] n 9 above.

[32] S. Derpmann, 'Solidarity and Cosmopolitanism' (2009) 12 Ethical Theory and Moral Practice 303, at 304. See also K. Bayertz 'Four Uses of Solidarity' in Bayertz (ed) n 7 above, who takes the moral dimension as the benchmark for his analysis of solidarity uses and the difficulties of positioning the positive obligations of solidarity in the context of the universalistic tendencies of modern ethics discussions.

[33] Derpmann, n 32 above, 305.

[34] M. Baurmann, 'Solidarity as a social norm and as a constitutional norm' in Bayertz (ed), n 7 above, 243.

[35] Space constraints prevent analysis of this nuanced term, which has been much influenced by the German concept of *Öffentlichkeit* and Habermasian applications. See H-J Trenz, 'In search of the European Public Sphere: between normative overstretch and empirical disenchantment' (ARENA working paper 12/2008) at <http://www.arena.uio.no> (last visited 5 July 2008).

[36] Stjernø, n 1 above, 326. Charity is also distinguishable as a one-way street lacking the reciprocity of solidarity. The relevance of the anthropological theory of gift to the sociological concept of solidarity is reviewed in A. Komter, *Social Solidarity and the Gift* (New York: Cambridge University Press, 2005).

[37] n 32 above, 305–306.

[38] Introduction, n 7 above at 2.

3. Rethinking solidarity in the EU: conceptual challenges

It almost goes without saying that classical approaches to solidarity did not have to embrace polities beyond the nation state to any significant degree. In this sense any discussion of solidarity's contemporary significance must engage with more recent attempts to explain and evaluate the complex connections, practices and tensions between units, levels and participants in the governance of the EU. More particularly, it must be asked whether solidaristic explanations compete with, complement or provide different insights from those to be found in the substance and rhetoric of discourses that focus upon how and why it is that the EU 'works' (or fails to) and the extent to which it constitutes a distinctive and cohesive phenomenon. On this level, solidarity can be seen as part of a mushrooming research agenda that uses the departure point of 'governance through...' for a wide range of legal, sociological, criminological or political inquiries.[39] The reach of solidarity, noted in the previous section, cuts into and across matters of values, identity and belonging, political commitment and the accommodation of relationships between institutions, individuals and states. The following discussion therefore addresses some key areas of intersection with other analytical concepts in order to provide an indication of both the potency and limitations of solidarity.

At the outset it might be reasonably safe to claim that any quest to reconfigure solidarity in the political, social and legal laboratory that is the evolving EU requires an approach that avoids the spatially bound and tightly organized solidarities of the past.[40] Cosmopolitan and highly mobile societies do not sit easily with the emergence of such 'thick' identities. In any event, the pursuit of a European identity may be a futile, indeed absurd,[41] exercise. At the very least, empirical evidence to support the emergence of any such identity yet is thin,[42] although this may be unsurprising given the brief lifespan (so far) of the EU and the lack of any seismic, unifying, identity-shaping event.[43] Instead, porous transnational boundaries and interdependencies provide ammunition to pursue recast notions of solidarity in forms to counter re-running the excesses of nationalism and strongly exclusionary practices that might be adopted by

[39] eg J. Simon, *Governing Through Crime, How the War on Crime Transformed American Democracy and Created a Culture of Fear* (Oxford: OUP, 2007); M. Findlay, *Governing Through Globalised Crime* (Devon, UK: Willan Publishing, 2008); A. Hamann and H. Ruiz Fabri, 'Transnational networks and constitutionalism' (2009) 6 Intl J of Constitutional Law 481.

[40] Wilde, n 4 above.

[41] Karagiannis, n 7 above, ch 12, 220; see also K-H. Ladeur, 'We, the European People...'—Relâche?' (2008) 14 Eur LJ 147.

[42] See J. Díez Medrano, 'Europeanization and the emergence of a European Society' IBEI working papers 2008/12 (Barcelona, January 2008); K. Kumar, 'The Question of European Identity: Europe in the American Mirror' (2008) 11 Eur J of Social Theory 87. For a different perspective on supranational identity-building, see H. de Schutter, 'Nations beyond nationalism' (2007) 50 Inquiry 378.

[43] Archetypal examples would be post-revolutionary constitutions, such as in the United States.

thicker identities. Here, it is not sameness but reflection upon and acceptance of difference that provides a foundation for solidarity. This is not to say that solidarity removes differences; rather it can re-evaluate the importance of differences and (re-)discover similarities.[44]

Many calls have been made to reinvent 'Europe', particularly by those of a cosmopolitan persuasion.[45] These approaches, which themselves vary widely,[46] emphasize new political visions of Europe (usually in contradistinction from neo-liberal concepts of a global market) and its re-anchoring as something more than a system or an efficiency-driven endeavour. As Calhoun has observed,[47] citizens need to be motivated by solidarity, not merely included by law. Who, after all, loves or identifies with an internal market? If there is a common baseline to the contributions of cosmopolitan approaches, it is in raising awareness of the reconfigured relationships between individuals, communities and, indeed, the world. As Rumford notes, 'Cosmopolitanism requires us to recognize that we are all positioned simultaneously as outsiders and insiders, as individuals and group members, as self and the other, as local and global.'[48] Europeanization in this context means a transformation in self-understanding as a result of a co-evolution of different levels of linkages (horizontally between European societies, vertically between EU/European societies, and transversally global/European).[49] But, of course, the logic of cosmopolitanism does not stop at, or within, Europe; we can speak of a cosmopolitan Europe but not of a particular European cosmopolitanism.[50]

At this point it might be asked whether reworking solidarity can perform any conceptual work that could not be done by cosmopolitanism, given that the latter notion has a longer pedigree[51] and is already used to describe and engage with transnational contexts in both political and social terms. Can either solidarity or cosmopolitanism shed greater light on how communities and institutions interact in settings such as the EU? On the surface, at least, there seems to be a tension between the universalist leanings of cosmopolitanism and the more anchored or exclusive type of community characteristic of traditional forms of solidarity.

[44] cf R. Rorty, who treats solidarity as the 'ability to see more and more traditional differences... as unimportant when compared with similarities with respect to pain and humiliation—the ability to think of people wildly different from ourselves as included in the range of "us"', see *Contingency, Irony, and Solidarity* (Cambridge: Cambridge University Press 1989) 192. In this sense solidarity has a more useful role than some (fruitless) search for a core essence of all human beings.

[45] eg, inter alia, U. Beck and E. Grande, 'Europe's Way Out of Crisis' (2007) 10 Eur J of Social Theory 67; Calhoun, n 8 above.

[46] See C. Rumford (ed) *Cosmopolitanism and Europe* (Liverpool: Liverpool University Press, 2007).

[47] n 8 above.

[48] n 46 above, Introduction at 3.

[49] V. Boon and G. Delanty, 'Cosmopolitanism and Europe: Historical Considerations and Contemporary Applications' in Rumford, n 46 above, 31.

[50] ibid 36.

[51] Traceable to the Cynics and Stoics in Ancient Greek thought; ibid 20.

For some, such as Derpmann, the apparent incompatibility of solidarity and cosmopolitanism is resolved by understanding that they cover different fields of moral deliberation.[52] Thus '[c]osmopolitan forms of solidarity do not extend to the universal moral community, but still transcend ethnic or national delimitations and thus emphasize the inclusive, rather than the exclusive component of solidarity.'[53] But, as Derpmann recognizes, this leaves open the question of how moral deliberation is conducted when these spheres conflict.

On this basis, it would seem that contemplation of a concept of cosmopolitan solidarity represents neither a tautology nor a contradiction in terms. Instead, the interesting prospect is that such an idea focuses upon the intersection of tendencies towards universal values (expressed for example as the promotion of fundamental human rights) and the need for a politically workable 'us' in terms of commitments and communities. In this sense, putting the ideas of cosmopolitanism and solidarity together addresses their common concern with issues of identification. Cosmopolitanism stresses a process of transformation without a particular end or aim,[54] so that, as Boon and Delanty claim, Europeanization is not a matter of *overcoming* national or parochial identifications but should instead be seen as a continuing process of *becoming*.[55] Solidarity's conceptual contribution—potentially at least—is accordingly to *give shape to* cosmopolitan processes in the EU. This does not mean predetermining that shape, although the rather 'leftist' leanings of solidarity historically may give it an appeal to those whose political agenda seeks to impose a brake on globalization or establish a more welfare-oriented redistribution of societal resources. But, it must be stressed, for the purposes of this chapter solidarity is not imbued with this (or other) prescriptive aspect. Its value lies in identification of the constraints and forces (especially legal) in the EU context which give a particular direction to the ordering of relations both within it and in facing its external context. In this sense solidarity may offer insights into the limits of what can be done together (ie by the EU and its peoples).

However, any attempt to sketch a particular European solidarity, in the sense of trying to identify relevant and sufficient transnational bonds, encounters theoretical problems similar to efforts to encapsulate cosmopolitanism. Historically, as Schwartz observes,[56] it has been the tension 'between particularistic bonds of attachment and more universalist impulses towards social justice' that has framed philosophical analysis of solidarity. Once the bonds themselves are universally inspired so it might follow that solidarity becomes thinner—a consequence

[52] n 32 above, 313.
[53] ibid 314.
[54] Boon and Delanty, n 49 above, 32.
[55] ibid 35, italics original.
[56] J. Schwartz, 'From domestic to global solidarity: the dialectic of the particular and universal in the building of social solidarity' (2007) 38 J of Social Philosophy 131,136.

which, for some, deprives solidarity of its intrinsic worth and character. Stjernø, summarizing the history of solidarity as an idea, detects this tendency:

> The main trend is towards a broad and inclusive idea of solidarity that has justice or social integration as the main objective. Modern theories vary most probably when it comes to the foundation of solidarity. Is this empathy, ethics, religion, interaction, social practice or interests?[57]

If solidarity derives from matters of choice (eg beliefs, values) rather than given and seemingly inalienable conditions (eg race, gender—yet even these may be only socially constructed categories), it intuitively seems more difficult to locate boundaries to the constituency.[58] However, this may be too much of a generalization. For example, a commitment to 'the environment' is in at least some sense more particularistic than the pursuit of universal 'justice' or 'democracy'.

Put another way, solidarity's capacity to give shape to cosmopolitanism is in effect tantamount to transnational norm-building. As Müller has argued,[59] it is possible to be attached to universalist principles *and* feel loyalty to a particular constitutional culture. Of course, quite what the EU's constitutional culture actually is remains a matter of some dispute. But from the perspective of this chapter it is not entirely implausible to suggest that a cosmopolitan solidarity of substance could form part of both the values underpinning that culture and a process for its establishment. Thus, whilst the universal and the particular may be seen as in a permanent and inevitable relationship, it is the dynamic and dialectical nature of that arrangement which is especially pertinent to the conceptualization of solidarity. There is an essential *political* dimension to solidarity which moderates its reach, touching both the creation and sustainability of the bonds which characterize it. As Schwartz observes:

> the bonds of *democratic* social solidarity are neither innately particularist nor inherently universal. Rather, bonds of solidarity can evolve through democratic contestation toward broader horizons of fellow feeling.[60] (emphasis original)

There is no room in this chapter to discuss the new governance models needed to provide the underpinning fora for that contestation to take place in the EU.[61] It is instead sufficient for the moment to stress the *transformative* capacity that the tension between universal and particular can yield, rather than the supposed

[57] n 1, 320.

[58] cf N. Karagiannis, 'European Solidarity with "the Rest of the World"' in Karagiannis, n 7 above, ch 12, who criticizes the dilemma set up by conceptualizing solidarity within the EU (social Model) and with the rest of the world (humanitarian model).

[59] J-W. Müller, 'A general theory of constitutional patriotism' (2008) Intl J of Constitutional Law 72.

[60] n 56 above—Schwartz cites the position of Islam faith immigrants into the EU.

[61] See B. Lange and N. Alexiadou's piece in this volume for a detailed exploration of education as an example. For an introduction to network governance issues, see C. Sabel and J. Zeitlin, 'Learning from difference: The new architecture of Experimentalist Governance in the EU' (2008) 14 Eur LJ 271. cf C. Joerges, 'Integration through de-legalisation? An irritated heckler' European Governance Papers (EUROGOV) No N-07–03, <http://www.connex-network.org/eurogov/pdf/egp-newgov-N-07–03.pdf.> (last visited 10 Aug 2008).

antimony which, as Schwartz has claimed, is historically inaccurate.[62] However, it is acknowledged that the political dimension essential to solidarity-in-fact requires any theorization to engage with the question of how to politicize a compound polity such as the EU.[63]

A further, wider challenge to solidarity (indeed described as its greatest threat by one leading scholar[64]) is how its collective dimension can be reconciled with tendencies towards self-interest. The latter is represented by the middle class, individualism and consumerism, with potentially lethal results for the creation and/or strength of solidarities. On the one hand, when morality is based on self-realization, universal moral criteria lose their significance and other people are only important in the context of intimate relationships.[65] On the other, in a reflexive and liquid modern society, social identity is ever more associated with being a consumer, eroding recognition that each human being is dependent on others. The result is that welfare arrangements previously based on solidarity are replaced by ones based upon individual purchasing power.[66] Social solidarity becomes one of the collateral casualties of consumerism.[67]

However, as Delanty has noted, social theory has moved on beyond a dichotomous view of the individual and society as locked in conflict where a gain in one is the loss of the other.[68] A more nuanced relationship can be theorized in which self-realization can be enhanced by participation in collective action.[69] Thus contemporary social movements—whether tied to ecology, feminism, gay rights or anti-globalization—are based upon individuated personal positions. But the *outcome* from actions taken is a collective identity for those movements. Nevertheless, it must be recognized that this observation only partly wards off scepticism as to solidarity's conceptual power. It does not, for example, connote any European characterization or specificity other than the extent to which particular causes find support within the population of the EU. To this extent these arguments may only attest to the process of cosmopolitanism whilst not negating the possibilities for developing solidarities.

So, in the light of recurring messages about the trajectory of lifeworlds in which fluidity, mobility and choice point towards thinner allegiances and commitments, can a concept of solidarity be meaningfully grounded in the EU at all?

62 n 56 above, 144.

63 See P. Magnette and Y. Papadopoulos, 'On the politicization of the European consociation: A middle way between Hix and Bartolini', *European Governance Papers* (EUROGOV) No C-08–01, <http://www.connex-network.org/eurogov/pdf/egp-connex-C-08–01.pdf.> (last visited 5 July 2008).

64 Stjernø, n 1, 321.

65 ibid 335.

66 ibid 337.

67 Z. Bauman, *Consuming Life* (Cambridge: Polity Press, 2007), especially 142–145.

68 G. Delanty, *Community* (London and New York: Routledge, 2003) 129.

69 See especially A. Melucci, *Challenging Codes: Collective Action in the Information Age* (Cambridge: Cambridge University Press, 1996).

It may be helpful to envisage solidarity constructed in terms of a virtuous circle of reinforcement as follows:

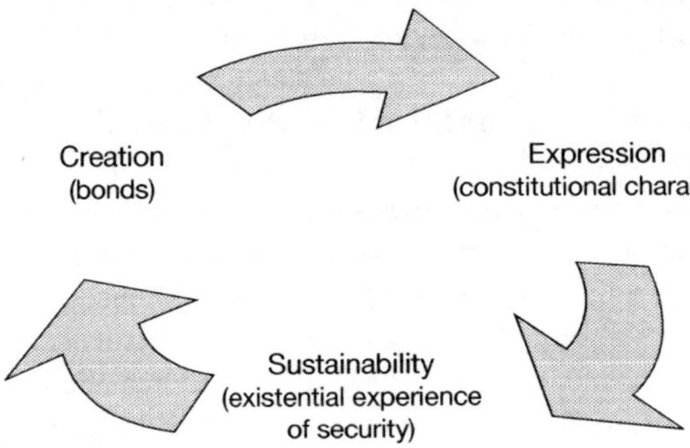

Figure 2. Solidarity's virtuous circle?

This approach attempts to capture both the dynamics of solidarity and the different kinds of analytical work that can be done by the concept. First, it acknowledges the interaction of theoretical and empirical dimensions of solidarity, recognizing that the scope of the concept itself connotes a social reality and/or aspiration.[70] The particularities of this arrangement—in other words, what gives it a distinctiveness in the EU context—can be seen not only in the mutually dependent processes of creation, expression and sustainability, but also in how each element is configured. Secondly, the model recognizes the linkages between disciplines and approaches which bite upon solidarity, both locating its breadth of conceptual power and informing its scope. Thus, as will be argued further below, the expression of solidarity is a strongly—though not uniquely—legal phenomenon (unlike, for example, sociological concepts such as community or cosmopolitanism). In contrast, not only the creation but durability of any such solidarity is dependent upon factors which are more overtly social and political. Thirdly, solidarity as understood here can perform a useful role in modifying or re-interpreting other concepts which are increasingly touted as the currency for understanding global and regional concerns. Security (or insecurity) is perhaps the most obvious such buzz-word of the twenty-first century so far, especially in the context of anti-terrorism measures, police powers and the demonization of 'others'.[71] It will be argued below that effective security can be understood as

[70] cf the Commission's use of the term in its social agenda Communications, nn 17 and 18 above.

[71] For contrasting approaches see, inter alia, M. Neocleous *Critique of Security* (Edinburgh: Edinburgh University Press, 2008), I. Loader and N. Walker, *Civilizing Security* (Cambridge: Cambridge University Press, 2007). The embedding of the security agenda can further be seen by research funding priorities, eg the UK Research Councils programme, Global Uncertainties: Security for All in a Changing World.

experienced through solidarity—which in turn postulates an enduring and reinforced character for the latter. The model's three interrelated constituent elements of creation, expression and sustainability are developed further below.

In relation to *creation*, the evolution of the EU to date exhibits a unique *combination* of bonds which, woven together, form more than a bare abstraction of solidarity. Relevant factors comprise identity, shared values and beliefs, positive rights and responsibilities, and levels of security and anxiety. Assessed separately in the EU context, these elements will score differently along the spectrum from thin to thick solidarities. But the *mix* of these political, legal and societal dimensions is both distinctive and more complex—to that extent suggesting a potentially 'thicker' set of linkages for solidarity than, for example, the notion of constitutional patriotism in its various Habermasian guises.[72] Bringing together these various associative factors (which individually will have different intensities) to provide a holistic concept of European solidarity implies a need to embrace a series of universal/particular relationships that cannot be turned into a simple binary model. Seen in this way, a theoretical model of European solidarity can credibly occupy a place that is neither an extremely thin 'legal rights' base nor a very thick statist or nationalist identity. It must of course be recognized that this positioning is in a state of flux and that the direction of travel in a cosmopolitan space does not have to be determined by or measured against previous historical benchmarks.

Turning to the *expression* of solidarity, this underlines the key role played by the legal framework in which solidarity operates and develops. Crucially, as the third section of this chapter claims, solidarity already occupies a significant place in the constitutional *acquis* of the EU and is explicitly enhanced by the ratified Lisbon Treaty. Put at its strongest, the positioning of solidarity as an emerging constitutional value suggests two interesting repercussions. First, solidarity becomes capable of shaping or directing other core values and legal institutions. Secondly, attributing a fundamental status to solidarity implies that it should apply unless there are good reasons for departing from it as a principle—in much the same way that the principles of equal treatment or non-discrimination have developed in the European legal order. On this basis, the expression of solidarity transforms existing legal relationships and takes on concrete content, especially in relation to two of the key drivers already employed by the Court of Justice in its constitutional jurisprudence—citizenship and fundamental rights.

The concept of citizenship is itself highly contested, and it should be remembered that its EU embodiment is only one of many possibilities.[73] The connections between citizenship and solidarity are superficially attractive. Indeed, Habermas famously referred to citizenship as 'an abstract, legally mediated solidarity between strangers'.[74] However, citizenship, as refined to date in EU law,

[72] eg, J. Bowman, 'Challenging Habermas' response to the European democratic deficit' (2007) 33 Philosophy & Social Criticism 736; also Müller, n 59 above.

[73] For general insights, see J. Ciprut (ed) *The Future of Citizenship* (Cambridge: MIT Press, 2008).

[74] J. Habermas, 'Why Europe needs a Constitution' (2001) Sept–Oct New Left Rev 5, 16.

remains anchored in mobility[75] and a rights methodology which has hitherto been constructed in the image (or, more accurately, shadow) of the market.[76] Its main role to date, whilst remarkable in the sense of expanding the reach of the EC Treaty, especially Article 12, has been untargeted and formal insofar as groups of non-economically active citizens have acquired extended rights through litigation. Recent cases, especially in relation to students, suggest that this particular trend is not unstoppable. On the one hand, there is evidence that a core feature of citizenship—equal treatment—may itself be a general principle that incorporates (and is limited by) concerns of solidarity. But on the other, this may not always be sufficiently strong to trump or prevent even legislative attempts at curtailment, such as the apparent discretion given by Directive 2004/38 to member states to impose temporal limitations on obligations to provide financial assistance to students.[77] There is accordingly a present ambiguity in the case law as to the relationship between citizenship and solidarity, illustrated by the Court's preferences and choices in language. For example, it might be asked whether the *Coleman* judgment[78] on the personal scope of EU secondary legislation against disability discrimination is properly seen as an expression of solidarity with all citizens rather than equal treatment as such. The primary carer of a disabled child was accordingly protected by construing Directive 2000/78 as targeting all forms of disability discrimination rather than protecting a limited group (the disabled).

Yet, it may still be observed that the rights field, however well cultivated, is insufficiently fertile to make a reality of citizenship's fabled 'fundamental status' tag.[79] The significant transformative capacity of citizenship is still unfulfilled in the political arena where contestation of electoral rights in the context of immigration and exclusion provides one of the biggest challenges for the EU polity.[80] As Delanty has observed,[81] Euroscepticism is now linked to a general hostility towards broadening the political community, and the extreme right now has a profile in countries whose social models have been challenged by the wider cultural transformation of Europe. Indeed, it may not be too much of an exaggeration to claim that traditional class conflict has been replaced by a conflict of migrants versus citizens.[82] Solidarity and citizenship thus occupy some common territory in addressing matters of inclusion/exclusion and treatment of 'others' and in having a political dimension which transcends rights-only agendas.

[75] Although some cases, so far in the context of children, may mark a limited shift here. See the case law summarized recently by A. G. Sharpston in Case C-353/06 *Grunkin and Paul* [2008] ECR I-7369.

[76] See Y. Borgmann-Prebil, 'The rule of reason in European Citizenship' (2008) 14 Eur LJ 328.

[77] See the Court's ruling in Case C-158/07 *Förster*, rejecting the more purposive approach canvassed by A. G. Mazák [2008] ECR I-8507.

[78] Case C-303/06 *Coleman v Attridge Law and Steve Law* [2008] ECR I-5603.

[79] Case C-184/99 *Grzelczyk* [2001] ECR I-6193.

[80] See particularly J. Shaw, *The Transformation of Citizenship in the European Union* (Cambridge: Cambridge University Press, 2007).

[81] G. Delanty, 'Fear of others: insecurity, xenophobia and Europe' (2008) 42 Social Policy and Adminstration 676.

[82] ibid.

Thus, there is perhaps potential in the exploration of synergies arising from the dynamics of solidarity and the *institution* of citizenship. As things stand, citizenship is a gradated, rights-led development in EU law, both in the case law and secondary legislation.[83] Seen in this way, it is tempting to describe it as at best a managed equality among tiers of strangers rather than solidarity. One nettle to grasp, accordingly, is whether solidarity can make a difference beyond the boundaries imposed by Article 20 TFUE, which only acknowledges nationals of member states as citizens of the Union.[84] Moreover, as Müller has pointed out, the notion of citizenship as solidarity is problematic in the first place if the latter connotes acting for the benefit of others.[85] However, it is suggested that solidarity—in this sense of embracing the needs of others—could influence and enlarge the content of citizenship rights. Indeed, the Court of Justice has shown some signs of this thinking in the thread discernible in the case law about 'sufficient integration' as a way of connecting migrants to participation in host state welfare arrangements.[86]

In contrast, the relationship of solidarity to fundamental rights seems rather more problematic. Rather than a situation in which citizenship and solidarity might be harnessed together, here there is potentially greater tension to the extent that solidarity may require the limitation of fundamental rights in specific situations. This operates on two linked levels: first, that of the general relationship between collective interests and individual rights and, secondly, in the framing of questions and problems (especially whether in favour of broader social justice or individual rights and freedoms). A particular example of this potential conflict is provided by the question of how solidarity and rights-led approaches play out in relation to typical providers of services of general economic interest. Is the relationship between utilities/customers, care homes/residents and other such combinations to be seen and their environments regulated through the lens of competition, consumer or citizenship law?[87] It could be imagined, for example, how solidarity and cohesion arguments could be harnessed in support of a putative right to receive basic services (energy, water, telecoms, digital television, high-speed broadband connectivity or whatever is deemed to constitute a twenty-first century must-have) across the whole territory and legal space of the EU on affordable terms. In these cases, the function of solidarity is to choose between alternative values housed within the EU Treaties.

[83] Dir 2004/38 exemplifies this approach and was recognized by the Court in its *Förster* judgment, n 77 above.

[84] A point taken up by M. Bell in this volume.

[85] n 59 above.

[86] Greater detail of the case law can be found in S. Giubboni's contribution to this volume.

[87] See P. Rott, 'Consumers and services of general interest: Is EC consumer law the future?' (2007) 30 J of Consumer Policy 49; P. Nebbia, 'Article 16 EC and unfair terms in the provision of public services to consumers' in M. Maresca (ed) *Diritto e Politiche Dell'Unione Europea* (Torino: G.Giappichelli Editore, 2007) 32. More generally, see M. Krajewski, U. Neergaard and J van de Gronden (eds) *The Changing Legal Framework for Services of General Interest in Europe: Between Competition and Solidarity* (The Hague: T M C Asser Press, 2009).

The third element of the virtuous circle model being envisaged, *sustainability*, provides a link between the dimensions of creation and expression which acknowledges the subjective component in classical characterizations of solidarity[88] and the consequent need to present the concept as embracing a 'lived' experience rather than a bare abstraction.[89] This existential dimension to solidarity, as it might be described, endows it with a capacity to challenge or re-appraise other paradigms. In particular, exploration of solidarity offers a significant counterpoint to the 'security fetishism' of this century.[90] This is not to deny that feelings of anxiety exist among European (and other) citizens—indeed, any existential solidarities are at risk of being undermined by such actual (even if misdirected or ungrounded) sentiments. Indeed, the list of insecurities[91] is seemingly inexhaustible—whether 'credit crunch' impoverishment, lack of 'belonging', job insecurity or general fears about immigration and the proliferation of counter-terrorism cultures.[92] However, the articulation of these problems and the framing of responses to them can be sharply distinguished according to whether conceptual foundations are couched in terms of solidarity or security.

In particular, solidarity is neither bounded nor hallmarked by the state in the way that security and its supporting apparatus is often promoted and sustained. As Neocleous has observed,[93] liberalism is a strategy of governance in which security is deployed as liberty. 'Securitizing' every issue provides opportunities for state intervention and those acts can in turn be justified in the name of 'balancing' the twin desiderata of liberty and security. For Neocleous, each step here is an illusion—insecurities are part of the human condition and so-called balancing is in fact a making of preferences in the absence of real argument. On this view, it might be argued that solidarity (by reviewing otherness) is an existential antidote to securitizing tendencies. However, it should also be recognized that the political power of 'security' can attempt to appropriate solidarity for its own ends—as witnessed by calls for 'international solidarity' in the so-called war on terror.

The conceptual challenge, accordingly, is whether rhetorically-charged notions of security and solidarity form counterpoints or linkages.[94] One possibility, it is suggested, is that the existential experience of security (in the sense of reduced

[88] eg Rehg's observation at text for n 31 above.

[89] cf the notion of 'practised' solidarity used by Müller, n 59 above, drawing upon H. Minckler, *Enzyklopädie der Ideen der Zukunft: Solidarität*; in J. Beckert et al (ed) *Transnationale Solidarität-Chancen und Grenzen* (Frankfurt a.M.: Campus, 2004).

[90] Neocleous, n 71 above, uses this term to argue that security is ideologically generated and developed as an interest of both capital and state, with the security industry acting as a partner to the state. cf Loader and Walker, n 71 above, who see security as a 'public good'.

[91] As to whether security or insecurity is the appropriate terminology, and whether security can exist as a condition at all, see R. Powell, 'Security' <http://ssrn.com/abstract=959266> (last visited 5 July 2008).

[92] See Delanty, n 81 above.

[93] n 71 above, 31.

[94] cf the subtitle of the Commission's 2005 paper: 'Strategic Objectives 2005–09: Europe 2010—A Partnership for European Renewal. Prosperity, Solidarity and Security' COM (2005) 12 final.

perception of certain risks and threats) forms an essential component in providing reinforcement (and, arguably, thickening) of the bonds of solidarity and their expression identified above.[95] This argument is perhaps double-edged for, as Neocleous has pointed out, a security-loyalty-identity mesh may be the state's means of ensuring that emergencies are 'normal' by mobilizing loyalty and identity for the purposes of maintaining security. Any rejoinder to this view, using the virtuous circle model of solidarity, must concentrate upon the comparison between (and therefore relative weight to be attached to) interests which are to be secured or secured against[96] and the type of values protected by and characteristic of European transnational solidarities. Whilst acknowledging that solidarity is vulnerable to being hijacked by amorphous security concerns, it is submitted that this is not inevitable and, further, that a solidarity built around social justice goals offers a different emphasis to omnipresent securitization. Or, to turn the dynamics around, a resurgent appraisal of solidarity may act at the very least as a reminder that security can be imagined as a social good rather than a state ideology.[97] In other words, a crucial test for solidarity's conceptual power is its ability to change the politics of security.

To summarize the model outlined above, solidarity is seen in terms of *bonds*, *expression* and *experience* in which constitutional (legal) and existential (sociological and political) dimensions predominate and are at the very least in a mutual (if not always directly causal) and dynamic relationship. Solidarity conceived this way is more than mere membership of a group or entity. Rather, it possesses an essentially active character, thereby implying a transformative capacity. Whether it can transform the contemporary obsession with security is perhaps the most pressing *political* issue for solidarity in the real world—and it may be necessary for that purpose to demonstrate that existential security is better served by transnational solidarities than nationalistic ideologies.

From a *legal* perspective, the most significant contribution from solidarity as a concept is that it can—unlike the process of cosmopolitanism—function as a constitutional principle that must uphold values and choose between priorities. Solidarity, it is argued in this chapter, can address the ways in which the legal and constitutional outcomes of cosmopolitan processes and tendencies are mediated and developed. By way of contrast, solidarity may in the future find itself in sharp competition with security as an ordering principle in the same way that solidarity is already engaged in conflict with market values as a dominant paradigm.

The remainder of this chapter therefore considers the strength of solidarity's actual and potential power in the development of EU law.

[95] cf Neocleous, n 71 above, ch 4.

[96] Powell, n 91 above, identifies four interests: way of life, means of life, rights and physical safety.

[97] Loader and Walker, n 71 above, claim that security is a state of well-being, in which people live in a political community, together and securely with risk (169).

4. Solidarity as a constitutional paradigm in the EU

I have dealt in greater detail elsewhere[98] with the extent to which solidarity already features in the EU's legal landscape. This presence, perhaps best described as persistent but diverse, is particularly significant for moulding the building blocks of an evolving legal architecture. In summary, there have been five areas where the Court of Justice has invoked or elaborated upon solidarity to shape the *acquis* of EU law, represented below.

Location/source	Solidarity's role	Expression and significance
Art 10 EC (now Art 4 TEU) duty	**Active** obligations to secure effectiveness of EU law	Applicable to EU and national institutions, especially national courts; transcends 1st and 3rd EU pillars; used by the ECJ as foundation for key constitutional principles securing protection of individual rights.
Fundamental rights: ECJ case law and EU Charter provisions	**Value signifier** in relation to social rights	Individual access to (and enjoyment of) social justice; eg healthcare, public services; Title II, Chapter IV of the Charter of Fundamental Rights is headed 'Solidarity'.
Market freedoms	**Modifier** of market imperative	Rule of reason in relation to justification of obstacles to single market; recognition of national solidarities and supporting solidarity as an EU concept.
EU citizenship	**Rights** building	Developing equal treatment principle in core citizenship rights; requiring member states to demonstrate financial solidarity towards those EU citizens sufficiently integrated into host society.
Competition rules, Arts 81–86 EC (now Arts 101–106 TFEU)	**Boundary** marker	Used to explain meaning of 'economic' to define 'undertaking'; solidarity systems excluded from EU competition rules; also invoked as justification for applying ex Art 86(2) to services of general economic interest and thus not applying the full rigour of competition rules.

Figure 3. The solidarity acquis

Moreover, there are additional illustrations to be found of solidarity in a Treaty context, most notably in relation to the various cohesion policies contained in Title XVIII TFEU.[99]

[98] M. Ross, 'Promoting solidarity: From public services to a European model of competition?' (2007) 44 CML Rev 1057.

[99] See also the sources of solidarity identified by C. Barnard in this volume.

Three points particularly emerge to underline the claim that solidarity is not just some occasional reference point or supplementary line of argumentation in existing jurisprudence. These relate to the transformative, constitutional and methodological dimensions of solidarity as a legal concept. First, ex Article 10 EC is perhaps the clearest example of the levels of activity and commitment which classical solidarity demands. If effectiveness[100] (of Treaty enjoyment) is the outcome demanded by the Court of Justice, then solidarity is the proactive means to deliver it. Solidarity here cuts across EU, national and local institutions[101] and across the former EU pillars,[102] thus providing the 'thickest' example of transnational legal bonds performing this kind of unifying role. This is not an attempt at replicating statism with one EU legal order but an accommodation of orders with solidarity as the essential value *and* instrument for keeping conflict and difference within manageable bounds. In this sense, solidarity as a cooperative and social justice-led concept is perhaps more credible in maintaining that accommodation than the discourse of supremacy and compliance. In this regard, solidarity may have a contribution to make to debates under the umbrella of legal pluralism as a means of understanding the operation and theoretical explanation of the EU.

Secondly, solidarity in a substantive sense bites on two fundamental questions affecting the very rationale of the European legal and political order. At one level, solidarity is central to the relationship between social and market values. As the Grand Chamber has recently observed, 'Since the Community has not only an economic but also a social purpose, the rights under the provisions of the Treaty on the free movement of goods, persons, services and capital must be balanced against the objectives pursued by social policy . . .'[103] Of course, this statement does not determine the outcome of that balance in any particular case, but if solidarity has indeed attained constitutional status then it acquires enhanced significance in that exercise. At the same time, solidarity issues have also acquired an importance in the resolution of competence allocation as between EU and member state levels. At its narrowest this can be seen in the on-going rumblings in the case law concerning the definition of an undertaking for the purposes of the competition rules.[104] More fundamentally perhaps, the recent CFI ruling in the *BUPA* case[105] has highlighted the legal chaos surrounding the respective powers of the EU and its

[100] See M. Ross, 'Effectiveness in the European legal order(s): beyond supremacy to constitutional proportionality?' (2006) 31 ELR 476; cf M. Dougan, 'When worlds collide! Competing visions of the relationship between direct effect and supremacy' (2007) 44 CML Rev 931.

[101] And, arguably, extends also to public bodies.

[102] eg Case C-105/03 *Pupino* [2005] ECR I-5285 and the notion of indirect effect.

[103] Case C-438/05 *Viking* [2007] ECR I-10779, para 79.

[104] eg Case C-49/07 *MOTOE* [2008] ECR I-4863.

[105] Case T-289/03 *BUPA* [2008] ECR II-81. This controversial judgment appears to give member states a significant area of discretion subject only to review against manifest error; see M. Ross, 'A healthy approach to services of general economic interest? The *BUPA* judgment of the Court of First Instance' (2009) 34 ELR 127. See also Case T-442/03 *SIC v Commission* [2008] ECR II-1161.

member states in the determination, support and regulation of public services.[106] On the one hand, the judgment starts from the premise that the identification of what constitutes a service of general economic interest is a matter for the discretion of member states and, accordingly, only subject to review under EU law for manifest error.[107] But on the other, the CFI also asserts that there are minimum (EU law) criteria to be satisfied in determining a service of general economic interest: 'notably, the presence of an act of the public authority entrusting the operators in question with an SGEI mission and the universal and compulsory nature of that mission.'[108] Given the heightened political sensitivity which attaches to the provision of public services, this arena may well provide the sternest test of whether solidarity has indeed acquired a *communautaire* meaning and application.[109] Or, to frame the issue in other terms, how does solidarity apply to subsidiarity—and vice versa?

Thirdly, but by no means least significantly, it should be noted that the treatment of solidarity in the above examples is entirely consistent with the methodologies and practices of the Court of Justice in rationalizing new constitutional steps. There is ample evidence, for example, of solidarity in the constitutional traditions of (some) member states[110]—a classic justification for the introduction of fundamental rights and other foundational principles (eg proportionality) into EC/EU law. Thus Article 2 of the Italian constitution[111] (under Fundamental Principles), Article 1 of the French constitution (institution of Community) and Article 2 of the Spanish constitution (National Unity, Regional Autonomy) all explicitly refer to solidarity. Whilst the term may still sound a little odd or unfamiliar to some lawyers in a few member states, solidarit*ies* arguably form a significant part of Europe's legal heritage and culture.[112] But of course, and this is hugely relevant for the virtuous circle of solidarity canvassed earlier, the fact that a concept has antecedents in member states does not demand that the EU level version of it has to correspond to most, or indeed any, of them. Moreover, the Grand Chamber

[106] More properly for the purposes of EU law, variously described as services of general economic interest, services of general interest, social services of general interest and even non-economic services of general interest.

[107] *BUPA*, n 105 above, paras 166–167.

[108] ibid, para 172.

[109] See *Analysis of the implications on Services of General Interest and proposals for implementation* Discussion paper drawn up by European experts, March 2008. Accessed via <http://www.ces.etat.lu/SIG_Document%20de%20reflexion.pdf> (last visited 5 July 2008).

[110] See T. Fiegle, '*Solidarité* and *Solidarität*: the concept of solidarity in France and Germany in the nineteenth century' in Karagiannis (ed), n 7 above, 48.

[111] 'La Repubblica riconosce e garantisce i diritti inviolabili dell'uomo, sia come singolo sia nelle formazioni sociali ove si svolge la sua personalità, e richiede l'adempimento dei doveri inderogabili di solidarietà politica, economica e sociale.' I am grateful to Cristina di Luigi, doctoral student at the University of Sussex, for bringing this to my attention.

[112] cf R. Cotterrell, 'Images of Europe in Sociolegal Traditions' in V. Gessner and D. Nelken (eds) *European Ways of Law—Towards a European Sociology of Law* (Oxford and Portland Oregon: Hart Publishing, 2007).

has recently reiterated its stance on the interpretation of EU concepts, to the effect that:

> It follows from the need for uniform application of Community law and from the principle of equality that the terms of a provision of Community law which makes no express reference to the law of the Member States for the purpose of determining its meaning and scope must normally be given an autonomous and uniform interpretation throughout the Union. [113]

Even if the above claims are too bold, it seems unarguable that solidarity will become a hotly debated concept since the ratification of the Lisbon Treaty.[114] The Treaty on European Union refers to a society 'in which pluralism, non-discrimination, tolerance, justice, solidarity and equality between women and men prevail.' Article 2 provides that the Union pursues 'a highly competitive social market economy'. Tasks in the same Article include the promotion of social justice and protection, intergenerational solidarity, economic, social and territorial cohesion, and solidarity among member states. On the external stage, the Union 'shall contribute to peace, security, the sustainable development of the Earth, solidarity and mutual respect among peoples.' Moreover, solidarity is described as a principle alongside equality with respect to the Union's action on the international scene. The conduct of foreign policy is stated to be based on the 'development of mutual political solidarity among Member States'. As regards the Treaty on the Functioning of the European Union, the chapter on the area of freedom, security and justice requires that policies and their implementation shall be governed by the principle of solidarity and fair sharing of responsibility, including its financial implications, between the member states.

Of course, there is a risk that these new developments constitute no more than a feel-good mantra. Moreover, as already shown in relation to current EU law, the Lisbon Treaty appears to continue using solidarity in a number of different senses and glaringly does not define it. Yet it would be difficult to dispute either its pervasiveness or significance under the new arrangements so that, like citizenship most recently before it, solidarity offers considerable creative opportunities for interpretation. What, for example is the scope of intergenerational solidarity—how dominant a paradigm does it represent in the establishment and regulation of welfare and social security programmes, environmental priorities, or the provision of educational and other public services?[115]

[113] Case C-66/08 *Szymon Kozlowski* [2008] ECR I-6041 para 42. The case on this point was concerned with the meaning of 'resident' and 'staying' in Framework Decision 2002/584/JHA on the European arrest warrant.

[114] OJ [2007] C306.

[115] See *BUPA*, n 105 above where intergenerational solidarity is discussed in the context of health insurance premiums; paras 292–293.

5. Some conclusions

I have argued that solidarity possesses considerable potential as a transformative concept in developing a commitment to social justice as part of a revitalised and cosmopolitan EU. As a concept, it holds significant power alongside, in relation to or in competition with, other key discourses currently being adopted to analyze the evolving structures and character of the EU. Manifestations of the notion are already embedded in the *acquis* of EU law and, moreover, the Lisbon Treaty confirms the centrality of solidarity in the EU's future constitutional arrangements. Indeed, if for no other reason, the elaboration and conceptualization of solidarity is inevitable with the Lisbon Treaty in force since so many elements of it will give rise to tests of justiciability and interpretation. Nevertheless, in presenting solidarity as potentially hugely influential, three particular caveats should be entered.

First, solidarity is certainly not being advocated as some unique prescription or panacea. Rather, the argument is that the concept is capable of being aligned with other law-rich ideas (especially citizenship, cohesion and effectiveness) as both a statement of values and adjudicatory mechanism in favour of social justice priorities. Solidarity is thus a concept 'with legs'—although whether it runs, stumbles or falls over is still to be seen. Secondly, the virtuous circle idea outlined in this chapter canvasses the interdependence of legal and existential elements to solidarity. However, I have concentrated upon those legal elements (partly present in bonds, more so in expression) which can be classified as constitutional contributions. Translating solidarity from powerful concept into lived experience demands political responses. Accordingly, the third but indispensable caveat is that the key bridge between the constitutional and the existential rests upon a recursive political context dependent, especially, upon an evolution in governance models.

3

Mission Impossible? Limits and Perils of Institutionalizing Post-National Social Policy

Wolfram Lamping

1. Introduction

'History tells us that EU social policy is not evolutionary in any simple way'.[1] In contrast, this peculiar European policy field is tightly constrained by governments' (legitimate) self-interests and the dominant market character of the European integration project.[2] Rather than driving on the main highway, 'Social Europe' often has to make various detours—and not seldom comes in by the backdoor. Despite the formidable obstacles and perils EU social policy faces,[3] since the 1970s many scientists have hankered after a strong, centralized EU social policy regime, based upon a pan-European solidarity space and equipped with strong regulatory and spending capacities and powerful enough to preserve the main elements of the so-called post-war 'European social model' at supranational level. Jürgen Habermas in particular, is well aware of the fact that a post-national entity, let alone European statehood, cannot function without a greater expansion of the social remit and the development of European forms of solidarity, expressing itself via a European public sphere.[4] Calling for European unity and interested in the future of post-national social policy, he views European

[1] M. Daly, 'Whither EU Social Policy? An Account and Assessment of Developments in the Lisbon Social Inclusion Process' (2007) 37 (1) J of Social Policy 1–19.

[2] W. Lamping, 'European Union Social Policy: Towards a Post-National Welfare State?' in K. Schubert, S. Hegelich, and U. Bazant (eds) *The Handbook of European Welfare Systems* (London/ New York: Routledge, 2009) 495–510.

[3] K. Anderson and W. Lamping, 'Europeanization or Persistence of National Differences? Opportunities and Obstacles to European Social Policy Integration' (Paper presented at the 57th Political Studies Annual Conference, April 21–23, 2007, University of Bath).

[4] J. Habermas, *The Inclusion of the Other: Studies in Political Theory* (Cambridge: MIT Press, 1998); ibid, 'The European Nation-State and the Pressures of Globalisation' (1999) 235 Left Rev 46–59; ibid, *The Postnational Constellation: Political Essays* (Cambridge: MIT Press, 2001).

integration as a response to the effects of globalization and the shortcomings of national welfare states unable to cope with new pressures and new risks. According to Habermas the establishment of a Europe-wide rights-based solidarity as well as the development of a post-national social policy—which Habermas believes are important tools for the formation of a post-national identity in Europe—are primarily a matter of political will and skill. Moreover, he assumes in most of the EU member states' populations a sort of strong permissive consensus in favour of deeper social policy integration.[5]

It is nevertheless hardly surprising that 'Social Europe' is still contentious and a long way from being more than a bold idea. We certainly witness an incremental social supranationalism in social policy and a segmented Europeanization of the national welfare states, but national welfare states still refuse to be amalgamated into a single European one. The more European integration approaches the 'solidarity core' of national welfare states (distribution, redistribution, public services), the greater the political resistance and the higher the necessity for the EU to justify itself and to prove the additional value of further supranationalization. National systems of social sharing and social transfers are still fundamental mechanisms of social closure. Social rights and the organization and financing of redistribution are still an essential part of the nations' politically constructed identity. The dilemma, however, is a double one: post-nationalist projects, such as the EU, mean (and require) to some extent creating a new sense of social solidarity among citizens without giving up national social solidarity communities. At the same time the institutionalization of an EU-wide social solidarity presupposes something which it simultaneously needs to develop: common values and the willingness to share.

The basic argument of this chapter is that it is time to (re)direct scholarly debates back to the unresolved and delicate challenges and dilemmas 'Europe' as a political and social community faces in terms of establishing social cohesion, solidarity and trust among strangers. Against this background this chapter argues, first, that supranational social solidarity should not be taken for granted given the fact that collectivity, membership, mutual commitment, identification, and a sense of belonging to a specific community of fellow citizens are still organized in and by member states. Second, (re)distribution matters: while the (regulatory) social policy regime of the EU is certainly considerable, especially in the 'periphery' of welfare states, national solidarity communities are still intact. National borders are the boundaries of distribution and redistribution as well as public/social services which are at the heart of national welfare statehood. Third, enhancing a common European social solidarity is an open process with a radically uncertain outcome, not least because the non- or not yet state European

[5] J. Habermas, 'Das illusionäre "Nein der Linken"' (2005) 6 Blätter für deutsche und internationale Politik 755–757; 'Europa: Vision und Votum' (2007) 5 Blätter für deutsche und internationale Politik 517–520.

polity still lacks the socio-structural and normative-political preconditions upon which nation-states have been built. Therefore, fourth, there is the foreseeable risk that European integration, in many ways, continues to weaken the member states and to de-structure the solidarity space within them, while not being able to reconstitute at supranational level that kind of solidarity which is both characteristic of and necessary for fully developed welfare statehood.

After having discussed some of the political, institutional and cultural obstacles to social policy integration, this chapter comes to the conclusion that the EU should be careful when it raises high expectations or when it announces high-flown and ambitious social policy projects which approach the sensitive core policies of national welfare statehood. Under these conditions, however, diversity might not be a problem, but a challenge. The central question for a 'Social Europe' is which (institutional, social, distributive etc) diversity can be acknowledged and accepted as legitimate—and which cannot.

2. Touching the social contract between citizens and the state: boundary shifting and boundary redrawing as a challenge to national welfare states

Abram de Swaan argued decisively in the 1990s that 'welfare states are national states', pointing to the fact that the normative concept of welfare statehood with its internal moral assumptions of justice, social coherence and individual well-being requires at least well defined territorial boundaries and an instinctive solidarity —even if this kind of solidarity has been a hierarchically imposed one.[6] According to Titmuss, the welfare state promotes feelings of solidarity and mutual obligation, and tends to generate a higher level of redistribution and social integration within the society.[7] Rothstein alludes to the point that welfare states represent conceptions of a legitimate social order.[8] They incorporate certain values into their institutions; to the extent that these values correspondent to the moral orientations and expectations of citizens, welfare state institutions can be expected to receive considerable public support. The welfare state, as Goodin argues, is 'first and foremost a political artefact',[9] and as such 'the product of historical accretion and political compromise'.[10] The (democratic) welfare state can

[6] A. de Swaan, 'Perspectives for Transnational Social Policy' (1992) 27 Government and Opposition 33 at 33; 'Perspectives for Transnational Social Policy in Europe: Social Transfers from West to East' in A. de Swaan (ed) *Social Policies Beyond Boarders: The Social Question in International Perspective* (Amsterdam: Amsterdam University Press, 1994) 101–115.

[7] R. M. Titmuss, *Commitment to Welfare* (London: Unwin University Books, 1968).

[8] B. Rothstein, *Just Institutions Matter: The Moral and Political Logic of the Universal Welfare State* (Cambridge: Cambridge University Press, 1998).

[9] R. E. Goodin, *Reasons for Welfare. The Political Theory of the Welfare State* (Princeton: Princeton University Press, 1988) 3.

[10] ibid.

be defined as 'a system of compulsory, collective, and largely nondiscretionary welfare provisions'.[11] Which programmes are to be included and which excluded from *the* welfare state varies according to time and place. Its *sine qua non*, however, is the institutionalization of 'solidarity'. It is the core of welfare statehood and part of its distinctive built-in moral grammar, although the scope and character of the concept varies between welfare states.

'Solidarity' has many faces. By solidarity I do not only mean the institutionalization of (collective) social rights guaranteed by the state, but primarily the establishment of redistribution (transfer programmes, benefits-in-kind), and non-discriminatory public services in order to achieve specific social policy ends (more social justice, equity, equality compared to the status quo *ante*). A specific kind of mutual commitment via social cooperation and social law which the members of a community perceive as legitimate are characteristic of solidarity within social groups as well as within nation-states. From an organizational perspective, however, this kind of 'solidarity can only be sustained in closed communities'.[12] It is conventional wisdom that without restrictions on entry to or exit from a solidarity community, governments lack effective means to maintain both the moral and especially, the organizational infrastructure of welfare states. In other words, social policies, especially those of high distributional relevance, necessarily discriminate between insiders and outsiders. Non-nationals generally have great difficulties entering the 'solidarity spaces' of other states.[13]

The nation-state has been the tried and tested home of social policy for more than 150 years. Therefore social and political space has been formed accordingly; ie there is a congruence between the social and political space. A post-national project like the EU, however, would require new concepts of solidarity reflecting that solidarity can no longer be conceived of as an exclusively national idea enforced by national boundaries and national social law. This, however, goes hand in hand with a redefinition of the concept of identity, since one can (theoretically) assume that the stronger the national identity is and the more people are emotionally attached to their country, the less they could support the transfer of sensitive nation building resources such as social security and protection and the

[11] ibid 12.

[12] H. Vollaard, 'Solidarity, Territoriality, and Healthcare: Cross-National Policy Learning in Europe' in D. Levi-Four, and E. Vigoda-Gadot (eds) *International Public Policy and Management* (New York: Marcel Dekker, 2004) 267.

[13] This is most striking in the area of means-tested (need-based) benefits which, usually financed by taxes, are closely linked to citizenship and the willingness of a collective to pay for those who are not in a position to help themselves (social assistance, basic incomes etc). In contrast to social security, member states explicitly want to reserve the right to social benefits unrelated to work or benefits to their own citizens and have great difficulty accepting nationals of EU member states who claim this benefit. Ferrera is right to argue that 'regarding social assistance, member states can still pull institutional levers to close off this sphere of national social sharing' (M. Ferrera, 'European Integration and National Social Citizenship. Changing Boundaries, New Structuring?' (2003) 36 (6) Comparative Political Studies 611–652 at 637).

less they might be willing to accept the costs of more solidarity (in terms of compromises, individual sacrifices, winners and losers, etc) at EU level.

The European welfare states still look national: there are national social security institutions, social rights and responsibilities are predominantly defined by national social law, social policy is financed by national resources, redistribution takes place within national borders, social policy laws are enacted by national legislatures, implemented by national bureaucracies and justified by national governments who still claim to be autonomous and sovereign in social policy matters. Yet, it is a truism that this is only half the story, since national social policy is increasingly transformed and redefined in the wake of European integration and EU-level accumulation of authority.[14] This is due to the fact that during the past two decades the influence of the EU on national welfare states has increased significantly. It is now generally acknowledged that most national social policy developments cannot be understood without taking into account the role of the EU. European integration has gradually de-bordered and redefined core principles of welfare statehood.

This development is part of a fundamental transformation of the concept and foundations of modern national statehood in Europe. Though we can describe and understand the driving forces of this process we do not really know the final results of this development. This is partly due to the fact that we witness a plurality of dissynchronous and discontinuing transformations among and within nearly all core areas of nation-states, ie resources, law, legitimation, sovereignty, and welfare[15]— all of which were in perfect and stable harmony during the 'trente glorieuses' of post-war Western welfare states. European integration, *eo ipso* and as such a project marked by high indefiniteness has become an additional source of stress for national welfare states. The establishment of an enlarged playing field in these spheres, ie the EU,[16] has not only sustainably changed the national 'rules of the game' in social policy and sectorally constrained governments' room for manoeuvre. The dynamics of market integration—not least via the EU's principles of free movement, free competition, and non-discrimination—as well as political initiatives from the Commission have resulted in sectorally considerable regulatory and political competencies in social policy. Since the end-1990s,

[14] W. Lamping, n 2 above; S. Leibfried, and P. Pierson, 'Social Policy. Left to Courts and Markets?' in H. Wallace, and W. Wallace (eds) *Policy-Making in the European Union* (4th edn, Oxford: Oxford University Press, 2000) 267–292.

[15] See eg S. Leibfried, and M. Zürn, 'Von der nationalen zur postnationalen Konstellation' in S. Leibfried, and M. Zürn (eds) *Transformationen des Staates?* (Frankfurt a.M.: Suhrkamp, 2006) 19–68.

[16] S. Bartolini, *Restructuring Europe: Centre Formation, System Building, and Political Structuring Between the Nation-State and the European Union* (Oxford: OUP, 2005); M. Ferrera, 'European Integration and National Social Citizenship. Changing Boundaries, New Structuring?' (2003) 36 (6) Comparative Political Studies 611–652; ibid, *The Boundaries of the Welfare State: European Integration and the New Spatial Politics of Social Protection* (Oxford: OUP, 2005); ibid, 'National Welfare States and European Integration: In Search of a "Virtuous Nesting"' (2009) 47 (2) J of Common Market Studies 219–233.

the European Court of Justice (ECJ) as well as the Commission have gradually approached the more sensitive areas of national welfare states.

Bartolini and Ferrera have analysed the problematic relationship between the opening pressures linked to European integration and the closure foundations of the nation-based welfare state. Their intellectual and argumentative point of departure is that European integration is an ongoing process of (and an important factor for) redrawing the boundaries of national welfare states ('spatial reconfiguration') which they demonstrate has significant consequences both for the distinct, clearly demarcated and long-standing national solidarity communities and for the EU as a new state-like territorial unit alike. National social policy is about defining and building boundaries, and it is about distinguishing between insiders and outsiders (territorial principle, compulsory insurance, public monopolies). European integration is about making boundaries more fluid (free movement, free and undistorted competition, non-discrimination) and turning outsiders into insiders and the out-space into the in-space. While national social policy at its very core is about defining spatial demarcations and locking their citizens in by defining exclusive sets of norms, rules and rights, European integration is about weakening or tearing apart these closure practices, constraining the scope and content of bounding decisions, and creating equals. The constant processes of boundary shifting has challenged the national social welfare territories, which were formerly sealed off from each other, and thus disrupted the traditional norms of social policy isolation and exclusiveness.[17]

In this respect, European social policy integration can be conceptualized as:

(i) a *bidirectional regime enlargement* in the sense that 'external' actors impact on domestic polities, economies and long-standing institutional equilibria while, simultaneously, national actors try to influence the supranational regime building process and exploit the supranational polity for their own interests. In this respect European integration has enhanced the room for manoeuvre of national governments/member states and at the same time substantially shaken national statehood, autonomy, sovereignty, and democracy, respectively, and rendered them increasingly nominal.

(ii) a constant but unequal *process of denationalization, deterritorialization and boundary shifting,* in the wake of which national authorities experience a loss of autonomous capacity to act and of sovereign social policy competences. This affects the normative self-perception and conceptual foundation of each and every *national* welfare state since national social policies define criteria for inclusion and exclusion. Welfare statehood without

[17] One striking example are the entry and exit rules defined by the meanwhile sophisticated system of coordination of national social security systems within the Union governed by a number of Council regulations. One core feature of these regulatory policies of positive integration is that they lead to a certain harmonization between member-state laws, but these laws are still implemented and 'materialized' within national frontiers.

boundaries and boundary control—ie without the ability to effectively prevent an external regime from encroaching on the 'social sovereignty' of member states or to effectively prevent 'mobile factors' from leaving the territory of national social law (closure of exit options) —is a new phenomenon and experience for member states.

(iii) a redefinition of *internal 'fraternity' and external 'unfraternity'*. The welfare state, which governments since the outset of national welfare statehood have perceived as a 'closed system' of national regulation and (though enforced) national solidarity is on the way to being made economically compatible and legally permeable. As a consequence, national solidarity communities (national territory, national boundaries, national politics and national citizens) are gradually drifting apart. This could give way to new concepts of solidarity which have to be defined by and refer to the fact that solidarity will no longer be an exclusively national idea enforced by national boundaries and national social law. Against this background, both European citizenship[18] and the Charter of Fundamental Rights further promote the dissociation of the nation-state and its citizens by defining European rights independent from nationality. They have at least the potential to enhance the Union's social legitimacy, strengthen transnational solidarity or even promote identification.

(iv) a simultaneous process of *supranational integration and national disintegration* in economic and social policy. In other words, supranational integration includes national disintegration processes because supranational integration cannot be achieved without fundamental economic and social policy change at the national level.

(v) a *critical juncture for national welfare statehood*. European integration coincides with and adds to welfare states' persistent and enormous internal and external challenges. In this respect the European welfare states are in a transitional phase, characterized by a high degree of strategic uncertainty vis-à-vis the ways and means of coping with the future—and not least with European integration which questions the core principles of national welfare statehood and national solidarity.

Each of these five processes has repercussions on national welfare states. They are caught between a process of eroding national boundaries and competencies, and a faltering, discontinuing, patchy process of EU-level boundary redrawing and capacity-building. In other words, in social policy, European integration cannot go any further without jeopardizing the legitimization capacities—and the normative und cultural foundations—of the nation-state. Van Kersbergen addresses the following questions: 'If social policies have institutionalized social solidarity

[18] cf T. Faist, 'Social Citizenship in the European Union: Nested Membership' (2001) 39 (1) J of Common Market Studies 37–58; L. Magnusson, and B. Strath, *A European Social Citizenship? Preconditions for Future Policies from a Historical Perspective* (Bruxelles: Peter Lang, 2004).

within the boundaries of the national state and have had such a beneficial impact on social and political integration under democratic conditions, does the weakening and even vanishing of national borders as a result of European integration threaten national integration and social solidarity?'[19] In contrast, I will in the following section explore whether fading, and indeed disappearing, national borders promote or even facilitate the institutionalization of European social solidarity as a sort of compensation for the national losses. Any progress in social policy integration which goes into that direction faces obstacles, dilemmas, and constraints of social policy integration which will be addressed in the following section.

3. Political, institutional, and cultural obstacles on the road to social policy integration

From a broader perspective one can identify, very briefly, some general aspects which allow for reflections on the perils of 'Europeanizing' social policy and institutionalizing transnational solidarity.

3.1 The constitutional asymmetry between negative and positive integration

Social policy appears to be a victim of the Treaty's imbalance and abeyance on the one hand and member states' jealousies on the other. *Economically*, member states, under the close scrutiny of the Commission and the ECJ, are obliged to 'act in accordance with the principle of an open market economy with free competition' (Article 120 TFEU). *Politically*, the EC/EU has been, by and large, able and willing to develop regulative social policy capacities only in those areas in which social policy is either a harmless means for facilitating market integration, or *in toto* does not really offend its members' sensibilities or go against their interests. This is the reason why member states still perceive the welfare state as an 'enclave' outside the integration process and consequently one of the last key realms of national policy competence.

The still inherent constitutional asymmetry in favour of 'negative integration' (ie market-building and market-making policies) at supranational level, and the dynamics giving European politics and policies a bias in favour of free trade and competition at the cost of market-correcting policies have been extensively analysed.[20] Every step of deepening the internal market threatens and put pressure on the existing national welfare regimes. Commission initiatives and

[19] K. van Kersbergen, 'The Politics of Solidarity and the Changing Boundaries of the Welfare State' (2006) 5 (4) Eur Political Science 377–394 at 382.

[20] cf eg F. W. Scharpf, 'Economic Integration, Democracy and the Welfare State' (1997) 4 J of Eur Public Policy 18–36; ibid, *Governing in Europe: Effective and Democratic?* (Oxford: OUP, 1999).

ECJ jurisprudence seeking to establish a liberal market regime via the abolition of restrictions on trade and the establishment of free competition are based on relatively simple and effective decision-making procedures. By contrast, the conceptualization and realization of 'positive integration' (ie market-correcting/redistributive policies) involve high decision-making costs, because a broad consensus needs to be reached among member state governments in the Council of Ministers. In other words, 'while the Commission and ECJ motors turn smoothly as they deepen negative integration, a lot of political support needs to be mustered up in the Council and the European Parliament to bring about positive integration and redistributive policies'.[21] Solidarity issues are still subject to intergovernmental negotiations which makes decision making much more complicated. The intergovernmental mode in the Council minimizes 'the risks of having to implement European policies that may violate interests and preferences that have very high political salience nationally'.[22] Decision -making in market-correcting, redistributive social policies remains highly political, as may still be seen with the Treaty of Lisbon (Article 153), which has increased qualified majority voting—and thus further reduced institutional barriers—with the exception of—inter alia—'social security and social protection', which is formally still well protected by unanimity (and governments' self-interests) in the Council.

Thus, in social security matters, governments have—at least theoretically—quite successfully avoided being rushed by the Commission's strategic initiatives or even being unexpectedly caught by surprise by individual governments. For the integration process as a whole, the veto power of governments is not simply a possibility for putting a spanner in the works, it is to the same extent a source of legitimacy ensuring that the output of Community decision processes in crucial policy fields is legitimate—and not more than nations and citizens can cope with. In these market-correcting areas, 'national policies are coordinated or standardized by agreements at the European level, but national governments remain in full control of the decision process, none of them can be bound without its own consent, and the transformation of agreements into national law and their implementation remains fully under their control'.[23] Under these circumstances of intergovernmental bargaining 'the problem-solving capacity of negotiated policy is strictly limited to solutions which are preferable to the status quo from the perspective of all participating governments'.[24] The problem is that 'high consensus requirements and the insistence on uniformity had the effect of drastically limiting political policy choices to issues on which member

[21] A. Héritier, 'Containing Negative Integration' in R. Mayntz, and W. Streeck (eds) *Die Reformierbarkeit der Demokratie. Innovationen und Blockaden. Festschrift für Fritz W. Scharpf* (Frankfurt a.M./New York: Campus, 2003) 101.

[22] F. W. Scharpf, 'Problem-Solving Effectiveness and Democratic accountability in the EU', Working Paper 03/1 of the Max Planck Institute for the Study of Societies, Cologne. 2003, p 12.

[23] F. W. Scharpf, 'Notes Toward a Theory of Multilevel Governing in Europe', Discussion Paper 00/5 of the Max Planck Institute for the Study of Societies, Cologne, 2000, p 13.

[24] ibid.

governments could agree'.[25] The logic inherent in institutional configurations of this type, where policy processes rely on the cooperation and good will of a large number of actors, tends to result either in deadlock or 'sub-optimal outcomes'. Solutions can be blocked by major conflicts of interest and/or reduced to the lowest common denominator—and that is what governments explicitly want in these sensitive policy areas.[26] Particularly in the social policy core areas, most obvious in social protection matters, it is much easier to block reforms than to enact them, given the considerable interest differences among the 27 governments. The price, however, of preserving national realms of sovereignty and autonomy is, as Scharpf correctly points out, that 'European policy is paralyzed by politically salient conflicts of interest or preference among its member states.'[27] Even though governments are meanwhile well aware of the fact that they are unable to cope with the new European policy challenges on their own, the supranationalization of substantial social policy competences, which some authors suggest, do not seem to be realistic in the foreseeable future.[28] In fact, despite the Treaty's impressive rhetoric, the notion of EU social policy and the areas of competence of the Community are still significantly limited because of the EU's peculiar institutional design and the imbalance between economic and political integration on the one hand and social integration on the other. Thus, institutional arrangements imbued with 'intergovernmentalism' especially the 'unanimity' requirement combined with prevalent diverging interests do not allow social policy—let alone redistribution—to really catch up with economic integration.[29]

3.2 Majoritarian decision-making in social policy?

Protagonists of parliamentarizing the EU according to national blueprints argue that 'the more citizens are involved in the decision-making process and its control, the more likely it is that they will accept the resulting political outcomes'[30]

[25] F. Scharpf, n 22 above, 23.

[26] F. W. Scharpf, 'Negative and Positive Integration in the Political Economy of European Welfare States' in Y. Mény/ M. Rhodes (eds) *The Future of European Welfare—A New Social Contract* (London: Macmillan, 1998) 155–177.

[27] F. Scharpf, n 22 above, 211.

[28] The history of social policy integration is a history of symbolic declarations which are uncontroversial as long as they have no formal standing. Once the debate over 'Social Europe' gets more concrete, or serious, deep divisions among governments unleash.

[29] Social policy played a minor role in the Convention process. The Draft Treaty of a Constitution for Europe (CONV 850/03) remained fairly vague and modest in its chapter on 'solidarity' (part II, title IV). Moreover, in its final report, the European Convention Working Group XI on 'Social Europe' went no further than to state in No. 3 of the 'Summary of Conclusion': 'On the competences of the Union in the social field, the Group considers in general that the existing competences are adequate.' Therefore a 'considerable number of Group members expressed their support for the limits placed on action at European level. In particular, they emphasised that these were areas in which the specific features of each Member State are very important' (CONV 516/1/03).

[30] M. Höreth, 'No Way Out For the Beast? The Unsolved Legitimacy Problem of European Governance' (1999) 6 (2) J of Eur Public Policy 249–268 at 258.

and, given the EP as a stage for European political debates, policy formulation, and conflict resolution, the more they are willing to identify with the 'European project'. EU-level majoritarian decision-making is, as mentioned before, linked to particular social and cultural preconditions which are only partially existent in the EU, and which can hardly be created by political intervention: both the European citizenry and the European public sphere are still fragmented along national lines; citizens still perceive themselves as members of their home countries, separated from 'the others' by high cultural, emotional and language barriers. A full parliamentarization of the supranational level, including a European government which rules on the basis of majoritarian parliamentary decisions, is, from the point of view of EU stability and coherence, a risky undertaking, since the Union still lacks the communicative and political foundations on which such a representative democracy in all its facets and with all its consequences could be based. This is particularly true in welfare-state politics.

Offe and Guggenberger allude to the fact that 'the principle of majority (…) is anything but a self-evident political principle',[31] though it is an effective tool and 'certainly the best of all the dissatisfying concepts which aim at producing binding decisions'.[32] Yet despite the indisputable advantages of this instrument, it has to be justified why citizens should accept decisions based on majoritarian decision-making as binding. Weiler is certainly right to stress that 'people accept the majoritarian principle of democracy within a polity to which they see themselves as belonging.'[33] The feeling of 'belonging', however, is generally the result of a long-term process influenced by a range of 'soft' factors, such as social, cultural, linguistic affinity and shared history. Majority decisions in a fragmented and still distant polity such as the EU, which do not result in positive-sum solutions, may bring about a substantial decline in the social (and political) legitimacy and lead to disintegration.

Parliamentarism—ie majoritarian decision-making plus the loyalty of the 'minority' in accepting the decisions taken by the majority though trying to revise them *democratically*—is a sophisticated mechanism of conflict resolution. There is an ongoing conflict between accepting majoritarian decisions as legitimate democratic (collective) self-determination and rejecting them as illegitimate 'foreign rule'. As such, this mechanism is unable to produce the moral infrastructure (trust, obedience, subordination, moderation, and the like) on which it should be based and which post-war Western European states, whatever their parliamentary systems, are generally able to produce reliably. Since the EU unsurprisingly still lacks these national socio-structural conditions and relationships, majoritarian

[31] C. Offe, 'Politische Legitimation durch Mehrheitsentscheidung?' in B. Guggenberger, and C. Offe (eds) *An den Grenzen der Mehrheitsdemokratie. Politik und Soziologie der Mehrheitsregel* (Opladen: Leske & Budrich, 1984) 150–183 at 187.

[32] ibid 188; author's own translation.

[33] J. Weiler, 'After Maastricht: Community Legitimacy in Post-1992 Europe' in W. J. Adams, (ed) *Singular Europe. Economy and Polity of the European Community After 1992* (Ann Arbor: University of Michigan Press, 1993) 11–41 at 22.

decision-making is a problematic vehicle for resolving highly normative and politically salient conflicts.

This holds especially true for expanding majoritarian decision-making within the Council. Within this body, the principle of unanimity ensures equal treatment and autonomy at the same time. It grants each participant an absolute veto and it forces all participants to negotiate and to seek compromises to which all actors involved can agree. Unanimity therefore has its price. Due to the high consent-building thresholds in politically salient policy fields where common problem-solving (concessions, compromises, etc) is not yet opportune, deadlock or decisions at the lowest common denominator are likely. Majoritarian decision-making allows for the blurring and shifting of responsibility, both necessary preconditions for more effective decision-making. Needless to say, majoritarian decision-making thus enlarges the strategic scope for more effective problem-solving even in contested and politicized policy fields. Unanimous decisions, as Scharpf argues, are highly legitimized decisions whereas majoritarian rule has to be legitimized as such before it grants democratic legitimacy to majoritarian decisions—especially when imposed on a dissenting minority.[34] This dispute has also been central to the negotiations about the draft EU constitution of 2004. While the French and German governments argued that, given a Union of 25 members, allowing individual countries to veto decisions is a recipe for paralysis, the British government in particular claimed that certain subjects are so sensitive that individual countries must retain the right of veto. The dilemma, however, is that both sides apparently are right.

Enlargement threatens to worsen some of the existing problems of European decision-procedures, resulting in a paralysis in decision-making particularly in an EU with 27 members. Regarding what he calls this 'enlargement crisis', Vobruba rightly states that:

> on the one hand, restricting the opportunities for representing national interests seems to be an appropriate measure. This would mean in particular extending the majority rule to more and even highly controversial political subjects. But, on the other hand, enlarging the EU without expanding the opportunities for representing national interests proportionately would create distribution conflicts which the EU would scarcely be able to master.[35]

Majoritarian decisions imply a defeat of *territorial* conceptions, differences and restrictions of welfare statehood in favour of a *functional* perspective based on the artificial idea of a European citizenry and a European unity. As long as 'solidarity' is still territorially limited and welfare states remain part of national 'identity' and self-conception, the prospects for majoritarian decisions in the social policy core sectors of distribution and redistribution are bleak. As long as national citizens do not

[34] F. W. Scharpf, 'Demokratieprobleme in der europäischen Mehrebenenpolitik' in W. Merkel, and A. Busch (eds) *Demokratie in Ost und West* (Frankfurt a.M.: Suhrkamp, 1999) 672.

[35] G. Vobruba, 'The Enlargement Crisis of the European Union: Limits on the Dialectics of Integration and Expansion' (2003) 13 (1) J of Eur Social Policy 35–62 at 41.

perceive European social policies and institutions (European taxes, European standards, European regulatory policies, European distributive programmes, and the like) as an attractive and convincing idea and as long as governments retain their welfare-state competencies, majoritarian decision-making will neither have a legitimatory nor a normative basis. Therefore Schmitter is right to state: 'Nothing could be more dangerous for the future of an eventual Eurodemocracy than to have it thrust upon a citizenry that is not prepared to exercise it, and that continues to believe its interests and passions are best defended by national not supranational democracy'.[36]

3.3 Eastern enlargement and the reinforcement of conflicts of distribution

EU enlargement(s) has further increased the already existing problem of institutional heterogeneity *and* the disproportionate distribution of wealth and economic opportunities within the EU of 27,[37] though recent studies reveal that interstate inequalities in the enlarged Union are gradually declining in the last years (while at the same time economic inequalities within nations are growing).[38] In this respect, Eastern enlargement has increased rather than decreased a protectionist stance towards their own social policy territory on the part of member governments and once again strengthened the market character of the EU project. More precisely, social policy (costs, financial contributions etc) and tax policy are still two major policy fields to which governments stick in order to increase their economic competitiveness given the harsh intra-EU competition. Pessimists argue that nothing more 'than the level of the lowest common denominator—today somewhere between Germany and Greece, tomorrow reflecting the even more extreme conditions of enlargement to the East',[39] would be the result of attempts to harmonize provision standards among member states—let alone attempts to converge organizational structures. Moreover, social policy is almost the only 'instrument' which governments can make use of in order to gain

[36] P. C. Schmitter, 'What is there to legitimise in the European Union and how must this be accomplished?', Jean Monnet Working Paper No. 6/01, Harvard Law School, 2001, p 5.

[37] cf eg M. Heidenreich, 'Territoriale Ungleichheiten in der erweiterten EU' (2003) 55 (1) Kölner Zeitschrift für Soziologie und Sozialpsychologie 1–28; ibid, 'Regional Inequalities in the Enlarged Europe' (2003) 13 (4) J of Eur Social Policy 313–333; D. Vaughan-Whitehead, *EU Enlargement versus Social Europe? The Uncertain Future of the European Social Model* (Cheltenham: Edward Elgar, 2003); W. Schmähl, 'EU Enlargement and Social Security. Some Dimensions of a Complex Topic' (2004) January/February Intereconomics 21–28.

[38] M. Heidenreich, and C. Wunder, 'Patterns of Regional Inequality in the Enlarged Union' (2007) 24 (1) Eur Sociological Rev 19–36 stress in their study that the slow convergence process in the enlarged Union may not increase popular support for the European integration process because the most important frame of reference is still the nation-state where regional inequalities are increasing.

[39] G. Danner, 'Torn Between National Interests and Community Requirements—the Position of European Health Policy' in B.-M. Bellach and H. Stein (eds) *The New Public Health Policy of the European Union. Past Experience, Present Needs, Future Perspectives* (München: Urban und Vogel, 1999) 65–71 at 66.

competitive advantages (taxes, contributions, wages). It is unlikely that the new East-European member states will hand over these instruments to 'Brussels'.

There is practically no possibility to reach agreements that could make poorer countries accept higher social standards or that could fix minimum standards acceptable for all. According to this line of argument, European economic and monetary integration is likely to erode the costly social policies of the richer European welfare states without them being replaced at European level. Given the EU's limited institutional capacities for managing such complex challenges, ie the distribution conflicts between member states and candidates as well as within both of these groups, Vobruba rightly states that eastward enlargement (the accession of net receivers) will form a restrictive framework for future social policy development in Europe.[40] As he notes, 'solving the enlargement crisis calls for institutional reforms and a considerable amount of redistribution (through social policy)'[41]—and at the same time systematically prevents it.

Eastern enlargement has even increased the EU's internal diversity: The EU is indisputably marked by very different welfare state regimes with widely divergent characteristic features (economic, structural, institutional, cultural and normative),[42] each of which is deeply embedded in national cultures and the biographies of national citizens. Social policies and institutional arrangements differ considerably from one country to another due to political balances of power, but especially due to different cultural notions of freedom, security, justice, solidarity, individual independence and responsibility and of the role of the state. Additionally, European welfare states, especially after Eastern enlargements, differ enormously in levels of economic development and thus in their ability to pay for social transfers. Without going into any detail, European welfare states are by no means variations of the same; rather, there are fundamental institutional and normative differences between them. It is evident that 'there is no unity among European welfare systems so compelling that all observers are forced to agree that these nations fit together in the same category'.[43] Indeed, '[t]he ideal of a European welfare state model does not leap automatically from the data. It has been constructed, argued for and maintained for particular reasons'.[44] The Commission's emphasis on shared values and normative objectives plus a common 'moral' agenda indicates that the 'European social model' idea has become an important element in the process of European state-building and 'identity creation' in the twenty-first century, the aim of which is to imitate nation-state building and to 'parallel the role of social policies in helping to define nation states and national identities

[40] G. Vobruba, n 35 above. [41] ibid 36.

[42] cf F. W. Scharpf, and V. A. Schmidt (eds) *Welfare and Work in the Open Economy. Vol 2. Diverse Responses to Common Challenges* (Oxford: OUP, 2000); or M. Ferrera, A. Hemerijck, and M. Rhodes, *The Future of Social Europe. Recasting Work and Welfare in the New Economy* (Oeiras: Celta Editora, 2000).

[43] P. Baldwin, 'Can we define a European Welfare State Model?' in B. Greve (ed) *Comparative Welfare Systems* (London: Macmillan, 1996) 29–44 at 33.

[44] ibid.

in the twentieth century'.[45] In this respect the Commission is well aware of the fact that a post-national entity cannot function without a greater expansion of the social remit and the development of European forms of solidarity and a European public sphere.[46] The problem is, however, that this policy space is already occupied by the member states, which are unwilling to withdraw from this terrain. The EU's new state-builders, however, have to start out from fundamentally different conditions—they face a world of deeply rooted, institutionally diverse welfare states which share specific values but certainly no common social model.

To sum up, the inclusion of new members can certainly be seen as a further source of conflict in the discussions about deepening and increasing EU responsibility in further policy domains. Eastern enlargement, in line with the increased competitive pressures of the single market and Economic and Monetary Union, is likely to make the adoption of common social standards more difficult and any progress of the EU in the areas of social security and social redistribution fairly unlikely to achieve in the years to come. It is especially the *enlargement dilemma* which tests the fluid resource of solidarity: the larger the EU grows and the more diverse it becomes, the greater the need to establish or strengthen solidarity between member states—yet the growing diversity of the EU systematically makes it more difficult to develop shared beliefs and a perception of commonality.

3.4 Social policy as a vehicle for political allegiance and popularity

Drawing on the work of Stein Rokkan and Albert Hirschman and anchored in the classical 'state-formation' and 'nation-building' perspective of political science, it has been variously demonstrated that the welfare state is a pivotal instrument of statecraft, that social policy was and still is a crucial instrument for state formation, that social policy fosters the consolidation, stability and legitimacy of liberal democracies,[47] and that it has the capacity to foster loyalty and allegiance to the nation-state and political support for governments.[48] Social

[45] M. Kleinman, *A European Welfare State? European Union Social Policy in Context* (Houndsmill/Basingstoke: Palgrave, 2002) 98.

[46] cf eg Commission (EC), 'Social Dimension of the Internal Market' COM (1988) 1148; Commission (EC), 'European Social Policy. Options for the Union' (Green Paper) COM (1993) 551; Commission (EC), 'European Social Policy—A Way Forward for the Union' (White Paper) COM (1994) 333; Commission (EC), 'The Future of Social Protection: A Framework for a European Debate' COM (1995) 466; Commission (EC), 'A Concerted Strategy for Modernizing Social Protection' COM (1999) 347; Commission (EC), 'Social Policy Agenda' COM (2000) 379; Commission (EC), 'Communication on the Legal Nature of the Charter of Fundamental Rights of the European Union' COM (2000) 644.

[47] M. G. Schmidt, 'Zur Leistungsfähigkeit von Demokratien' in Katenhusen/Lamping (eds) *Demokratien in Europa. Der Einfluss der europäischen Integration auf Wandel, Leistungsfähigkeit und neue Konturen des demokratischen Verfassungsstaates* (Opladen: Leske & Budrich, 2003) 269–283.

[48] cf K. van Kersbergen, 'The Politics of Solidarity and the Changing Boundaries of the Welfare State' (2006) 5 (4) Eur Political Science 377–394; E. Roller, *Einstellungen der Bürger zum Wohlfahrtsstaat der Bundesrepublik Deutschland* (Opladen: Leske & Budrich, 1992).

policy—especially the policies of interpersonal and intertemporal redistribution and the establishment of public services—has become an important source of legitimacy for modern nation states.

'Phase four'[49] of the ideal-type state-building process in Western Europe is marked by the growth of agencies of redistribution, the building of public welfare services, the development of nationwide policies for the equalization of economic conditions—'negatively through progressive taxation, positively through transfers form the better-off strata to the poorer, from the richer to the backward regions'[50]. Social policy, thus, is linking the territorial, membership, and citizenship dimensions of national statehood. In particular, it has been the institutionalization of public schemes (social insurances etc) which served to stabilize the internal sovereignty of the European nation states and to establish strong (symbolic and material) ties of loyalty and solidarity with and among their citizens.

Drawing on the growing literature on nationalism and social policy, Banting argues that in Canada 'social programmes have emerged as instruments of nation-building.[51] For central government social policy has been seen as an instrument of territorial integration, part of the glue holding together a vast country subject to powerful centrifugal tendencies'. Béland and Lecours show how processes of identity formation often involve a social policy dimension.[52] This successful connection between the welfare state, democracy and the nation-state, during a fairly long historical period which has not at all come to an end, makes any attempt to shift authority and responsibility to the supranational level a risky project—not least because member states' populations still generally support their national welfare states.

Kersbergen convincingly shows that national publics accept the efforts of their national state elites to built new trans or supranational political institutions on the condition that this guarantees or reinforces economic and social security *in the national context*.[53] The more citizens perceive European integration to threaten their (economic and social-psychological) security and well-being, the less likely they will support the EU.[54] According to this utilitarian line of argument, European integration depends upon a double allegiance consisting of a primary allegiance to the nation state and its political elite and a secondary

[49] S. Rokkan, 'Dimensions of State Formation and Nation-building: a Possible Paradigm for Research on Variations within Europe' in C. Tilly (ed) *The Formation of National States in Western Europe* (Princeton: Princeton University Press, 1975) 562–600 at 572.

[50] ibid.

[51] K. Banting, 'Canada: nation-building in a federal welfare state' in: H. Obinger, S. Leibfried, and F. G. Castles (eds) *Federalism and the Welfare State. New World and European Experiences* (Cambridge: Cambridge University Press, 2005) 89–137, at 90.

[52] D. Béland, and A. Lecours, 'The Politics of Territorial Solidarity. Nationalism and Social Policy Reform in Canada, the United Kingdom, and Belgium' (2005) 38 (6) Comparative Political Studies 676–703; see also the contributions in N. McEwen, and L. Moreno (eds) *The Territorial Politics of Welfare* (London: Routledge, 2005).

[53] van Kersbergen, n 19 above.

[54] C. E. De Vries, K. van Kersbergen, 'Interests, Identity and Political Allegiance in the European Union' (2007) 42 (2) Acta Politica 307–328.

or derived allegiance to the EU. This secondary allegiance, however, exists only to the extent that European integration facilitates nation states to provide the resources upon which primary allegiance hinges.

Moreover, despite the fact that retrenchment initiatives are generally associated with high electoral costs and deeply rooted interests,[55] the fact that social policy is, even after the 'trente glorieuses' (1945–1975), ie in times of austerity and distributive conflicts, an important vehicle for increasing governments' popularity and for producing party political allegiance should not be underestimated. Given the electoral importance of social policy, governments—(re-)elected by their national constituency—have quite successfully prevented social policy core competences from being transferred from the national to the European level. With regard to both the constant drain of competences to the supranational level and the irresistible forces of 'negative integration' which further reduce national policy-making, national governments prefer to hang on to whatever remains of social policy competences than to sacrifice them for the uncertain sake of the European 'project'—and for the benefit of 'Brussels'. Moreover, the influence of powerful and well-entrenched interest groups, but particularly the electoral behaviour of those (growing and heterogeneous) groups that depend on public services and welfare transfers, or even on work income from welfare state institutions and thus have come to base their life plans on the continuation of existing institutions, make governments tend towards a certain 'welfare state conservatism'. Thus, It is obvious that governments would have to face fierce opposition should they agree to the transfer of social policy core competences to the supranational level and the replacement of particular national welfare arrangements with qualitatively different European solutions[56]—especially when these European solutions or institutions are beyond direct electoral control. Apparently it is not only governments who want this. According to Eurobarometers, the Union's restricted role also seems to be in accordance with citizens' expectations. Thus, in contrast to a large number of cross-border policy issues like 'foreign policy', 'fight against organized crime and drug trafficking', 'single currency', 'protection of the environment', 'immigration policy', 'defence policy', or 'agriculture and fishing policy', which over the years have constantly received the support of the large majority of EU citizens as a matter of European concern and where Europeans accept joint EU decision-making, things are different in typically 'national' issues such as health policy, taxation, social welfare and pension policy where a large—and over time constant—majority of people, accustomed to specific features of their welfare state, is in favour of decisions

[55] P. Pierson, *Dismantling the Welfare State. Reagan, Thatcher, and the Politics of Retrenchment* (Cambridge: Cambridge University Press, 1994); ibid, 'The Path to European Integration. A Historical Institutionalist Analysis' (1996) 29 (2) Comparative Political Studies 123–163; ibid, 'Irresistible Forces, Immovable Objects: Post-industrial Welfare States Confront Permanent Austerity' (1998) 4 J of Eur Public Policy 539–560.

[56] F. W. Scharpf, n 23 above, 22.

being made only by national governments. In contrast to, eg, foreign policy or environmental policy, in social protection/social security, that is the inner core of welfare statehood, the degree of Europeanization is low. Its cross-border scope is also low, but its *distributional relevance* is fairly high. Asked whether decisions should be made by the national government or made jointly with the EU, with regard to health policy 33 per cent are in favour of decision-making at European level. The figures for social welfare are 32 per cent, 29 per cent for taxation, and 26 per cent for pensions.[57]

Citizens' emotional ties to their nation-states may be ambivalent from time to time, yet the bond and deep commitment to their respective welfare state is particularly strong and vivid. It is unlikely that the emotionally charged national 'welfare-state identity'—irrational as it is—can be set aside by an act of sheer will or by rational means. Undoubtedly, there exists a *general* and *abstract* desire among European citizens to solve (even more) problems at EU level, but depending on the *concrete* nature of the problem, citizens can at times be very choosy. Here, social policy apparently makes the difference.

3.5 Social trust, identity, and the boundaries of transnational solidarity

The EU is still a compound entity of different societies each with their specific historical, cultural, economic and social distinctiveness. It seems to be unlikely that in the years to come the EU will 'homogenize and "Europeanize" the constituent societies of the EU in the same way as political elites were able to unify national societies in the process of 19th century national building'.[58] Against this backdrop, Offe's sober conclusion that 'the prospects for uniting a "European society", i.e. the supranational equivalent and extension of national societies, are exceedingly discouraging'[59] is plausible. The consequences are momentous. While there is considerable readiness to integrate markets and to allow a supranational regime—ie other member governments (via the Council) and citizens from other

[57] See Eurobarometer 70, p 50; published in December 2008. According to the findings of Hooghe, both political elites and the public are anything but enthusiastic about Europeanizing high-spending, distributional policies, in particular policies such as social and health policy—for different reasons (L. Hooghe, 'Europe Divided? Elite vs. Public Opinion on European Integration' (2003) 4 (3) Eur Union Politics 281–304, at 296). One can therefore assume that citizens perceive these policies as 'policies of an intra-national problem scope' (E.-V. Trüdinger, 'Have They Gone too Far? Attitudes Towards the Transfer of Policies on the EU level', in D. Fuchs, R. Magni-Berton, and A. Roger (eds) *Euroscepticism. Images of Europe among mass publics and political elites* (Opladen: Barbara Budrich, 2009) 135–155, at 142) to be best dealt with at national level according to national policy traditions.

[58] C. Offe, 'Is There, or Can There be, a European Society?' in Katenhusen and Lamping (eds) *Demokratien in Europa. Der Einfluss der europäischen Integration auf Wandel, Leistungsfähigkeit und neue Konturen des demokratischen Verfassungsstaates* (Opladen: Leske & Budrich, 2003) 71–89, at 73–74.

[59] ibid 74.

member states (in the EP) non-accountable to the other citizenries—to make legally binding political decisions in specific areas which were formerly exclusively national issues, the prospects for 'Europeanizing' the (re)distributive core policies of national welfare statehood are gloomy. Redistributive, market-correcting social policy and the democratic fight for social rights have a lot to do with common history, common cultural norms, homogeneity, a cohesive and robust we-identity or at least a feeling of somehow belonging together, the maturity to make compromises and, especially, the willingness to accept the costs of social policies. If those who discuss the EU in categories of 'statehood' and 'European nationality' are right, it must be said that there is as yet, due to the lack of socio-structural preconditions, no 'spirit of solidarity' or European community, and no sound feeling of being committed to the people of other member states—which, as many argue, is an important precondition when it comes to resolving distributional conflicts.

Social trust is not only a main category of (national and post-national) welfare statehood, rather it is a significant indicator for the integration of the EU. The focus here is not so much on what trust is, but rather on what trust does in a society from a functional perspective. Social trust, defined here as 'the belief that others will not deliberately or knowingly do us harm, if they can avoid it, and will look after our interests, if this is possible'[60], is very unevenly distributed among the nations. Welfare state institutions are of central importance in building social trust among members of a society. Social trust is at the centre of welfare statehood, both as trust in (reliable) institutions and as trust in 'the others' in the sense of reciprocity, obligation to the strange fellow citizens, cooperation, empathy, an understanding of the common interest and the common good. In return, the social institutions of the welfare state shape citizens' attitudes and expectations.

According to the analyses of Delhey, social trust is still restricted mainly to the own national 'solidarity community', whereas transnational trust is dependent upon a number of aspects, such as a feeling of cultural affinity. Delhey argues that within the EU-15, social trust has gradually, though to a different extent, grown, but Eastern enlargement has, according to his findings, resulted in a significant decrease in social trust across the EU—due to a growing heterogeneity and cultural, economic and political disparity.[61] In other words, the political price of Eastern enlargement obviously is a disintegrative effect on the EU as such and a slowdown of future social policy integration in particular. This is in line with the empirical results of Mau who, with regard to the centrifugal forces within the EU-25, argues that European citizens are quite hesitant when it comes to transfering social policy competencies to the supranational level, primarily because most of them expect the EU to decrease social standards rather than to preserve

[60] J. Delhey, and K. Newton,' Predicting Cross-National Levels of Social Trust: Global Pattern or Nordic Exceptionalism?' (2005) 21 (4) Eur Sociological Review 311.

[61] J. Delhey, 'Nationales und transnationales Vertrauen in der Europäischen Union' (2004) 32 (1) Leviathan 15–45; ibid, 'Does Enlargement Make the European Union Less Cohesive? An Analysis of Trust Between EU Nationalities' (2007) 45 (2) J of Common Market Studies 253–279.

the existing level of social security.[62] This scepticism is particularly pronounced among citizens from mature welfare states with encompassing social benefits, such as the Nordic countries, Germany or France.

In addition, there is an ongoing debate about the effects of 'diversity' and 'heterogeneity' on the welfare state. With regard to the US society, Nathan Glazer argues that the greater social diversity is, the greater the resistance among citizens towards redistribution—and the greater the likelihood of a mere residual welfare state marked by low interpersonal and interregional redistribution.[63] In their study, Delhey and Newton come to the conclusion that high trust countries are characterized by, inter alia, ethnic homogeneity, wealth and income equality.[64] Generalized trust, ie trust in people we may not know, or who may not be like us, is strongly associated with ethnic homogeneity,[65] whereas a liberal and multiculturalist immigrant policy can make it more difficult to sustain a robust welfare state because there might be concerns that such policies erode the interpersonal trust and social solidarity and make strong redistributive policies rather unlikely.[66] Against this background the argument by Sykes that 'at a time of rapid economic and political change with the attendant socio-economic threats and uncertainties, finding a European solidarity on which trans-European politics might be based is still a somewhat distant target' seems to be convincing.[67] In contrast, in their cross-national study, Hooghe et al come to the conclusion that at the country level hardly any indicators for migration or diversity proved to be strongly and consistently related to generalized trust.[68] Their results suggest that the pessimistic conclusions about the negative effects of ethnic diversity on generalized trust cannot be confirmed at the aggregate level across European countries.

3.6 Limits to the 'Integration by Law' and the role of the ECJ

European integration is a process of transforming deeper structures of solidarity, legal order and justice away from the segmentally differentiated European family of nations and towards an emerging European society. The ECJ assumes a crucial role

[62] S. Mau, 'Soziale Ungleichheit in der Europäischen Union' (2004) B 38 Aus Politik und Zeitgeschichte 38–46; ibid, 'Europäische Solidaritäten' (2008) 21 Aus Politik und Zeitgeschichte 9–14.

[63] N. Glazer, Affirmative *Discrimination: Ethnic Inequality and Public Policy* (Cambridge: Harvard University Press, 1987).

[64] J. Delhey, and K. Newton, n 60 above.

[65] ibid 324.

[66] K. Halvorsen, 'Legitimacy of Welfare States in Transitions from Homogeneity to Multiculturality: A Matter of Trust' in S. Mau, and B. Veghte (eds) *Social Justice, Legitimacy and the Welfare State* (Aldershot: Ashgate, 2007) 239–259.

[67] R. Sykes, 'The Future for Social Policy in Europe?' in R. Sykes, and P. Alcock (eds) *Developments in European Social Policy. Convergence and Diversity* (Bristol: Policy Press, 1998) 251–264, at 252.

[68] L. Hooghe, T. Reeskens, D. Stolle, and A. Trappers, 'Ethnic Diversity and Generalised Trust in Europe. A Cross-National Multilevel Study' (2009) 42 (2) Comparative Political Study 198–223.

in this process, or rather power struggle, of enforcing a genuinely European legal order against national varieties of law.[69] A lack of consensus and political will among member governments, non-decisions at EU-level, a clear tendency amongst governments to ignore the (intended or unintended) effects of the single market on national welfare states, and ambiguous and vague Treaty provisions very often have brought the ECJ onto the social policy agenda. The ECJ has succeeded in establishing a strong transnational constitutionalism and a 'normative supranationalism' through its case law.[70] As a key EU institution, the ECJ has become a major point of reference (and source of hope) not least for EU citizens as an institution which they perceive as both guaranteeing and enhancing their civil and social rights within the EU and which they, on the whole, regard as a highly legitimized institution. Mény's statement that the 'power courts have acquired through constitutional review is significant since they are in charge of protecting, but also defining and redefining, citizens' rights without being accountable to the electorate'[71] is particularly true of the ECJ.

Momentous social policy rulings—not least in health policy[72] demonstrate that the Court has been capable of imposing substantial policies *which were not in accordance with the core interests of most member states.* Meanwhile it is interesting to observe how the Court has turned the tables, forcing national authorities to take the European dimension in social policy into consideration. Moreover, its capacity to activate transnational debates on the content, effects and political consequences of its rulings is remarkable. The specific quality and added value of such discourses on rights should therefore not be underestimated. The ECJ is a 'stage' for argumentative communication and agreement on Community norms. It gives citizens and interest groups alike an opportunity to make their voice heard and to shape the European agenda. The integration of member states' social policies is mainly an integration by ECJ case law via assertive citizens claiming their European (economic) rights (which their member states had politically excluded or at least restricted) and increasingly perceiving the EU as one market: it is mainly single market law to which the Commission and the ECJ are able to directly refer in order to impose prohibitions and obligations on member states, or to establish rights of individuals, groups and organizations against their home countries. When it came to capturing national 'welfare strongholds', that is, when it came to 'conquering' a territory still 'occupied' by member states, the ECJ has been the one and only actor legitimized and able to cut the Gordian knot and to make these core areas of national competence EU-compatible while incrementally

[69] I. Münch, 'Constructing a European Society by Jurisdiction' (2008) 14 (5) Eur LJ 519–541.

[70] J. Weiler, 'Community, Member-States and European Integration' (1982) 21 (1) J of Common Market Studies 39–56.

[71] Y. Mény, 'De La Démocratie en Europe: Old Concepts and New Challenges' (2003) 41 (1) J of Common Market Studies 1–13, at 6.

[72] cf W. Lamping, 'European Integration and Health Policy—a Peculiar Relationship' in M. Steffen (ed) *Health Governance in Europe. Issues, Challenges, Theories* (London: Routledge, 2005) 18–48; D. Martinsen, 'Towards an Internal Health Market with the European Court' (2005) 28 (5) West Eur Politics 1035–1056.

introducing a new set of European economic (and indirectly social) rights. From the point of view of *re-balancing negative and positive integration*, some authors, such as Fritz Scharpf among others, hope that, given the high legitimacy of the ECJ, 'judicial activism', which has so far mainly served the advancement of negative integration, might to the same extent be able to 'contribute as much to the expansion of social rights as it did to the protection of economic freedoms'.[73]

What makes things more complicated, however, is that the ECJ is the '*ersatz*-legislator' in a supranational regime where its rulings, covering an ever broader range of subjects, function as a substitute or surrogate for politics. At the time when the ECJ was successfully extending its own legitimacy and role (which governments accepted), the EC dealt with a far narrower range of issues (single market programme) than it does today. Social security and protection is one, but not the only, policy area which has to a large extent been integrated by the ECJ and not by democratic policy-making. In the absence of political guidance, the ECJ continues to decide autonomously on core aspects of the EU social policy regime. Most of its decisions have been based on the Treaty as an extremely 'incomplete contract'[74] which gives both the Commission and, in particular, the Court ample room for manoeuvre exploiting the Treaty's ambiguity and legal uncertainty, ie the Court enjoys considerable discretion in applying and interpreting the meaning of the Treaty. Yet, Martinsen is right to stress that 'the consequences [of the ECJ jurisdiction,] are political, and the response to legal integration needs to be political as well'.[75] In this respect, the ECJ jurisprudence functions as a substitute or surrogate for politics. As yet, there is certainly no lack of judicial power; what is lacking in social policy integration is democratic politics. These democratic politics—which are essential for institutionalizing social solidarity—not only face many obstacles discussed earlier. While 'integration through law' (ECJ case law, cooperation with national courts; obedience by national governments etc) has been an accelerator of European integration, the price of democratic politics—in terms of party-political, ideological struggles, conflicts and compromises etc—seems to be less promising for those interested in efficient and effective supranational policy-making.

Against this background, most social scientists, especially those in favour of accelerating European integration, tend to perceive 'law' as a simple and technical instrument or tool which can be 'activated' whenever necessary or required. Nevertheless, we should redraw the attention to the foundations of European integration which go far beyond the *formal, instrumental, abstract, teleological* integration through law principle.[76] Post-national law is hardly able to generate legitimacy, acceptance, and identity—nor to institutionalize a new

[73] F. W. Scharpf, n 20 above, 201.

[74] A. Stone Sweet, *The Judicial Construction of Europe* (Oxford: OUP, 2004) 24.

[75] D. Martinsen, n 72 above, 1050.

[76] cf also U. Haltern, 'Pathos and Patina: The Failure and Promise of Constitutionalism in the European Imagination' (2003) 9 (1) Eur LJ 14–44; ibid, 'Integration Through Law' in A. Wiener, and T. Diez (eds) *European Integration Theory* (Oxford: OUP, 2004) 177–196.

European, non-state *contrat social* put in place either top-down or as the pure sum of the supranational plus the national constitutional and social rights. The aspect of deepening the social policy dimension of European integration, ie to establish and institutionalize 'social solidarity' among European citizens, cannot be addressed through the legal lens *alone*. Under such circumstances it is more than doubtful that law will be able to perform the tasks associated with it in member states.

Though, eg, Habermas argues that, moving toward post-nationalism, it is time 'for loyalty to be based on abstract procedures and principles', law alone can hardly make European citizens feel responsible for one another during the state-making process such as European integration.[77] The crucial point is that a formal perspective on the integration through law does not answer the question of its legitimacy. Being a community of law is an important aspect, but this perspective does underestimate that the integration process is a political issue whose *social* legitimacy is still generated predominately at national level.

4. Solidarity and Europe reconciled—is that possible?

To date, European social policy integration has been a permanent conflict between European forces of change and national forces of resistance and persistence. It comes as no surprise that social policy at EU level has been scattered to date, consisting of 'what seem at best loosely connected fields'[78]. Moreover, so far there is, as Leibfried and Pierson stress, no European welfare law granting individual entitlements vis-à-vis 'Brussels', there are no direct taxes or contributions, and no funding of a 'social budget' to back such entitlements, and there is no 'Brussels' welfare bureaucracy to speak of.[79] There is considerable redistribution at the EU level, such as the European Social Fund and the European Globalization Adjustment Fund, but it is, as Daly emphasizes, 'interstate in nature and within that sectoral and spatial rather than among income groups and risk categories'.[80] 'Solidarity', as defined above, is still a matter of member states. This points to two important aspects: first, the future role of national welfare states, and second the prospects for establishing a post-national, European solidarity community in social policy.

National welfare states will remain the primary institutions of European social policy and will in any foreseeable future be the primary 'agency of

[77] J. Habermas, *The Inclusion of the Other*, n 4 above, 117–118.

[78] M. Daly, 'Whither EU Social Policy? n 1 above, 1.

[79] S. Leibfried, and P. Pierson, 'Social Policy. Left to Courts and Markets?' in H. Wallace, and W. Wallace (eds), n 14 above; S. Leibfried, and P. Pierson, 'Semi-Sovereign Welfare States: Social Policy in a Multi-Tiered Europe' in S. Leibfried, and P. Pierson (eds) *European Social Policy. Between Fragmentation and Integration* (Washington, DC: Brooking Institution Press, 1995) 43–77.

[80] M. Daly, 'Whither EU Social Policy? n 1 above, 1.

socialization', but they will do so in the context of an increasingly constraining multi-tiered institutional context.[81] Though the EU still lacks redistributive social policy competencies, European social policy integration can be conceputalized as a constant, but unequal rights-based process of denationalization, de-territorialization and boundary rebuilding, *one* consequence of which is that national authorities experience a continuing loss of autonomous (de facto) capacity to act and of sovereign (legal) social policy competencies. Nevertheless, national schemes for the protection (or insurance against) life risks are still in place. The organization, financing, and regulation of the systems of social security is still a national core competence (at least as long as these systems are compatible with EU primary and secondary law). The national level has to continue guaranteeing social cohesion, inclusion and protection (especially with regard to economic globalization) and to fulfil citizens' expectations, even though its own power is increasingly restricted (not least by EU internal market imperatives. The EU, however, has only limited political power and legal authority to compensate for the member states' restrictions in social policy —for the reasons discussed earlier. As long as the EU will not be able adopt these functions, the Union should be more protective of the inner core of national welfare statehood, thus leaving substantial scope for national social policy making in the hands of national governments, instead of undermining the institutional and normative foundations of welfare states (internal market regime, competition law, marketization, etc).[82]

What are the implications for establishing *European solidarity*? What we see so far is an emerging European society of autonomous individuals superimposing itself upon the traditionally existing Europe of nations.

> Individualisation (...) is the vehicle of overcoming Europe's segmented differentiation into nations and of producing a new transnational European society composed of empowered individuals and a plurality of self-organizing associations of autonomous individuals. (...) the corresponding tensions will fuel conflicts on Europeanisation versus preserving national collective solidarity for still a long time to come.[83]

Put more precisely, due to an accumulation of case law, in which the ECJ applied the 'four freedoms' to the system of social security, the 'community of common destiny' (national territory, national boundaries, national politics and national citizens) is drifting apart in favour of citizens (or social consumers) experiencing

[81] S. Leibfried, and P. Pierson, 'Semi-Sovereign Welfare States: Social Policy in a Multi-Tiered Europe', n 79 above; S. Leibfried, and P. Pierson, 'Social Policy. Left to Courts and Markets?' in H. Wallace, and W. Wallace (eds), n 14 above.

[82] W. Lamping, 'Grenzverschiebungen. Das Verhältnis von Sozialpolitik und Wirtschaftspolitik auf EU-Ebene und die Neubestimmungen des "Sozialen"' in A. Evers, and R. G. Heinze (eds) *Sozialpolitik. Ökonomisierung und Entgrenzung* (Wiesbaden: VS-Verlag, 2008) 115–135.

[83] I. Münch, 'Constructing a European Society by Jurisdiction', n 69 above, 541.

the EU as a virtually borderless 'single social area'[84] whose new boundaries are set by non-EU countries. This, however, is a process of individualization rather than one of creating a supranational solidarity community. Certainly, the ECJ (very often in collaboration with the Commission) plays an important role in defining and developing uniform EU social policy standards and social rights in specific, primarily market—or labour-related policy areas. Through its case law the ECJ is redefining in particular the *vertical* relationship between the individual and the state by defining social rights and entitlements (which certainly can have distributive and redistributive effects *within* the national welfare state). But the ECJ jurisdiction is not redefining solidarity at the *horizontal* level, ie between states or between European citizens in terms of European solidarity spaces.

The argument thus far has been that social solidarity is closely linked to the (re)distribution of resources—and that the 27 national 'welfare castles' have not yet lowered their drawbridges in matters of (re)distribution. Against this background, the question what solidarity could be, or should look like, *beyond the rights-based homogenization via ECJ case law and the coordination of social security schemes and entitlements,* has not yet been sufficiently elaborated on in academic debates; neither have the preconditions of furthering social policy integration nor the consequences of a too ambitious deepening of the 'social dimension'.

Instead we observe that the process of Europeanizing social policy is developing as a peculiar, *issue-specific, fragmented* and *incremental* process, which is necessarily patchy and inconsistent from the point of view of those in favour of strong and far-reaching EU competencies in social policy. This process mirrors what is politically possible rather than what might be normatively desirable. Social policy integration, depending on the policy sector, has been a pragmatic, although often technocratic and juristic process. Member state governments see their role as policy-makers diminishing, but remain hesitant to actively shape European social policies and to accept a growing transfer of competences, if they want to defend the European level of social protection in the competitive environment of a liberalized world economy.

5. Concluding remarks

Any debate about designing 'Social Europe' or any attempts to construct transnational solidarity communities should take two perspectives into consideration:[85] The first perspective is a careful investigation of the conditions

[84] M. Threlfall, 'European Social Integration: Harmonization, Convergence and Single Social Areas' (2003) 13 (2) J of Eur Social Policy 121–139.

[85] cf R. Breton, 'Identification in Transnational Political Communities' in: K. Knop, S. Ostry, R. Simeon, and K. Swinton (eds) *Rethinking Federalism: Citizens, Markets, and Government in a Changing World* (Vancouver: UBC Press, 1995) 40–58.

conducive or detrimental to the moulding of an overarching, transnational system into a meaningful object of identification for individuals of different national units. The second requires a thorough examination of the conditions under which individuals are likely to define their own identities in relation to the larger, more encompassing collectivity and of the factors that can affect the nature of the emerging identification. These perspectives are crucial when it comes to deepening social policy integration.

With respect to European social policy integration, Habermas' post-national hopes seem to be ahead of their time because social policy in a non-state which lacks the basis of a collective, shared identity and common values cannot simply be based upon abstract principles—let alone the role of law as a 'mediator between the ideal and the real of social solidarity'.[86] The welfare state is a demanding, and fragile, project. No one can predict how much 'solidarity' is needed to build and sustain a post-national welfare state; yet one precondition for establishing it is certainly to accept and promote the *political* nature of the process of European integration.

Spinner-Halev argues that 'post-nationalism means forgetting about national memories'[87]: 'We cannot easily bear the legacy of the past and move towards post-nationalism'.[88] In fact, 'solidarity' created by national identity has been, and still is, crucial to national institution-building—and has a built-in mechanism towards inequality vis-à-vis outsiders. In order to achieve equality and equity within the EU, ie while moving towards post-nationalism, identity should be gradually separated from the concept of the state. Though this argument is certainly striking since a strong national identity often contains support for a deepening of the EU, in social policy this seems to be easier said than done. The EU has not succeeded in developing a collective European identity that is in any way an alternative to the national one. Nor does such a post-national, European identity, though co-existing or nested with the national or sub-national ones, per se ensure the institutionalization of a fully-fledged EU welfare state, but, theoretically, there is good reason to think it is necessary for one. If citizens perceive themselves as being a part of a European community of solidarity, they could accept an increase in EU social policy-making activities and the institutionalization of transnational solidarity spaces or schemes. However, there is reason to believe that the EU could be damaged by raising too high expectations as to what a 'Social Europe' could be and do. The key to 'Social Europe' could be a greater acknowledgement and acceptance of diversity, because otherwise there is the risk that the EU could be damaged by self-delusion and an overestimation of its own capabilities.

[86] M. Murphy, 'Between Facts, Norms and a Post-National Constellation: Habermas, Law and European Social Policy' (2005) 12 (1) J of Eur Public Policy 143–156, at 144.

[87] J. Spinner-Halev, 'Democracy, Solidarity and Post-nationalism' (2008) 56 (3) Political Studies 604.

[88] ibid.

To conclude, instead of provoking disappointment, European social solidarity, especially when it comes to distribution and redistribution across borders, should be extended gradually and carefully, always balancing the requirements of a deeper European integration *and* the willingness and ability of Europeans to show solidarity.[89] In the meantime, European social rights, most of which derived from the European market building programme, should not be mistaken for 'solidarity'. Citizens' attitude towards the EU still seems to be more instrumental than emotional. The development and institutionalization of 'solidarity', however, has often been a reaction to crises at national level. It might be that huge European crises make European citizens accept the EU to play a greater role in social solidarity. It may be that in such a situation the three main questions (Can there be a European welfare state? Should there be a European welfare state? Which additional value could it provide?) would be answered in the affirmative.

[89] Also argued by S. Mau, 'Europäische Solidaritäten', n 62 above,14.

4

Solidarity and the Commission's 'Renewed Social Agenda'

*Catherine Barnard**

1. Introduction

The word solidarity has made a number of appearances in key constitutional documents in recent years not least in the Preambles of the Constitutional Treaty,[1] the Lisbon Treaty[2] and the Charter of Fundamental Rights.[3] It was also listed in the tasks of the Community in Article 2 EC[4] and now in the statement of the Union's values laid down in Article 2 TEU.[5] Given these extensive and positive references, it comes as no surprise that the Commission has seized upon the concept to give weight to its two major policy documents examining the future of social policy in the EU, 'Opportunities, Access and Solidarity: towards a new social vision for 21st Century Europe' of 2007 and 'The Renewed Social Agenda: Opportunities, Access and Solidarity' of 2008. These communications, strongly imbued with Third Way thinking, develop the policies the Commission

* I am grateful to Nicholas Gilbert-Morin from DG Empl, Simon Deakin, Susan Millns, and Malcolm Ross for helpful discussions. In this chapter 'EU' refers to the Treaty on European Union pre-Lisbon; 'TEU', the Treaty on European Union post-Lisbon; 'EC' refers to the European Community Treaty; 'TFEU' refers to the Treaty on the Functioning of the European Union. The post-Lisbon Treaty numbers are used as far as possible throughout this text.

[1] 'Believing that Europe, reunited after bitter experiences, intends to continue along the path of civilisation, progress and prosperity, for the good of all its inhabitants, including the weakest and most deprived; that it wishes to remain a continent open to culture, learning, and social progress; and that it wishes to deepen the democratic and transparent nature of its public life, and to strive for peace, justice and solidarity throughout the world'.

[2] 'DESIRING to deepen the solidarity between their peoples while respecting their history, their culture and their traditions'.

[3] 'Conscious of its spiritual and moral heritage, the Union is founded on the indivisible, universal values of human dignity, freedom, equality and solidarity'.

[4] 'The Community shall have as its task...the raising of the standard of living and quality of life, and economic and social cohesion and solidarity among states'.

[5] 'The Union is founded on the values of respect for human dignity, freedom, democracy, equality, the rule of law and respect for human rights, including the rights of persons belonging to minorities. These values are common to the Member States in a society in which pluralism, non-discrimination, tolerance, justice, solidarity and equality between men and women prevail.'

has pursued over the last decade to help fulfil the (over) ambitious Lisbon strategy objectives of making Europe the most successful, knowledge-based economy in the world by 2010.

The aim of this chapter is to examine the concept of solidarity as used in these two documents and how it relates to 'opportunities' and 'access'. At first glance, solidarity seems to be employed as much for its rhetorical value as its substance. On closer examination, it appears that solidarity helps to offer a social justice counterweight to the potentially neo-liberal direction that an agenda based purely on access and opportunities might lead the EU. In this way, the use of solidarity ensures that the 'Renewed Social Agenda' does not break so radically from the social democratic traditions of most (old) EU states. More specifically, this chapter will argue that solidarity, as used in these documents, is employed to serve a variety of functions ranging from, at a meta-level, an objective of EU social policy to, at a more micro-level, an instrument to help foster cohesion and community, particularly through the use of structural funds. The article considers this variety of uses and concludes with a discussion of whether solidarity is a sufficiently sturdy vehicle to steer Union social policy through the challenges of the next decade, especially at a time when a severe recession has hit most of the member states. However, we begin by placing the discussion of the term solidarity in the 2007 and 2008 Communications in the broader context of the use of solidarity by the other EU institutions.

2. Solidarity and the Union Institutions

2.1 Solidarity and its use in the Treaty and secondary legislation

Article 3 TEU uses the term solidarity in three different ways: first, it talks of 'solidarity between generations';[6] secondly, it talks of 'solidarity among member states',[7] and thirdly, it refers to 'solidarity and mutual respect among peoples' in respect of the Union's relations with the outside world.[8] This demonstrates the multi-faceted nature of the principle of solidarity. There is also a 'Solidarity' Title in the Charter of Fundamental Rights 2000 which embraces a range of social rights (eg workers' rights to information and consultation, collective bargaining

[6] Art 3(3), para 2 provides 'It shall combat social exclusion and discrimination, and shall promote social justice and protection, equality between women and men, solidarity between generations and protection of the rights of the child.'

[7] Art 3(3), para 3 continues: 'It shall promote economic, social and territorial cohesion, and solidarity among Member States.'

[8] Art 3(5) says 'In its relations with the wider world, the Union shall uphold and promote its values and contribute to the protection of its citizens. It shall contribute to peace, security, the sustainable development of the Earth, solidarity and mutual respect among peoples, free and fair trade, eradication of poverty and protection of human rights and in particular the rights of the child, as well as to the strict observance and the development of international law, including respect for the principles of the United Nations Charter'.

and industrial action, protection in the event of unjustified dismissal, fair and just working conditions, prohibition of child labour and protection of young people at work, social security and social assistance, healthcare, environmental and consumer protection).

Not only does solidarity appear in these constitutional documents but it has also been used by the Union legislature as a guiding principle to justify what are, in essence, 'sacrifices'[9] by certain undertakings/companies to assist others in their sector. This usage of solidarity was first seen in the 1970s in respect of the anti-crisis policy in the iron and steel sector, where the reference to solidarity in the Preamble to the European Coal and Steel Community (ECSC) Treaty provided the basis for the Commission to justify a variety of interventionist measures.[10] Subsequently, this idea of solidarity between producers in a specific sector has been extended beyond coal and steel to a number of areas covered by the Treaties, notably agriculture, fisheries and transport. For example, in respect of agriculture, the Court recognized in *Eridania Zuccherifici*[11] that, in dividing quotas between individual undertakings on the basis of their actual production under the system established by Regulation 1785/81,[12] the Council was acting in accordance with the principles of regional specialization and solidarity.[13]

Solidarity is also the guiding principle behind the cohesion policies set out in Title XVIII TFEU (on economic, social and territorial cohesion and the structural funds) and subsequently fleshed out by detailed regulations. The Commission describes the Structural Funds (ERDF, EAGGF, ESF and FIFG), the Cohesion Fund, the funds aimed at preparing the CEECs for accession (ISPA, Phare and Sapard) and the Solidarity Fund collectively as instruments of solidarity.[14]

2.2 Solidarity and the Court of Justice

The Court of Justice has also used solidarity in a variety of contexts. For example, it has invoked the principle of solidarity to defend certain social welfare schemes from the application of competition law. So, in *Poucet and Pistre*[15] the Court held that certain French bodies administering a basic pension scheme

[9] Joined cases 26 and 86/79 *Forges de Thy-Marcinelle et Monceau SA v Commission (concrete reinforcement bars)* [1980] ECR 4155, para 10.

[10] Joined cases 154, 205, 206, 226 to 228, 263 and 264/78, 39, 31, 83 and 85/79 *SpA Ferriera Valsabbia and others v Commission* [1980] ECR 4046, para 59.

[11] Case 250/84 *Eridania zuccherifici nazionali SpA and others v Cassa conguaglio zucchero and the Italian Ministry of Finance and the Treasury* [1986] ECR 5804, para 20.

[12] OJ 1981 L177/4.

[13] For more detail, see C. Barnard, 'Solidarity and New Governance in the Field of Social Policy?' in G. de Búrca and J. Scott (eds) *New Governance and Constitutionalism in Europe and the US* (Oxford: Hart Publishing, 2006).

[14] See also the use of ESF in particular to help address the economic crisis: <http://ec.europa.eu/social/main.jsp?langId=en&catId=736>

[15] Joined Cases C-159/91 and C-160/91 *Poucet and Pistre v AGF and Cancava* [1993] ECR I-637.

for self-employed persons were not to be classified as undertakings for the purpose of competition law due to the solidaristic elements of the schemes administered. It was a non-funded scheme, operated on a redistributive basis with active members' contributions being directly used to finance the pensions of retired members. The scheme had a social objective, providing cover for the beneficiaries against the risks of sickness or old age regardless of the individuals' financial status and state of health at the time of affiliation. Unlike capitalization schemes where the amount paid in is reflected in the amount paid out, solidarity in this scheme was reflected in the grant of pension rights where no contributions had been made and of pension rights that were not proportional to the contributions paid.

By contrast, in *Albany*,[16] a case involving a capitalization scheme, the Court said that a pension fund charged with the management of a supplementary pension scheme set up by a collective agreement to which affiliation was compulsory by the public authorities for all workers in that sector, was an undertaking within the meaning of Article 101 TFEU (ex Article 81 EC). However, it did say that the solidarity elements in the scheme[17] justified the exclusive right of the fund to manage the supplementary scheme under Article 106(2) TFEU (ex Article 86(2)) and so there was no breach of Article 106(2) TFEU respectively.

The Court has also used solidarity to justify obstacles to free movement. This can be seen in *Tas-Hagen*[18] where Dutch law made payment of benefits to civilian war victims conditional on the fact that they were resident in the territory of the Netherlands at the time when their application was submitted. The Court ruled that this law was liable to dissuade Dutch nationals from exercising their freedom to move and to reside outside the Netherlands and so breached Article 21(1) TFEU.[19] The Dutch Government argued that the residence requirement could be justified by the need to 'limit the obligation of solidarity with civilian war victims to those who had links with the population of the Netherlands during and after the war'. While the Court accepted that 'this aim of solidarity may

[16] Case C-67/96 [1999] ECR I-5751, para 87.

[17] The solidarity was reflected by the obligation to accept all workers without a prior medical examination, the continuing accrual of pension rights despite exemption from contributions in the event of incapacity for work, the discharge by the fund of arrears of contributions due from an employer in the event of the latter's insolvency and by the indexing of the amount of the pensions in order to maintain their value. The principle of solidarity was also apparent from the absence of any equivalence, for individuals, between the contribution paid, which is an average contribution not linked to risks, and pension rights, which are determined by reference to an average salary. Such solidarity makes compulsory affiliation to the supplementary pension scheme essential. Otherwise, if 'good' risks left the scheme, the ensuing downward spiral would jeopardize its financial equilibrium (para 75). This would increase the cost of pensions for workers, particularly those in small and medium-sized undertakings with older employees engaged in dangerous activities, to which the fund could no longer offer pensions at an acceptable cost (para 108).

[18] Case C-192/05 *Tas-Hagen v Raadskamer WUBO van de Pensioen- en Uitkeringsrad* [2006] ECR I-10451, paras 34–35. See also Case C-350/07 *Kattner Stahlbau GmbH v Maschinenbau- und Metall- Berufsgenossenschaft* [2009] ECR I-000, para 87.

[19] Case C-192/05 *Tas-Hagen* [2006] ECR I-10451, para 32.

constitute an objective consideration of public interest',[20] on the facts it found the residence requirement to be disproportionate.

In the cases considered so far, the Court has used solidarity as a 'buttress' against the single market.[21] In the famous case of *Grzelczyk*[22] the Court used solidarity in the citizenship context in a more positive way to justify requiring host state authorities to provide some temporary financial support (the Belgian minimum income guarantee, the so-called minimex) to the migrant citizen.[23] The case concerned a French national studying at a Belgian university who supported himself financially for the first three years of his studies but then applied for the minimex at the start of his fourth and final year. While Belgian students could receive the benefit, migrant students could not[24] because, under Article 1 of the Students' Directive 93/96 (now Article 7(1)(c) of the Citizens' Rights Directive 2004/38), they should have had sufficient resources to fund their studies. The Court said that while a state could decide to withdraw a residence permit from a student having recourse to social assistance,[25] such actions could not be the *automatic* consequence of a migrant student having recourse to the host state's social assistance system.[26] The Court continued that beneficiaries of the right of residence could not become an 'unreasonable' burden on the public finances of the host state.[27] Therefore, the Belgian authorities had to provide some temporary support (the minimex) to the migrant citizen, as they would to nationals, given that there exists 'a certain degree of financial solidarity' between nationals of a host member state and nationals of other member states.[28] However, that support would continue only for so long as the student did not become an unreasonable burden on public finances. Thus, in the name of financial solidarity between EU citizens, Grzelczyk received the minimex for a certain period of time.[29]

Grzelczyk does, however, present a paradox in the context of the solidarity debate. If, as we shall see, solidarity is in part about fostering the interest of the collective, allowing the individual to succeed runs the risk of undermining solidarity for the collective (think of the *Daily Express* headline '92,000 East Europeans Milk Our Benefits'[30]).The precedence of the rights of the individual over those of the collective were also starkly revealed in the controversial decisions

[20] ibid para 35.

[21] T. Hervey, 'Social Solidarity: a Buttress against Internal Market law?', in J. Shaw (ed) *Social Law and Policy in an Evolving European Union* (Oxford: Hart Publishing, 2000).

[22] Case C-184/99 [2001] ECR I-6193.

[23] For fuller discussion, see A. Somek, 'Solidarity decomposed: being and time in European citizenship' (2007) 32 ELR 787.

[24] Case C-184/99 *Grzelczyk* [2001] ECR I-6193, para 29.

[25] ibid para 42.

[26] ibid para 43.

[27] ibid para 44.

[28] ibid.

[29] Solidarity can also be used to explain the decision in Case C-413/99 *Baumbast and R v Secretary of State for the Home Department* [2002] ECR I-7091.

[30] Whitehead, *Daily Express*, 23 May 2007, 1.

of *Viking*[31] and *Laval*.[32] Both cases concern an important and well-established form of collective association, namely membership of trade unions and participation in their activities. The background to these cases was the 2004 enlargement and its creation—overnight—of a pool of migrant labour willing to work for significantly less than labour in the old member states.[33] Most importantly, these migrants saw free movement as their ticket to greater prosperity. This inevitably led to a sense of threat, a 'them and us' situation, which, as the Commission noted in its 2007 'Social vision' Communication, fuelled 'a perception of insecurity, isolation, inequity and inequality'[34] and undermined any sense of transnational solidarity, however tenuous, that the Court claimed existed in *Grzelczyk*.

Viking concerned the selling of a Finnish vessel to an Estonian subsidiary, reflagging the vessel in Estonia and employing an Estonian crew in place of a (higher paid) Finnish crew. *Laval* concerned a Latvian company carrying out a building contract in Sweden using Latvian workers and paying them below the Swedish—but not the Latvian—collectively-agreed wage rates. In both cases trade unions either threatened (*Viking*) or actually took (*Laval*) preventive industrial action. The industrial action in *Viking* was extensive: it included the 10 million strong International Transport Workers' Federation launching a solidarity campaign blacking Viking's vessels.

Employers sought to challenge this industrial action—which was legitimate under national law—as being incompatible with Union law. The Court agreed. It found that Article 49 TFEU (ex Article 43 EC) and Article 56 TFEU (ex Article 49 EC) applied to trade unions and that the collective action constituted a restriction on free movement. The question therefore was whether the industrial action could be justified. It is here that Advocate General Poiares Maduro's opinion in *Viking* is of particular interest for our purposes.

He distinguished between two types of industrial action: (1) collective action in the interests of the jobs and working conditions of the *current crew*; and (2) collective action to improve the terms of employment of seafarers throughout the *Union*. In respect of the first type of industrial action, he said this was compatible with EU law provided that cases of intra-Union relocation (Finland-Estonia) were not treated less favourably than relocations within the national borders (one part of Finland to another).[35] However, he added a caveat: this presumption of

[31] Case C-438/05 *Viking Line ABP v The International transport Workers' Federation, the Finnish Seaman's Union* [2007] ECR I-10779 (hereinafter '*Viking*'); preceded by judgments in the High Court, [2005] EWHC 1222, [2005] 3 CMLR 29 (QB) and Court of Appeal, [2005] EWCA Civ 1299, [2006] 1 CMLR 27. For a full discussion of these cases see the chapters by Barnard, Dashwood, Deakin, Novitz, Rönnmar and Sciarra in (2007–2008) 10 CYELS.

[32] Case C-341/05 *Laval un Partneri Ltd v Svenska Byggnadsarbetareförbundet* [2007] ECR I-11767 (hereinafter '*Laval*'). See R. Eklund, 'The *Laval* Case' (2006) 35 ILJ 202.

[33] According to Wagstyl, Cienski, Eddy and Escritt, ('Gone west: why Eastern Europe is labouring under an abundance of jobs', Financial Times, 16 January 2008), hourly labour costs are about €28 in Germany compared to €8 in the Czech Republic, €7.50 in Poland and €4 in Romania.

[34] COM (2007) 726, 3.

[35] Case C-438/05 *Viking* [2007] ECR I-10779, para 65.

legality of such industrial action (if that is what he intended) did not apply to collective action that merely sought to prevent an undertaking that has moved elsewhere from lawfully providing its services in the member state in which it had previously been established.[36] In other words, while the Finnish Seamen's Union could take collective action to try to stop Viking relocating from Finland, once Viking had relocated to Estonia it could not take such action. He said:

> [T]o allow those kinds of action would carry the risk of creating an atmosphere of constant retaliation between social groups in different Member States, which could gravely threaten the common market and the *spirit of solidarity* embedded in it.[37]

In respect of the second type of collective action, Advocate General Poiares Maduro said that coordinating the national unions so as to promote a certain level of rights for seafarers was consistent with the unions' right to collective action because it constituted a reasonable method of counter-balancing the actions of undertakings who sought to lower their labour costs by exercising their rights to freedom of movement. However, he then distinguished between the situation where, on the one hand, all national unions were *obliged* to support collective action by any of their fellow unions and, on the other, where they had a choice to offer such support. Only the latter situation was permissible.

Thus, Advocate General Poiares Maduro showed himself highly sensitive to the conflicting directions in which solidarity among workers pointed: on the one hand solidarity between all EU workers must not be jeopardized by allowing Finnish workers to block services provided by Estonian workers and, on the other, solidarity among Finnish workers meant they should be allowed to protest to protect their jobs. The Court, on the other hand, was considerably less nuanced. In *Viking* it noted that while 'the right to take collective action for the protection of workers is a legitimate interest which, in principle, justifies a restriction of one of the fundamental freedoms guaranteed by the [Treaties]',[38] the collective action would not be justified if, as the Court suggested on the facts, it were established that the jobs or conditions of employment at issue were not jeopardized or under serious threat.[39] For good measure, the Court added that if the collective action could be justified it had to be proportionate. Here the Court of Justice suggested that industrial action should be the last resort; and the British courts had to verify whether the Finnish Trade Union had exhausted all other avenues under Finnish law before the industrial action was found proportionate.[40]

[36] ibid para 67.
[37] ibid para 68. Emphasis added.
[38] ibid para 77.
[39] ibid para 81.
[40] ibid para 87. The Court of Appeal will not have the opportunity to rule on these issues since the parties settled the case. The terms of the settlement remain confidential (<http://www.itfglobal.org/news-online/index.cfm/newsdetail/1842>). It is, however, known that the *Rosella* is now registered in Sweden.

In *Laval* the Court recognized that 'the right to take collective action for the protection of the workers of the host State against possible social dumping may constitute an overriding reason of public interest within the meaning of the case-law of the Court which, in principle, justifies a restriction of one of the fundamental freedoms guaranteed by the [Treaties]'.[41] But it said that using collective action to secure Laval's signature on the collective agreement could not be justified,[42] nor could it be justified for a national system to be so unclear as to what is required of the foreign service provider in terms of pay.[43] Thus, in both *Viking* and *Laval* the Court sent a strong indication to the national courts that collective action taken by trade unions contravened Articles 49 and 56 TFEU.

3. The Meaning of 'Solidarity'

The brief review of the use made by the Union institutions of 'solidarity' shows that while the principle has been used in a variety of ways by the institutions, at no stage has there been any attempt to define the term. The EU institutions appear to apply the elephant test: you know it if you see it. The one exception is Advocate General Fennelly in *Sodemare*[44] who described solidarity as the 'inherently uncommercial act of involuntary subsidization of one social group by another'.[45] His approach reflects the 'brotherhood side of solidarity', a phrase coined by Ferrera. Having described solidarity as a 'rather illusive concept and a complex social good',[46] Ferrera continues:

> On the one hand, it connotes a trait of whole social aggregates, ie a high degree of 'fusion' or internal union, cohesion and commonality of purpose of a given group (the term 'solidarity' comes from the Latin *solidus* – a firm and compact body). On the other hand, it connotes a particular set of ties among the members of such group: *sharing ties,* ie transactions aimed at pooling (a part of) each member's resources for some common purpose (we might call this the "brotherhood" side of solidarity).[47]

[41] Case C-341/05 *Laval* [2007] ECR I-11767, para 103.
[42] ibid para 108.
[43] ibid para 110.
[44] Case C-70/95 *Sodemare SA, Anni Azzurri Holding SpA and Anni Azzurri Rezzato Srl v Regione Lombardia* [1997] ECR I-3395.
[45] ibid para 29.
[46] M. Ferrera, 'Towards an "Open" Social Citizenship? The New Boundaries of Welfare in the European Union' in G. de Búrca (ed) *EU Law and the Welfare State: In Search of Solidarity* (Oxford: OUP, 2005) 19–20.
[47] See also S. O'Leary, 'Solidarity and Citizenship Rights in the Charter of Fundamental Rights of the European Union' in G. de Búrca (ed) *EU Law and the Welfare State: In Search of Solidarity* (Oxford: OUP, 2005) 55. O'Leary, citing the work of Tinga and Verbraak, says solidarity refers both to 'the interdependency of people as a basis for social cohesion and also to diffuse solidarity in large aggregates (territorial or community groupings, states, insurance schemes, etc) in which members of one social group are willing to subsidize another'.

In his ground-breaking book, *Solidarity in Europe*,[48] Steinar Stjernø considers much of the theoretical writing on the meaning of the principle of solidarity. He concludes that a key distinction can be made between, on the one hand, conceptions that understand solidarity as being norms contributing to social integration (Comte, Durkeheim) and, on the other, conceptions that understand solidarity as being a relationship between members of a more or less specified group (Lerous, Marx, Weber). In the second group, solidarity is about interpersonal relationships that bind a group of people together in social relationships. When a group is so defined, 'solidarity is seen as being a force that includes and excludes. In this understanding, solidarity integrates and divides'.[49] He asks whether these variables point to a necessary core in the idea of solidarity. He argues that all the concepts he examined point to two necessary values 'that an individual should identify with others, to some degree, and that a feeling of community should exist between the individual and (at least some) others, and, as a consequence it can be argued that all these ideas of solidarity imply some sort of inclusiveness'.

Social policy, particularly in Continental Europe, is the context in which the principle of solidarity is traditionally associated. It is one of the main policy areas where there is a redistribution of resources between members of the community, so it is not surprising that the principle—which, as we shall see, had already been relied on by the Commission in earlier social policy documents—formed the cornerstone of the Commission's 'Opportunities, Access and Solidarity' communications on the future of European social policy. We shall consider the type of solidarity envisaged by these documents below. First, however, we shall trace the path the Commission followed to arrive at this agenda.

4. Paving the Way for the Social Agenda

The phrase 'Opportunities, Access and Solidarity' was first used in the Commission's Citizens' Agenda of 2006 'Delivering results for Europe'.[50] This document was part of the Commission's response to the 'no' votes to the Constitutional Treaty in France and the Netherlands. In the introduction to its Citizens' Agenda, the Commission identified the paradox that 'the European Union has never been more needed but rarely more questioned'. It therefore suggested that:[51]

> A new Citizens' Agenda for Europe must deliver peace, prosperity and *solidarity* in a new context, globalisation. It should deliver an open and fully functioning single market and effectively turn the four freedoms into reality; promote *solidarity, opportunity, access* and sustainability; and increase security.

[48] S. Stjernø, *Solidarity in Europe* (Cambridge: Cambridge University Press, 2005).

[49] ibid 85.

[50] COM (2006) 211. The theme was picked up again in the Commission's single market review: 'A Single Market for 21st century Europe' COM (2007) 724, 10.

[51] Emphasis added.

Under the heading 'Opportunity, access and solidarity', it continued: 'The drive for a deeper and wider economic integration should go hand in hand with further support for one of Europe's most unifying and fundamental values: solidarity.' It then pledged to undertake a 'social reality stocktaking exercise' prior to launching an 'agenda for access and solidarity'.

The stocktaking exercise started in February 2007,[52] based on a background paper written by the Bureau of European Policy Advisers (BEPA).[53] In November 2007 the Commission produced its Consultation Paper 'Opportunities, access and solidarity: towards a new social vision for 21st century Europe' ('the 2007 Social Vision Communication').[54] In May 2008 the Commission hosted a social agenda forum[55] to provide 'a platform for stakeholders —representatives from member states, European Institutions, social partners, civil society and experts—to discuss the outcome of the social reality stocktaking exercise and the broad policy orientations for a renewed Social Agenda'. This was followed up by the launch, in July 2008, of the Commission's 'Renewed Social Agenda: Opportunities, Access and Solidarity' ('the 2008 Renewed Social Agenda Communication'),[56] which aimed to put into practice some of the ideas floated in the 2007 Communication, together with the Social Agenda package. This package contained a number of policy documents[57] in a wide range of areas, including health and education of migrant

[52] <http://ec.europa.eu/citizens_agenda/social_reality_stocktaking/index_en.htm> (last visited on 25 July 2008). An interim report was issued to the Spring European Council (<http://eur-lex.europa.eu/LexUriServ/LexUriServ.do?uri=CELEX:52007DC0063:EN:NOT>) and a summary of the conclusions was drawn up (<http://ec.europa.eu/citizens_agenda/social_reality_stocktaking/docs/sec_2008_1896_en.pdf>)

[53] <http://ec.europa.eu/citizens_agenda/social_reality_stocktaking/docs/background_document_en.pdf> (last visited on 24 January 2010).

[54] COM (2007) 726.

[55] <http://ec.europa.eu/employment_social/emplweb/social_agenda/ec_conference_en.html>

[56] COM (2008) 412.

[57] Commission (EC), 'Renewed social agenda: Opportunities, access and solidarity in 21st century Europe' (Communication) COM (2008) 412; Commission (EC), 'A Community framework on the application of patients' rights in cross-border healthcare' (Communication) COM (2008) 415; Commission (EC), 'A renewed commitment to social Europe: Reinforcing the Open Method of Coordination for Social Protection and Social Inclusion' (Communication) COM (2008) 418; Commission (EC), 'Non-discrimination and equal opportunities: A renewed commitment' (Communication) COM (2008) 420; Commission (EC), 'Solidarity in the face of Change: the European Globalisation Adjustment Fund (EGF) in 2007—Review and Prospects' (Communication) COM (2008) 421; Commission (EC), 'Improving competences for the 21st Century: An Agenda for European Cooperation on Schools' (Communication) COM (2008) 425; Green Paper, 'Migration & Mobility: challenges and opportunities for EU education systems' COM (2008) 423. In addition a number of staff working documents were adopted: 'Restructuring and Employment: the contribution of the European Union', 'Report on the implementation of the European social partners' Framework Agreement on Telework'; 'The role of transnational company agreements in the context of increasing international integration'; Community Instruments and Policies for Roma Inclusion'; 'First biennial report on the situation of social services of general interest in the EU'; Report on the EU contribution to promoting decent work for all in the world'; 'A renewed social agenda for Europe: Citizens Wellbeing in the Information Society'; 'Efficiency and effectiveness of social spending'. The documents can be found on <http://ec.europa.eu/social/main.jsp?catId=547> (last visited 24 January 2010).

children, as well as four concrete legislative proposals for hard law instruments[58] (for a revised directive on European Works Councils; a revised directive implementing the agreement concluded by the European Community Shipowners' Associations (ECSA) and the European Transport Workers' Federation (ETF) on the Maritime Labour Convention; a new directive on discrimination in the fields of goods and services in respect of disability, age, sexual orientation, religion and belief; and a directive on healthcare services[59]).

The conclusion of the 2007 and 2008 Communications was the culmination of an ongoing process dating back to at least 2000 and probably before,[60] re-examining traditional tenets of labour law, and social policy more generally, to adapt it to changes brought about by globalization, new technology and an ageing population. For example, the Lisbon strategy of 2000[61] said there was a need to 'modernize' the European social model[62] in order to balance social protection, competitiveness, welfare provision and sound finance. Various Commission documents then considered how this balance might be achieved.[63] One answer lay in a shift in thinking away from viewing social policy as a burden on the economy to seeing it instead as a necessary input into its success.[64] This was reflected in the Commission's 2000 Social Policy Agenda[65] which said that

[58] The fact that there are only four hard law proposals is in part explained by the institutional calendar (and in particular the Parliamentary timetable which limits the number of dossiers that can be submitted given that there was not much time left in the Parliamentary session).

[59] Proposal for a Council Dir implementing the agreement concluded by the European Community Shipowners' Associations (ECSA) and the European Transport Workers' Federation (ETF) on the Maritime Labour Convention, 2006 and amending Dir 1999/63/EC (COM (2008) 422) now adopted as Dir 2009/13 (OJ L124/30); proposal for a Council Dir on implementing the principle of equal treatment between persons irrespective of religion or belief, disability, age or sexual orientation (COM (2008) 426); proposal for a European Parliament and Council Dir on the establishment of a European Works Council or a procedure in Community-scale undertakings and Community-scale groups of undertakings for the purposes of informing and consulting employees (Recast) (COM (2008) 419 f/2) now adopted as Dir 2009/38 (OJ [2009] L122/38); proposal for a Dir of the European Parliament and of the Council on the application of patients' rights in cross-border healthcare (COM (2008) 414).

[60] The roots could be traced back even earlier—to the Commission's Green Paper and White Paper on Social Policy (COM (93) 551; COM (94) 333 respectively); White Paper on Growth, Competitiveness and Employment Bull Supp 6/93; Green Paper on the New Organisation of Work (COM (97) 127).

[61] E. Szyszczak, 'The New Paradigm for Social Policy: A Virtuous Circle' (2001) 38 *Common Market Law Review* 1125; V. Hatzopoulos, 'A (More) Social Europe: Apolitical Crossroad or a Legal One Way? Dialogues between Luxembourg and Lisbon' (2005) 42 CML Rev 1599.

[62] Lisbon Presidency Conclusions, 23 and 24 March 2000.

[63] 'Partnership for a New Organisation of Work' COM (97) 127 final; 'Modernising and Improving Social Protection in the European Union' COM (97) 102 final; 'Modernising the Organisation of Work' COM (98) 592.

[64] Commission (EC), 'Social Policy as a Productive Factor' (Luxembourg: OOPEC, 1996); Commission (EC), 'White Paper on Social Policy' COM (1994) 333, introduction, para 5, 'the pursuit of high social standards should not be seen as a cost but also as a key element in the competitive formula'; Commission (EC), 'Mid-term review of the Social Policy Agenda' COM (2003) 312, 'A major guiding principle in the Social Policy Agenda was to strengthen the role of social policy as a productive factor. This has been extended during the past years in particular through the promotion of quality as the driving force for a thriving economy, more and better jobs and greater social cohesion.

[65] COM (2000) 379, 6.

'modernising the European social model and investing in people will be crucial to retain the European social values of solidarity and justice while improving economic performance'. It continued that 'growth is not an end in itself but essentially a means of achieving a better standard of living for all. Social policy underpins economic policy and employment has not only economic but also a social value'.[66]

One essential corollary of the idea that social policy is an input into growth is the need for quality since quality jobs are more likely to keep people in employment and thus socially included. As the Commission has said, quality of social policy implies a high level of social protection, good social services, real opportunities for all and the guarantee of fundamental and social rights.[67] The Heads of State meeting at Nice in December 2000 agreed that '[q]uality of training, quality in work, quality of industrial relations and quality of social policy as a whole are essential factors if the European Union is to achieve the goals it has set itself regarding competitiveness and full employment'.[68] Thus, quality is seen as a 'key element' in the link between competitiveness and social cohesion. In this way, developments at EU level dovetail with the International Labour Organisation's (ILO) 'Decent Work' agenda.[69]

In the specific context of employment, the emphasis on quality of working life and employability of the workforce has coalesced around the neologism 'flexicurity'.[70] Underpinning this idea is the aim to create a 'labour market which is fairer, more responsive and inclusive, and which contributes to making Europe more competitive'.[71] As the Commission explains in its 2007 paper, 'Towards Common Principles of Flexicurity: more and better jobs through flexibility and security',[72] '[f]lexicurity promotes a combination of flexible labour markets and adequate security'. It says flexicurity is not about deregulation, giving employers freedom to dissolve their responsibilities towards employees and giving them little security. Instead, flexicurity is about bringing people into good jobs and developing their talents. Employers have to improve their work organization to offer jobs with a future. They need to invest in their workers' skills. The Commission calls this 'internal flexicurity'. However, the Commission also recognizes that keeping the same job is not always possible. 'External flexicurity' attempts to offer safe

[66] COM (2000) 379, 13.

[67] ibid.

[68] European Council's Social Policy Agenda, Annex I to the Nice Presidency Conclusions, para 26.

[69] <http://www.ilo.org/public/english/decent.htm> (last visited 15 August 2008).

[70] See more generally J. Kenner, 'New Frontiers in EU Labour Law: From Flexicurity to Flex-security' in S. Currie and M. Dougan (eds) *Fifty Years of the Treaty of Rome* (Oxford: Hart Publishing, 2009).

[71] Commission (EC) 'Modernising labour law to meet the challenges of the 21st century' (Green Paper) COM (2006) 708, 4. See S. Sciarra, 'EU Commission Green Paper "Modernising labour law to meet the challenges of the 21st century"' (2007) 36 ILJ 375, 378.

[72] COM (2007) 359, 5.

moves for workers from one job into another, and good benefits to cover the time span between jobs, if needed. This is the so-called 'lifecycle' approach to work.

In respect of security, which is meant to complement flexibility, the Commission focuses not on job security but 'employment security'. Employment security means staying in employment, within the same enterprise or in a new enterprise. It concludes 'The philosophy behind flexicurity is that workers are more prepared to make such moves if there is a good safety net'. Once again, the emphasis is not on deregulation but investment in employment and skills with a social safety net to catch those in transition. This, says the Commission, is the way to 'maintain and improve competitiveness whilst reinforcing the European social model'. The European Social Models (sic), it says, are based on 'social protection, social cohesion and solidarity'.[73] The concept of solidarity is therefore the bridge between the flexicurity agenda and the renewed social agenda.

Having examined the background policy documents leading up to the 2007 and 2008 Communications, we turn now to consider these documents in some detail and, in particular, the notion of solidarity that they manifest.

5. The 2007 'Social Vision' Communication

5.1 The content of the Communication

In its 2007 Communication the Commission identifies three main social realities facing Europe at present. The first is the rapid change of European society—increased life expectancy, declining birth rates, generation fracture, changing family patterns, migration, high levels of unemployment in certain parts of Europe, and newly-emerging social problems (stress, depression, obesity). The second reality is 'globalization', technological progress and economic developments affecting the way EU citizens live and work, whose benefits are not shared evenly across the EU. The third reality is that the EU itself has changed, growing to encompass 500 million citizens. It is also more diverse; 'the accession of new Member States has extended the benefits of peace, freedom and prosperity across the EU and to neighbouring countries'.

In order to respond to these social realities, the Commission proposed a 'new social vision' which has 'opportunities, access and solidarity' at its core:[74]

- Opportunities—to start well in life, realize one's own potential and make the most of chances offered by an innovative open and modern Europe;
- Access—new and more effective ways to get an education, progress in the job market, obtain quality healthcare and social protection and participate in culture and society.

[73] <http://eur-lex.europa.eu/LexUriServ/LexUriServ.do?uri=COM:2007:0359:FIN:EN:PDF> 7 (last visited 24 January 2010).

[74] COM (2007) 726, 6.

- Solidarity—to foster social cohesion and social sustainability, and make sure that no individual is left behind.

The Commission continues:

This vision reflects an increasingly accepted view that whereas society cannot guarantee equal outcomes for its citizens, it must become much more resolute in fostering equal opportunities... The central ambition is to achieve a wider distribution of 'life chances' to allow everyone in the EU to have access to the resources services, conditions and *capabilities* in order to turn the theoretical equality of opportunities and active citizenship into a meaningful reality.[75]

5.2 The influence of Third Way thinking

The 2007 paper, consistent with the earlier social policy documents discussed above, is strongly imbued with 'Third Way' thinking, aiming at a genuine synthesis between the state and the market.[76] While there is much debate as to the meaning of the phrase 'Third Way', both in theory and in practice,[77] at its core lies the idea of replacing the egalitarian goal of achieving greater equality through redistributing wealth using welfare state mechanisms (ie equality of outcomes), with the goal of creating the conditions for the eradication of social exclusion (ie equality of opportunity).[78] As Collins puts it:[79]

The objective is to provide every citizen with the necessary resources in terms of education, training, skills and other financial support, so that they can participate fully in the opportunities afforded by a flourishing market economy. Inequalities of wealth can be tolerated provided that real equality of opportunity is available to all citizens...

There is a direct link here with Sen's capability theory[80] expressly, but briefly, referred to by the Commission in its 2007 paper (see the quote at the top of this page), namely expanding the '"capabilities" of persons to lead the kind of lives they value—and have reason to value'. He continues that these capabilities can

[75] COM (2007) 726, 6. Emphasis added.

[76] This ultimately led to the adoption of the phrase 'social market economy' in Art 3(3) TEU which, as the Final Report of Working Group XI 'Social Europe' of the European Convention, explained (<http://register.consilium.eu.int/pdf/en/03/cv00/CV00516-re01en03.pdf> para 17), underlines 'the link between economic and social development and the efforts made to ensure greater coherence between economic and social policies'. See C. Joerges and F. Rödl, '"Social Market Economy" as Europe's Social Model?' EUI Working Paper LAW No 2004/8.

[77] H. Collins, 'Is there a Third Way in Labour Law?' in J. Conaghan, R. M Fischl and K. Klare (eds) *Labour Law in an Era of Globalisation: Transformative Practices and Possibilities* (Oxford: OUP, 2002), 459.

[78] ibid 451. See also T. Blair, writing in favour of true equality ie 'equal worth and equal opportunity, not an equality of outcome focused on incomes alone': *The Courage of our Convictions* (London: Fabian society, 2002), quoted in S. Fredman, 'The Ideology of New labour' in C. Barnard, S. Deakin and G. Morris (eds) *The Future of Labour Law: Liber Amicorum Sir Bob Hepple QC* (Oxford: Hart Publishing, 2004) 14.

[79] Collins, n 77 above, 452.

[80] A. Sen, *Capability as Freedom* (Oxford: OUP, 1999) 18.

be enhanced by public policy (eg education, training, healthcare and a career of their choosing) but also the direction of public policy can be influenced by the effective use of participatory capabilities by the public.[81] For this reason human rights and democratic freedoms, including freedom of association, the right to participate in economic and political decision-making, are so important.[82]

Collins adds that implicit in the Third Way ideal is that markets produce a fair distribution of wealth for most people, and so lead to a reduction in poverty, provided that everyone has a fair opportunity to participate in the market. In contrast with pre-Third Way politics, there is no commitment on the part of the state to ensure an acceptable redistribution pattern occurs because this is 'impracticable, unaffordable, ineffective, and counter-productive owing to the problem of welfare dependency'.[83] Instead, individuals have the responsibility to take up the opportunities for achieving a decent standard of living that are facilitated or provided by the state. This is one aspect of what Fredman terms 'civic responsibility'[84] which is one of the hallmarks of Third Way thinking (the others being the facilitative state, equality, and community and democracy). The corollary of civic responsibility is that if individuals fail to take advantage of the opportunities offered to them, the consequences rest with them, not the state (and its welfare system).

These Third Way ideas can be seen in the notions of 'opportunities' and 'access' which structure the Commission's 'Social Vision' Communication: getting *access* to the necessary education, training and healthcare (provided by the 'facilitative' state and/or employers) enables individuals to take advantage of the *opportunities* available to them on the market. And the market means the employment market because, according to Third Way thinking, the principal cause of social exclusion is unemployment (or at least the inability to get a decent job to which the 'Quality' agenda, discussed above, is intended to respond). In respect of the question of (equal) opportunities, the Third Way adopts a substantive, rather than formal, approach. It recognizes that many of those currently excluded from the labour market (the young, the old, ethnic minorities, women with caring responsibilities, the disabled) face formal barriers to their participation, especially discriminatory barriers (hence the significance of the 'Article 13 EC' (now Article 19 TFEU) Directives (2000/43 and 2000/78) which extend the prohibition of discrimination to socially excluded categories such as ethnic minorities, the disabled and older workers). They also face substantive barriers such as the absence of child and eldercare, as well as financial barriers created by the 'poverty trap'.

The seven areas for action outlined by the Commission in its 'Social Vision' Communication are intended to respond to these barriers: investing in youth, particularly the education of the very young; investing in fulfilling careers, assisting in the shift from a job-for-life to employment for life and 'safe and innovative

[81] ibid.

[82] B. Hepple, 'Labour Law, inequality and global trade', Sinzheimer Lecture 2002, 10–11. Cf Case C-438/05 *Viking*, considered above nn 31–40.

[83] ibid.

[84] n 77 above, 12.

working conditions'; investing in longer and healthier lives; investing in gender equality including addressing pay gaps, reviewing the tax systems to improve work incentives, developing affordable and accessible childcare and eldercare and spreading family-friendly practices; investing in active inclusion and non-discrimination, investing in mobility and successful integration; and investing in civic participation, culture and dialogue.

5.3 The presentation of solidarity

So what role is there for solidarity in the Commission's Third Way view of social policy? The addition of 'solidarity' to the duo of 'opportunities' and 'access' indicates that the state, in some form, should provide a safety net for those who cannot take advantage of the opportunities available to them. In this way, the EU hopes to avoid some of the criticisms levelled at the UK's execution of Third Way principles: in the UK if the individual does not take advantage of what is offered, the individual, not the state, suffers the consequences; there is little or no safety net.

However, it is important not to exaggerate the function of solidarity in the 2007 Communication. Although 'solidarity' has joined 'opportunities' and 'access' as defining features of the new social vision, it is striking just how little the word itself is mentioned: after the initial description of solidarity,[85] the word is used just twice more in the paper.[86] This gives the sense that solidarity was too politically sensitive[87] or—worse—was simply added as a make-weight. The one area where solidarity is mentioned concerns the need to build and maintain a collective identity of any society. We are told:

> Traditional bonds such as family, social group and religion are weakening. There is a trend to individualisation of values and an atomisation of culture – a focus on the individual and the consumer rather than on society as a whole...At the same time, new forms of solidarity are emerging, including through leisure and cultural activities.[88]

Later, the Communication adds:

> Active participation in collective activities such as culture, sport, civic and political activism contributes to the coherence and solidarity of Europe's communities and can thus help fight risks of atomisation and isolation. Voluntary work and civic engagement also play a prominent role in strengthening social cohesion.[89]

[85] COM (2007) 726, 6.

[86] 'Active participation in collective activities such as culture, sport, civic and political activism contributes to the coherence and solidarity of Europe's communities and can thus help fight risks of atomization and isolation' (p 9) and 'European societies in which pluralism, non-discrimination, tolerance, justice, solidarity and equality between women and men prevail' (p 9).

[87] Earlier drafts of the 2007 Communication contained no reference to solidarity at all, merely to 'Opportunities and Access'. The paper was drafted by Secgen (Secretariat-General) and was not subject to the usual inter-service consultation. DG Empl had only one opportunity to comment on this document. The absence of solidarity in the title was one of the principal bones of contention.

[88] COM (2007) 726, 5.

[89] ibid 9.

This reflects the 'community and democracy' strand of Third Way thinking. It contains the idea of creating an 'espace de solidarité': a place where people can connect with each other to overcome a growing sense of isolation brought about by the individualistic pursuit of economic success.[90] This is resonant of Stjernø's first and second understandings of solidarity: that it is about norms contributing to social integration as well as being about interpersonal relationships that bind a group of people together in social relationships. It also reflects Durkheim's views that only when there is a strong social solidarity and a powerful collective conscience that individuals will have the platform on which to express their individualism; otherwise they risk being isolated by the pressures of the modern market economy and getting lost, resulting in alienation and '*anomie*'—a sense of purposeless anonymity.[91] As Hutton says, '[h]uman beings depend for their humanity on association, and this requires that they participate in a collective consciousness and shared belief system that allows them to empathise with the conditions of others'.[92] Viewed from this perspective, the Court of Justice's decisions in *Viking* and *Laval* seem all the more problematic to the extent that they appear to favour the needs of the individual employer (and the migrant service provider in *Laval*) over the collective interests of the Finnish and Swedish trade unions.

6. The 2008 'Renewed Social Agenda' Communication

6.1 The content of the Agenda

The 2007 Communication is generally upbeat, progressive and imaginative. It talks about everyone having 'ladders of opportunity' and the need to create a 'well-functioning, confident and buoyant society which invests in its human capital and creates opportunities for individuals to move on throughout their life cycle'.[93] It is, however, an exercise in kite-flying. By contrast, the 2008 Communication is much more stolid and predictable but also more practical since it has to put a number of these ideas into operation. It recognizes the need for a 'renewed social agenda' to respond to new challenges facing the EU ('Technological advances, globalisation and an ageing population'). At each stage of the EU's development, it notes, social policy has had a role to play. For example, in the 1980s the Social Agenda was 'conceived as a means of securing assent to the industrial restructuring that the "1992" agenda involved and the focus was on employment protection and the need to secure consensus between the social partners in order

[90] See more generally P. Xuereb, 'The Future of Europe: Solidarity and Constitutionalism: Towards a Solidarity Model' (2002) 27 ELR 643.

[91] W. Hutton, *The World We Are In* (London: Abacus, 2002) 91.

[92] ibid 87.

[93] COM (2007) 726, 7.

to facilitate industrial change'.[94] According to the Commission, the position is different today where 'a much wider social agenda is needed that allows Europe to take full advantage of the opportunities brought about by globalisation, to help citizens adapt to changing realities and to show solidarity with those who are affected negatively.'

Once again the goals of this renewed social agenda—all of 'equal importance'[95]—are opportunities, access and solidarity. For the Commission, creating *opportunities* means 'generating more and better jobs and facilitating mobility'.[96] It continues:

> In societies where each individual is regarded as being of equal worth, no barriers of any kind should hold people back. This means ensuring the chances for all to develop their own potentials (sic) while respecting Europe's diversity and tackling both overt and indirect discrimination and fighting racism and xenophobia.[97]

Once again, this rhetoric is strongly inspired by the Third Way thinking—in particular equal opportunities and the facilitative state.

In respect of providing *access*, the Commission recognizes that 'given the very different starting points in life, opportunity cannot be ensured without improving access for the most disadvantaged'.[98] In practice this means that all citizens must have access to good quality education, social protection, healthcare and services that can help to overcome inequalities in starting points and to enable all to enjoy longer, healthier lives. Europe's youth must be equipped to take advantage of opportunities. All Europeans should also have access to education and skills development throughout their life (for example, second chance schools or life-long learning) so as to be able to adjust to change and start afresh at different points in their life. In other words, to exploit opportunities, individuals need access to enable them actively to participate and integrate in the societies in which they live.[99] Here the state has an important facilitative role in investing in these individuals to enhance their capabilities to enable them to compete for opportunities available to them.

The final goal of the 2008 Communication is demonstrating *solidarity*: 'stepping up efforts to fight poverty and social exclusion and explore new ways to help individuals adjust to globalisation and technological change'.[100] The Commission continues:[101]

> Europeans share a commitment to social solidarity: between generations, regions, the better off and the less well off and wealthier and less wealthy Member States. Solidarity is part of how European society works and how Europe engages with the rest of the world. Real equality of opportunity depends on both access and solidarity. Solidarity means

[94] COM (2008) 412, 5.
[95] ibid 6. [96] ibid.
[97] ibid 4. Elsewhere, the Commission talks about 'fostering gender equality, supporting families and tackling new forms of social exclusion'.
[98] ibid 6. [99] ibid 4. [100] ibid. [101] ibid 6.

action to help those who are disadvantaged – who cannot reap the benefits of an open, rapidly changing society....

We consider in more detail this approach to solidarity below. For the present it is sufficient to note first, that the Commission recognizes that solidarity, in a variety of guises, goes to the heart of European identity and it is one of the ways that Europe asserts is distinctiveness from the United States.[102] The Commission makes this point explicit earlier in the Communication where it notes that '[s]hared social values', including solidarity, are 'intrinsic to feelings of European identity, having underpinned the foundations of the European project from the beginning'.[103] As Weiler has noted,[104]

Europe prides itself on a tradition of social solidarity which found political and legal expression in the post-war welfare state,[105] which all states of all political colours embraced as an ideal and as a programmatic commitment for years.... Like the eventual rejection of the death penalty, this commitment became a source of identity, even pride—especially in comparison with the United States.

The second point to note about solidarity is that the Commission sees the trio of opportunity, access and solidarity as intimately interconnected. A neo-liberal vision of the Third Way would focus on access and opportunity only; there would be no social safety net. This has not been the EU's way: as we have seen from the earlier policy documents, the Commission still envisages a role for the welfare state to provide 'good benefits' albeit, as the 2007 *Flexicurity* document shows, to facilitate the change from one job to another.

As with the 2007 Communication, the Commission identifies seven priority areas for action in its 2008 Renewed Social Agenda. These broadly overlap with those areas identified in 2007 Communication, albeit with some changes in emphasis. Children and youth are still the number one priority. Investing in people, more and better jobs and new skills stays at number two, now spanning a wide range of issues including modernizing labour markets, anticipating change and restructuring, flexicurity,[106] structural funds and immigration. Mobility has become the third priority area of action and includes a reference to developing a 'fifth freedom', promoting the mobility of specific groups like researchers, young entrepreneurs, young people and volunteers. This section of the Communication

[102] Hutton, n 91 above, 84.

[103] COM (2008) 412, 4.

[104] J. H. H. Weiler, 'A Constitution for Europe? Some Hard Choices' (2002) 40 J of Common Market Studies 563, 569.

[105] 'Universal health coverage, free education from kindergarten through to university, generous welfare for the less fortunate, notably the unemployed, have been the proud hallmark of this commitment'.

[106] See further the Commission's Green Paper, 'Modernising labour law to meet the challenges of the 21st Century' COM (2006) 708 final and the follow up, 'Towards Common Principles of Flexicurity: More and Better Jobs through flexibility and security' COM (2007) 359 considered above, nn 70–71.

also identifies that the *Viking*, *Laval* (and *Rüffert*[107]—see below) decisions have been 'widely discussed' and declares that:

The Commission is committed to ensuring that there is no contradiction between the fundamental freedoms of the Treaty and the protection of fundamental rights and will thoroughly assess, discuss and respond to issues of concern, including through providing interpretative guidelines if needed.[108]

Longer and healthier lives and combating poverty and social exclusion are the fourth and fifth priorities. The sixth priority area is 'fighting discrimination'. While gender is referred to under this broad rubric it has lost the independent status it enjoyed as a priority area in the 2007 Communication. Specific reference is now made to the position of the Roma community.[109]

The seventh priority area for action in the 2007 Communication, investing in civic participation, culture and dialogue, has been abandoned altogether,[110] in part because the Commission had no accompanying policies, although there is a brief reference to 'civic participation' later in the document.[111] This seventh area has been replaced by the heading 'Opportunities, Access and Solidarity on the global scene', which covers matters such as global cooperation, cooperation with the ILO and promoting corporate social responsibility.

6.2 Solidarity in the 2008 Consultation Paper

So what does the 2008 paper tell us about the Commission's approach to solidarity? At a rudimentary level, the term is used more extensively throughout the 2008 document than in the 2007 Communication. This may reflect the fact that the 2008 Communication was drafted by DGEmpl (Directorate General on Employment, Social Affairs and Equal Opportunities) which had pushed for the inclusion of solidarity in the original 2007 document (on which it had been consulted but did not draft). Solidarity is also used in a wider range of situations than in 2008: for example, when talking about climate change, the 2008 Communication says that the EU can help harness new opportunities for economic development and the creation of 'green jobs' 'while acting in solidarity with

[107] Case C-346/06 *Rüffert v Land Niedersachsen* [2008] ECR I-1989.

[108] See also 'A Single Market for 21st century Europe' COM (2007) 724, 10, 'The single market has prompted new trends in intra-EU mobility. Some workers have difficulty adapting and see these wider processes as a threat, particularly when they affect their local communities. These are legitimate concerns, which must be addressed. Workers' rights need to be guaranteed and a level playing field maintained, notably through the correct application of EU labour law'.

[109] See Commission Staff Working Paper, 'Community Instruments and Policies for Roma Inclusion' COM (2008) 420.

[110] This is surprising since many of the respondents 'expressly supported the consultation document on this point': Commission Staff Working Paper, 'Report on the Public Consultation on Europe's Social Reality and on a new Social Vision for 21st century, SEC (2008) 1896, 13.

[111] ibid 18.

vulnerable groups'.[112] When describing children and youth as a priority area, the Commission refers to developing new forms of 'intergenerational solidarity'. On the global stage, the Commission talks of 'solidarity beyond EU borders'.[113]

Given the breadth of the contexts in which solidarity is invoked, the dilution of the community/democracy approach to solidarity, through abandoning the seventh priority area for action in the 2007 Communication, is all the more remarkable. On the other hand, the different contexts in which solidarity is envisaged in the 2008 Communication does reflect the notion of 'civic responsibility' underpinning the Third Way agenda. As Fredman explains, the Third Way uses the notion of responsibility to distance itself from the neo-liberal conception of the autonomous individual who is free to pursue his or her own rational self-interest. She continues 'Instead, it stresses the responsibility of individuals to one another and to the community as a whole, whether through bearing a fair share of taxes to ensuring opportunities for all, caring for the environment, or participation in democratic and other civic structures.'[114] She adds 'Civic responsibility translates, too, into the pivotal notion of solidarity, which means mutual dependence and a sense of togetherness'.[115] Fredman emphasizes that in the Third Way literature civic responsibility is multilateral: on the state to provide relevant opportunities and to intervene where differential market reward is not a true reflection of personal responsibility and effort, on employers towards their workers as well as to their shareholders, and, of course on individuals.[116] However, in the UK, she notes, the implementation of civic responsibility places responsibility primarily on the shoulders of workers, 'with little or no attention paid to the responsibilities of business'.[117] Where duties are imposed on employers they are not explained in terms of mutual responsibility but are portrayed as beneficial to business and are shaped as far as possible to minimize business responsibilities.[118]

It could be argued that the 2008 Communication, in contrast with the 2007 Communication, also places much emphasis on the responsibilities of the individual with little reference to the responsibilities of others. For example, it says that the focus of the renewed social agenda 'needs to be on **empowering and enabling** individuals to realise their potential while at the same time helping those who are unable to do so'.[119] Later, under the heading 'opportunities', the Commission adds that there must be 'chances for all to develop their own potential'.[120] However,

[112] ibid 6.
[113] ibid 14.
[114] Fredman, n 78 above, 12–13.
[115] ibid 29.
[116] ibid 13.
[117] ibid 21.
[118] ibid.
[119] ibid 3, emphasis in the original.
[120] cf the emphasis on corporate social responsibility (CSR) in Council Resolution on the follow-up to the Green Paper on corporate social responsibility 2002/C 86/03, [2002] OJ C86/3; Commission (EC), 'Corporate Social Responsibility: A Business Contribution to Sustainable Development' (Communication) COM (2002) 347.

this criticism should not be pushed too far because in other related documents the Commission takes a multilateral view of responsibility. Take for example, the Commission's 2007 Communication 'Towards Common Principles of Flexicurity'.[121] One of those common principles says 'Flexicurity implies a balance between rights and responsibilities for employers, workers, job seekers and public authorities'; another says 'Flexicurity requires a climate of trust and dialogue between public authorities and social partners, where all are prepared to take responsibility for change, and produce balanced policy packages'.[122]

While, as Fredman shows, the approach to civic responsibility has strong solidaristic elements and this can be found in related policy documents, it is surprising that the heavy reliance on the principle of solidarity in the 2008 'Renewed Social Agenda' is not carried through in the accompanying policy documents in the Social Agenda package which might be deemed to have solidaristic elements.[123] Beyond references to the title of the 2008 Communication, these documents contain very few express uses of the word solidarity. This is particularly noteworthy in the policy documents and legislative proposals on non-discrimination where, as we have already seen, there is the most obvious link between solidarity and non-discrimination, an area which might have been fruitful to explore, a point we return to below. The one policy document in which there is more extensive reference to solidarity concerns healthcare where, starting with the European healthcare strategy,[124] the Commission regularly refers to the values of 'universality, access to good quality health care, equity and solidarity'.[125]

6.3 The uses of solidarity in the 2008 Communication

While it might be easy to be cynical about the regular references to solidarity in the 2008 communication, there is evidence that, in DG Empl at least, there is a genuine commitment to solidarity as the core of social policy and the basis of the sort of society the EU wishes to preserve (create?). While it is not clear that the Commission has thought deeply as to the meaning of the term, the 2008 Communication does suggest that the Commission (intentionally or unintentionally) uses the term in the following ways:

- Solidarity as a goal or an objective;
- Solidarity as an interpretative or guiding tool;
- Solidarity as a means;
- Solidarity as a process;
- Solidarity as an instrument.

[121] COM (2007) 359.
[122] ibid 10.
[123] See the documents referred to in n 57 above.
[124] COM (2007) 630.
[125] COM (2008) 412, 11.

Of course, there is considerable overlap between these various uses but there may be some distinctive features of each use, which we now consider.

6.3.1 *Solidarity as an objective*

Starting from the highest level, solidarity is the *objective* of EU social policy. Its aim is to ensure that 'individuals and regions that cannot cope' are not left behind.[126] In practice, as we have seen with the 2007 Communication, solidarity seems to be allied with a notion of equal opportunities: under the heading of 'Demonstrating solidarity' the Communication says 'Real equality of opportunity depends on both access and solidarity. Solidarity means action to help those who are disadvantaged'.[127] The use of the solidarity as an objective is perhaps the most important function in political terms: while social policy is being modernized—and this will cause pain to some—the process of modernization does not involve a total break with the past. Solidarity is there to provide a bridge between the old and the new and to catch those who cannot take advantage of the opportunities available to them.

6.3.2 *Solidarity as an interpretative principle*

The second use of the solidarity principle is as an *interpretative or guiding tool* to steer other policies towards creating social cohesion. The seed of this approach was already sown in the European Convention's 'Social Europe' Working Group where 'Some members considered that recognition of the role of the "social economy" should be made in the Treaty, allowing for its development on the basis of social solidarity'.[128] How might this work in practice? Take the question of social spending as against social investment. As Fredman notes, social spending on welfare, with its redistributive connotations, makes some better off at the cost of others. Social investment spent on creating opportunities through education, training and healthcare makes everyone better off. Yet she argues these are not alternatives: 'Measures (such as education and training) which prevent social exclusion, cannot fully substitute for measures (such as unemployment benefit) which protect individuals who are in fact excluded'.[129] A solidarity reading would suggest that Fredman is right and that the social welfare safety net should not be removed altogether, a point the Commission has already recognized. In the quote referred to (p 93) above, the Commission said that individuals should be empowered to realize their potential while at the same time 'helping those who are unable to do so'.

The interpretative function of principles and rights has long been recognized. For example, Lyon-Caen, writing about the role of social rights,[130] argues that

[126] ibid 4. [127] ibid 6.

[128] <http://register.consilium.eu.int/pdf/en/03/cv00/CV00516-re01en03.pdf>, para 33.

[129] Fredman, n 78 above, 15.

[130] A. Lyon-Caen, 'Lessons from the European Experience' in B. Hepple (ed) *Social and Labour Rights in a Global Context: International and Comparative Perspectives* (Cambridge: Cambridge University Press, 2002), 186–189.

they can serve four functions: (1) to orientate the interpretation of other rules; (2) to provide a justification for the adoption of rules, mechanisms or institutions; (3) to control the generation of norms in ways that can offer protection against the excess of legislative opportunism; (4) to control mechanisms of implementation. Translating this into the context of solidarity, his categories (1) and (2) overlap with the interpretative approach under discussion. There is little evidence that the Commission has directly envisaged the control function of solidarity (categories (3) and (4)), although the reference to mainstreaming (considered below) might be read in this respect. However, there are indications in the Court's case law on the restructuring cases of the 1970s in the iron and steel sectors (cases considered in section 2.1 above) that solidarity has the potential to play that role.

6.3.3 Solidarity as a means

So far we have considered the use of solidarity in the 2008 Communication as a meta-objective of social policy and as an interpretative tool. The third use of solidarity is, as Stjernø recognizes in his first understanding of solidarity, as a *means* to help build that community. In this context solidarity is closely linked to integration. This understanding is reflected in the Commission's observation that solidarity means '*fostering* social inclusion and integration'.[131] This is an active and ongoing process, a process which involves some bootstrapping: solidarity is needed to create a community; repeated references to the existence of solidarity help to define the characteristics of the community that has been created. It could be argued that it was this understanding of solidarity which guided the Court in its decision in *Grzelczyk*.

In the 2008 Communication, solidarity as a means is used in two distinct areas identified in the document: immigration and social welfare. In the context of immigration policy the Commission says that 'immigration has to be accompanied from the start by efforts to facilitate successful integration'. The Commission's Common Immigration Policy for Europe[132] provides for coordinated action with a view to promoting 'prosperity, solidarity and security'.[133] In respect of social welfare, receipt of social assistance serves an important integrationist function.[134] Social welfare also offers a life-belt, as the Commission notes in its 2008 Communication: solidarity means 'giving support to those who are exposed to temporary, transitional problems of globalisation and technological change'.[135]

[131] COM (2008) 412, 6.

[132] COM (2008) 359.

[133] COM (2008) 412, 6.

[134] See, eg, Case C-111/91 *Commission v Luxembourg* [1993] ECR I-817; Case C-85/96 *Martínez Sala* [1998] ECR I-2691, para 28; Case 65/81 *Reina v Landeskreditbank Baden-Württemberg* [1982] ECR 33, para 17; Case C-237/94 *O'Flynn v Adjudication Officer* [1996] ECR I-2617. E. Ellis, 'Social Advantages: A New Lease of Life' (2003) 40 CML Rev 639, 648.

[135] COM (2008) 412, 6.

6.3.4 Solidarity as a process

The fourth use of solidarity is as a *process* 'fostering... participation and dialogue'.[136] In the 2008 Renewed Social Agenda communication, the Commission says:

> Opportunities, access and solidarity for all can only be achieved in partnership between the European Institutions, Member States, Regional and Local Authorities, Social Partners, Civil Society and other stakeholders, including external partners as relevant.

The most developed—and Constitutional—example of participation has been through the social dialogue.[137] The Commission claims that the right of social partners to be consulted prior to any employment or social affairs initiative from the Commission, to negotiate themselves on issues submitted by the Commission or to conclude autonomous agreements on their own initiative, has had 'many positive results'[138] (listing, for example, the collective agreements on parental leave, on violence and stress at work, on telework and on the ILO Convention on seafarers). This view might be contested: in the 15 years in which the social partners have enjoyed the possibility of negotiating collective agreements, the number produced, particularly those resulting in an intersectoral directive, can be counted on the fingers of one hand. It is perhaps for this reason that the Commission calls on 'the Social Partners to make full use of the possibilities offered by the European Social Dialogue'.[139]

6.3.5 Solidarity as an instrument

The fifth and final use of solidarity in the 2008 Communication is as an *instrument* to help foster solidarity as an objective of the EU. The 2008 Agenda talks about 'solidarity mechanisms'.[140] It also refers to '*stepping up* efforts to fight poverty and social exclusion and explor[ing] new ways to help individuals adjust to globalisation and technological change'.[141] In practical terms this means the use of EU funds. Here the 2008 Communication is most explicit. For example, it talks of 'Cohesion Policy and the Structural Funds' making a vital contribution to the promotion of opportunities, access and solidarity. In particular, it notes the role of the 2007–2013 Programme on employment and social solidarity (PROGRESS) helping to apply EU Law, creating a shared

[136] ibid. See also 4: individuals should be able to 'actively participate and integrate in the societies in which they live'.

[137] See A. Reale, 'Representation of Interests, Participatory Democracy and Lawmaking in the European Union: Which Role and Which Rules for the Social Partners?' Jean Monnet Working Paper 15/03. On the subject of more general consultation, see Commission (EC), 'Towards a reinforced culture of consultation and dialogue—Proposal for general principles and minimum standards for consultation of interested parties by the Commission' COM (2002) 277.

[138] COM (2008) 412, 16.

[139] ibid.

[140] ibid 3.

[141] ibid 4, emphasis added.

understanding of the EU objectives and priorities and strengthening partnerships with key EU and national stakeholders, and the function of the (underused[142]) European Globalisation Adjustment Fund (EGF).[143] It also means more emphasis on education and training,[144] and greater involvement of the scientific community in developing knowledge and evidence-based policies.

6.4 Implications of these uses of solidarity for future legislative and executive action at EU level

So how will the EU put its ambitious objectives—of opportunities, access and solidarity—into action? The 2007 'Social Vision' Communication is vague, talking of:

> setting policy frameworks for action; upholding Europe's values and ensuring a level playing field; sharing experiences and good practices; supporting action at local, regional and national level; raising awareness and building a strong knowledge base.

This vagueness is understandable. One of the distinguishing features of Third Way thinking is a move away from the vision of the state as provider to the position of the state as 'facilitator'.[145] In practical terms this means two things: first, that the state cannot legislate in a traditional command and control manner. Instead, law is there is to give 'shape and support to these new understandings and as a last resort to help resolve differences and disputes if they should arise'.[146] Reflexive law appears to respond to this imperative. With this type of law-making, the essential objective of the legislation is laid down (eg to inform and consult the workforce) but the details are left to the parties to work out.[147]

However, in the areas identified in the Communications requiring particular attention by states—education, training and healthcare—there is no direct role for the EU since it has no express competence to act in these fields nor does it have the capacity to act, as the Commission notes in the introduction to its 2008 Communication:[148]

[142] Commission (EC), 'Solidarity in the face of Change: The European Globalisation Adjustment Fund (EGF) in 2007—Review and prospects' COM (2008) 421. cf <http://ec.europa.eu/social/main.jsp?langId=en&catId=736> where the Commission proposes amendments to the EGF to make it more efficient in responding to the current financial crisis.

[143] COM (2008) 412, 17.

[144] See the Green paper on 'Migration and Mobility: challenges for the EU's educational systems' COM (2008) 423 which accompanied the social agenda package.

[145] S. Fredman, 'The Ideology of New Labour' in C. Barnard, S. Deakin and G. Morris (eds) *The Future of Labour Law: Liber Amicorum Sir Bob Hepple QC* (Hart Publishing: Oxford, 2004) 10–11.

[146] T. Blair, Foreword to the White Paper, *Fairness at Work*, Cm 3968 (London: HMSO, 1998).

[147] See further C. Barnard and S. Deakin, '"Negative" and "Positive" Harmonisation of Labor Law in the European Union', 2002 (8) Columbia J of Eur Law 389–413.

[148] COM (2008) 412, 3.

Actions in the social field are primarily the responsibility of the Member States and have to be taken closest to the citizen at national and sub-national level.[149] The EU's powers and responsibilities in the social field are limited. However, the EU, with its blend of shared values, common rules and solidarity mechanisms, is uniquely placed to work in partnership with the Member States and stakeholders and foster cooperation to manage socio-economic change, particularly the change driven by globalisation and technology.

It is in this context that Open Method of Coordination (OMC) techniques have an important role to play. While leaving key policy choices to the member states, OMC tries to encourage member states to improve these choices through 'promoting common objectives and common indicators and through comparative evaluations of national policy performance'.[150] This is consistent with the now well established idea, dating back to the European Employment Strategy, of the EU coordinating activities of the member states in areas of common interest rather than acting as a super-state relying on centralized, uniform, top-down forms of regulation.[151] Here solidarity could be used as an interpretative or guiding tool to shape the relevant common objectives, for example, targets on getting young people (back) into employment, with notions of the quality of the work that they can be asked to perform.

OMC is not the only tool in the Commission's kit. The Commission also refers to EU funding and mainstreaming all EU measures to check that they promote opportunities, access and solidarity. It is in the context of mainstreaming that the Commission specifically points to EU rules on public procurement which 'leave ample opportunities for authorities to take into account social considerations when selecting the best offer'[152]. Yet in *Rüffert,*[153] a case which followed *Laval* closely, the Court ignored the public procurement issue entirely. The case concerned a German State law requiring building contractors to observe the minimum terms of a collective agreement governing public works. However, the main contractor in the case had employed a Polish subcontractor which was paying its workers wages below the rate set out in the German collective agreement. As Advocate General Bot noted, 'The possibility of integrating social requirements into public procurement contracts has already been recognised by the Court'[154]

[149] See also ibid 7 'Actions to move towards these goals are primarily the responsibility of the Member States at national, regional and local levels'.

[150] F. Scharpf, 'The European Social Model: Coping with the Challenges of Diversity' (2002) 40 J of Common Market Studies 645, 666.

[151] D. Trubek and M. Nance, 'EU Law as Reflexive Coordination: The Strange Case of the Posted Workers Dir' unpublished paper on file with the author.

[152] The Handbook on socially responsible public procurement, which the Commission is due to publish shortly, will provide detailed guidance and practical illustrations in this context.

[153] Case C-346/06 *Rüffert v Land Niedersachsen* [2008] ECR I-1989.

[154] Citing Case 31/87 *Beentjes* [1988] ECR 4635 and Case C-225/98 *Commission v France* [2000] ECR I-7445.

and is now enshrined in Directive 2004/18.[155] In the light of this he concluded that:

> Since the contract performance condition relating to the minimum remuneration of workers laid down in the disputed provisions of the Landesvergabegesetz complies with the principle of non-discrimination on the basis of nationality, and since it complies with the principle of transparency, it must, in my opinion, be considered to be consistent with [Union] law.[156]

The Court took a different line. It focused only on the Posted Workers' Directive 96/71 and found that because Germany had not complied with the technical requirements of the Directive (ie it had not fixed a rate of pay according to one of the procedures laid down in the first and second indents of the first subparagraph of Article 3(1) and in the second subparagraph of Article 3(8) of Directive 96/71[157]) there was a breach of Directive 96/71. There was also a breach of Article 56 TFEU because the requirement on undertakings performing public works contracts, and indirectly on their subcontractors, to apply the minimum wage laid down in the collective agreement was a restriction on freedom to provide services[158] which could not be justified on the grounds of worker protection due to the breach of the Posted Workers' Directive.[159]

The *Laval* and *Rüffert* cases show how easy it is for the Court to use the Treaties, in particular Article 56, to limit the protection provided by Union secondary legislation, the Posted Workers' Directive, which itself is based on the free movement of services provisions in the Treaties. This highlights the point noted by Scharpf, that since effective welfare-state policies remain located at the national level, they cannot overcome the constitutional asymmetry that constrains national solutions, namely the primacy of European economic law. He therefore advocates a search for solutions which have the character of European law, to establish constitutional parity with the rules of European economic integration but which are sufficiently differentiated to accommodate the existing diversity of national welfare regimes.[160]

[155] At the time of the dispute Dir 93/37/EEC on the coordination of procedures for the award of public works contracts (OJ [1993] L199/54) was the relevant Dir. This Directive was repealed and replaced by Dir 2004/18/EC (OJ [2004] L134/114). Art 23(1) provides: 'The contracting authority may state in the contract documents, or be obliged by a Member State to do so, the authority or authorities from which a tenderer may obtain the appropriate information on the obligations relating to the employment protection provisions and the working conditions which are in force in the Member State, region or locality in which the works are to be executed and which shall be applicable to the works carried out on site during the performance of the contract.' Art 26 of Dir 2004/18, headed 'Conditions for performance of contracts', reads: 'Contracting authorities may lay down special conditions relating to the performance of a contract, provided that these are compatible with Community law and are indicated in the contract notice or in the specifications. The conditions governing the performance of a contract may, in particular, concern social and environmental considerations. For further discussion see C. Barnard, 'British Jobs for British Workers': The Lindsey Oil Refinery Dispute and the Future of Contracting in an Integrated EU Market' (2009) 38 ILJ 245.

[156] Case C-346/06 *Rüffert v Land Niedersachsen* [2008] ECR I-1989, para 134.

[157] ibid para 31. [158] ibid para 37.

[159] ibid para 38.

[160] F. Scharpf, 'The European Social Model: Coping with the Challenges of Diversity' (2002) 40 J of Common Market Studies 645, 666.

This suggests that there is still a role for the EU to enact employment laws but based on the social policy provisions of the Treaties which can be less easily circumvented by interpretation of the four freedoms. In the 2008 Communication the Commission recognizes that legislation is envisaged (although, as we have seen, the legislative proposals accompanying the social agenda are, in fact, fairly minimal). If the Commission was prepared to be more ambitious, solidarity could have a role to play. For example, it could be used to justify a more active legislative approach towards those identified in the *Modernising Labour Law* Green Paper as currently suffering from inequality in the labour market, such as workers in 'three way relationships' (temps) and those engaged in 'economically dependent work' (essentially the dependent self-employed).[161] Such individuals need to have a 'ladder of opportunity so as to enable them to improve their mobility and achieve successful labour market transitions'.[162] Hepple makes this point clearly:[163] achieving true equality of opportunities in the Third Way sense—what Hepple describes as 'equality of capabilities'—depends not only on active labour market policies (such as education and training) but also on the need to expand labour law to dependent workers who fall outside its coverage[164] and introduce a new conception of work that embraces both employed and self-employed paid labour and by reconciling paid work and family work.

Solidarity might also give the Commission the excuse to break away from the paradigm of proposing social legislation primarily to address market failures. As Prosser points out, this is an inadequate explanation to account for much regulation and that in reality other justifications can be found in the protection of rights and the maintenance of social solidarity.[165] Take, for example, the Directive on Transfers of Undertakings 2001/23.[166] By protecting employees' terms and conditions of employment when they are transferred it is essentially an employment rights measure, as the Preamble to the revised Directive recognizes.[167] It also has solidaristic elements since workers' representatives must be informed and consulted before any such transfer occurs. Yet, partly as a result of the legal basis of the Directive (Article 115 TFEU (ex Article 94 EC)) the Court's interpretation of the Directive has been motivated at least in part by market failure arguments, namely by a desire to ensure a level playing field of costs so that the financial burden of restructuring an enterprise is the same in all member states.[168] This results

161 COM (2006) 708, 11 and 13.

162 COM (2007) 720, 9.

163 Hepple, n 82 above, 31.

164 See the work done in this respect by M. Freedland, *The Personal Employment Contract* (Oxford: OUP, 2003) and the discussion in the special issue of the ILJ, March 2007.

165 T. Prosser, 'Regulation and Social Solidarity' (2006) 33 J of Law and Society 364.

166 OJ [2001] L82/16.

167 The 3rd Preambular para provides: 'It is necessary to provide for the protection of employees in the event of a change of employer, in particular, to ensure that their rights are safeguarded.

168 Case C-382/92 *Commission v UK* [1994] ECR I-2435: 'By harmonising the rules applicable to transfer of undertakings, the [Union] legislature intended both to ensure comparable protection of workers' rights in the different Member States and *to harmonise the costs which such protective rules entail for [Union] undertakings* (emphasis added).

in decisions such as *Katsikas*,[169] where the Court recognized the worker's right to refuse to be transferred but allowed national law to prescribe the consequences for the worker of his or her refusal. As a result, some member states have said that the employee's contract of employment is treated as terminated, thereby negating in practice the employee's right to refuse to be transferred. A directive embedded with notions of solidarity might have produced the result that workers must not be prejudiced as a result of their decision not to be transferred.

The principle of solidarity could also have a transformative effect in the field of discrimination law, justifying the enactment of more creative measures which depart from the formal model of equality and focus on the question of disadvantage.[170] In this respect the Commission's proposal on goods, facilities and services is a disappointment since it largely fits within the existing formal model of equality. While this may respond to political realities, it does tend to suggest that, at present, solidarity serves as little more than a rhetorical device.

In the absence of much legislative activity, let alone ground-breaking legislative activity, it leaves only fundamental rights to respond to Scharpf's call for 'Constitutional parity' with the economic freedoms. Yet, as *Viking* and *Laval* show, even fundamental rights risk being read subject to a strong integrationist, rather than social, imperative. This raises the question as to how the 2007 and 2008 Communications deal with the question of fundamental rights.

6.5 Fundamental rights

In his influential (albeit uncited) report, 'The Transformation of work and the future of labour law in Europe: a Multidisciplinary perspective',[171] Alain Supiot argues that the required overhaul of employment law and the traditional approach to the welfare state must be 'linked to a comprehensive view of social rights based on solidarity'.[172] He continues that 'Such solidarity must not be conceived of merely in terms of a response to individual need' since this would lead to a shift from the welfare state to a 'charity state', nor should they be framed as a form of passive protection for individuals based on a catalogue of specified risks. Instead, he advocates, 'a form of solidarity that would ensure individual and collective security in the face of contingencies that can arise at any time and anywhere'.[173] He commends the Charter of Fundamental Social Rights 1989 in terms of its substantive guarantees. Presumably, he would now approve of the Charter of Fundamental Rights 2000, not least because in the Solidarity Title it envisages protection for individuals from various contingencies (eg dismissal) but also an active role for the state in terms of, for example, social assistance and provision of healthcare. Supiot also argues for

[169] Joined Cases C-132,138 and 139/91 [1992] ECR I-6577.
[170] H. Collins, 'Discrimination, Equality and Social Inclusion' (2003) 66 MLR 16.
[171] (1999) 138 ILR 31. A full version of the report has been published in English, A. Supiot, *Beyond Employment: Changes in Work and the Future of Labour Law in Europe* (Oxford: OUP, 2001).
[172] (1999) 138 ILR 31, 44.
[173] ibid 44.

procedural guarantees involving the participation of a range of actors, particularly representative bodies, in defining and implementing their rights.[174]

These substantive and procedural guarantees, linking labour law and social law, form the core of what Supiot describes as social citizenship based on the notion of social integration and not just the notion of work.[175] Building on Supiot's work, Deakin and Browne link social rights to capability theory.[176] They argue that social rights have a value not just in themselves but in terms of their pro-competitive effect, in the sense of encouraging enterprises to invest in human capital and avoid the destructive social effects of low wage competition.[177]

In the light of this literature, and the economic and social justifications for social rights, it is striking that the 'Renewed Social Agenda' communications of 2007 and 2008, in stark contrast to the Commission's 2000 Social Agenda,[178] pay such little overt attention to fundamental rights.[179] The only clear reference to rights comes in the introduction to the 2008 Communication:

> The fundamental social objectives of Europe have not changed: a strong commitment to harmonious, cohesive and inclusive societies respecting fundamental rights in healthy social market economies. This is clearly spelt out in the objectives of the Union and the Charter of Fundamental Rights of the European Union.[180]

Given the reference to 'solidarity' in the title of the 2007 and 2008 Communications it is particularly surprising that the *Solidarity* Title of the Charter of Fundamental Rights is not expressly referred to.[181] One explanation for this might be that the Commission did not want its 'Renewed Social Agenda' to become mired in the debate about Protocol (No 30) to the Lisbon Treaty (on the application of the Charter of Fundamental Rights of the European Union to Poland and to the United Kingdom) and whether this gives the UK and Poland (and soon the Czech Republic) an opt-out from the Charter as a

[174] See further C. O'Brien, 'Reframing Deliberative Cosmopolitanism: Perspectives on Transnationalisation and Post-national Democracy from Labour Law' (2008) 9 German LJ 1035–1037. (<http://www.germanlawjournal.com/article.php?id=983>).

[175] A. Supiot, *Beyond Employment: Changes in Work and the Future of Labour Law in Europe* (Oxford: OUP, 2001) 228.

[176] S. Deakin and J. Browne, 'Social Rights and Market Order: Adapting the Capability Approach' in T. Hervey and J. Kenner (eds) *Economic and Social Rights under the EU Charter of Fundamental Rights* (Hart Publishing: Oxford, 2003) 42. More generally, see S. Deakin and F. Wilkinson, *The Law of the Labour Market: Industrialization, Employment, and Legal Evolution* (Oxford: OUP, 2005) and S. Deakin, 'The "Capability" Concept and the Evolution of European Social Policy' in M. Dougan and E. Spaventa (eds) *Social Welfare and EU Law* (Hart Publishing: Oxford, 2005).

[177] n 176 above, 42.

[178] See also the emphasis on fundamental rights in Commission (EC), *Promoting Core Labour Standards and Improving Social Governance in the Context of Globalisation* COM (2001) 416, 10.

[179] Although cf the 2007 Communication 'EU legislation will remain essential to uphold the rights of citizens as set out in the Treaty, including through ensuring a better compatibility between national rules.' (p 10).

[180] COM (2008) 412, 4. cf 'A Single Market for 21st century Europe' COM (2007) 724 where somewhat surprisingly there is more reference to rights than in a document on the social agenda.

[181] cf the Commission's 2000 Communication, 'Social Policy Agenda' COM(2000) 379, para 4.2.4 'To ensure the development and respect of fundamental social right as a key component of an equitable society and of respect for human dignity'.

whole (unlikely)[182] or at least from the Solidarity Title, Title IV (possibly).[183] A more generous explanation is that fundamental rights are now so much part of the EU constitutional furniture that it is no longer necessary to make repeated references to them.

However, as *Viking* and *Laval* show, reference to fundamental rights is not necessarily transformative. Early in the judgments in these two cases the Court said that:

> the right to take collective action, including the right to strike, must therefore be recognised as a fundamental right which forms an integral part of the general principles of Union law the observance of which the Court ensures.[184]

Yet as we saw above, one of the paradoxes of the *Viking* and *Laval* judgments is that cases which, for the first time, give express recognition to the right to strike as a fundamental human right, do not lead to enhanced protection of that right. In fact, the Court has so limited the right to take collective action that it has successfully undermined much collective solidarity which exists at national level and has traditionally been the *raison d'être* of the trade union movement.

7. Conclusions

Anthony Giddens has written:[185]

> Third way politics—modernizing social democracy—can develop a political programme that is integrated and robust. Far from displacing social justice and solidarity, third way politics... represents the only effective means of pursuing those ideals today.

As this article has shown, Third Way politics has played an important role in shaping the future direction of EU social policy. The version of Third Way politics which the Commission appears to favour is imbued with notions of solidarity and social justice. It thus avoids some of the criticisms levelled at the UK's neo-liberal interpretation of the Third Way, particularly today when (blind?) faith in the market's ability to deliver now looks misplaced.

[182] C. Barnard, 'The "Opt-Out" for the UK and Poland from the Charter of Fundamental Rights: Triumph of Rhetoric over Reality?' in S. Griller and J. Ziller (eds) *The Lisbon Treaty: EU Constitutionalism without a Constitutional Treaty* (Wien/NewYork: Springer 2008).

[183] There is a perplexing irony about the UK and Polish position. The UK has a Labour government. The Labour party's origins lie in the workers' movement. Yet it is a labour government which has highlighted the Solidarity Title as problematic. This problem is more acute in Poland where the Solidarity movement was so influential in challenging the Communist regime. This point was admitted by the Polish Government in Declaration 62 on the Protocol:

> Poland declares that, having regard to the tradition of social movement of 'Solidarity' and its significant contribution to the struggle for social and labour rights, it fully respects social and labour rights, as established by European Union law, and in particular those reaffirmed in Title IV of the Charter of Fundamental Rights of the European Union.

This Declaration appears to undermine significantly any potential use of the Art 1(2) 'opt-out' in respect of Poland.

[184] *Viking*, para 44. *Laval*, para 91.

[185] A. Giddens, *The Third Way and its Critics* (Cambridge: Polity Press, 2000) 29.

The strength and weakness of the Commission's 'Renewed Social Agenda' is its ambition. It does not shy away from identifying the difficult issues, nor does it concentrate on the more familiar territory of employment law and policy. As the 2008 Communication states: 'This agenda cannot be confined to traditional social domains; it must be cross-cutting and multi-dimensional, covering a wide range of areas from labour market polices to education, health, immigration and intercultural dialogue'.[186] Later it adds: 'Solidarity means fostering social inclusion and integration, participation and dialogue and combating poverty'.[187] But herein lies the rub: how can solidarity—in any of its guises—possibly combat poverty? The risk is the EU is setting itself up for a fall because the essential features of the welfare state still rest within the hands of the member states. As the Laeken declaration of 2001 noted,[188] although citizens demand that the EU be empowered to do 'something' about these big issues they are often disappointed that when the EU does act, expectations are often not fulfilled.

Is solidarity therefore a principle that can guide EU social policy through the choppy waters of the next decade, particularly as the economic crisis continues to bite deeply? On its own, the answer must be no but the ideals it espouses of inclusion and integration are ones with which it is difficult to disagree. Solidarity is, however, a work in progress. The Commission has been instrumental in working out the different contexts in which it can be used and what it might mean in those different contexts. To a social lawyer, the fact that solidarity is identified as the backbone to the 'Renewed Social Agenda' and identified as one of the values of the Union's approach can only be a good thing. However amorphous and difficult to define, solidarity is a distinctive feature of the European social model(s).[189] This is an important step for starting to rebuild citizens' confidence in the EU. The problem for the Commission is the low level of coverage that the Agenda itself received in the general press.[190] The Commission now needs to work on communicating its ideals and following them through with something more concrete than just policy documents.

[186] ibid 3.

[187] ibid 6.

[188] This point was noted more generally in the 2001 Laeken Declaration: 'Citizens often hold expectations of the European Union that are not always fulfilled. And vice versa—they sometimes have the impression that the Union takes on too much in areas where its involvement is not always essential. Thus the important thing is to clarify, simplify and adjust the division of competence between the Union and the Member States in the light of the new challenges facing the Union. This can lead both to restoring tasks to the Member States and to assigning new missions to the Union, or to the extension of existing powers, while constantly bearing in mind the equality of the Member States and their mutual solidarity.' <http://www.ena.lu/laeken_declaration_future_european_union_15_december_2001-020003970.html>

[189] M. Jepsen and A. S Pascual, 'The European Social Model: an Exercise in Deconstruction' (2005) 15 J of Eur Social Policy 231.

[190] In the UK the coverage focused almost exclusively on the healthcare proposal: D. Charter, 'Patients to travel for treatment in Europe—and the NHS will pay, The Times, 3 July 2008, 16; 'UK "will not back health tourism"', The Independent, 3 July 2008; J. Chapman, 'Be an EU tooth tourist; Brussels plan to let patients travel abroad for free treatment includes dental work', Daily Mail, 3 July 2008.

5

The Price of Letting Courts Value Solidarity: The Judicial Role in Liberalizing Welfare

Gareth Davies

1. Introduction

Welfare states have traditionally had a high degree of closure, not just to persons, but to providers. On the supply side, it is not easy to enter the market either because of very strict, sometimes exclusionary regulations, or because the field is dominated by (quasi-) monopolistic, (quasi-) public institutions. One cannot simply open a university or hospital in the way that one could open a shop, and even if one could, one probably would not get any customers because established financial incentives would steer them towards existing players.[1] On the demand side, consumers usually have a limited amount of choice of provider, and even when consumer choice is a principle built into the system, it is often deprived of some of its substance by rules severely standardizing the range of services which may be offered; you can have any treatment you want as long as it's the one that the state approves. And if one can and does simply opt-out and go to a foreign or alternative or simply new provider of services then the chances are that this has dire financial consequences; the state only pays if you use its preferred institutions.[2]

These regulatory and institutional aspects of the welfare state restrict competition and free movement of services, something of increasing importance now that the concept of economic activity in the relevant law—that of the EU internal market—is coming to encompass activities that not very long ago were seen as

[1] See eg K. Stöger, 'The freedom of establishment and the market access of hospital operators' (2006) 17 Eur Business L Rev 1545; Case C-153/02 *Neri v ESE* [2003] ECR I-13555; E. Manganaris, 'The principle of supremacy of Community law in Greece—from direct challenge to non-application' (1999) 24 ELR 426.

[2] See eg Case C-372/04 *Watts* [2006] ECR I-4325; Case C-385/99 *Müller-Fauré and van Riet* [2003] ECR I-4509; Case C-157/99 *Geraets-Smits and Peerbooms* [2001] ECR I-5473; Case C-158/96 *Kohll* [1998] ECR I-1931; Case C-76/05 *Schwarz* [2007] ECR I-6849; joined cases C-11/06 and C-12/06 *Morgan* and *Bucher* [2007] ECR I-9161.

inherently non-market.[3] That change is likely to snowball since the potential markets involved, for health, education, and social insurance, are vast. Health and social insurance dwarf any other industry found in the developed world.[4] This ensures that lobbying for increased opportunities to participate in that market—to share in the potential profits—will be intense and well-backed. Since liberalization—used here to mean an increase in the scope of free choice allowed to providers and consumers—can also be presented as a force for increased efficiency and empowerment of individual consumers, there is a conjunction of perspectives and interests that seems likely to keep the process going for some way yet.[5]

The initial fears that such a process arouses are that consumers who are either poor or particularly needy of services—for example the chronically ill—will be unable to get what they need. Free markets means free pricing which means that not everyone will have the same purchasing power, and some will not have enough. Hence if the widely shared European ideal of universal access to important welfare services, on more or less equal terms, is to be maintained there is a need for policies balancing, limiting, or managing the relevant market.[6]

In practice, the powers-that-be have taken this lesson to heart. In the Treaty, secondary legislation, and case law of the Court of Justice there is repeated acknowledgment that both free movement and competition may be limited where this is necessary to protect other important social interests, notably universal access to solidarity-based welfare services or the maintenance of the institutions that provide them. One may think here of the acknowledgment that paying for hospital treatment abroad at the will of the patient could undermine the stability of health systems, and the subsequent partial subordination of free movement to that latter interest, or the restrictions on competition accepted in a number of social insurance cases in the interests of maintaining solidarity-based systems, but there are also numerous other examples of careful balancing and acknowledgment of the risks of over-liberalization.[7]

However, the justifications that are acknowledged here could be described as 'functional' and contrasted with more subtle social justifications which have not been explicitly addressed. It is the contrast between these two types of justifications which is the subject of this chapter. It will be suggested that the latter

[3] See G. Davies, 'The process and side-effects of harmonisation of European welfare states', Jean Monnet Working Paper 02/06, <http://www.jeanmonnetprogram.org> 17–28.

[4] ibid 81–83.

[5] See G. Davies, 'The effect of Mrs Watts' trip to France on the NHS' (2007) Kings LJ 158, 165–166; Case T-289/03 *BUPA v Commission* [2008] ECR II-81.

[6] F. Scharpf, 'The European social model: coping with the challenges of diversity' (2002) 40 J of Common Market Studies 645.

[7] Case C-385/99 *Müller-Fauré* [2003] ECR I-4509, annotated by M. Flear (2004) 41 CML Rev 209; Case C-159/91 *Poucet and Pistre* [1993] ECR I-637; Case C-70/96 *Sodemare* [1997] ECR I-3395; Case C-264/01 *AOK* [2004] ECR I-2493; Case C-115/97 *Brentjens* [1999] ECR I-6025; C-219/97 *Drijvende Bokken* [1999] ECR I-6021; Case C-218/00 *Cisal* [2002] ECR I-691; Case C-475/99 *Ambulanz Glöckner* [2001] ECR I-8089; Case T-289/03 *BUPA v Commission* [2008] ECR II-81.

sort—which might perhaps be called communitarian, given their valuing of unity and mutual obligation over individual choice[8]—are simply too amorphous for judicial review, and that this raises severe problems for the application of internal market law, with the risks involved being on the one hand a possible collapse into protectionism, or even nationalism, and on the other a dismantling of social cohesion which threatens quality of life, solidarity, and ultimately identity.

2. The role of institutions

Restrictions on market freedom serve to reduce diversity and restrict innovation—that is one objection to them. However, it is also an advantage. They create a degree of uniformity and of institutional stability. They also create a sense of institution; even if on a formal legal level providers of services are independent or diverse, if regulation constrains them so tightly that they are forced to operate in the same way, offer the same services at the same prices, and treat their clients identically, then the distinction between the providers becomes less apparent to the client and accordingly less important. The more these providers are regulated, the more they seem to customers to be part of a single body. This explains why continental social-insurance based systems, where provision of services is privatized but highly regulated, are nevertheless perceived as containing public welfare institutions.[9] This institutional perception, and reality, has (at least) three consequences for the public which are worth noting: uniformity, shared experience, and aligned interests.

2.1 Uniformity

Equality is a nebulous concept, most significantly because it acquires useful meaning only if one can answer the question 'equality of what' with reasonable precision.[10] It is a transitive concept that is often used intransitively, with a consequent loss of clarity. In the context of welfare, the view that all citizens should be treated as 'equal' by the system is usually uncontroversial. However, translating this into concrete policy immediately raises less easily resolved issues.[11] Do

[8] See eg A. Etzioni, *New Communitarian Thinking* (University Press of Virginia, 1996); C. Newdick, 'Citizenship, free movement, and healthcare: cementing individual rights by corroding social solidarity' (2006) 43 CML Rev 1645, at 1645–1646.

[9] B. Rothstein, 'Social capital in the social democratic welfare state' (2001) 29 Politics and Society 207,

[10] See eg A. Sen, 'Equality of what?' in R. Goodin and P. Pettit (eds) *Contemporary Political Philosophy: An Anthology* (Oxford: Blackwell 2005); R. Dworkin, 'What is equality? Part 1: equality of welfare' (1981) 10(3) Philosophy and Public Affairs 185–246, and 'What is equality? Part 2: equality of resources' (1981) 10(4) Philosophy and Public Affairs 283–345; E. Anderson, 'What is the point of equality?' (1999) 109 Ethics 287–337.

[11] W. Korpi and J. Palme, 'Inequality, and Poverty in the Western Countries' (1998) 63(5) American Sociological Rev 661–687.

student loans violate equality, or reflect the idea of 'equal opportunity'? Can 'equality' in healthcare be coherently limited to ensuring everyone has basic essential services, or must it entail ensuring identical services to all citizens, and perhaps even prohibiting the purchase of extra luxury? Does a desire for equality for all children in the education system mean that there must be compulsory mixing of different social groups to avoid ghettoization, or does freedom of choice for every parent, the same terms offered to all, best embody the ideal? The risk of discussing such issues in terms of equality, particularly in its more complex forms, is that informed consideration of substantive social issues comes to be displaced by sterile theory. It may then become attractive to retreat, or advance, to an apparently simpler and more formal notion of equality, that of uniform treatment, a value found to a great extent in continental European social-democratic welfare states.[12] Although it is well-known that treating all the same works to the advantage of some and the disadvantage of others, nevertheless the attractiveness of uniformity is the high level of transparency, predictability, and certainty that it brings.[13] The idea that all children, patients, and students will have the same rules, treatment, and principles applied to them is relatively easy to build a social consensus around, and by making equality functional and comprehensible—if arguably less equal—can turn it into a collective value that has a social as well as functional role. It minimizes group identity in favour of broader collective identity. That is controversial, but in some societies attracts support that is not purely majoritarian assertiveness.[14] A republican uniform treatment ideal can help us feel bonded with our fellow denizens, whoever they may be and however we may differ from them, as well as reinforcing, in some eyes, an image of the state as neutral between groups.

This uniformity is much easier to achieve in a tight, institutionalized welfare system. Diverse provision and consumer choice can be defended and explained in equality terms, but it is the more amorphous 'equality of opportunity' or 'freedom of choice for everyone on the same terms' which comes into play. The reality is that diversity will result in different qualities of service and experience, and those differences will be understood as part of the system rather than merely a defect in it. The social value which markets embody is, of course, individualism more than equality; they allow us to emphasize what makes us different, not what makes us the same. The role of a market-based welfare system in social cohesion and community-building is distinctively different from that of a uniformity-based one.

[12] See G. Esping-Anderson, *The Three Worlds of Welfare Capitalism* (Oxford: Polity Press, 1990).

[13] See J. Baldock, 'On being a welfare consumer in a consumer society' (2003) 2 Social Policy and Society 65, at 67.

[14] On this issue see eg C. McCrudden, 'Theorising European equality law' in C. Costello and E. Barry (eds) *Equality in Diversity: The New Equality Directives* (Irish Centre for European Law, 2003) 1, 20–31, and citations therein; A. Vakulenko, 'Islamic dress in human rights jurisprudence: a critique of current trends' (2007) 7 Human Rights L Rev 717.

2.2 Shared experience

In a modern European welfare state almost all citizens participate in recognizably similar institutions and have a similar relationship with them. It is hard to think of any other institution or socially constructed context which is shared in the same way by people of almost all incomes, classes, races, religions and lifestyles. The media is more divided, and public transport is less used by the rich, and neither, in any case, touch on the crucial and vulnerable moments of life in the way that welfare services do. There was, briefly, perhaps a time when all Britons watched the BBC, but within the realm of the social and governmental it is now probably the institutions of the welfare state that offer the broadest and deepest shared experience. If we look for a project that we are all participating in, an interaction with the state that is common to us all, and a positioning in the public sphere that does not depend upon our background or social position, then the institutionalized, uniform, welfare state provides this. This is a political sphere where we can recognize the experiences of others whose life is otherwise dramatically different from our own, and as such it contributes to our sense that we are part of a community, doing something together, and living linked lives.[15]

2.3 Aligned interests

There is an obvious conflict of interests between those who have money and those who do not. In the context of welfare that conflict can be extended to those who have a limited need for welfare services—perhaps no longer in need of education, or work-related social insurance, or apparently in good health—and those with a particularly high need—the chronically ill being a notable example. Creating a system in which privileged groups agree to subsidize others is a political challenge that has to be met in order for ideals of universality to be maintained.

One way of doing this is to appeal to morality or philanthropy. Another way is to create shared institutions that service all groups. Of course, some groups would be advantaged by creating separate institutions for themselves, but this requires an extra energy or initiative. If they are already invested in the shared institution, part of it, used to it, comfortable with it, then the chance is greater that they will be prepared to fight for its maintenance and improvement—which then also benefits the less privileged users too.[16] By contrast, if there is fragmentation of service provision, then it is likely that providers will partly come to service consumer groups defined along the lines of social division, wealth and class and religion and race and so on. Moreover, the links between the groups are then embodied only in the system of taxation and redistribution, not in shared institutions. In these more distanced circumstances it is a smaller intellectual leap for some groups to

[15] B. Rothstein, n 9 above, 234.

[16] ibid.

imagine being cut free, able to invest only in themselves. Fragmentation threatens political support for solidarity.[17]

It does this in one more way too. In many contexts people are prepared to pay for security and predictability. It is a truism that insurance is a bad buy except when it is for catastrophic events—losses which one could not otherwise afford. Apart from these, it is better value to bear the risk oneself, since insurance companies will always take care that their premiums on average amount to more than one is likely to receive. Yet people buy insurance even for affordable risks, because it brings a certainty and predictability which reduces stress and improves quality of life. And why not? What better thing to spend money on?

Monopolistic welfare institutions can be understood partly in similar terms. Individuals might be able to get a better deal if they were not part of the bigger system and did not have to subsidize the less fortunate. However, they cannot be sure that their own good fortune will continue. Moreover, most people have some others that they care about. They cannot be sure that these will also continue to be light users of the welfare state. Paying over the odds today is also paying an insurance premium in a broad sense; contributing to the political sustainability of a system which ensures that one does not need to worry about the financing of one's future welfare. By contributing to solidarity now, one strengthens a social norm, and strengthens a system embodying that norm, which one may need in the future.[18]

The greater the sense of institution, or of system, the better this works.[19] The individual's financial contribution to solidarity is the same in a market or a non-market system, but this is not all that matters. They also make a participatory contribution, by using an institution that others use. Here they can stand among those they do not know and feel a sense of belonging and connection. A system in which bad luck might well project them into different schools, hospitals, systems, is one they will feel less inclined to invest in. Those different institutions may be nominally 'equivalent'—access to basic services may be guaranteed—but there is fear of the unknown and there is the fact that different is never quite equal. Knowing that a particular, known, trusted, institution is yours and your family's whatever your circumstances—that can motivate a privileged individual to buy into the system now and keep defending it. And one may note here that the privileged can be good at defending; they have political ability and power. If they opt out, they care less.

Groups whose interests are apparently opposed can therefore come to perceive that they have a shared self-interest, the one group because they need now, and the other group because they realize that they may need tomorrow. This virtuous position relies on trust that 'philanthropy' today will be returned tomorrow if it

[17] See J. Kääriäinen and H. Lehtoninen, 'The variety of social capital in welfare state regimes —a comparison of 21 countries' (2006) 8 Eur Societies 27; M. Meier Jaeger, 'Welfare regimes and attitudes towards redistribution: the regime hypothesis revisited' (2006) 22 Eur Sociological Rev 157.

[18] J. Hassler, J. V. R. Mora, K. Storesletten, and F. Zilibotti, 'The Survival of the Welfare State' (August 2001) CEPR Discussion Paper No 2905. Available on <http://ssrn.com>.

[19] ibid 3.

is needed, and that trust is strengthened when institutions are shared. There is no other service provider to which the privileged can turn; they have to maintain this one. That serves as a guarantee for the future. Of course, systems can be changed, but this takes time and energy. No-one wants to be the first to opt-out, because being alone outside the system is not advantageous even for most net payers. Inertia, and the risk entailed in being the first to try and exit the system, mean that the guarantee entailed in the monolithic system is not empty, albeit not cast-iron either.

2.4 An insight from Hirschman's voice and exit

Hirschman described how customers of an organization have two tactics they can use to influence its behaviour; voice or exit. Which of these they are likely to choose for in particular circumstances, and which choice leads to more desirable results for themselves or the organization, was described in his classic *Voice, Exit and Loyalty*, which was partly intended as a rebuttal of economists' tendency to adopt the over-simplified assumption that markets always work by customers switching provider (exiting) when they are not satisfied.[20] He suggested that they might also remain as customers but try and persuade the organization to change (voice), and that this might sometimes be an efficient and desirable course of action.[21]

One of the points he makes in the course of his discussion is that exit can actually be a boon to monopolists.[22] One might assume that any business desires as many customers as possible, and the monopolist is particularly happy to have all of them, with the extra pricing opportunities that this entails. Yet he suggests that there is often a minority of customers who are particularly demanding, and a majority who are somewhat more inertial, more likely to accept whatever service they are offered without fuss. This comment certainly resonates in an analysis of welfare states. He then points out that if these demanding customers are denied exit—as for example where education or healthcare is provided via a single homogenous and quasi-monopolistic provider or system—they are likely to channel their energies into voice, demanding that the organization improve its services. Their complaints use up resources, and can be costly and tiresome, and may put the organization in the position of either having to spend much money on rebutting and defending—and in the modern world dealing with lawsuits—or improve quality, which is likely to reduce profits, since the organization has all the customers it can get anyway.

By contrast, if there is a certain limited exit option—not too easy or widespread perhaps, but possible, one geared to the wishes of the demanding customers—then these may well take it. The organization is then left with the

[20] A. O. Hirschman, *Exit Voice and Loyalty. Responses to Decline in Firms, Organizations and States* (Cambridge, Mass: Harvard University Press, 1970).

[21] ibid ch 3 (30–43).

[22] ibid ch 5 (55–61).

majority of passive customers, whom it can milk for high profits while offering second-rate services. In other words, losing your most expensive and difficult customers is not always bad news, if profit is what you care about.

Hirschman, an organizational scientist, is interested in the possibilities for business organizations to recover and improve, and this concern resonates once again in the context of welfare. He sums up the possibility of limited competition in a largely monolithic system in terms of 'freedom to deteriorate' for the dominant institution: there is no longer anyone forcing it to maintain quality.[23] Limited competition 'comforts and bolsters' the 'lazy monopolist'.[24]

It hardly seems controversial to suggest that this may be very relevant to welfare services. If limited competition is introduced, the customers who may take advantage of it are the same ones who are most able to look after their own interests, most demanding of the system, and most capable of wielding political power and influence to force that system to improve. Others, probably the majority, will be inclined to accept what they get, stick with the institution they know, and will experience slowly degrading services.

This is particularly so as a result of the complex and sensitive nature of welfare services. This makes it hard for a customer to truly judge the quality of what he receives. Hospitals simply wanting to come high in customer satisfaction rankings would probably do better to teach their staff to smile a lot and provide free tea than invest in the latest treatments and advances. An analogous statement could be made of education. Secondly, because of the importance of the services to the individual, there will be a high motivation for customers to stick with what they know; the natural reaction to risk is to be conservative. Only those very confident with the system and the issues will trust their judgement enough to change. Finally, it is the nature of these services that they change with society. Both education and healthcare are quite different now than even a few decades ago. This means that deterioration can take the form of standing still or even improving slowly, since it may be that technological and social changes mean that the potential is there for rapid and significant improvement. But like a frog in slowly warming water, the customer whose welfare services slowly improve, and only degrade in a relative sense, is even less likely to be provoked to resistance than Hirschman's passive customer prepared to accept slow deterioration in absolute terms. Unless very well informed about the possibilities, and able to understand them, how is the relative victim even to know he is a victim?

The argument above does not hold if those exiting instead of using voice would in fact have used voice to further their own interests only. Then they were selfish participants, and their loss is no loss to others.[25] However, while specific patient groups do have specific interests, they also have many shared ones, and a generally

[23] ibid 60.
[24] ibid 59.
[25] I am grateful to Georgio Monti for drawing my attention to this caveat.

well-working system benefits all. It is therefore assumed here that reforms that active and politically agile patient groups would like would also, on the whole and on balance, tend to benefit more passive groups too, so that the exit of these reform forces could work as described above.

3. Courts and welfare systems

3.1 Judicial review of welfare regulation

Governments making policy should be concerned with more than the most immediate and direct issues, but also with longer term ones. In designing welfare systems the most effective treatment and teaching right now is important, but so is ensuring that the system is stable, enjoys support, and can go on developing and surviving. Further, the system is part of society as a whole, and contributes to its cohesion and identity. Governments concerned about the quality of life of their citizens—which might be influenced by trust in society, social division and the criminal and social costs it brings, and the perception and actual pursuit of equality—must look at welfare institutions in context, and consider the contribution they make beyond the concrete services they provide.

They therefore have many legitimate reasons to structure their systems in ways which may be, to some extent, restrictive of change and individual freedom—of competition therefore—yet not all of those reasons can be expressed in terms of the narrowly functional requirements to provide the highest-quality services at the lowest cost to all customers now. The 'communitarian' reasons described above are broader, less direct, and to do with building relations and cohesion in society. They are well expressed in terms of social capital.[26]

Can courts review such reasons? The structure of EU law is such that it falls to the Court of Justice, and national courts acting under its supervision, to decide whether public measures restricting competition and free movement (or entry and exit, as one could put it) are justified by sufficiently weighty reasons of policy.[27] They must balance the pros and cons to decide if a measure is to be struck down. Yet communitarian reasons are subtle, non-quantitative, subjective, unprovable—the very essence of the kind of judgements that politicians make and courts rightly shy away from. In any other judicial review context it would probably be beyond question that judges would not second guess the judgement of authorities on such issues.[28] They would engage in marginal, or purely procedural, review.

[26] B. Rothstein, 'Social capital in the social democratic welfare state' (2001) 29 Politics and Society 207.

[27] See J. Temple Lang, 'Privatisation of Social Welfare: European Union Competition Law Rules' in M. Dougan and E. Spaventa (eds) *Social Welfare and EU Law* (Oxford: Hart, 2005) 45, 55–64; E. Szyszczak, *The Regulation of the State in Competitive Markets in the EU* (Oxford: Hart, 2007) 36–41.

[28] See C. Newdick, n 8 above, 1651–1653.

However, marginal review in the context of EU law brings its own problems. Deferral to authority is not a 'safe' option here, because there is authority on two levels, and public authorities with policy interests in either possible decision. The European public authority's choice to pursue open markets because of the social and economic advantages these bring confronts the national public authority's choice to close the markets in the name of other social interests. Both are legitimate political policy-makers. Each accepts that they must sometimes bow to the other, the EU via its exceptions to economic law, and states via their acceptance of the supremacy of EU law.[29] Hence a judicial deference to policy choices and enthusiasm for marginal or procedural review offers no way out. Even though the Court of Justice pays intermittent lip service to deference to member states, notably in the context of Article 106 TFEU, marginal review is a structurally inadequate response to the situation, which cannot be made adequate by judicial repetition.[30] Marginal review of which authority? Marginal review of national decisions amounts to marginalization of EU ones, overruling the legislator on the importance of entry and exit. It creates incentives for misuse of national discretion at the cost of EU law, and is a non-sustainable legal position. On the other hand, marginal review of EU choices disregards complex policy balancing done by national authorities, and is ultimately destructive of good policy and inefficient. What is judicial deference from one perspective is judicial activism from the other. A substantive engagement with the balancing process is unavoidable if law is to be a constructive social tool and if Treaty goals are to be taken seriously.

The conventional language of the internal market might speak of protectionism in a context like the above. This is one of the bogeymen of integration, and given the many social and economic dangers it brings, quite rightly so. Overcoming it has always been at the heart of EU policy, is one of the reasons for the existence of the EU, and so any judge should, and will, assume that public authorities at all levels, including the national—they joined the EU—must be taken to reject it. A strict line against protectionism is deferential, not activist.

Yet from the 'outside' it is difficult to determine whether restrictions on entry and exit are motivated by protectionism or legitimate social concerns. This is precisely what a judge cannot be expected to get to the bottom of, because the line between the two is itself contestable and because of evidential reasons. However, if a governmental assurance that motives are good is sufficient, then adjudication of the issue becomes a farce. This would effectively give member states an opt-out, and so undermine the effectiveness of EU law that this fact alone could provide a challenge to the legality of such limited review.[31] There is implicitly a requirement to examine national measures more substantively and critically.

[29] Case 6/64 *Costa v ENEL* [1964] ECR 585.

[30] See W. Sauter, 'Services of general economic interest and universal services in EU law' (2008) 33 ELR 167, at 186–188.

[31] See Case C-213/89 *Factortame* [1990] ECR I-2433; M. Accetto and S. Zleptnig, 'The principle of effectiveness: rethinking its role in Community law' (2005) 11 Eur Public L 375.

3.2 Essentialism in judicial reasoning

At the moment the Court is fairly deferential to member state concerns in this area, and uses three particular legal arguments to express that deference. One is the old but still oft-repeated rule of thumb that it is for member states to determine what sort of social welfare system they wish to have, while the Court will merely decide whether the operation of that system is compatible with the requirements of EU law.[32] Of course, this distinction between the nature of the system and its operation cannot withstand a moment's rigorous thinking. If a system is required to operate differently, its nature changes, however marginally. The Court seems to be trying to express some kind of essentialism, a doctrine that the core principles and structures of the system are for the member states to determine, while others may be subject to market law requirements.[33] Essentialism is always a philosophically troublesome doctrine, and no less here than elsewhere.[34] In particular, the vulnerability of welfare systems to financial pressure means that tinkering with what, conceptually or philosophically, seems a non-core element of the system may well have effects that touch the core deeply, via the banal mechanism of significantly increasing costs.[35]

Yet, despite its intellectual problems one could understand the Court's approach as an attempt to respect the social concerns around welfare. It is a recognition that the 'nature' of the system embodies concerns judges cannot meaningfully engage with, and so they will confine themselves to more practical, functional, measurable, *reviewable* issues—the 'operation'. In practice, the Court's nature/operation distinction appears to have no obvious impact on its judgments—the cases where member states have (partially) lost can certainly not be explained on the basis that the judgments did not affect core aspects of the principles or practice of the system: they did.[36] However it does provide a peg on which judgments can be hung, a way of putting judicial deference in the less defeatist language of the division of competences.

3.3 The use of evidence

A second technique that the Court is fond of is the acceptance of unpersuasive evidence. When it finds that a measure is necessary or unnecessary, justified or unjustified, it does so in sonorously objective tones, as if its decision is the inevitable

[32] eg Case C-103/06, *Derouin*, judgment of 3 April 2008, paras 23–25; Case C-385/99 *Müller-Fauré and van Riet* [2003] ECR I-4509, para 100, and citations therein.

[33] For analogous reasoning in other contexts, see Case 15/74 *Centrafarm v Sterling* [1974] ECR 1147; Case C-274/96 *Bickel and Franz* [1998] ECR I-7637; Case C-148/02 *Garcia Avello* [2003] ECR I-11613.

[34] D. J. Levinson, 'Rights Essentialism and Remedial Equilibration' (June 1999) University of Virginia Law School, Legal Studies Working Paper No 99–5. Available on <http://ssrn.com>.

[35] C. Newdick, n 8 above.

[36] eg concerning core principles of the relevant service provision: Case C-372/04 *Watts* [2006] ECR I-4325; Case C-385/99 *Müller-Fauré and van Riet* [2003] ECR I-4509; Case C-157/99 *Geraets-Smits and Peerbooms* [2001] ECR I-5473; Case C-65/03 *Commission v Belgium* [2004] ECR I-6427; Case C-147/03 *Commission v Austria* [2005] ECR I-5969.

conclusion of careful perusal of the evidence. However, a quick look at the cases on welfare, particularly those concerning free movement, reveals that it makes highly speculative and controversial assertions. The claim, for example, that allowing patients to travel at will for non-hospital medical treatment will not significantly undermine the finances of health systems, whereas allowing them to travel at will for hospital treatment would, may be true, but one can be quite sure that it is not self-evidently so on the basis of the evidence presented.[37] There is still plenty of research to be done on this issue, and frankly nobody knows quite what would happen.[38] The Court decided on what seemed like a reasonable middle position on the basis of evidence that may have been suggestive, but was not conclusive. Perhaps one should understand this—certainly as a UK lawyer—as a simple application of the civil law 'balance of probabilities' approach to deciding a case. An alternative interpretation is that in these complicated welfare contexts states discharge their evidential duty if they can make a reasonable case, or raise a presumption, that their measures are necessary and justified. They do not have to prove it; that would be too hard. The question that remains open is how courts would respond to counter-evidence from litigants—they do not appear to have seriously attempted to rebut state claims of necessity in cases so far, at least insofar as one can judge from the opinions of Advocate Generals and the judgments.[39] The question is made more complex by the fact that formally it is for national courts to assess evidence, according to national rules.[40] Although in practice the Court of Justice often does decide issues of fact, it also often expressly refers them back.[41] Not just the how, but the who, of determining what is in reality necessary or not remains legally ambiguous.

Both of these techniques of reasoning give judges room for flexibility. But that flexibility is only in a good cause if the judges do in fact judge, at least to some degree, the substantive issue. They do have to decide whether measures really are socially important or just protectionist, and implicitly this is what they are doing when they decide cases nominally on a functional basis, but with gaps in logic and evidence. Those gaps are where the other, judicially unnameable, subjective and political, arguments do their work. Judges are therefore deciding on the social value and social sustainability of welfare systems, and weighing this against other interests, and they are probably aware that they are doing so, but they admit none

[37] See *Watts*, ibid para 75; *Müller-Fauré and van Riet*, ibid para 93; See also *Commission v Austria*, ibid paras 64–66; G. Davies, 'Health and efficiency: Community law and national health systems in the light of *Müller-Fauré*' (2004) 67 MLR 94, at 104.

[38] J. V. McHale, 'Framing a right to treatment in English law? *Watts* in retrospective' (2007) 14 Maastricht J of Eur and Comparative L 263, at 278–282.

[39] See n 37 above.

[40] See eg K.Lenaerts, D. Arts and I. Maselis, *Procedural Law of the EU* (2nd edn, London: Sweet & Maxwell, 2006) 187–193.

[41] ibid; G. Davies, 'Abstractness and concreteness in the preliminary reference procedure' in Niamh Nic Shuibhne (ed) *Regulating the Internal Market* (Cheltenham: Edward Elgar, 2006) 210. Also available as 'The Division of Powers between the European Court of Justice and National Courts on <http://ssrn.com> and as ConWeb Working Paper 2004/04, <http://www.bath.ac.uk/esml/conWEB>.

of it; they speak exclusively the language of functional requirements—quality of service, accessibility, price—and of competence and evidence.

3.4 Solidarity as a legal justification

The third legal technique that the Court (increasingly) relies on is the reference to solidarity.[42] This has been used in a number of cases as a justification for restrictive measures.[43] The Court understands the concept in a narrowly functional way, using it simply to mean redistribution within the system.[44] It has found at times that systems founded 'on the principle of solidarity' are therefore not economic activities, and so not subject to internal market rules.[45]

This is not particularly persuasive. Neither solidarity nor compulsory membership make an activity non-economic in the normal—economic—sense of the words. The fact that a system entails redistribution certainly does not, for example, mean that it is not an economic activity. There are few more redistributive activities than flying, in which business class passengers pay most of the costs of those sitting in the cheaper seats behind them. The Marxist 'from each according to his abilities' approach is now conventional business technique, more often criticized as abuse of capitalist power, under the label of 'price discrimination', than as incipient socialism. Compulsory membership is more interesting, but even this need not render an activity non-economic; the fact that an individual is required to purchase a service from a given provider does not mean that there is not a genuine exchange of value, or that the provider is not engaging in an activity which could take place on a market, the two core elements which the Court uses in defining economic activity.[46] The same argument holds when looked at from a more everyday perspective; the fact that an organization has a monopoly over certain customers does not mean that it does not behave in a ruthlessly commercial way—in fact it may well encourage it—and that it redistributes between those customers does not affect this logic in the least. Thus compulsory participation in a system based on solidarity provides no rational reason to classify the system as non-economic.

[42] See M. Ross, 'Promoting solidarity. From public services to a European model of competition' (2007) 44 CML Rev 1057; C. Barnard, 'EU Citizenship and the Principle of Solidarity' in M. Dougan and E. Spaventa (eds) *Social Welfare and EU Law* (Oxford: Hart, 2003) 157.

[43] Case C-159/91 *Poucet and Pistre* [1993] ECR I-637; Case C-70/96 *Sodemare* [1997] ECR I-3395; Case C-264/01 *AOK* [2004] ECR I-2493; Case C-115/97 *Brentjens* [1999] ECR I-6025; C-219/97 *Drijvende Bokken* [1999] ECR I-6021; Case C-218/00 *Cisal* [2002] ECR I-691; Case C-244/94 *FFSA* [1995] ECR I-4013; Case C-67/96 *Albany* [1999] ECR I-5751; C-180/98 *Pavlov* [2000] ECR I-6451.

[44] ibid.

[45] Case C-205/030 P, *FENIN* [2006] ECR I-6295; Case C-159/91, *Poucet and Pistre* [1993] ECR I-637; Case C-70/96 *Sodemare* [1997] ECR I-3395; Case C-264/01 *AOK* [2004] ECR I-2493; Case C-115/97 *Brentjens* [1999] ECR I-6025; C-219/97 *Drijvende Bokken* [1999] ECR I-6021; Case C-218/00 *Cisal* [2002] ECR I-691.

[46] See G. Davies, 'The process and side effects of harmonisation of European welfare states', n 3 above, 18–21.

More importantly, compulsory membership and internal solidarity do not provide functional reasons for restricting competition. Solidarity can be achieved quite straightforwardly in a system without compulsory membership, and without shared institutions, by requiring everyone to pay tax, which is then redistributed. For example, subsidized health insurance and commercial provision of healthcare, or subsidized education vouchers and commercial provision of education, achieve the core solidarity effect of ensuring universal access with differing degrees of financial contribution.[47] Yet such approaches do not replace markets for healthcare and education by monopoly institutions, or even public institutions. Solidarity as such, in a functional sense, does not steer policy away from or towards markets and competition, except where the extremes of market freedom are approached. It is organizationally neutral. It does not therefore, if understood functionally, provide a coherent argument against the claimed merits of liberalization and fragmentation of welfare.

Thus when the Court says that economic law does or should not apply because an institution embodies solidarity, it makes no sense to interpret this as meaning that the application of economic law would undermine this solidarity; in most cases it need not do this at all. Nor does it make sense to interpret the statement as meaning that where solidarity is present there is no economic activity; this is not true either, as the Court in fact recognizes in other cases. [48] Solidarity—often in the form of public subsidy—can be importantly present even while individuals also provide remuneration that covers a great deal, perhaps the majority, of the value of the service,[49] or while an organization engages in activity on a market.[50] Subsidy does not have to be a hundred per cent of cost to matter.

The remaining, and best interpretation of the use of solidarity is that it serves as a cipher for communitarian reasons; where institutions embody solidarity this both reflects, demonstrates, and bestows, a special social value and role. This is why, at least sometimes, economic law should not be allowed to deconstruct them, and so why it should not apply, or its application should be restricted. On this reading of the cases the Court, when it allows restrictions on economic law, is implicitly acknowledging the communitarian reasons for restricting competition and prizing monopolistic institutions, even though it cannot voice those reasons explicitly, lacking the vocabulary to do so, and perhaps aware of the controversy it would arouse.

Thus, a judicial awareness of subtle social values is again to be found in the gaps in judicial reasoning, and in the fact that social values often do prevail over purely economic ones, without the reasons provided for this being fully convincing;

[47] See eg F. Paulucci, A. Den Exter and W. van de Ven, 'Solidarity in competitive health insurance markets: analysing the relevant EC legal framework' (2006) 1 Health Economics, Policy and Law 107.

[48] V. G. Hatzopoulos, '*Killing* National Health and Insurance Systems but *healing* Patients? The European Market for Health Care Services After the Judgments of the ECJ in *Vanbraekel* and *Peerbooms*' (2002) 39 CML Rev 683, at 705–713; G. Davies, 'The process and side effects of harmonisation of European welfare states', n 3 above, 20–21.

[49] eg Case C-109/92 *Wirth* [1993] ECR I-6447; Case C-76/05 *Schwarz*, judgment of 11 September 2007.

[50] Case C-41/90 *Höfner and Elsner* [1991] ECR I-1979; cases in n 43 above.

there is more going on in the case law than judges choose to say. Solidarity is the blanket under which this furtive communitarianism takes place.

4. Conclusions

There is much to be said for courts saying openly what they are doing, but the fact that the Court of Justice does not is the result of the difficult position it has been put in. Decisions have been placed in the judicial sphere which do not ideally belong there. It can ignore communitarian justifications, leading to bad decisions, or it can consider them but mask them in conventional legal language, or it can start speaking in the language of social capital, cohesion, voice and exit, and such social-theoretical terms. It is not hard to see why it avoids this latter path. It is interesting language, but it is not easy language to rest a proof on—judicial authority is quite possibly maintained more by tactical omissions than by full but subjective explanations, particularly in a court that often seems to have difficulty expressing itself clearly anyway and is heir to, among others, minimalist and legalist continental traditions.[51]

The major reason why the Court has been lumbered with its difficult task is the diversity of national welfare systems and rules, which makes detailed regulation at EU level practically impossible.[52] EU law in this area is inevitably at a relatively abstract and principled level, with the consequence that judges have lots of work left over to do.

This provides a reason to be sceptical of proposals for legislation on Services of General (Economic) Interest.[53] The fact that there is a problem, a conflict of interest, and a dissatisfaction with leaving these matters to courts, does not mean that legislation is a solution. It will run up against the same diversity of systems, and very likely be forced into the same kind of relatively abstract rules as the Court has developed. The consequence will be that the nature of the judicial balancing required does not really change.

The parties who could do more to 'solve' the problem of balancing the immeasurable are member states. If the Advocate General's opinions and the judgments are a fair guide then the nature and quality of their arguments in the cases are unimpressive, and suggest some branches of government are not engaging with the obligations EU membership entails. On the contrary, EU demands are neither new nor unpredictable, and it is surely reasonable to expect states to proactively look for a defensible compromise between their own social policy and the EU policies of openness and integration. A true picture of the extent to which

[51] M. Lasser, 'Anticipating Three Models of Judicial Control, Debate and Legitimacy: The European Court of Justice, the Cour de cassation and the United States Supreme Court' Jean Monnet Working Paper 1/03. Available at <http://www.jeanmonnetprogram.org>.

[52] F. Scharpf, 'The European social model' n 6 above.

[53] See the Commission's 'White Paper on Services of General Interest' COM (2004) 374 final, 12 May 2004.

they are doing this would require an extensive—but very worthwhile—empirical survey. A survey of the case law provides many examples of manifestly indefensible practices, and suggests that more could certainly be done.[54] Taking subtle concerns about exit seriously will be easier if judges, and the Commission, can see that states are genuinely attempting to engage with the positive aspects of it too.

It would be a shame to see the picture solely in terms of the tensions between openness and cohesion, liberty and solidarity, welfare and the market, however. There are at least two other interpretations possible which deserve consideration. The liberalization of welfare can be understood as a statement or suggestion that Europe is politically mature, and no longer needs closed institutions to maintain its social cohesion—it can now have the best of both worlds, of freedom and solidarity. The compulsory, institutional maintenance of certain values treats these as delicate flowers, and is prepared to sacrifice other interests to protect them. But if those flowers are surprisingly robust and have grown strong roots the sacrifice may be redundant, and even harmful; a system that restricts freedom unnecessarily comes into discredit. Whether solidarity is a sufficiently rooted value that citizens will maintain their commitment to each other even if given the freedom to fragment and reorganize is of course difficult to predict. Ultimately the answer will be known only by experiment, and the cautious liberalization that the EU is imposing may be that experiment. The fear that it evokes may then be understood as a fear of ourselves, that we are in fact not ready for freedom—perhaps given the chance we will rush off and be selfish and abandon the weak to their fate. To use the European's (unjustified) stereotype of the United States; are we just Americans waiting to be released, or do we really have rooted European social values?[55]

The liberalization project can also be understood as part of the creation of a Europe-wide expression of welfare solidarity, which is less the creation of an EU welfare empire than an attempt to place national societies firmly in the context of neighbouring ones that share similar values, and thereby to turn the logic of communitarian monopoly on itself; if shared participation in a common project strengthens bonds, then making states transparently part of a wider community of states committed to welfare and solidarity should perhaps achieve the same effect on a larger scale.[56] Reaching the right compromise between national openness and national institutions is not a balance between cohesion and freedom, but about trying to use freedom to actually strengthen that cohesion—at least that may be the dream.

[54] It is unlikely that their lawyers advised the Dutch, British, Greek, or German governments that they had a reasonable chance in *Müller-Fauré*, *Watts*, Case C-444/05 *Stamatelaki* [2007] ECR I-3185, Case C-8/02 *Leichtle* [2004] ECR I-2641, *Schwarz*, and many others.

[55] G. Davies, 'The process and side-effects of the harmonisation of European welfare states', n 3 above, 63–64.

[56] J. Habermas, *The Post-National Constellation* (Cambridge: Polity Press, 2000).

6

When Patients Exit, What Happens to Solidarity?

*Clemens M. Rieder**

Within the last decade or so we have been able to observe the unfolding of a European healthcare framework that allows patients, under certain circumstances,[1] to *exit* the member state where they are insured and *enter* another member state for treatment, while the member state in which they are insured still carries all or at least a certain percentage of the treatment costs; the purpose of this chapter is to study closer the implications of the exit entitlement on solidarity.

The development of exit/entry was originally mostly driven by the case law of the European Court of Justice; one need only mention the well-known cases from *Kohll*[2] and *Watts*[3]. Now the EC Commission has taken on the matter and has drafted a legislative proposal for a Directive on Cross Border Health Care.[4] Certainly one could ask the question about why there is all this fuss about EU healthcare law when less than one per cent of German patients, for example, went abroad for treatment and in 2006 only 350 British patients did

* I am grateful to Prof Chris Hilson and Prof Chris Newdick for their comments; all errors, however, remain mine. The author can be contacted at c.rieder@rdg.ac.uk.

[1] V. Hatzopoulos, 'Killing National Health and Insurance Systems but Healing Patients? The European Market for Health Care Services after the Judgments of the ECJ in Vanbraekel and Peerbooms' (2002) 39 CML Rev 683; T. Hervey, 'The Current Legal Framework on the Right to Seek Health Care Abroad in the European Union' (2006/07) 9 The Cambridge Ybk of Eur Legal Studies 261, 268; C. Rieder, 'The EC Commission's New Adopted Baby: Health Care' (2007/08) 14 The Columbia J of Eur L 145; A. Serrano, 'Recent Developments. Improvements in Cross-Border Access to Health Care Within the European Union' (2002) 43 Harvard Intl LJ 553; P. van Nuffel, 'Patient's Free Movement Rights and Cross-Border Access to Healthcare' (2005) 12 Maastricht J of Eur and Comparative L 253.

[2] Case, C-158/96 *Raymond Kohll v Union des Caisses de Maladie* [1998] ECR I-1931.

[3] Case C-372/04 *The Queen on the application of Yvonne Watts v Bedford Primary Care Trust and Secretary of State for Health* [2006] ECR I-4325.

[4] Commission (EC), 'Proposal for a Directive of the European Parliament and of the Council on the Application of Patients' Rights in Cross-Border Health Care' COM (2008) 414 final.

so.[5] Having said that, a few observations must be made as to why the study of EU healthcare law is, nevertheless, a fruitful exercise. First, the extent to which patients are able to go abroad depends largely on whether they need to request such authorization or how easy it is to receive prior authorization. Secondly, the EU healthcare framework provides a 'generic door' through which patients can exit; to what extent this door will be used depends on the awareness people have of its existence. Thirdly, one could make the argument that the extent of the existence of EU healthcare may serve as an indicator regarding the level of integration achieved.

Particularly this latter aspect certainly stems from the fact that European public healthcare systems have been based on solidarity in order to pool the risk of sickness of the individual among all people in a given society ('universalism') or a particular group within a given society ('segmentalism').[6] Due to lack of space it is impossible to study in more depth how solidarity is generated; for our purposes it suffices to say that, as found by the US Supreme Court in *Baldwin v G.A.F. Seelig*, national solidarity is produced by a feeling or a reality of 'sink or swim together'[7] but also that solidarity finds itself 'at the crossroads between "liberty" and "equality", between "self-interest" and "altruism"'.[8]

While the cohesion of a group, for example, on the national level appears to be of considerable importance, EU healthcare law, according to the concerns of its critics, dissolves this very cohesion as it introduces an exit option.[9] In other words, if we study the relationship between exit and solidarity, we are not so much in search of a form of supranational solidarity but rather the main concern is that the supranational EU healthcare framework contributes to or fosters *inequality*, which may amount to a form of *injustice*[10] as it 'divert[s] resources from the poorly represented, less visible, less articulate groups typically composed of disabled, mentally ill and elderly patients'.[11] Whether this is really the case may be questioned if one considers Alter's argument, which claims that, on the contrary, '[l]itigation is thus often a tool of the weak, used because actors

[5] BBC, 'Health Care across Europe's Borders', 19 December 2007, available at <http://news.bbc.co.uk/1/hi/uk/7147971.stm>.

[6] See K. Anderson in this volume.

[7] *Baldwin v G.A.F. Seelig* 294 US 511, 523 [1935].

[8] M. Ferrera, *The Boundaries of Welfare. European Integration and the New Spatial Politics of Social Protection* (Oxford: OUP, 2005) 2044.

[9] See, for example, Ch. Newdick, 'Citizenship, Free Movement and Health Care: Cementing Individual Rights by Corroding Social Solidarity' (2006) 43 CML Rev 1645.

[10] R. Gilbar and H. Bar-Mor, 'Justice, Equality and Solidarity: The Limits of the Right to Health Care in Israel' (2008) 16 Med L Rev 225, 226.

[11] Newdick, n 9 above, 1646; cf also J. Schwartz 'From Domestic to Global Solidarity: the Dialectic of the Particular and Universal in the Building of Social Solidarity' (2007) 38 J of Social Philosophy 131, 133; A. Somek, 'Solidarity Decomposed. Being and Time in European Citizenship' U of Iowa Legal Studies Research Paper (No 07/13, 2007) 55; M. Maduro, 'Reforming the Market or the State? Article 30 and the European Constitution: Economic Freedom and Political Rights' (1997) 3 ELR 5 60.

cannot use the political system to address their concerns'.[12] Horowitz's argument goes in a similar direction as he asserts that '[d]eprived social groups have joined the advantaged in the march to the courthouse'.[13]

Be that preliminary discussion as it may; having mentioned the concepts of *equality* and *justice*, one cannot avoid Rawls and his 'difference principle'[14], which brings both aspects together. According to Rawls, justice requires 'equality in the assignment of basic rights and duties'.[15] If there exists inequalities of any kind in the access of exit this requires *justification*, which will only be satisfied when 'the difference in expectation is to the advantage of the representative man who is worse off'.[16]

This chapter will apply Hirschman's concept of exit, voice, and loyalty[17] in order to analyze whether the EU healthcare framework meets the conditions of the 'difference principle' and, consequently, can be considered a just system, which appears to be a key feature for its acceptance.

1. Hirschman's theory of exit, voice, and loyalty

Brian Barry, in a review article, predicted, with regards to Hirschman's theory, that '[t]here is no doubt that [Hirschman's] *Exit, Voice, and Loyalty* has the features necessary for an "in" book...: the theory can be stated in a few words but at the same time has unlimited range of application'.[18]

EU healthcare cases portray a history of patients who, being disappointed with the 'offers' provided by their member state of affiliation, consequently started looking for better 'bargains' abroad. They wished to make a change, which is in no way different from what an ordinary consumer would do if she/he is dissatisfied with the quality or price of a product.[19] While some may not like the idea of labelling the patient as a 'consumer', Hirschman's theory can be applied on a more abstract level that should then allow us to draw valuable conclusions. Additionally, it may be added that consumerization is a development currently taking place particularly in the field of healthcare; this is certainly supported by the internet, which may be a contributing factor in that '[t]he "gatekeeping" role of the doctor, or other health professional, is reduced or absent'.[20] Having said

[12] K. Alter, *The European Court's Political Power. Selected Essays* (Oxford: OUP, 2009) 23.

[13] D. Horowitz, *The Courts and Social Policy* (Washington: The Brookings Institution, 1977) 11.

[14] J. Rawls, *A Theory of Justice. Revised Edition* (6th edn, Cambridge, MA: Harvard University Press, 2003) 68.

[15] ibid 13. [16] ibid 68.

[17] A. Hirschman, *Exit, Voice, and Loyalty: Responses to Decline in Firms, Organizations, and States* (Cambridge, MA: Harvard University Press, 1970).

[18] B. Barry, 'Review Article: "Exit, Voice, and Loyalty"' (1974) 4 British J of Political Science 79, 82.

[19] K. Dowding et al, 'Exit, Voice and Loyalty: Analytical and Empirical Developments' (2000) 37 Eur J of Political Research 469, 470.

[20] T. Hervey and J. McHale, 'Law, Health and the European Union' (2005) 25 Legal Studies 228, 232.

that, it is, however, worth pointing out that, in most of the EU healthcare cases, patients *were advised* to use facilities in other member states by their doctors.

The mechanism at work with exit is that '[t]he customer who, dissatisfied with the product of one firm, shifts to that of another, uses the market to defend his welfare or to improve his position'.[21] However, already at this point it should be flagged that there are different levels of exit. The form of exit chosen by people who live in gated communities, who very visibly have decided to detach themselves from the rest of society by using their own security guards, or those who send their children to private schools, have a tendency to completely exclude and withdraw themselves permanently from society; and, as a consequence, they may no longer be willing to pay a substantial amount of (solidaristic) tax.[22] Exit under the EU healthcare framework, on the other hand, follows a radically different approach as people have no intention of excluding or withdrawing themselves from the solidaristic system as they, in return, want the home solidarity community to pay for their treatment; thus in a sense these people have an interest in the existence of a functioning solidarity community.

The following sections will analyze the three elements of Hirschman's theory; exit, voice, and loyalty, and relate them to national solidarity in the light of a supranational healthcare framework.

2. Exit

The fulcrum for our purposes is exit; this section will examine what the considerations are when people are allowed to exit a system. Certainly, a major concern in the context of healthcare is that planning will become more difficult when people are given the chance to choose the system (member state) where they want to be treated.[23] Having said that, it should be recalled that when the Court ruled on this particular issue it did not give patients absolute freedom as it was aware that providing an accessible healthcare system requires planning.[24] The early *Pierik*[25] rulings were certainly the most far reaching and liberal in this perspective as they

[21] Hirschman, n 17 above,15.

[22] J. Guéhenno, 'From Territorial Communities to Communities of Choice: Implications for Democracy' in W. Streeck (ed), *Internationale Wirtschaft, Nationale Demokratie. Herausforderungen für die Demokratietheorie* (Frankfurt/Main: Campus, 1998) 137, 143.

[23] T. Hervey and L. Trubek, 'Freedom to Provide Health Care Services Within the EU: An Opportunity for a Transformative Directive' (2006–2007) 13 Columbia J of Eur L 623, 635.

[24] Case C-157/99 *B.S.M. Geraets-Smits v Stichting Ziekenfonds VGZ and H.T.M. Peerbooms v Stichting CZ Groep Zorgverzekeringen.Geraets-Smits* [2001] ECR I-5473, para 78; the latest example is Case C-169/07, *Hartlauer Handelsgesellschaft mbH v Wiener Landesregierung, Oberösterreichische Landesregierung,* nyr, for further references.

[25] Case 117/77 *Bestuur van het Algemeen Ziekenfonds Drenthe-Platteland v G. Pierik* [1978] ECR 825 and Case 182/78 *Bestuur van het Algemeen Ziekenfonds Drenthe-Platteland v G. Pierik (No 2)* [1979] ECR 1977.

gave patients access to the best available treatment in Europe; however, no longer can they be considered good law.

In the aftermath of the recent integration rounds, the terminology of and categorization in 'new' and 'old' member states developed, which is an expression of economic differences between these two groups of member states; as a consequence of the current economic standing of the new member states they only can afford less spending in healthcare if one compares the absolute figures. There is certainly a danger that even if only a small number of patients become entitled to leave, this would, nevertheless, put a heavy burden on those systems that are exited; it would be particularly problematic when people leave the member state where they are insured invoking Article 22 of Regulation 1408/71 (replaced by Regulation 883/2004 at the beginning of 2010), which reimburses patients in accordance with the tariffs of the destination state but which requires prior authorization under all circumstances as a safeguard. The reimbursement of patients who rely on Article 49 EC (now Article 56 of the Treaty on the Functioning of the European Union), which does not need prior authorization for primary care, is limited anyway to the amount they are entitled to in accordance with the legislation of the member state of affiliation; in other words, patients who choose this latter track will not cost a member state more than she/he would cost if the treatment were to be received at home.

However, while there is a distinction in absolute figures regarding the money spent on healthcare, this difference is less critical if one compares the figures in the percentage of the GDP that member states spend on healthcare, which ranges between six and seven per cent.[26] The only exception to this finding are countries in two groups that Casas calls 'New Familialistic' countries (such as Poland and Slovakia) and 'New Liberal' countries (such as the Baltic states), which spend an average 3.7 per cent of their GDP on healthcare.[27] These findings, however, lead to the conclusion that, generally speaking, the spending difference is for most of the new member states, excluding the 'New Familialistic' and 'New Liberal' countries, only a temporary problem. Nevertheless, given the importance which healthcare law has apparently developed for the EU it comes as a surprise that healthcare law so far has not played any significant role in the screening process of candidate countries.

2.1 The exit mechanism

What is a key issue of exit is that 'exiters' send out alarm signals to other people that something is going astray[28] and 'although exit of some customers is essential for bringing the mechanism [competition as recuperation/making aware of problems] into play, it is important that other customers remain unaware of, or unperturbed by, quality decline'.[29] There is a danger that 'too much [happens]

[26] R. Casas, 'European Integration and Social Inequalities from an Empirical Perspective' in L. Magnussen and B. Stråth (eds) *European Solidarities. Tensions and Contentions of a Concept* (Brussels/New York: P.I.E. Peter Lang, 2007) 89–90.

[27] ibid 90. [28] Hirschman, n 17 above, 24–25. [29] ibid 25.

too soon'[30] and that by abandoning a product *en masse* customers will ruin a firm or organization. Whether this is a real danger in the context of healthcare is to be examined when we analyze the motives as to why people exit a system.

2.2 Reasons for exiting

If we study the case law as to why patients leave their system of affiliation, broadly speaking we can identify three categories that carry a different risk of mass exodus. The first category, which is called *covered treatment*, addresses the danger that patients may exit in order to receive treatment in another member state that is not available and/or not covered in their home state; the second category describes patients who are exiting because they seek *better quality* in a different system; and finally patients in category number three want to *shorten their waiting times* through exit.

The case of Mr Peerbooms[31] may serve as an example in the first category. Mr Peerbooms was a Dutch patient who underwent treatment in Austria, which would not necessarily be considered treatment covered by the Dutch solidarity community but would be according to Austrian legislation. As a matter of fact, according to EU law, prior authorization for treatment only has to be granted when treatment is considered to be covered by the legislation of the member state a patient is insured with. The Dutch national court involved, however, concluded that this particular treatment could not be considered 'normal', which means that in accordance with the ruling of the ECJ in this case the treatment has to be 'tried and tested by *international* medical science'.[32] The Dutch national court, however, found that the treatment that was received by Mr Peerbooms could not be considered 'normal' and, therefore, could not be covered by social security and following this finding Mr Peerbooms was not reimbursed. The Dutch national court was rightly criticized for the relatively little effort it undertook in establishing whether the treatment in question was 'normal' from an international perspective.[33]

In this group of patients any form of mass exodus in the context of hospital treatment is rather unlikely as member states do not have to authorize all forms of available treatments as was once required in the *Pierik*[34] rulings; having said this, this fact need not necessarily be a positive thing as the case of *Peerbooms*[35] clearly indicates. As a consequence of the treatment Mr Peerbooms received in Austria he awoke from a coma and did not need further treatment; leaving the personal benefits for Mr Peerbooms aside, the Dutch society as a whole also benefitted as a consequence of the Austrian treatment: no longer was Mr Peerbooms in need of an expensive hospital bed in order to monitor his condition.

[30] ibid 24. [31] *Geraets-Smits and Peerbooms*, n 24 above.
[32] ibid para 94 (emphasis added).
[33] F. Urlesberger, 'Ein gemeinsamer Markt für Kranke—Zweiter Anlauf' (2003) 38 Zeitschrift für Arbeitsrecht und Sozialrecht 265.
[34] Both *Pierik* rulings, n 25 above. [35] *Geraets-Smits and Peerbooms*, n 24 above.

Closely related to the issue of 'covered treatment' is the matter of 'quality of treatment', as sometimes it may be rather uncertain whether a particular treatment is just of better quality or already amounts to a different form of treatment, which would then become more an issue of whether it amounts to 'covered treatment'. *Kohll*[36] would be an example where a patient wanted to move because of real or assumed better quality of dental treatment in another member state. Again, better treatment can contribute to minimizing costs in the longer run as, for example, complications after the treatment are less likely. In this context one oddity may be added, which is highlighted by Le Grand: according to a US study, if patients do not use the facility treatment near to them but go further away, as a rule, the treatment becomes even more effective. 'One interpretation of this is that exercising choice is good for one's health: that the sense of control that choice gives has a powerful effect on individuals' ability to respond to treatment and their speed of recovery'.[37] If a system delivers poor quality of healthcare, from a societal perspective this is a waste of money, as it produces complications as a consequence of a treatment received, which leads to additional costs, let alone the fact that it is very undesirable from the individual's perspective.

However, to what extent in the future people would be entitled to leave a system because of its poor quality is difficult to predict; after all, Article 35 of the Charter on Fundamental Rights, which speaks of a 'high level of human health protection', has only been invoked once by the Advocate General in *Stamatelaki*,[38] the most recent case dealing with cross-border healthcare where a patient insured in Greece received cancer treatment in a private hospital in the UK.

The last group of patients who decided to exit did so because of waiting times that were considered to be too long; the case of Ms Watts[39] would fall into this category. Ms Watts went to France in order to receive a hip replacement sooner than she was scheduled for under the NHS regime. In the context of waiting times, Newdick brings up the issue of opportunity costs. He argues that 'if Peter secures access to resources otherwise intended for Paula, then Paula's treatment may have to be cancelled, delayed, or diluted as a result'.[40] The costs that arise from Peter's earlier treatment are then called opportunity costs. The concept of opportunity costs 'is not simply concerned with the *cost* of treatment, it also assesses the alternative ways in which that sum could benefit others'.[41] McHale's argument is on a similar line: 'if the NHS were required to pay the

[36] *Kohll*, n 2 above.

[37] J. Le Grand, *The Other Invisible Hand: Delivering Public Services through Choice and Competition* (Princeton: Princeton University Press, 2007) 101–102.

[38] Opinion of A. G. Colomer in Case C-444/05 *Aikaterini Stamatelaki v NPDD Organismos Asfaliseos Eleftheron Epangelmation (OAEE)* [2007] ECR I-3185, para 40.

[39] *Watts*, n 3 above.

[40] Ch. Newdick, 'Preserving Social Citizenship in Health Care Markets: There May Be Trouble Ahead' (2008) 2 McGill J of L and Health 93, 104.

[41] Newdick, n 9 above, 1650.

cost of some of its patients having treatment abroad earlier than they would receive it in the United Kingdom, this would require additional resources'.[42] While prima facie the argument seems convincing, both scholars ignore the simple fact that being on a waiting list itself is not cost free to patients, hospitals and ultimately the taxpayers. A Canadian study clearly indicates that the per-patient costs on a waiting list rise with waiting times.[43] Studies in only four fields of healthcare including total joint replacement or sight restoration revealed costs of 14.8 billion Canadian dollars (9.5 billion euros) as a consequence of waiting lists, which is according to this study only the tip of the iceberg.[44] Thus Newdick's argument loses at least some of its strength, as by shortening the waiting time for Peter, Paula may not necessarily have to suffer since money is actually saved by shortening waiting times. Generally, waiting lists have a potential to regulate themselves as the exodus will either stop once a sufficient number of people have left the system or waiting times at the more popular destination states have grown.

So far, exit has by and large been described as something that only concerns the individual; however, what needs to be taken into consideration is that 'my strength comes not from threatening my own Exit, but from threatening that of all those who have *not yet noticed* the decline in quality but who would Exit if they had'.[45] Thus from this perspective exit has a societal dimension; in other words the voice aspect of exit (which is to be considered in the next section) only emerges if the individual is to be understood as part of a collective. This brings us to the second element of Hirschman's triad, which is 'voice'.

3. Voice

This section, as a first step, will look into the relationship between exit and voice and, secondly, study voice on its own in more depth. For Hirschman voice is

> any attempt at all to change, rather than to escape from, an objectionable state of affairs, whether through individual or collective petition to the management directly in charge, through appeal to a higher authority with the intention of forcing a change in management, or through various types of actions and protests, including those that are meant to mobilize public opinion.[46]

[42] J. McHale, 'Rights to Medical Treatment in EU Law' (2007) 15 Med L Rev 99, 106.

[43] The Centre for Spatial Economics, *The Economic Cost of Wait Times in Canada* (January 15, 2008) 41.

[44] ibid 45–46.

[45] M. Laver, 'Exit, Voice, and Loyalty Revisited: The Strategic Production and Consumption of Public and Private Goods' (1976) 6 British J of Political Science 463, 465 (emphasis added).

[46] Hirschman, n 17 above, 30.

3.1 The relationship between voice and exit

The relationship between exit and voice can be understood either positively or negatively. According to Hirschman, who argues in favour of a negative relationship between voice and exit, those patients who exit no longer have any interest in exercising voice, which becomes particularly problematic if we are dealing with a 'lazy'[47] state monopoly; here the system becomes less and less efficient. Hirschman cites as an example the Nigerian Railroad Cooperation to make his point where:

> exit did not have its usual attention-focusing effect because the loss of revenue was not a matter of utmost gravity for management, while voice did not work as long as the most aroused and therefore the potentially most vocal customers were the first to abandon the railroads for the trucks.[48]

While the example is in itself convincing, as indicated, EU healthcare law is structured differently and the danger that in the departure of the more critical patients the system becomes highly inefficient is rather limited for several reasons. First, as there is only limited movement in the EU most of the patients will be citizens/voters of the member state in which they are insured. Secondly, as it is certainly not popular to receive healthcare far away from home (because this means being separated from one's family, the obstacle of a different language or additional costs for the patients because of, for example, travelling expenses) politicians cannot ignore the state of the healthcare system as this certainly leads to voter dissatisfaction.[49] Thirdly, from a financial perspective patients, even when leaving, cannot be forgotten by the system as it has to pay for them and those who leave the system still have to contribute to it. Thus, taking all these considerations together, a patient only exits from certain aspects of the healthcare system and only temporarily.

Thus, what is to be preliminarily concluded here is that exit through EU healthcare law does not deprive voice of its force; and even if people are leaving they still may contribute in changing/improving the home system.

3.2 The mechanism of voice

Voice is an invaluable tool to feed back information into the system and to highlight where and whether there are problems unfolding that prevent it from delivering 'good service', which may in the context of healthcare mean 'good quality', 'efficiency' or 'equity'[50] just to mention a few. While voice is certainly an appropriate tool to bring identified problems to the attention of the 'system', what remains to be seen is under what conditions it works best.

[47] cf Hirschman, n 17, 59. [48] ibid 45.

[49] cf A. Obermaier, 'The National Judiciary—Sword of the European Court of Justice Rulings: The Example of *Kohll/Decker* Jurisprudence' (2008) 14 ELR 735, 745–747.

[50] Le Grand, n 37 above, ch 1.

As said, Hirschman's claim, that people would always develop voice if they are only locked in, overlooks the fact that exercising voice carries costs. For example, the matter of retaliation may be an obvious cost factor related to voice.[51] Birch tells the story where he had to undergo brain surgery. Whereas the operation was a success the nursing was rather poor; and yet when he complained he experienced rather painful retaliation.[52] In healthcare we face a certain dilemma: those people who are in the system, as for example patients in a hospital, will be very reluctant to exercise voice despite the fact that they would have first-hand knowledge of existing problems. On the other hand, those people who are currently not in the system and who certainly have less knowledge 'could exercise voice without fear of retaliation... [b]ut rarely do so because of a special variety of the Olson thesis, namely that the possibility of going into hospital is not normally a salient factor in the thinking of healthy people'.[53]

Apart from retaliation we also find other factors that are considered by an individual when making the choice whether to exercise voice or stay silent. Factors to be taken into consideration are group size and the complexity of the issue. An example of this latter aspect might be: '[a] citizen complaining to a local government about a street light not working may expect almost immediate action, but if one voiced concern over the general course of the government then one may allow several years to see if satisfaction might be achieved'.[54] The matter of healthcare is usually a complex one and even if a patient is willing to exercise voice in order to change things what remains to be the case is that a patient almost always fights against the clock.

Furthermore, as mentioned above, group size plays another decisive role. Only in very small groups are the benefits of exercising voice likely to outweigh the costs[55] as the costs of turning opinions of larger groups are much greater for an individual not having ready access to the media or a party infrastructure. The problematic issue with costs and voice is that while exit is a binary concept (leave or stay) voice is of a bigger variety as it leaves a 'choice... not normally merely between voice and no voice but between larger and smaller amounts of voice (including zero) each associated with a given cost'.[56] In these larger communities voice is probably better understood in terms of Hilson's terminology of 'political opportunity',[57] which is of a 'collective nature',[58] or 'legal opportunity'[59] which is more of an 'individualistic voice [mechanism]'[60] expressed via the courts.

Suffice to say here is that if one tries to take advantage of 'political opportunities' a person can only be successful if a sufficiently big group out of a constituency

[51] A. Birch, 'Economic Models in Political Science: The Case of Exit, Voice, and Loyalty' (1975) 5 British J of Political Science 69, 75–79.

[52] ibid 78. [53] ibid 79. [54] Dowding, n 19 above, 475.

[55] Barry, n 18 above, 92. [56] ibid 89.

[57] C. Hilson, 'New Social Movements: The Role of Legal Opportunity' (2002) 9 J of Eur Public Policy 238, 242.

[58] Le Grand, n 37 above, 32. [59] Hilson, n 57 above, 243–244.

[60] Le Grand, n 37 above, 32.

can be attracted who shares one's own opinion. Given these circumstances it does not come as a surprise that contrary to what Hirschman would expect, sometimes people 'suffer in silence'[61] without attempting to actually change the status quo.

Things are slightly different in the context of 'legal opportunities'. Here costs most likely consist of litigation costs and it is certainly not necessary to participate in some sort of 'popularity contest' where a substantial amount of people have to be convinced that the case is important enough which may require a person to spread her/his healthcare problem across the tabloids in order to gain sufficient support for the cause, even though this may be the (undesired) *result* of a court case.

However, sometimes a combination of both approaches may do the trick as demonstrated by the case of Ms Rogers, who was suffering from a rare form of breast cancer that required very expensive treatment by the NHS.[62] A sign of effectiveness of 'legal opportunities' is the fact that many legal actions by consumers are settled out of court as there is a reluctance 'to allow consumer dissidence to become too public'.[63] At the same time '[l]itigation strategies are at best crude instruments for policy change, entailing the risk that adverse decisions could regress policy, and are thus usually adopted only after other political avenues have failed'.[64] Nevertheless, what can be observed in the EU context is that the ECJ cases eventually lead to some political activism by the EC Commission on the European level. As one can imagine, both opportunities, as with many other issues in life, are more accessible for those who have more economic potential.[65] While this in itself is regrettable, it can also be considered an element of 'organic solidarity due to the division of labor'.[66] Those who have more economic capacity are more likely to exercise voice, which, however, can result in a better system *for all*. At the end of the day it should not matter so much *who* brings a problem to the table as long as it is unveiled.

4. Loyalty

The regulating mechanism that can influence the likelihood of a person exercising exit or voice is expressed in the concept of loyalty. Hirschman understands this

[61] Barry, n 18 above, 92

[62] For details see *R (on the application of Rogers) v Swindon NHS Primary Care Trust* [2006] EWCA Civ 392; or as The Sun titled: Thornton, 'No-drug "death Sentence"', 7 February 2006, available at <http://www.thesun.co.uk/sol/homepage/news/article37037.ece>.

[63] Laver, n 45 above, 465.

[64] K. Alter and J. Vargas, 'Explaining Variation in the Use of European Litigation Strategies. European Community Law and British Gender Equality Policy' (2000) 33 Comparative Political Studies 452, 457.

[65] Schwartz, n 11 above, 133.

[66] E. Durkheim, *The Division of Labor in Society* (London: Collier-Macmillan Limited, 1933, translated by Simpson) 111.

relationship in a way that '[a]s a rule, then, loyalty holds exit at bay and activates voice'.[67]

Particularly in the field of healthcare it seems fair to assume that a person tries to maximize utility which means that she/he tries to have access to the best healthcare available. Loyalty 'tends to check our preference for exit over voice'.[68] It works as a 'psychological attachment which increases the cost of exit'.[69] Needless to say, loyalty is the most 'ambiguous element of Hirschman's original scheme'.[70]

When it comes to healthcare though, it appears to be the case that loyalty does not play a decisive role if one considers the following Eurobarometer figures, which describe under what conditions patients were willing to exit their system of affiliation: 91 per cent of the respondents would be willing to travel abroad for treatment that is not available at home, 78 per cent would if they could receive better quality treatment and 69 per cent would go if they were treated by a renowned specialist. Finally, a majority of 64 per cent would, in principle, travel to another member state in order to shorten waiting times.[71] Thus, what can be concluded from these findings is that it is not so much loyalty that prevents patients from exiting but rather an aspect of convenience.

If we speak of loyalty, however, it becomes necessary to distinguish between loyalty (self-chosen) and coercion (determined from the outside).[72] As argued before, if exit is closed (sign of coercion) then voice is unlikely to generate. Thus, only self-chosen loyalty (resulting from convenience) may have the potential to generate voice. Needless to say, making this distinction between loyalty and coercion may at times be difficult as the line can be a very fine one. This is even more the case as sometimes coercion comes in the guise of loyalty. For example, loyalty is traditionally attributed to those who serve in the armed forces. However, it need not necessarily always be the case that a person joins the armed forces out of loyalty for her/his country: other elements such as 'structural violence'[73] in a society may have contributed to a person joining the forces. The practice of poverty drafting applied by the US army supports this assumption; here recruiters search, in particular, for new recruits amongst the poor and promise them education and money for their services[74] (even if this amounts to just 1,200 US dollars[75] a month for a private first class in the red-zone in Iraq). In much the same way, a very restrictive approach to

[67] Hirschman, n 17 above, 78.

[68] G. Fletcher, *Loyalty. An Essay on the Morality of Relationships* (Oxford: OUP, 1993) 5.

[69] Ferrera, n 8 above. [70] ibid 35.

[71] Eurobarometer, *Cross-Border Health Services in the EU.* Analytical Report (2007) 11.

[72] Laver, n 45 above, 480.

[73] J. Galtung, 'Twenty-Five Years of Peace Research: Ten Challenges and Some Responses' (1985) 22 J of Peace Research, 141.

[74] J. Key (as told to L. Hill), *The Deserter's Tale. The Story of an Ordinary Soldier Who Walked Away from the War in Iraq* (Publishers Group West, 2007) 223.

[75] ibid 229.

prior authorization in the context of healthcare can hardly be described as loyalty.[76]

At the same time, Birch highlights the fact that loyalty has something to do with '"allegiance" and "fidelity"'[77] and thus argues that it is doubtful if it is really the loyalist who is asking the critical questions and who is, therefore, exercising effective voice.[78] According to him it is safe to say that '[i]n the normal usage of political language, loyalty means a *disposition to accept* rather than a *disposition to criticize*'.[79] Here we find a principle at work already mentioned; if loyalty is so strong that it actually bars exit then we can hardly expect voice to develop.

We should now have sufficient arguments to come to an overall conclusion to whether the EU healthcare framework fulfils the conditions as required by Rawls' 'difference principle'.

5. Conclusion

All these previous considerations taken together did not really bring any arguments to light that would suggest that supranational solidarity corrodes national solidarity. One could almost argue the opposite in that a system that allows for exit is more sensitive to critique and flaws occurring in the system. This sensitivity is important if we recall that solidarity in a national context always has an aspect of reciprocity inborn; this, however, means that in order for people to be willing to contribute to a solidarity system that is not exclusively based on a form of altruism but also on forms of reciprocity, efficiency of the system is certainly an important factor in order to preserve the willingness of the people to further contribute to the system.

Generally, the case law of the ECJ makes problems of the system more transparent and so the Court plays a key role in this framework as it allows patients to exit by using their voice. The Court creates a 'generic door' that can be used not only by those people who actually brought the case but equally by others; this, however, strengthens the force of voice that multiplies if there is a credible '*threat of exit*'[80] available. It also has to be highlighted that EU healthcare case law is an example where 'legal opportunities' attract 'political opportunities'; taking this into consideration it does not seem to be a coincidence that the UK Government's policy of using private hospitals in order to reduce waiting lists happened at a similar time when European judgments were delivered on the free movement of patients.[81]

[76] cf M. Sandel, *Justice What's the Right Thing to do?* (Allen Lane, 2009) 82.
[77] Birch, n 51 above, 74. [78] ibid.
[79] ibid at 75 (emphasis added). [80] Hirschman, n 17 above, 82 (emphasis added).
[81] G. Davies, 'The Effect of Mrs Watts' Trip to France on the National Health Service' (2007) 18 King's LJ 158, 166.

At the same time, patients, even when they exit, remain sufficiently linked with their 'domestic system' as they still generally have to contribute to the system. Taking all these considerations together, Davies' observation—that an 'individual who has learnt to exit that system and receive treatment elsewhere may come to see national authorities as merely a source of funds, and will have a reduced personal interest in the quality or availability of national facilities'[82]—is not necessarily correct.

If one applies Durkheim's already mentioned division of labour, one could even argue that the relationship between those who exit and those who stay is somehow one of organic solidarity; as in Durkheim's division of labour some people have the potential to exit and thereby strengthen their voice whereas other people may have only the ability to vote (or do nothing and just complain). However, the group who can exit, in doing so, improves the quality of the system for all. If this, however, is the case, then in line with Rawls' difference principle a possible unequal access to exit is justified and does not amount to injustice as understood by Rawls.

[82] G. Davies, 'The Community's Internal Market-Based Competence to Regulate Healthcare: Scope, Strategies and Consequences' (2007) 15 Maastricht J of Eur and Comparative Law 215, 235.

7

EU Environmental Solidarity and the Ecological Consumer: Towards a Republican Citizenship

*Chris Hilson**

1. Introduction

Within political theory, solidarity, justice and citizenship are closely inter-related concepts. Solidarity has been expressed as a preparedness[1] or, more strongly, a duty to share resources with others in need in a spirit of mutual support. Such solidarity duties or duties of justice—which are typically institutionalized via collective action such as the welfare state—are frequently said to be owed only to fellow citizens within a confined political community. However, in exploring environmental solidarity in this chapter, a broader approach is adopted. Rather than just being about the distribution or redistribution of goods, environmental solidarity is conceived of here as also involving a just avoidance of bads such as pollution. In addition, the article argues for a set of solidarity duties that are potentially global in nature and not owed only to those within, for example, one's own state.

The first part of the chapter will explore some examples of solidarity at work within existing EU environmental and natural resources law and policy. As will be seen, these are principally solidarity commitments of the former kind above—in other words, they involve collective, often redistributionary, resource commitments on the part of member states and the EU institutions themselves. Where these schemes are redistributionary, while they may eventually filter down to individuals, they do not currently give rise to individual rights claims by citizens. This

* I am grateful, for their comments/conversations, to John Barry, Richard Bellamy, Martha-Marie Kleinhans, Stuart Lakin, participants at the MLR workshop, 'Seeking Solidarity in the European Union—Towards Social Citizenship and a European Welfare State?', University of Sussex, 7 May 2008, and also to Laura Graham for her research assistance in connection with this chapter. All errors remain my own.

[1] S. Stjernø, *Solidarity in Europe: The History of an Idea* (Cambridge: Cambridge University Press, 2005) 326.

stands in stark contrast with the way in which much of the existing legal literature has examined solidarity recently, which has been in the context of individual rights claims by EU citizens trying to exit from their existing solidarity communities and gain access to new ones in other member states.[2] Though of course collective member state provision is also central there, the relevant case law and literature raise the key question of the link between solidarity and individual citizens. The aim of the current chapter is to interrogate this link in the context of the environment. The second part of the chapter thus starts by drawing some contrasts between the 'mainstream' EU solidarity case law, and solidarity in the context of the ecological citizen consumer. It proceeds to argue for a republican model of ecological citizenship, at the heart of which lie broader solidarity duties of the latter type above, which are to be exercised in the private sphere of the market.

2. Collective EU environmental solidarity

In the context of EU environmental and natural resources law and policy, references to solidarity can be found in numerous official documents and provisions concerning sustainable development, energy, climate change and disaster assistance. With sustainable development, the Commission's Strategic Objectives 2005–2009[3] set the EU's sustainable development objective in the context of solidarity, both intragenerationally within the EU and globally,[4] and also intergenerationally.[5] The report states that:

> Our common project brings with it a responsibility to offer mutual support and to protect and manage our surroundings together. A healthy European society depends on the effective delivery of this common project.[6]

It goes on to state that 'solidarity needs a concrete expression, both at present and with future generations',[7] through economic and social cohesion, sustainable management and protection or safeguarding of the EU's environment, natural resources and energy supply, reform and management of social protection systems, and preservation and strengthening of common EU values.[8]

[2] See eg C. Newdick, 'Citizenship, Free Movement and Health Care: Cementing Individual Rights by Corroding Social Solidarity' (2006) 43 *CML Rev* 1645; M. Dougan and E. Spaventa, 'Wish You Weren't Here…New Models of Social Solidarity in the European Union' in M. Dougan and E. Spaventa (eds) *Social Welfare and EU Law* (Oxford: Hart, 2005); C. Barnard, 'EU Citizenship and the Principle of Solidarity' in Dougan and Spaventa (eds), ibid; A. Somek, 'Solidarity Decomposed: Being and Time in European Citizenship' (2007) 32 ELR 787; S. Giubboni, 'Free Movement of Persons and European Solidarity' (2007) 13 Eu LJ 360.

[3] 'Europe 2010: A Partnership for European Renewal: Prosperity, Solidarity and Security', COM (2005) 12 final (26 January 2005).

[4] On global solidarity, see ibid 12.

[5] On solidarity with future generations, see ibid 9.

[6] ibid 8. [7] ibid. [8] ibid.

In relation to energy policy, the Presidency conclusions of the 8/9 March 2007 Brussels European Council emphasized the need to enhance security of energy supply 'in a spirit of solidarity between Member States.'[9] A Eurobarometer survey from around the same period would seem to support this, having found that 'Europeans express a strong level of solidarity on the issue of energy: almost eight out of ten (79%) EU citizens agree that in the case of a sudden shortage of oil and gas, the affected Member State should be able to rely on the reserves of other EU countries, while only 17% is opposed to this.'[10]

With climate change, there has been an emphasis on solidarity both in terms of prior adaptation measures and also in terms of emergency response to climate-related natural disasters. The Green Paper on Adapting to Climate Change stressed that adaptation 'will require solidarity among EU Member States in order to ensure that the poorer and disadvantaged regions and those regions that will be hardest hit by climate change will be able to take the necessary measures.'[11] While the Green Paper also covers the need for the EU to support adaptation actions in developing countries—particularly in light of the EU's historically greater share of responsibility for anthropogenic greenhouse gas emissions—it does not use the term solidarity in this context.[12]

Perhaps the most prominent example of solidarity in the environmental field lies in relation to the EU Solidarity Fund, set up under Council Regulation 2012/2002,[13] which is designed to allow the Union to show solidarity with the populations of regions in EU and accession states affected by major disasters, by providing them with financial assistance. This includes disasters caused by climate change, which is likely to give rise to an increased incidence of extreme weather incidents such as flooding, droughts and accompanying forest fires. Although not in the end thought to have been caused by climate change,[14] the severe flooding which affected the UK in the summer of 2007 provides a good example of a natural disaster which prompted a successful application to the

[9] Council, 7224/1/07 REV 1.

[10] 'Eurobarometer: Europeans support greater EU action on energy and climate change', Press Release IP/07/280, 5 March 2007. However, breaking these figures down, the main report (Flash EB Series No 206a, *Attitudes on Issues related to EU Energy Policy*, April 2007) states that the lowest levels of solidarity were found in Austria (65%), Romania (69%), Hungary and the UK (both 72%), while highlighting that, even in these states, 'the overwhelming majority are in favour of shared reserves' (at 20). The demographic figures show that: women tend to be marginally more solidaristic than men; the young and especially the old less solidaristic than the in-between age groups; the educated more solidaristic than the less educated; and rural dwellers less solidaristic than urbanites (Annex, 49).

[11] 'Adapting to Climate Change in Europe—Options for EU Action' COM (2007) 354 final, 29 June 2007,12.

[12] ibid 22–23.

[13] Council Regulation 2012/2002 establishing the European Union Solidarity Fund [2002] OJ L311/3.

[14] Centre for Ecology and Hydrology, 'Summer 2007 Floods: A Very Singular Event—11th March 2008' at <http://www.ceh.ac.uk/news/news_archive/2008_news_item_05.html> (last visited 16 April 2008).

Fund.[15] And while the Regulation states that assistance should mainly be mobilized in the case of natural disasters, man-made disasters are also included. In 2006 for example, the UK submitted an application for assistance from the Fund in connection with the fire and explosions at the Buncefield oil storage depot in Hertfordshire in December 2005.[16] In the event, that particular application was withdrawn because it fell too far below the required thresholds, but the Fund has been successfully mobilized in at least one man-made pollution incident—the 'Prestige' oil tanker disaster off the Spanish coast in mid-November 2002.[17]

In addition to more general provisions on solidarity,[18] the Treaties also contain some specific environmental examples along similar lines to those above. Article 122(1) of the Lisbon Treaty on the Functioning of the European Union (TFEU) (ex 100(1) EC) for example, provides for appropriate measures to be taken if severe difficulties arise in the provision of certain products. The Lisbon formulation specifically mentions energy as a notable example of such a product and also introduces the explicit language of solidarity in connection with such action. The need for solidarity in relation to energy supply is also mentioned in Article 194 TFEU under the new Energy Title XXI. In addition, Article 122(2) TFEU (ex 100(2) EC)—while not using the explicit language of solidarity—provides for Council assistance to member states in the case of natural disasters or exceptional occurrences beyond their control. The precise relationship between this provision and the Solidarity Fund remains unclear. Although the latter is more expansive in scope in certain respects (being available to accession and not just member states), in others it is arguably more restrictive than the Treaty Article (in requiring a disaster to be 'major'). Matters are further complicated by an explicit Solidarity Clause in Title VII TFEU which additionally provides for assistance to member states in the event of natural or man-made disasters or terrorist attacks.[19]

3. European citizenship and environmental solidarity

The above clearly demonstrates that there are numerous examples of collective institutional mechanisms involving solidarity and the environment within the EU policy framework. However, the principal aim of this chapter is to interrogate the link between European citizenship and environmental solidarity. While the above collective arrangements might be said to engage citizenship insofar as they may be seen as a means of attempting to foster a common European identity, they do

[15] See Decision of the European Parliament and of the Council (EC) 2008/267 of 11 March 2008 on the mobilization of the EU Solidarity Fund [2008] OJ L85/7. The UK was awarded €162,387,985.

[16] 'European Union Solidarity Fund Annual Report 2006' COM (2007) 632 final, 25 October 2007, 3–4.

[17] ibid. <http://www.ceh.ac.uk/news/news_archive/2008_news_item_05.html>.

[18] See eg the Preamble and Arts 2–3 of the Lisbon TEU.

[19] Art 222 TFEU.

not currently involve individual citizens' rights or duties,[20] which (particularly the latter) are the focus of this chapter. Before considering the place of the individual citizen in this rights/duties sense specifically in relation to environmental solidarity, it is worth starting with a more general exploration of the way in which solidarity and the individual European citizen have been approached by the Court of Justice.

What one finds is a troubled relationship between the European citizen and solidarity. As far as individual entitlements are concerned, the EU is not a direct provider of solidaristic welfare services and neither, many would claim, could it be, since it lacks the relevant socio-cultural ties which form the basis of effective solidarity communities. Such ties are typically found at national level and the role of EU law, through the Court, has been to force member states to open up their solidarity entitlements to nationals from other member states relying on their free movement rights. This began, pre-Maastricht, with the 'market citizen'[21] relying on the economic freedoms, such as free movement of workers or freedom to provide and receive services, in order to secure equality of access, with host state nationals, to domestic, solidarity-based, social rights. In this respect, as Giubboni has noted, there is a decided tension between the (single) market and national solidarity.[22] Post-Maastricht, with the creation of formal EU citizenship, the market citizen has been transformed by the Court's citizenship case law into a social citizen, 'freed from the requirements and limits of economic integration'.[23] However, even here, EU citizenship is linked, if not with market actors, then with the rights of individuals to move and reside within the EU and thereby acquire access to national social rights.[24] There may not be the same tension between the market and national solidarity therefore, since these cases do not involve market actors acting instrumentally in the service of the single market. However, they still involve a tension between individualism—with individuals arguing for universal entitlement—and a more particularist approach whereby entitlement is available only to those within the national solidarity community and not more widely to outsiders from other member states.[25] In addition—and potentially in contrast with the ecological citizen outlined below—the relevant cases do not involve the exercise of political citizenship (rights) —only movement and residence rights and associated social rights.[26]

[20] cf T. Faist, 'Social Citizenship in the European Union: Nested Membership' (2001) 39 J of Common Market Studies 37, 51.

[21] On which see further M. Everson, 'The Legacy of the Market Citizen' in J. Shaw and G. More (eds) *New Legal Dynamics of the European Union* (Oxford: Clarendon, 1995).

[22] Giubboni, 'Free Movement of Persons and European Solidarity', n 2 above.

[23] ibid 368.

[24] As well as certain political rights.

[25] Somek, n 2 above, 815.

[26] S. O'Leary, 'Solidarity and Citizenship Rights in the Charter of Fundamental Rights of the European Union' in G. de Búrca (ed) *EU Law and the Welfare State: In Search of Solidarity* (Oxford: OUP, 2005) 39, 75.

How then does this compare with the individual citizen in relation to environmental solidarity in the EU? One obvious point of comparison lies in the context of rights, which are often seen as the principal currency of citizenship.[27] The free movement citizen described above relies on EU economic or citizenship freedoms or rights in order to secure national welfare rights. These welfare rights are associated with a Durkheimian organic solidarity found in market-based societies characterized by interdependence stemming from the division of labour, and provide a form of insurance against social risks such as unemployment or sickness.[28] Environmental rights can easily be seen in similar terms: thus, according to Turner, these rights can be seen as guarding against environmental as opposed to social risks, thereby providing not social security but what he terms 'ontological security'.[29] Instead of social interdependence based on the division of labour, one has environmental interdependence, both within existing political communities and also—based on the cross-border and even global nature of many environmental processes—between them.

In an EU context, the above has particular resonance in relation to the Charter of Fundamental Rights, which famously contains a number of expressly named 'solidarity rights'. Menendez states that 'the term *rights to solidarity* points correctly to those rights which aim at complementing the *market* (private property and contractual exchange) with *solidaristic* obligations to *share* social wealth.'[30] However, while this perfectly characterizes the various rights to benefits found within the Charter's solidarity chapter, it does not capture the essence of the more regulatory rights such as the (rather limited) right to environmental protection in Article 37.[31] What the two types of right share in common is, rather, their positioning as a response to risk. Alternatively, rather than speaking of the sharing of wealth, one might argue that the relevant solidarity rights are more concerned with ensuring justice—whether this involves the just sharing of goods in the case of social welfare type rights, or also the just avoidance of bads in the case of environmental justice.[32]

However—to borrow Dobson's typology[33]—the focus here will not be on 'environmental' citizenship with its liberal emphasis on solidarity *rights*, but rather on 'ecological' citizenship, which places more of a republican emphasis

[27] In part due to the abiding influence of T. H. Marshall—see his *Citizenship and Social Class: And Other Essays* (Cambridge: Cambridge University Press, 1950).

[28] D. Beland and R. Hansen, 'Reforming the French Welfare State: Solidarity, Social Exclusion and the Three Crises of Citizenship' (2000) 23 West Eur Politics 47, 51.

[29] B. S. Turner, 'The Erosion of Citizenship' (2001) 52 The British J of Sociology 189.

[30] A. Menendez, 'The Sinews of Peace: Rights to Solidarity in the Charter of Fundamental Rights of the Union' in E. Eriksen et al, *The Chartering of Europe* (Oslo: Arena, 2001) 201, at 205 (emphasis in original).

[31] This distinction between benefits-based and regulatory rights also stems from Menendez, ibid.

[32] The environmental justice movement in the US is closely associated with fighting the tendency for environmental bads to be disproportionately distributed in communities inhabited by the poor and people of colour—see eg V. Been, 'Analysing Evidence of Environmental Justice' (1995) 11 J of Land Use and Environmental L 1.

[33] A. Dobson, *Citizenship and the Environment* (Oxford: OUP, 2003).

on the idea of solidarity obligations or duties.[34] Of course, the notion of duty is not exactly missing from the welfare-based accounts encountered earlier in the chapter. However, these tend to be straightforward Hohfeldian correlatives:[35] the reverse side of the individual's right to welfare is a solidarity duty owed *by the state*. They are not duties owed *by individuals* in the same way as the individual possesses rights.

Not of course that individualized duties are strangers to European law: the Charter preamble states that '(e)njoyment of these rights entails responsibilities and duties with regard to other persons, to the human community and to future generations'; and Article 20 TFEU (ex 17(2) EC) on Union citizenship declares that '(c)itizens of the Union shall enjoy the rights and be subject to the duties provided for in the Treaties. However, the nature of these duties remains rather underdeveloped to say the least. At national level, citizen duties might typically relate to things such as the payment of taxes, sending one's children to school, performing national service or jury service, obeying the law, or (in a limited number of countries) voting. With the exception of the last two, none of these are activities which arise at supranational level as part of EU competence, which to an extent makes it easy to see why individual duties owed by EU citizens have been under-specified. However, the aim of this chapter is precisely to suggest ways in which EU citizenship can be recast in ecological terms based on solidaristic duties owed in relation to the environment. In fact, the Charter—quoted above—already provides a head-start in this respect, since it explicitly speaks of duties to future generations, which is of course a key component of the environmental principle of sustainable development. Similarly, the EC's 5th Environmental Action Programme spoke powerfully of the 'shared *responsibility*' we all have for the environment—in other words, not just business and government, but also individual citizens.[36]

These duties might take a variety of forms. While space precludes a full treatment within the scope of this chapter, the aim here will be to focus on one possible candidate—the duty of ecological consumption (including, often more appropriately, non-consumption), as an example of market citizenship.[37] My contention

[34] Dobson, ibid, distinguishes his 'post-cosmopolitan' ecological footprint-based version of ecological citizenship from a republican approach (while acknowledging a number of shared points of contact). My approach is, in contrast, more firmly rooted in republicanism and hence I do not adopt Dobson's 'post-cosmopolitan' frame. Nb also that while emphasizing duties rather more than liberals, republicans are not wholly rights-sceptical—they simply support different types of right (see eg C. Hilson, 'Legitimacy and Rights in the EU: Questions of Identity' (2007) 14 J of Eur Public Policy 527). Similarly, liberalism can be seen as supporting some private environmental duties, though not to the same extent as the republican account offered here (see eg D. Bell, 'Liberal Environmental Citizenship' (2005) 14 Environmental Politics 179, 190).

[35] W. Hohfeld, *Fundamental Legal Conceptions* (London: Yale University Press, 1964).

[36] 'Towards Sustainability', COM (92) 23 final, 27 March 1992.

[37] Seyfang has also made a case for sustainable consumption as an example of ecological citizenship—see G. Seyfang, 'Shopping for Sustainability: Can Sustainable Consumption Promote Ecological Citizenship?' (2005) 14 Environmental Politics 290. However, her argument is very much based on Dobson's post-cosmopolitan approach (n 33 above), as opposed to the republican one adopted here.

is, first, that this provides an example of a republican European market citizenship which, far from conflicting with solidarity as we found with the ECJ's case law, is in fact quite in tune with it; and second, that while consumerism is often seen as an example of naked self-interest, this need not be so. Overall, the aim is to tease out the implications of ecological consumerism for solidarity and citizenship and to assess whether it makes sense to speak of an identifiably *European* ecological citizen consumer.

4. The ecological citizen consumer

The role of the green European consumer has been aided by informational regulatory instruments such as the EU Eco-label[38] and energy labelling of products,[39] although of course green choices are often made outside the scope of these formal schemes (particularly in member states like the UK, where the visibility and impact of the eco-label has been modest).

To what extent can these then be regarded as instruments of solidarity to be employed by republican ecological citizens? One of the problems, one might think, from the perspective of solidarity and republican citizenship, is that consumer decision-making in the market place is typically seen as a *self-interested* activity. In contrast, solidarity and citizenship are said to require an other-regarding stance. Perhaps the best known republican proponent of this position is Sagoff, who has stated:

> As a citizen, I am concerned with the public interest, rather than my own interest; with the good of the community rather than simply the well-being of my family... In my role as a consumer, in other words, I concern myself with personal or self-regarding wants and interests; I pursue the goals I have as an individual.[40]

However, while solidarity clearly entails communal rather than self-interested decision-making, it is far from clear that consumers are unable to adopt a communal stance.[41] In other words, the contrast Sagoff draws between citizens and consumers is too stark. Just as citizens, like the consumers assumed by neo-classical economics, are capable of acting selfishly, so too consumers are able to act in a non-self-interested manner.

[38] Council Regulation (EC) 1980/2000 of the European Parliament and of the Council on a revised Community Eco-label Award Scheme [2000] OJ L237/1.

[39] Council Dir 92/75/EEC on the indication by labeling and standard product information of the consumption of energy and other resources by household appliances [1992] OJ L297/16.

[40] M. Sagoff, *The Economy of the Earth: Philosophy, Law and the Environment* (Cambridge: Cambridge University Press, 1988) 8.

[41] See eg R. Keat, 'Citizens, Consumers and the Environment: Reflections on the Economy of the Earth' (1994) 3 Environmental Values 333, 344; J. Barry, *Rethinking Green Politics: Nature, Virtue and Progress* (London: Sage, 1999) 66–67.

Non-self-interested market activity is variously and usually interchangeably described as ethical or political consumerism—with the latter broadly defined, for example by Micheletti et al as 'the use of market purchases by individuals, groups, and institutions, who want to take responsibility for political, economic, and societal developments.'[42] However, for the purposes of this chapter, there is an important distinction to be drawn between political and ethical consumerism: while the latter involves moral or ethical duties,[43] the former is underpinned by a stronger, political, justice-based duty. The ecological citizen consumer is practising political consumerism: she is acting not through self-interest, but solidaristically out of concern for the potential environmental harm she may be causing to other current humans and also future generations. That this is a matter of politics, justice and solidarity rather than altruism or morality is a point that will be argued for later, below.

Unlike our free movement EU citizen (market or social) from earlier in the chapter, the EU ecological market citizen can thus be seen as engaging in a form of political participation. From a republican citizenship perspective, one might seek to contest this both in terms of the *sphere of activity* and also in terms of *democratic equality*. With the former, the claim might be made that the political activity of citizenship can only take place in the collective public sphere and that whatever takes place in the individual private sphere of the market cannot be regarded as a form of citizenship practice. However, Dobson, borrowing from feminist theory where the personal has long been regarded as political, rightly contests this, arguing that many private acts have public implications.[44] For ecological citizenship, the lines between the individual and collective, the private and the public, between what is citizenly and what is not, are much more fluid. That this is perfectly in tune with republicanism is confirmed by Barry, who argues that the privileging of the public sphere stems back to Greek times when the private sphere was seen as one of privation, which is no longer necessarily the case.[45]

This brings us on to the question of democratic equality. One might claim that globally informed political consumerism (in its broadest sense) has filled a democratic deficit in that it makes up for the lack of effective global democratic

[42] M. Micheletti et al, 'Introduction' in M. Micheletti, A. Follesdal and D. Stolle (eds) *Politics, Products and Markets: Exploring Political Consumerism Past and Present* (London: Transaction Publishers, 2004) xxv.

[43] Duties which are arguably 'imperfect' in nature. Some may deny whether ethical consumerism involves duties at all, regarding it, at best, as supererogatory in nature.

[44] Dobson, n 33 above, 52–56. cf R. Lister, *Citizenship: Feminist Perspectives* (Basingstoke: Macmillan, 1997), who draws a distinction between 'citizenship politics' and 'personal politics': campaigning for a more equal share of housework in the public sphere would constitute the former; arranging a fairer division of labour in one's own home would amount to the latter and, being solely within the private sphere, would not involve acting as a citizen (28). However, many environmental actions, including consumer decision-making, affect others and thus have a political dimension beyond the household (Dobson's 'public implications') in a way which chore division does not.

[45] J. Barry, 'Resistance is Fertile: From Environmental to Sustainability Citizenship' in A. Dobson and D. Bell (eds) *Environmental Citizenship* (London: MIT Press, 2006) 26.

institutions able to exert control over companies and states.[46] In addition, one might argue, like Micheletti, that political consumerism, which is typically practised by women (as shoppers for their families), provides a means of political expression for those who have often found themselves excluded from more traditional forms of political participation.[47] However, from a republican perspective, one has to call into question the credentials of political consumerism as far as democratic equality is concerned. If representative democracy is supposed to be one person, one vote, then the marketplace, where the rich have more votes, can hardly be seen as democratic.[48] Political consumerism may include women but it may well end up being principally well-off and well-educated middle-class women who are enfranchised.

To what extent does this argument from democratic equality—central to modern republicanism[49]—sound the death knell for arguments about ecological consumerism as a form of political, citizenship practice? My claim is not that consumerism can act as a replacement for representative democratic institutions, but that it can act as a site for practising and inculcating citizenship *virtues*—an idea also central to republicanism.[50] The market is often seen as something that necessarily undermines citizenship. As Marquand states:

> The soil in which citizenship grows often becomes barren. And one of the more insidious threats to its fertility is the possessive hedonism which lies at the heart of the free-market model of man and society and perhaps the liberal-individualist conception of citizenship itself.[51]

However, the market need not necessarily be undermining of citizenship. In making trade-offs between self-interest and the interests of others in purchasing goods and services, the consumer is acting in a citizenly manner which will stand her in good stead for reaching the similar sorts of accommodation and trade-off that are needed in the more conventional political process. Inequality of access for practising these virtues matters of course, but it arguably matters less than with formal political processes, and in any event, one might argue that the well-off have always benefited from better access to virtue-supporting associational life within civil society.

The tendency in the literature on civic virtue is to see civil society as a place where virtue is inculcated for service in the public sphere.[52] However, what I am arguing

[46] Micheletti et al, n 42 above, xii–xiii.

[47] M. Micheletti, 'Why More Women? Issues of Gender and Political Consumerism' in Micheletti et al, n 42 above, 251. However, cf feminists such as MacGregor, who have criticised the notion of ecological duty on the basis that it is likely to be a duty unequally borne by women (S. MacGregor, 'No Sustainability Without Justice' in Dobson and Bell (eds) n 45 above, 116–117).

[48] D. Stolle and M. Hooghe, 'Consumers as Political Participants? Shifts in Political Action Repertoires in Western Societies', in Micheletti et al, n 42 above, 284.

[49] See eg C. Sunstein, 'Beyond the Republican Revival' (1988) 97 Yale LJ 1539, 1541.

[50] See further Barry, n 45 above. See also Barry, n 41 above.

[51] D. Marquand, *The New Reckoning: Capitalism, States, and Citizens* (Oxford: Polity, 1997) 47, cited by Barry, n 45 above, 26.

[52] W. Kymlicka, *Contemporary Political Philosophy: An Introduction* (2nd edn, Oxford: OUP, 2002) 304–306.

for is essentially the opposite—in other words that civic virtue (literally, according to Dagger, a disposition to further the public over the private good)[53] practised by citizens in the public sphere can and should also be practised in the private sphere.

One might also point to consumerism's incompatibility with republicanism in the sense that the market simply aggregates preferences untested instead of subjecting them to prior scrutiny and debate whereby they might be changed.[54] However, in this respect, the act of voting and the act of shopping are not that dissimilar: one can just as easily go into the voting booth with one's preferences untested.[55] What is important is the need for citizens to engage with debate in the public sphere—debate one finds today not just in relation to conventional politics, but also in relation to consumer politics. Indeed, debates around the latter (consider, for example, recent issues such as food miles and fair trade) are often more prominent than the former.

Next, market-based consumer purchasing (and, typically also its associated informational labelling regimes) is of course *voluntary* rather than legally compulsory in nature. In the *Sodemare* case, Advocate General Fennelly defined solidarity in his Opinion as the 'inherently uncommercial act of *involuntary* subsidization of one social group by another.'[56] However, this—like a number of the other issues under discussion—is arguably an example of the is/ought problem: just because many people are used to conceiving of solidarity in terms of compulsory tax or insurance-based welfare systems, does not mean that solidarity cannot have a place outside of this context. One can be under a civic duty without this being inscribed in a system of *legal* regulation or compulsion. Only if too many people fail to act in accordance with their civic duties and free-ride need solidarity be legally institutionalized. In addition, one might argue that, where solidarity is legally obligated, this is in fact a weaker example of the term. An example of this argument, which arguably goes too far to the other extreme, is provided by Bayertz who states that 'terming what is coerced from the taxpayer under the threat of authoritative measures "solidarity" amounts to no less than a euphemism.'[57]

Another potential problem in arguing for ecological consumerism as an example of solidarity and citizenship practice is that both solidarity and citizenship are often considered to require a degree of *reciprocity* based on a form of social contract.[58] With solidarity, it has been argued that reciprocity is an important element, which separates it from notions of charity or altruistic help.[59] For that

[53] R. Dagger, *Civic Virtues: Rights, Citizenship and Republican Liberalism* (Oxford: OUP, 1997) 14.

[54] M. Sagoff, n 40 above, 10–11.

[55] R. Dagger, n 53 above, 105. This is what Dagger (104–108) refers to as the 'citizen as consumer' (as opposed to the premise of this chapter, which is the 'consumer as citizen').

[56] Case C-70/95 *Sodemare v Regione Lombardia* [1997] ECR I-3395 [29], emphasis added.

[57] K. Bayertz, 'Four Uses of "Solidarity"' in K. Bayertz (ed) *Solidarity* (Dordrecht: Kluwer, 1999) 24.

[58] Dobson, n 33 above, 44–45.

[59] H. Thome, 'Solidarity: Theoretical Perspectives for Empirical Research', in Bayertz (ed) n 57 above, 126.

reason, it has been claimed that it is inappropriate to speak of solidarity with future generations, because no such reciprocity is possible.[60] One might make a similar point about ecological consumerism motivated, not by concern for future generations, but by concern for environmental harm to current humans elsewhere with whom one does not stand in a formal, reciprocal, citizenship relationship. If there is no reciprocity there either, can there be solidarity in that context?

Thus, with both liberal and republican versions of citizenship, the suggestion is that it is only proper to speak of citizenship rights in the context of reciprocal citizen duties owed towards the state. Under such theories, it becomes problematic to conceive of the sort of 'unreciprocated and unilateral'[61] obligations involved in ecological consumerism amounting to *political* obligations of *citizenship* as such rather than moral obligations or supererogatory action of a charitable or humanitarian type which might be owed or practised globally.[62]

One possible republican response might be to argue that a specific, unilateral ecological *civic* duty (as opposed to a moral one or lesser, supererogatory practice) can be grounded in the duty of citizens of the republic to maintain it. In the Victorian era up until the 1950s in the UK, this often translated into a sense of civic pride and duty in the maintenance of the public environment—both in terms of the collective provision of grand civic buildings and also the individual's duty to maintain domestic front gardens, pick up litter and so on.[63] In more recent times, this duty might be recast as one of maintaining a functioning ecosystem on which the survival of the republic and its future generations depends.[64] In an interdependent world, this of course means paying attention not only to the effects of one's consumption decisions on the territory of one's own particular political community or republic, but also to global effects. However, the obvious limitation of such an approach is that a civic duty would appear to lie only where such global effects would impact on one's own republic, as in the case of global warming. If consumption would simply lead to the degradation of a foreign republic's environment with no knock-on effects for one's own, then there would be no such duty. For that reason, the republic-maintenance approach cannot be considered an entirely satisfactory one for present purposes.

Another, more convincing response to the unilateral duty question is the one offered by Dobson. He argues that while reciprocity is too demanding and thus an unnecessary condition for citizenship obligations, moral[65] commitments are

[60] A. Wildt, 'Solidarity: Its History and Contemporary Definition', in Bayertz (ed) n 57 above, 217.

[61] Dobson, n 33 above, 47.

[62] See eg Miller, a nationalist republican who argues in favour of moral international duties of justice, but against seeing these in terms of citizenship (D. Miller, *Citizenship and National Identity* (Cambridge: Polity, 2000) 81.)

[63] Although often with less care for the natural environment.

[64] On maintenance of the republic, see further J. Barry and K. Smith, 'Civic Republicanism and Green Politics' in D. Leighton and S. White (eds) *Building a Citizen Society: The Emerging Politics of Republican Democracy* (London: Lawrence and Wishart, 2008).

[65] And *a fortiori*, lesser supererogatory actions.

insufficient.[66] However, he argues that it is the notion of causal responsibility for injustice which renders an obligation a political one of citizenship rather than a moral one.[67] With charity, even assuming one has a moral duty to give,[68] if I walk on by, I have not positively caused the relevant harm myself, merely omitted to prevent it; with environmental harm caused as a result of my consumption behaviour, in contrast, I am actively causing harm and therefore I am under a citizenship duty to prevent it. What marks out a duty as a citizenship as opposed to simply a moral one is, therefore, a sense of causal responsibility. Of course, the line between the two will not always be easy to draw. Giving aid personally after a tsunami on the other side of the world may only be seen as, at best, a moral obligation rather than a citizenship one in Dobson's terms, as I can in no sense be said to have caused the tsunami. However, what if I give aid to the victims of severe floods in a country from the South? Does this move across from potential moral obligation to a stronger solidarity-based, citizenship obligation because my consumption lifestyle may have caused climate change involving an increased likelihood of violent weather patterns? Dobson implies that the causal relationship need only be plausible in a precautionary sense—as in this scenario—for citizenship duties to become engaged.[69] There would thus be no need to establish something like the civil standard of proof in terms of the balance of probabilities.

While Dobson characterizes his approach as post-cosmopolitan,[70] my claim here is that it can just as easily be viewed in republican terms. Central to republicanism is the idea of supporting freedom as non-domination.[71] Where pollution harms or threatens to harm others, a relationship of dominance exists[72] and the state and individuals are thus under a political duty to prevent it.[73] Unlike the republic-maintenance approach, this has the advantage of supporting a fully global approach to civic duty. The potentially controversial step here is, however, to argue that individuals and not just their states are subject to civic duties to prevent domination.[74] However, within the literature on justice, Cohen has argued that, contra Rawls, duties of justice are owed not only by the basic structure

[66] Dobson, n 33 above, 125.

[67] ibid 48–49; 125.

[68] Which some would contest.

[69] A. Dobson, 'Thick Cosmopolitanism' (2006) 54 Political Studies 165, 174.

[70] Because based on material reality as opposed to cosmopolitan idealism—see eg Dobson, n 33 above, 99, 110, 114.

[71] P. Pettit, *Republicanism: A Theory of Freedom and Government* (Oxford: OUP, 1999).

[72] S. Slaughter, 'The Republican State: An Alternative Foundation for Global Environmental Governance' in J. Barry and R. Eckersley (eds) *The State and the Global Ecological Crisis* (Cambridge, Massachusetts: MIT Press, 2005).

[73] Another route would be to argue, as Miller does, that states have a duty to respect the self-determination of other states and that to degrade those states' environments is to fail to fulfil such a duty (D. Miller, *On Nationality* (Oxford: Clarendon, 1995), 103–104).

[74] For a similar, implicit, criticism of Dobson's approach, see T. Hayward, 'Ecological Citizenship: Justice, Rights and the Virtue of Resourcefulness' (2006) 15 Environmental Politics 435, 441. This step would also be needed to apply Miller's approach (n 73 above) here as an alternative, and would not necessarily be one he would endorse.

of society (namely the state), but also by individuals when making legally unconstrained choices within that structure.[75] While Pogge's critique of Cohen's monism[76]—based, inter alia, on the difficulty of assessing the limits of an individual's duties and their incompatibility with other important values such as individual autonomy—is well made,[77] it arguably applies with less force in the context of duties which appear to have more in common with corrective justice (in terms of avoiding harm and domination in the form of bads) than of Rawlsian distributive justice (which focuses principally on the distribution of primary goods, including income and wealth).[78] A personal duty to sacrifice one's life plan in order to achieve a just arrangement of benefits may appear to go too far; however, a personal duty to restrain from behaviour that can be seen as causing harm to others does not appear so far-fetched.

This leads on to a further possible issue of concern, which is again a common feature of solidarity and citizenship, and that relates to the territorial scope of the relevant solidarity and citizenship community. For republicans, citizenship and solidarity are typically regarded as territorially bounded. On this view, one cannot be solidaristic to everyone; and similarly, citizenship rights and duties are not universal in scope but are, rather, limited to members of a particular, territorially-defined, community. There is a strong link with the notion of identity here. Membership, as a citizen, of a solidarity community, rests on shared historical and cultural ties and thus on a common cultural identity. One is (and should be) more likely to offer solidaristic support to those with whom one has common ties and who are fellow members of one's community. And such ties are of course predominantly found within the nation state.[79] One might—as advocates of constitutional patriotism do—seek to argue for the possibility of a common, civic European identity providing an appropriate platform for membership as European citizens within an associated European civic solidarity community. Indeed, elements of the Court of Justice's case law on free movement and solidarity could be said to implicitly stand for such a claim.[80] However,

[75] G. A. Cohen, 'Where the Action Is: On the Side of Distributive Justice' (1997) 26 Philosophy and Public Affairs 3.

[76] As opposed to Rawls' dualism, which argues for a separation between the duties of justice owed by the basic structure and the choices of individuals.

[77] T. Pogge, 'On the Site of Distributive Justice: Reflections on Cohen and Murphy' (2000) 29 Philosophy and Public Affairs 137.

[78] One may argue (see eg D. Miller, 'Social Justice and Environmental Goods' in A. Dobson (ed) *Fairness and Futurity* (Oxford: OUP, 1999)), that environmental goods can and should be added to Rawls' list of primary *goods*, or (eg D. Bell, 'Environmental Justice and Rawls' Difference Principle' (2004) 26 Environmental Ethics 287, 291–293) that environmental justice should incorporate both 'bads' and 'goods'. However, I have framed environmental justice here as involving an attempt to avoid the unjust imposition only of *bads*, because this is the extent of the obligation of justice (and indeed solidarity) owed by *individuals* (as opposed to eg states, which may have solidarity obligations in respect of goods too, as we saw at the start with many of the EU policy examples).

[79] Miller, n 62 above, 31–32.

[80] eg the health cases such as Case C-372/04 *Watts v Bedford Primary Care Trust* [2006] ECR I-4325.

many republicans would reject this, arguing that solidarity typically remains state-based and that a federal EU solidarity community does not exist.

To what extent can ecological consumerism be seen as an example of republican citizenship given these typical territorial assumptions? With my republican version of Dobson's justice-based approach to ecological duty described earlier, one would appear to run into difficulties. After all, republicanism does typically presume a bounded political community and my approach to citizenship does not possess one: the harm-based duties are owed not just to those within the confines of one's own narrow political community, but also to others globally and to future generations. Of course, much of this is entangled with notions of reciprocity and mutuality discussed earlier. Connected with that, I would again argue that one should draw a distinction between the just distribution of goods and the just avoidance of domination and harm or bads. While the typical, state-based territorial assumptions of republicanism hold good for the former, my contention is that the latter requires republicans to adopt a broader geographical compass if they are to remain true to the principle of global freedom as non-domination.

Finally, there is the important question of whether the sorts of ecological consumer duties discussed here can rightly be described as ones owed by EU citizens. The answer to this is that such duties are inevitably owed by all citizens whose consumption behaviour has the capacity to cause harm to others—whether at home or abroad. Many citizens from EU member states will fall into this category, as will those in other countries with significant ecological footprints such as the United States. They are thus appropriately characterized as both national and EU citizenship duties, though by no means ones which are unique to the EU.

5. Conclusion

To return to the mainstream Court of Justice case law on solidarity, one thus finds a tension between solidarity and the market citizen. Solidarity is something that the mover within the single market is potentially threatening, either in his home state,[81] or else within the destination state where he may not be entirely welcome. The job the Court seems to have created for itself is to be at the same time both the source of and the balancer of this tension. However, if one then compares this with solidarity in the context of the European ecological citizen consumer, one finds no such tension. There we have a market actor who is able to act perfectly in tune with solidarity. While the market citizen is normally seen as the poor cousin within the EU law family, what one finds if one steps outside the confines of formal EU case law, is that the market citizen can begin to be seen in an altogether more favourable light.

[81] Newdick, n 2 above.

8

Irregular Migrants: Beyond the Limits of Solidarity?

Mark Bell

1. Introduction

In developing its case law on the rights of EU citizens, the Court of Justice has referred to the principle of social solidarity.[1] This principle is invoked to justify why scarce social or economic entitlements should be extended beyond the inner circle of domestic nationals to include those from other member states. There is an assumption that the category of 'Union citizen' binds together nationals of the member states with a reciprocal bundle of rights; all are entitled to travel to any other member state and to receive equal treatment with nationals of the host state. The reciprocal nature of the solidarity principle reflects the fact that whilst the UK must provide equal treatment for French citizens on its territory, similarly France must extend such treatment to UK nationals present in its territory.

The linkage of social solidarity to Union citizenship creates difficulties when the position of third country nationals is considered. They lack the ties of shared citizenship, whilst the extension of social and economic entitlements cannot easily be based on a reciprocal view of solidarity. Apart from international agreements between third countries and the Union, any conferral of rights to third country nationals does not guarantee that EU citizens would be treated in a similar manner if present in the third country. Nevertheless, there has been a gradual trajectory in favour of providing a core set of rights and obligations to third country nationals. The Tampere Agenda of the European Council declared:

The European Union must ensure fair treatment of third country nationals who reside legally on the territory of its Member States. A more vigorous integration

[1] See further C. Barnard, 'Solidarity and new governance in social policy' in G. de Búrca and J. Scott (eds) *Law and new governance in the EU and the US* (Oxford: Hart Publishing, 2006) 153, 170; O. Golynker, 'Student loans: The European concept of social justice according to Bidar' (2006) 31 ELR 390.

policy should aim at granting them rights and obligations comparable to those of EU citizens.[2]

This approach was subsequently given the label of 'civic citizenship'[3] and it is best reflected in the Long-Term Residents Directive.[4] This includes a wide-ranging right to equal treatment in the labour market, education and training, the recognition of qualifications, social protection, tax benefits, access to goods and services and free movement within the territory of the member state.[5] Although the Directive contains numerous limitations, such as significant exceptions to the right to equal treatment,[6] it remains premised on recognition of third country nationals' entitlement to a measure of social solidarity, in the form of equal treatment in key areas of social and economic life.

Looking back to the Tampere principle, it is notable that the European Council carefully circumscribed its commitment; fair treatment of third country nationals would be only for those 'who reside legally on the territory of its Member States'. This is also reflected in the Long-Term Residents Directive, which is limited to those who are legally resident.[7] More broadly, EU immigration policy discourse tends to emphasize a firm dichotomy between legal and irregular migrants.[8] A recent illustration can be found in the Commission's 2008 Communication 'A common immigration policy for Europe: principles, actions and tools'.[9] This echoes the Tampere agenda, calling for 'fair treatment of third country nationals who reside legally on the territory of the Member States', combined with 'stepping up the fight against illegal immigration'.[10]

The exclusion of irregular migrants from the acquisition of rights in EU law conveys a message that solidarity, as expressed in social and economic entitlements, is primarily owed in respect of EU citizens and, subject to limitations, legally resident third country nationals. The placing of irregular migrants outside this circle of solidarity is, on the face of it, unsurprising. By definition, an irregular migrant has no clear authority to be present on Union territory and may face compulsory return to the country of origin. Superficially, it would seem to

[2] Bulletin—EU, 10–1999.

[3] Commission (EC), 'Communication on a Community immigration policy' COM (2000) 757, 22.

[4] Dir 2003/109/EC of 25 November 2003 concerning the status of third country nationals who are long-term residents, [2004] OJ L16/44. This Directive does not apply to the UK, Ireland and Denmark.

[5] ibid Art 11(1).

[6] L. Halleskov, 'The Long-Term Residents Directive: a fulfillment of the Tampere objective of near-equality?' (2005) 7 Eur J of Migration and L 181.

[7] Dir 2003/109/EC, n 4 above, Art 3(1).

[8] Throughout this chapter the term 'irregular migrants' will be used to denote those persons who are present in the EU, but lack legal permission to be resident or where the legality of their residence is unclear. This term is increasingly preferred to 'illegal' immigration which has been criticized for its stigmatizing effects: para 7, Parliamentary Assembly of the Council of Europe, Resolution 1509 (2006) on the human rights of irregular migrants.

[9] COM (2008) 359. [10] ibid 17–18.

follow that those lacking any right to be within the EU cannot complain if they are then denied access to social and economic entitlements. Indeed, states are commonly concerned to ensure such exclusion in order to reduce any incentives for irregular migration.

This chapter suggests that the picture is more complex and that there is a case for reconsidering the extent to which irregular migrants should receive social solidarity. It begins this discussion with an examination of the social reality of irregular migration in Europe. This is followed by an analysis of solidarity principles emerging from international and European human rights instruments and their approach to irregular migrants. The final section turns to consider in more depth EU law and policy on irregular migration and whether there is any evidence of this reflecting the basic solidarity principles which can be found within human rights law.

2. The social situation of irregular migrants in Europe

Any quantification of the scale of irregular migration is inherently uncertain because of the covert nature of the phenomenon.[11] In 2007, the Commission estimated that there were two to eight million irregular migrants in the Union.[12] One indicator of the scale of irregular migration is regularization programmes, which provide an opportunity for irregular migrants to emerge from their clandestine position in society. These have revealed substantial populations in certain member states. During the last two decades, almost four million people were regularized in France, Spain, Italy, Portugal and Greece.[13]

Irregular migration is closely associated with participation in undeclared work.[14] The expansion of the service sector has generated a constant demand for cheap, flexible and mobile labour.[15] Key sectors of the labour market include hotel and catering; entertainment (eg bars, restaurants); domestic

[11] V. Mitsilegas, 'Measuring irregular migration: implications for law, policy and human rights' in B. Bogusz, R. Cholewinski, A. Cygan and E. Szyszczak (eds) *Irregular migrants: theoretical, European and international perspectives* (Leiden: Martinus Nijhoff Publishers, 2004) 29.

[12] Commission (EC), 'Proposal for a Directive providing for sanctions against employers of illegally staying third-country nationals—impact assessment' SEC (2007) 603, 6.

[13] Commission (EC), 'A common immigration policy for Europe', Press release MEMO/08/402, 17 June 2008.

[14] Undeclared work has been defined as 'the paid production and sale of goods and services that are unregistered by, or hidden from the state for tax, benefit and/or labour law purposes but which are legal in all other respects'; C. Williams, 'A critical evaluation of public policy towards undeclared work in the European Union' (2008) 30 J of Eur Integration 273, 274.

[15] C. Sole and S. Parella, 'The labour market and racial discrimination in Spain' (2003) 29 J of Ethnic and Migration Studies 121, 130.

assistance (cleaning, childcare).[16] Indeed, the Commission has acknowledged that 'whole industries' in the EU are dependent on irregular migrants working for low wages in order to maintain international competitiveness.[17] It is also important to recognize a significant gender dimension to the experience of irregular migration. Some types of work which are commonly associated with irregular migrants tend to be performed by more women than men, such as cleaning. In particular, domestic work by irregular migrants is dominated by women; the private context in which this work takes place creates a high vulnerability to exploitation.[18]

It is not difficult to find evidence of the precarious situation faced by irregular migrants. In 2007, Médecins Sans Frontières conducted a survey of 600 seasonal migrant workers in southern Italy, of whom 72 per cent had no residence permit.[19] The situation of the migrants was stark:

- Two-thirds lived in abandoned buildings with no running water, toilet or electricity;
- 53 per cent had no bed;
- 72 per cent had health problems, mostly of a chronic nature;
- 90 per cent had no employment contract.

Although less dramatic, a recent qualitative study in Ireland confirmed the vulnerability of irregular migrants within the workplace. Individuals were denied employment rights, such as holiday pay or overtime, and were threatened by their employers with being deported if they sought to challenge their working conditions.[20] Moreover, illness or injury sparked fear: a fear of losing one's job and a fear of being discovered by the authorities if treatment was sought. Problems in accessing healthcare have also been recorded in research conducted by the Platform for International Cooperation on Undocumented Workers (PICUM). A comparative study of the situation in 11 member states found that irregular migrants faced serious practical and administrative obstacles which often culminated in denial of healthcare.[21] For example, in Amsterdam, a survey of gynaecologists revealed that 33 per cent of pregnant women who were irregular migrants were unable to access a general practitioner.[22]

[16] F. Quassoli, 'Migrants in the Italian underground economy' (1999) 23 Intl J of Urban and Regional Research 212, 221.

[17] Commission (EC), n 12 above, 7.

[18] V. Mantouvalou, 'Servitude and forced labour in the 21st century: the human rights of domestic workers' (2006) 35 ILJ 395, 397.

[19] Médecins Sans Frontières, 'Migrants employed in agriculture in southern Italy continue to work and live in deprivation and unhealthy conditions': <http://www.msf.org/msfinternational/countries/europe/italy/index.cfm> (last visited 15 August 2008).

[20] Migrant Rights Centre Ireland, 'Life in the shadows—an exploration of irregular migration in Ireland' (Dublin: Migrant Rights Centre Ireland, 2007).

[21] PICUM, 'PICUM's main concerns about the fundamental rights of undocumented migrants in Europe in 2006' (Brussels: PICUM, 2006) 9.

[22] ibid.

Although the brief evidence above merely provides a snapshot of the everyday situation of irregular migrants in Europe, it reveals two facts of salience to this chapter. First, irregular migrants are a sizeable group within the population. Given the scale of the phenomenon, realistically not all of these persons will eventually return to their countries of origin, nor could forced removal be effectively applied in respect of the entire group.[23] Indeed, the pattern in many European countries has been to address this social reality through periodic regularization programmes.[24] Secondly, there is evidence that, as a consequence of their residence situation, irregular migrants are vulnerable to exploitation, such as abusive working conditions. This poses the question of how states respond to a group within society that is de facto resident on a long-term basis, albeit without a clear legal status. The evidence of exploitation calls into question whether it is acceptable to place irregular migrants completely outside any notion of social solidarity.

3. Irregular migrants and human rights law

3.1 International human rights instruments

In seeking to explore what element, if any, of solidarity is owed in respect of irregular migrants, international human rights law is a helpful starting point. This makes it clear that states incur certain obligations even in respect of those with no legal entitlement to be present on their territory. The Universal Declaration of Human Rights is arguably premised on a basic notion of *human* solidarity; certain rights are owed to everyone as an inherent part of personhood. Article 1 declares that 'all human beings are born free and equal in dignity and rights', whilst Article 2(1) states 'everyone is entitled to all the rights and freedoms set forth in this Declaration, without distinction of any kind ...'. Subsequent international human rights instruments have also recognized that the fundamental nature of those rights generally presumes their application to all persons.[25] Whilst there may be less debate over applying the right to life or freedom from torture in respect of irregular migrants, difficulties arise when social and economic rights are engaged, such as rights relating to the labour market, education, healthcare or housing. It is evident that the right to non-discrimination, even if it applies to

[23] para 4, Parliamentary Assembly of the Council of Europe, Resolution 1509 (2006) on the human rights of irregular migrants.

[24] Commission (EC), 'Study on the links between legal and illegal migration' COM (2004) 412, 10.

[25] For an overview, see R. Cholewinski, *Irregular migrants: access to minimum social rights* (Strasbourg: Council of Europe Publishing, 2005); D. Weissbrodt, 'The protection of non-citizens in international human rights law' in R. Cholewinski, R. Perruchoud and E. MacDonald (eds) *International migration law—developing paradigms and key challenges* (The Hague: TMC Asser Press, 2007) 221.

'everyone', has not been assumed to require states to open their labour markets to any person who happens to find themselves on national territory. The right to non-discrimination in the International Convention on the Elimination of All Forms of Racial Discrimination is subject to the proviso that: 'this Convention shall not apply to distinctions, exclusions, restrictions or preferences made by a State Party to this Convention between citizens and non-citizens.'[26] In recent years, the UN Committee on the Elimination of Racism has argued that this proviso cannot be taken as a carte blanche for any differential treatment of non-citizens.[27] Noting that irregular migrants are one of the main groups subject to contemporary forms of xenophobia, it has recommended that differences in treatment based on immigration status must be objectively justified by reference to a legitimate aim and proportionality.[28]

The International Convention on the Protection of the Rights of All Migrant Workers and Members of their Families is the main international human rights document which attempts to provide a roadmap for states on those social rights which should be available for all migrants, whether regular or irregular.[29] It presents a package of law and policy, seeking to balance rights for irregular migrants with measures which seek to promote lawful migration and diminish irregular migration. As regards employment, the Convention provides that irregular migrants should have equal treatment with national workers in respect of:

- remuneration;
- conditions of work (working time, rest periods, paid holidays, health and safety, protection from termination);
- terms of employment (minimum working age);
- the right to join and participate in trade unions.[30]

In essence, the Convention endeavours to sever immigration law issues from labour law issues. It does not confer any rights of entry or residence for irregular migrants, but it requires that those who are present and active in the labour market be able to receive equal treatment in the areas listed above. In order that these rights are not rendered meaningless, states must ensure that 'employers shall not be relieved of any legal or contractual obligations, nor shall their obligations be limited in any manner by reason of any such irregularity'.[31] The employer-employee relationship in labour law is thus separated from the relationship between the migrant and the state in respect of immigration law.

Although the Convention is in force since 2003, it has been neither ratified by any EU member state, nor does there seem any imminent prospect of a change

[26] Art 1(2).
[27] General recommendation no 30: discrimination against non-citizens, 1 October 2004.
[28] ibid para (4).
[29] The Convention entered into force on 1 July 2003. Available at: <http://www2.ohchr.org/english/law/cmw.htm> (last visited 15 August 2008).
[30] Arts 25 and 26. [31] Art 25(3).

in outlook. MacDonald and Cholewinski note that states increasingly cite the role of the EU as an obstacle to ratification.[32] Whilst EU law generally sets minimum requirements and hence does not prevent states adhering to more generous international standards, a perception has emerged that the extent of European integration in the immigration policy field would now jar with any individual state unilaterally proceeding to ratification. The Convention is not, though, the only international instrument which legitimizes the view that irregular migrants are entitled to basic labour law protections. International Labour Organisation (ILO) Convention No 143 on migrant workers starts from the premise that each state party 'undertakes to respect the basic human rights of all migrant workers'.[33] In respect of those workers who entered irregularly and who cannot be regularized, the Convention requires 'equality of treatment for himself and his family in respect of rights arising out of past employment as regards remuneration, social security and other benefits'.[34] Such workers must also have the possibility to raise a dispute about their employment rights before a competent institution, either themselves or through a representative.[35] Although the obligations are more modest than the UN Migrant Workers Convention, only five EU member states have ratified this Convention (Cyprus, Italy, Portugal, Slovenia and Sweden).

3.2 European human rights instruments

Given the reluctance to accept international human rights instruments relating to irregular migrants, greater influence is likely to be exerted by the Council of Europe's human rights instruments, which have been ratified by all EU member states.

3.2.1 The European Convention on Human Rights

The European Convention on Human Rights (ECHR) follows the premise of universality found in other international human rights instruments. Therefore, its rights can be invoked by irregular migrants present within the territory of a contracting state. The largest body of case law relating to irregular migrants concerns residence rights, typically situations where an irregular migrant is contesting a national decision to remove her to a third country. In this area, the ECHR seems increasingly willing to accept that rights to private and family life under Article 8 ECHR can translate, in some circumstances, into an obligation to

[32] E. MacDonald and R. Cholewinski, 'The Migrant Workers Convention in Europe—obstacles to the ratification of the international convention on the protection of the rights of all migrant workers and members of their families: EU/EEA perspectives' (Paris: UNESCO, 2007) 68–69.

[33] Art 1, Convention concerning migrations in abusive conditions and the promotion of equality of opportunity and treatment of migrant workers, No 143 (1975).

[34] ibid Art 9(1). [35] ibid Art 9(2).

provide residence rights to irregular migrants.[36] There has been less opportunity for the Court to consider the extent to which irregular migrants may be entitled to fundamental social rights. A glimpse of the Court's outlook is provided in *Siliadin v France*.[37] The case concerned an irregular migrant performing domestic work in highly abusive conditions. From the age of 15, she worked for almost two years without pay doing housework and caring for the family's children. She had no room, simply a mattress on the floor of the children's bedroom. Given her fear of arrest by the police if she were to challenge her working conditions, the Court held that she had, in practice, no 'free will' but was compelled to accept the abusive conditions creating a situation of servitude.[38] The Court found that the applicable French legislation did not provide 'practical and effective protection' against servitude and consequently there was a breach of Article 4 ECHR. This decision provides a clear indication that states cannot adopt an attitude of indifference in respect of the treatment of irregular migrants in the labour market. The fact that such individuals may have infringed national immigration legislation does not remove from the state any duty to provide protection against extreme forms of exploitation. Whilst the Court seemed particularly influenced by the fact that the individual concerned was a minor when she first arrived in France, the judgment may be read as recognizing a minimum bond of social solidarity with irregular migrants, insofar as the state has a positive duty to protect all persons from ending up in a situation of servitude.

3.2.2 The European Social Charter

The European Social Charter (ESC) is much more detailed than the ECHR in its approach to social rights in areas such as the labour market, education, housing and healthcare. Yet, its application to irregular migrants seemed to be excluded by the limitation on its personal scope of application. Paragraph 1 of the Appendix to the 1996 Revised ESC states that its provisions 'include foreigners only in so far as they are nationals of other Parties lawfully resident or working regularly within the territory of the Party concerned'. In other words, the protection of the ESC did not appear to extend to any third country nationals.

In *International Federation of Human Rights Leagues (FIDH) v France*,[39] the complaint concerned changes to French law on access to healthcare in relation to persons not lawfully resident on French territory. The new rules provided that those with less than three months of residence were restricted to emergency healthcare where there was an immediate threat to life. For those with more than three

[36] See further D. Thym, 'Respect for private and family life under Article 8 ECHR in immigration cases: a human right to regularize illegal stay?' (2008) 57 Intl and Comparative LQ 87.

[37] Application No 73316/01, 26 July 2005.

[38] ibid para 119. The Court states that she was 'at the least' a victim of forced labour during the period when she was a minor. See further Mantouvalou, n 18 above, 404.

[39] Complaint No 14/2003, 8 September 2004.

months of residence, a flat-rate charge would be payable in respect of non-hospital treatment and a daily charge for hospital stays.[40] FIDH argued that these restrictions breached Article 13 of the Revised ESC on the right to social and medical assistance, as well as Article 17 on the rights of children and young persons.

The principal barrier to this complaint was the restriction to the personal scope of the Charter. In a striking decision, the European Committee of Social Rights set aside the Charter's express wording in this area. It noted that 'in the circumstances of this particular case' the exclusion of third country nationals 'treads on a right of fundamental importance to the individual since it is concerned with the right to life itself and goes to the very dignity of the human being.'[41] Given the connection between access to healthcare and maintaining human dignity, it held that the denial of medical assistance to 'foreign nationals, within the territory of a State Party, even if they are there illegally, is contrary to the Charter'.[42] Although this decision makes it clear that the Charter can be invoked by irregular migrants, this principle may be limited to those rights that are intimately linked to protecting fundamental human dignity. To date, the Committee has not clarified further which rights that may entail (or exclude).

In 2006, the Parliamentary Assembly called for a clarification of the rights of irregular migrants within Council of Europe instruments.[43] The Committee of Ministers readily acknowledged that irregular migrants were entitled to the civil and political rights contained in the ECHR.[44] Yet, in respect of social and economic rights, it declared that it was 'up to each Member State to adopt specific measures, as appropriate'.[45] The Committee of Ministers expressed its view that 'neither the European Social Charter nor the revised Charter contain provisions relating to irregular migrants'. This position creates an ill-disguised conflict with the approach of the European Committee of Social Rights in *FIDH v France*.

3.2.3 The EU Charter of Fundamental Rights

Any contemporary consideration of human rights standards in the EU obviously needs to address the EU Charter of Fundamental Rights. The Charter commences with an apparent emphasis on the universality of human rights, declaring that 'human dignity is inviolable'.[46] This is reinforced by the regular use in many of its provisions of expressions such as 'everyone' or 'no one'.[47] For example, Article 5(1) states that 'no one shall be held in slavery or servitude'. In the light of *Siliadin v France*, there can be little doubt that such provisions would be interpreted as

[40] ibid para 16. [41] ibid para 30. [42] ibid para 32.

[43] Parliamentary Assembly of the Council of Europe, Resolution 1509 (2006) on the human rights of irregular migrants.

[44] para 2, Reply adopted by the Committee of Ministers on 13 December 2006 at the 983rd meeting of the Ministers' Deputies; CM/AS (2006) Rec 1755, 15 December 2006.

[45] ibid. [46] Art 1; [2007] OJ C303/1.

[47] S. Peers, 'Immigration, asylum and the European Union Charter of Fundamental Rights' (2001) 3 Eur J of Migration and L 141, 146.

applying to irregular migrants. Many of the socio-economic rights found within the Charter are located in Chapter IV, entitled 'Solidarity'. For the most part, this continues the open-ended extension of rights; Article 30, for example, states that 'every worker has the right to protection against unjustified dismissal …'. The only specific restriction is in respect of social security, where rights are limited to 'everyone residing and moving legally within the European Union'.[48] Tensions emerge, though, when Article 15 is examined. This introduces an explicit delineation of rights in relation to work:

2. Every citizen of the Union has the freedom to seek employment, to work, to exercise the right of establishment and to provide services in any Member State.

3. Nationals of third countries who are authorised to work in the territories of the Member States are entitled to working conditions equivalent to those of citizens of the Union.

The second paragraph is an unsurprising reiteration that EU free movement rights remain limited to citizens of the Union. This is confirmed later in the Charter where Article 45(2) states that free movement rights 'may' be granted to nationals of third countries who are 'legally resident' in the Union. Paragraph three is more perplexing as it apparently excludes irregular migrants from the right to equivalent working conditions. Yet it is contradicted by Article 31(1) which states that '*every* worker has the right to working conditions which respect his or her health, safety and dignity' (emphasis added). One way of reconciling these provisions would be to read Article 31(1) as guaranteeing a minimum threshold of basic working conditions required to uphold human dignity, to which irregular migrants are also entitled, whilst working conditions which go beyond this minimum standard are restricted to legal migrants, in accordance with Article 15(3). Although such a reading would be consistent with the text of the Charter, it exposes a significant divergence from the approach of the UN Migrant Workers Convention, which requires equal treatment in working conditions for all migrant workers, whether legal residents or irregular migrants.

3.3 Overview on human rights and solidarity

Taking an overview of the various sources of international and European human rights law, there is no doubt that the principle of solidarity, informed by a universalistic concept of human dignity, extends to include irregular migrants. Where the law remains ambiguous is in respect of how far solidarity and human dignity require states to extend social and economic rights to irregular migrants. *FIDH v France* reflects the view that there are minimum social rights to which irregular migrants are entitled and which cannot be used as a lever to discourage or penalize such migration. Similarly, *Siliadin* implies a positive duty on the state to prevent irregular

[48] Art 34(2).

migrants falling into de facto servitude. Yet whether in the non-ratification of the UN Migrant Workers' Convention or the hedged statements of the Committee of Ministers, there is a marked reluctance amongst European states to make firm commitments to a minimum set of social rights for irregular migrants.

4. EU law and policy on irregular migrants

This section turns to consider in more detail EU law and policy on irregular migrants. In analyzing whether it reflects any semblance of the solidarity principle, it will be relevant to consider whether irregular migrants are recognized as bearers of fundamental human rights and, if so, the extent to which that encompasses any social rights.

4.1 Constructing a policy on irregular migration

Irregular migration became a Community competence by virtue of the amendments to the EC Treaty introduced by the Treaty of Amsterdam 1999. Article 63(3)(b) EC defined the competence in the following terms: 'illegal immigration and illegal residence, including repatriation of illegal residents'.[49] The reference to 'repatriation' indicates from the outset that policy in this field is directed towards combating illegal immigration. Indeed, the reference to 'immigration', rather than 'immigrants', has given rise to an ongoing debate regarding the extent to which the Union has competence to address issues relating to irregular migrants which are not directly connected to their entry or exit.[50] A more rounded outlook was presented in the 1999 Tampere Conclusions:

> The European Council is determined to tackle at its source illegal immigration, especially by combating those who engage in trafficking in human beings and economic exploitation of migrants.... The rights of the victims of such activities shall be secured with special emphasis on the problems of women and children.[51]

In the period since then, an elaborate legislative framework has been constructed on many aspects of immigration and asylum law. Progress in relation to irregular migration has been notably slower.[52] The Commission first set out the main parameters of this policy in a 2001 communication.[53] Despite the balanced sentiment found in the Tampere Conclusions, the agenda reflected in this paper reverted to an overwhelming emphasis on immigration control. The main thrust of the measures suggested aimed at preventing irregular migration through better

[49] Art 63(3)(b) EC is now replaced by similar wording in Art 79(1)(c) TFEU.

[50] See below in the discussion of the Dir on employer sanctions. [51] para 23.

[52] S. Peers, *EU Justice and Home Affairs Law* (2nd edn, Oxford: OUP, 2006) 297.

[53] Commission (EC), 'Communication on a common policy on illegal immigration' COM (2001) 672.

enforcement of border controls. A focus on repression is also evident in the discussion of irregular migrants engaged in employment, where the measures considered are purely in terms of penalizing the employers of irregular migrants.[54]

The orientation towards prevention and repression of irregular migration has continued to dominate much of the subsequent development of this policy field.[55] This is epitomized by the growing focus on compulsory return of irregular migrants to their countries of origin. A Green Paper on returns was published in 2002.[56] The tone of this document is revealing. It refers to the 'problem of refugees' and advances the unproven contention that 'forced returns' are necessary to ensure 'public acceptance' of legal migrants.[57] In 2005, this was taken a step further when the Commission proposed the 'Returns Directive'.[58] The basic philosophy of the proposal is a presumption that all irregular migrants should be returned to their country of origin, voluntarily or forcibly. This is coupled with a ban on re-entering any EU state, which would be applicable for five years.[59] Despite widespread criticism from human rights organizations,[60] the Directive was adopted in December 2008.[61] The Directive is more flexible than the Commission's original proposal. For example, it permits member states to grant residence permits to irregular migrants for 'compassionate, humanitarian or other reasons' (Article 6(4)). Nevertheless, the basic formula in the Directive is compulsory return and the threat of a re-entry ban for up to five years. Moreover, it permits up to 18 months detention prior to forced removal, including for reasons beyond the control of the individual migrant (Article 15).

The preoccupation with return denies the social reality of the scale of irregular migration and the numerous practical obstacles to implementing the forced removal of millions of residents. This was briefly acknowledged in the Commission's 2003 Communication on 'immigration, integration and employment'. This admitted that many irregular migrants could not be returned for 'legal, humanitarian or practical reasons'.[62] Nevertheless, the Commission has since voiced its hostility to 'wide-scale regularisation measures'.[63] This hardening

[54] ibid 23.

[55] eg Commission (EC), 'Communication on the development of a common policy on illegal immigration, smuggling and trafficking of human beings, external borders and the return of illegal residents' COM (2003) 323.

[56] Commission (EC), 'Green paper on a Community return policy on illegal residents' COM (2002) 175.

[57] ibid 8.

[58] Commission (EC), 'Proposal for a Directive on common standards and procedures in Member States for returning illegally staying third-country nationals' COM (2005) 391.

[59] ibid Art 9(1).

[60] See joint letter from Amnesty International and the European Council on Exiles and Refugees (13 May 2008).

[61] European Parliament and Council Directive (EC) 2008/115 on common standards and procedures in Member States for returning illegally staying third-country nationals [2008] OJ L348/98.

[62] Commission (EC), 'Communication on immigration, integration and employment' COM (2003) 336, 26.

[63] Commission (EC), 'Study on the links between legal and illegal migration' COM (2004) 412, 17.

of attitudes is evident in contemporary policy developments. In October 2008, the European Council approved the 'European Pact on Immigration and Asylum', which includes a policy commitment from all member states to refrain from any mass regularizations in the future.[64]

What seems to be missing from the existing policy framework is any sustained attention to the fundamental rights of irregular migrants. Where rights-discourse enters into the policy documentation, this is normally in terms of protecting rights during the process of return.[65] There is little evidence of recognition of the social and economic rights of irregular migrants outside of the immigration process. A telling example is the Commission's 2008 Communication on 'a common immigration policy for Europe'.[66] This aims to install new governance mechanisms for the future development of immigration policy, akin to the open method of coordination. Policy would be organized around three pillars: prosperity, solidarity and security. In this context, 'solidarity' is defined purely in terms of solidarity between member states in managing immigration, whereas irregular migrants are dealt with under the 'security' heading. Although this pillar does include reference to securing access for irregular migrants to services that are essential to guaranteeing fundamental rights,[67] the prime emphasis is on controlling and repressing irregular migration.

4.2 Sanctioning employers of irregular migrants

In 2009, a Directive was adopted on sanctioning employers of 'illegally staying third-country nationals'.[68] This offers a concrete and contemporary illustration of the extent to which the Union recognizes any legitimate claim to minimum social rights by irregular migrants. The Directive's underpinning goal is combating irregular migration by suppressing the participation of irregular migrants in undeclared work. Member states are required to prohibit the employment of irregular migrants and to impose financial penalties on any employer in breach of this provision. Such employment must be punishable as a criminal offence in any of the following circumstances:

- where the offence is repeated;
- where it involves simultaneous employment of a significant number of irregular migrants;
- where it is accompanied by 'particularly exploitative working conditions';
- where the employer knows that the employee is a victim of trafficking;
- where the infringement involves illegal employment of a minor.[69]

[64] Council, 'European Pact on Immigration and Asylum' 13440/08 ASIM 72, 24 September 2008, 7.
[65] Commission (EC), n 55 above, 10. [66] COM (2008) 359. [67] ibid 13.
[68] European Parliament and Council Directive (EC) 2009/52 providing for minimum standards on sanctions and measures against employers of illegally staying third-country nationals [2009] OJ L168/24.
[69] Art 9.

The counterpart to the repressive dimension to the Directive is a small, yet significant, step in the direction of recognizing that the irregular migrants affected enjoy certain minimum rights in respect of the period of employment completed. Article 6 requires the employer to pay any outstanding remuneration to the irregular migrant. If the employer's activities constituted a criminal offence, and if the migrant cooperates in proceedings against the employer, then a limited-duration residence permit may be granted for the duration of these proceedings (Article 13(4)). Finally, procedures shall be established to enable irregular migrants to lodge complaints against their employers via third parties such as trade unions (Article 13(1)). These third parties may engage 'on behalf of or in support of' an irregular migrant in proceedings related to the implementation of the Directive (Article 13(2)).

Whilst the Directive marks a shift away from the exclusive focus on the immigration law situation of irregular migrants, it falls short of the standards found in the UN Migrant Workers Convention or ILO Convention No 143. The Directive focuses exclusively on remuneration issues, whereas the international instruments recognize irregular migrants as having an entitlement to a broader range of labour law protections. Fundamentally, the Directive continues to intertwine labour law issues with immigration law issues, with the result that the latter overwhelms the former. When the Employer Sanctions Directive is combined with the Returns Directive, the likely consequence for an irregular migrant who exposes mistreatment at work will be removal from the member state. Even in the more extreme instances of exploitative working conditions, the Employer Sanctions Directive only promises a time-limited residence permit which will expire once the migrant's participation in the prosecution of the employer is complete. It is difficult to escape the impression that the irregular migrant is being treated in an instrumental fashion; her presence will be tolerated only so long as it is directly valuable for the law enforcement authorities.

A coalition of trade unions and European NGOs has argued that the vulnerability of irregular migrants to abusive working conditions can only be effectively addressed by disentangling labour law from immigration law.[70] The ILO Committee of Experts has identified labour inspectorates as having the potential to play a constructive role,[71] not least because they generally enjoy the right to enter workplaces without prior warning. They have, though, warned that this depends on confining the role of labour inspectors to the enforcement of labour law. The confidence of irregular migrants to bring complaints to labour

[70] para 5, ETUC, PICUM and Solidar, 'Joint comments of ETUC, PICUM and Solidar on expected Commission proposals to fight "illegal" employment and exploitative working conditions', 26 April 2007.

[71] See further PICUM, 'PICUM's comments on the communication from the Commission on "Policy priorities in the fight against illegal immigration of third-country nationals" COM (2006) 402', 12 February 2007, 6.

inspectorates is undermined in some EU states where such bodies are under a subsequent duty to report such individuals to the immigration authorities.[72]

5. Conclusions

The overall trajectory of EU law and policy on irregular migration has been towards repression; an immigration control agenda is dominant.[73] The Commission has repeatedly contended that the public will only accept the integration of legally resident third country nationals if they are convinced that a robust approach has been adopted in respect of irregular migrants.[74] This has been reduced to an unswerving commitment to return as the cornerstone of the policy, combined, more recently, with an extinguishing of the possibility for regularization. One of the effects of this outlook has been to treat irregular migrants as mere objects of immigration policy; undesirables who must be physically removed from EU territory. There is limited recognition of irregular migrants as individuals entitled to protection of their fundamental human rights. Moreover, the focus on immigration control overshadows and compromises measures designed to combat the exploitation of irregular migrants.

International human rights instruments provide a different perspective on irregular migrants. Without suggesting that border controls should be abandoned, there is recognition that irregular migrants are entitled to a minimum level of protection from the state, which should be ensured irrespective of immigration control issues. Whilst the language of solidarity is typically not expressly found in such instruments, the underpinning principle of human dignity implies that a degree of solidarity can be claimed by everyone. In respect of social and economic rights, there is little consensus on the extent of the obligations which flow from the basic concept of human dignity. Nevertheless, benchmarks can be found, such as the UN Migrant Workers' Convention or European human rights case law. If the EU is to provide a fairer reflection of the legitimate claims to basic social solidarity from irregular migrants, then law and policy need to be rebuilt, beginning with a foundation of fundamental human rights.

[72] ibid.

[73] Cholewinski, n 25 above, 20.

[74] eg in the following Commission documents: 'Green paper on a Community return policy on illegal residents' COM (2002) 175, 8; 'Communication on policy priorities in the fight against illegal immigration of third-country nationals' COM (2006) 402, 10.

9

A Certain Degree of Solidarity? Free Movement of Persons and Access to Social Protection in the Case Law of the European Court of Justice

*Stefano Giubboni**

1. Introduction

When the rules on the citizenship of the Union appeared in the Maastricht Treaty, most commentators received them very lukewarmly. The European citizenship was built as a complementary institution and a mere addition to national citizenship—as unnecessarily specified by Article 2 of the Amsterdam Treaty. Even the most well-disposed observers saw it as a simple consolidation of subjective legal positions, which were already recognized by Community legislation. Most of them saw Union citizenship as a status summarizing rights that already existed in the system, even though with little practical relevance; and few were confident that this status could strengthen the dimmed legitimacy of Community institutions, even though only symbolically, as was the intention of the revisers of the treaties.[1]

The criticism most frequently made of the notion of citizenship of the Union is that it could not free itself of its mercantile legacy and of the 'market citizen' model that has always dominated the Community construction.[2] The citizenship

* University of Perugia and URGE—Unità di Ricerca sulla Governance Europea, Collegio Carlo Alberto, Moncalieri (Turin). This chapter is based on a presentation given at the Sussex Law School MLR sponsored workshop on 'Seeking Solidarity in the European Union—Towards Social Citizenship and a European Welfare State'. I am very grateful to all participants, and particularly to Malcolm Ross and Charlotte O'Brien, for their useful discussion and suggestions. The usual disclaimer applies.

[1] See eg J. H. H. Weiler, 'European Citizenship and Human Rights', in A. Winter (ed) *Reforming the Treaty on the European Union—The Legal Debate* (The Hague, London, Boston: Kluwer, 1997) 57.

[2] See *ex plurimis* M. Everson, 'The Legacy of the Market Citizen', in J. Shaw, G. More (eds) *New Legal Dynamics of European Integration* (Oxford: Clarendon Press, 1995); and for a

of the Union was weakened since its inception on the very grounds that should have been its strength. It was deprived, in fact, of true political meaning and content, thus ending up reaffirming the central position of the paradigm of the economic player, the 'market citizen', without even promising an authentic universalization of the freedom of movement and residence within member states. And even though the European Commission tried to instil some optimism about its potential,[3] only few believed that the limitations posed by secondary legislation—as expressly reaffirmed by the Treaty[4]—could make it possible to overcome the traditional and clear-cut functional demarcations (between economically active and inactive individuals) for accessing free movement and related-rights in the host state.

Today, if we look retrospectively at the powerful interpretative innovations that have been introduced by the Court of Justice's case law since the end of the 1990s, it is hard to understand why the potential of Articles 17 and 18 of the EC Treaty (now Articles 20 and 21 of the Treaty on the Functioning of the European Union—TFEU) was so underestimated. By now, the Court of Justice has accustomed us to its role of 'judge-as-artist', a moulder of a truly European social dimension, which can open '*des horizons meilleurs aux citoyens, sans tourner les dos au rèalités et aux situations concretes*',[5] as Advocate General Ruiz-Jarabo Colomer has recently written. In fact, it is now difficult to account for the amount of caution and scepticism expressed when the rules on citizenship of the Union were read for the first time.[6]

Beyond any reasonable expectation, the Court of Justice upheld the views of those (few, to be honest) who believed that the capacity for institutional self- regeneration and change were implicit in those weak provisions.[7] The transformative potential of the institution that was cautiously designed by these rules was perceived to be marginal at the beginning of the 1990s, but then took centre stage later. Now, one can well argue that the 'European citizenship constitutes a unique experiment for stretching social and political bonds beyond national boundaries'.[8]

Thus, since the Court recognized the citizenship of the Union as a 'fundamental status of nationals of the Member States, enabling those who find

retrospective insight, M. Bell, 'Civic Citizenship and Migrant Integration' (2007) 13 Eur Public L 311, especially 313.

[3] See for instance Commission (EC), 'Second Commission report on citizenship of the Union' COM (1997) especially 15.

[4] See current Article 18(1) of the EC Treaty.

[5] Opinion delivered on 20 March 2007 in Joined Cases C-11/06 and C-12/06 *Rhiannon Morgan v Bezirksregierung Köln and Iris Bucher v Landrat des Kreises Düren* [2007] ECR I-9161, point 1.

[6] The author of this chapter did not refrain from an exercise of critical reading either. See S. Giubboni, 'Libertà di circolazione e protezione sociale nell'Unione europea' (1998) Giornale di Diritto del Lavoro e di Relazioni Industriali 81.

[7] See for this terminology D. Kostakopoulou, 'Ideas, Norms and European Citizenship. Explaining Institutional Change' (2005) 68 MLR 233.

[8] See again D. Kostakopoulou, 'European Citizenship: Writing the Future' (2007) 13 Eu LJ 623 especially 624.

themselves in the same situation to enjoy the same treatment in law irrespective of their nationality, subject to such exceptions as are expressly provided for',[9] the effects of Articles 12 and 18 EC (Articles 18 and 21 TFEU) in the form of cross-border access to social protection systems have expanded to the extent that the traditional boundaries of these systems have been questioned and perhaps irreversibly undermined. The status of citizen of the Union requires, as reaffirmed by the Court in *Grzelczyk*,[10] 'a certain degree of financial solidarity between nationals of a host Member State and nationals of other Member States, particularly if the difficulties which a beneficiary of the right of residence encounters are temporary'.

This chapter intends to reconstruct critically the tortuous course that the Court's case law followed to reach this result. A critical overview of the Court's case law—from the famous *Martínez Sala*[11] decision to the latest judgements—provides food for thought about the spectacular and controversial outcome of a long season of renewed judicial activism. Some commentators have even stated that a new paradigm of social solidarity has at last emerged on a pan-European scale, which has redefined the boundaries of domestic welfare systems and the requirements for belonging to the resulting redistribution communities.[12]

I am not arguing that the Community project was alien to forms of solidarity among member states nationals before the case law reached this turning point. It is fair to recall that at least some of the 'existing accounts of European Union citizenship do not adequately capture its origins and growth', and that 'European rights have political origins'.[13] The rules on the free movement of workers—established in 1968 with a well-known provision in Regulation 1612 on social advantages—rested on the association between free access to labour market and full equality of treatment in host member states in almost all spheres of social and economic life. However, in the last decade, the case law on Articles 12 and 18 EC (now Articles 18 and 21 TFEU) has undoubtedly extended the scope of application of this association between equal treatment and solidarity,[14] far beyond

[9] Case C-184/99 *Rudy Grzelczyk v Centre public d'aide sociale d'Ottignies-Louvain-la-Neuve* [2001] ECR I-06193, para 31.

[10] ibid para 44.

[11] Case C-85/96 *Martínez Sala v Freistaat Bayern* [1988] ECR I-02691.

[12] See eg for a partially critical approach O. Golynker, 'Jobseekers' Rights in the European Union: Challenges of Changing the Paradigm of Social Solidarity' (2005) 30 ELR 111; M. Dougan, E. Spaventa, 'Wish You Weren't Here…'. New Models of Social solidarity in the European Union', in M. Dougan and E. Spaventa (eds) *Social Welfare and EU Law* (Oxford and Portland, Oregon: Hart Publishing, 2005) 181; and for an approach mostly in line with that of the Court, H. Verschueren 'European (Internal) Migration Law as an Instrument for Defining the Boundaries of National Solidarity Systems', (2007) Eur J of Migration and L 307.

[13] W. Maas, 'The Genesis of European Rights' (2005) 43 J of Common Market Studies 1009.

[14] See also Bell, n 2 above, 313 (according to him, the fundamental status of European citizen was shaped 'around twin principles of equality and solidarity'), and in the same vein M. Ross, 'Promoting Solidarity: From Public Services to a European Model of Competition?' (2007) 44 CML Rev 1057, especially 1065.

what could be expected from the wording of Community primary and secondary rules, to include all nationals of the Union simply on account of their sharing this 'fundamental status'. This new paradigm of social solidarity—within the limitations that will be analyzed later in this chapter—is supposed to have an innovative element: inclusiveness. Social solidarity is projected beyond the traditional beneficiaries of the economic freedoms established in the Treaty. For this reason, later in the chapter attention will be devoted to the rights of movement and residence, and the relevant entitlements to social protection recognized by the Court's case law to the persons who do not play, or have ceased to play, an active role on the labour or service market; ie the 'residual' category of Community citizens for whom Directive 90/364/EEC was intended.[15]

This case law, which Community legislators have only partially codified in a revision of the main instruments of secondary legislation in this area,[16] is a source of unresolved interpretative tensions. The relationships between the outcomes of interpretations reached by the Court's case law and the explicit contents of secondary legislation—Directive 2004/38/EC and Regulations 1408/71 and 1612/68 in particular—are far from being clear and final.[17] Above all, the case law of the Luxembourg judges seems to have a strong tendency to go beyond the boundaries of the current EU regulatory framework. The interplay between the role of the Court of Justice and that of European and domestic legislatures generates mounting tension. From this perspective, this case law has a constitutional dimension,[18] anticipating the establishment of a more incisive role to be played by the Court of Justice, together with new paradigms of European social solidarity. And the Court seems resolute to defend the prerogatives afforded to citizens of the Union by the Treaty, much further than Community legislature seems ready to grant.[19] The sensitive issues raised by this interplay will be tackled in the critical reflections at the end of this chapter.

2. Free movement and social protection of economically inactive European citizens

Directive 90/364/EEC[20] introduced for the first time a right of movement and residence for the citizens of the Union who did not benefit from the freedoms established by the founding treaty since they were not, and may not have been, engaged in any economic activity. However, the Directive extended this freedom

[15] See below ss 2–4.

[16] Dir 2004/38/CE and Reg 833/2004. The latter is not yet in force, since the relevant implementation provisions are still missing.

[17] See s 5.

[18] Dougan, 'The Constitutional Dimension to the Case Law on Union Citizenship' (2006) 31 ELR 613.

[19] See s 6.

[20] Today repealed and replaced by Dir 2004/38/EC.

of movement within the European space with extreme caution. Member states were mainly interested in preventing this extension placing undue pressure on their welfare systems. This resulted in the introduction of a strict means requirement— 'a sort of reverse means test (or affluence test)'[21]—making the right of residence of an economically inactive citizen conditional on a dual requirement. On the one hand, the person concerned was required to have sufficient economic resources, especially to avoid becoming a burden for the social assistance of the host member state; and on the other, he/she was required to have insurance fully covering the risk of illness.

This solution had self-evident intrinsic limitations. It institutionalized a glaring disparity of treatment and introduced two different citizenship rights,[22] with very different implications. On the one hand, there was the right of economically active citizens who were fully entitled to access the social protection systems of the member states because of their presumed contribution to the economic life and prosperity of the host country. On the other hand, there was the right of citizens who were not engaged in economic activities and were therefore excluded, on principle, from a cross-border access to the domestic systems of social solidarity. The underlying rationale was more that of 'poor laws' than that of a typical modern social citizenship, to make use of Marshall's categories.[23] The Directive was underpinned by a Victorian ethic which was hardly suited to the new European dimension. In fact, 'a person who is not actively involved in economic life must take care of his or her vital necessities in a manner congruent with taking his or her own responsibility, without enjoying the right to rely on public funds of the State of residence'.[24]

Also, the limits and conditions provided for in the Directive seemed to be reaffirmed and legitimized *ex post* by the restrictive wording in the Maastricht Treaty codifying the rights of movement and residence of European nationals. This is, in fact, the most frequent reading of the formula that expressly excludes the

[21] M. Ferrera, 'Towards an "Open" Social Citizenship? The New Boundaries of Welfare in the European Union', in G. de Búrca (ed) *EU Law and the Welfare State. In Search of Solidarity* (Oxford: OUP, 2005) 11, at 31.

[22] The issue of 'two citizenships' is harshly criticized by J-M. Belorgey, 'La protection sociale dans une union de citoyens' (1998) Droit Social 160.

[23] T. H. Marshall, in his seminal work *Citizenship and Social Class* (1950) pointed out that the system of poor laws reformed by the 1834 law resulted in the poor waiving the fundamental civil right to personal freedom, and in particular the freedom to move within national territory. In practice, this denies the principle of full equality of status on which the uniform recognition of modern citizenship rests. Although I am aware that the comparison with mid-nineteenth century England is way too extreme, a certain similarity with the picture outlined by the 1990 Directive is irrefutable. The status of being poor of a European national accessing social assistance in the host member state authorizes the latter to send him/her back to his/her country of origin. The comparison is convincingly proposed by S. Leibfried, 'Towards a European Welfare State? On Integrating Poverty Regimes into the European Community', in C. Jones (ed) *New Perspectives on the Welfare State in Europe* (London/New York: Routledge, 1993) 145.

[24] C. Tomuschat, in his note commenting the above-mentioned *Martínez Sala* judgment (2000) 37 CML Rev 449, at 455.

limitations and conditions of the treaty or of the provisions adopted to give it the effect contained in Article 18(1) of the EC Treaty (Article 21 TFEU).

The picture that was unfolding at the beginning of the 1990s—resulting from a simple (perhaps too simple) linking of the text of the Directive and the provisions of the Treaty—appeared sufficiently clear. The three Residence Directives 'stood as powerful evidence of a political consensus that residency and equal treatment is a privilege to be enjoyed by those who can afford it, devoid of any concern to confer comparable rights upon those who cannot'.[25] If this is the meaning of the political compromise that was originally wanted and established by the Treaty and Community law, there is no doubt that with a 'radical'[26] reading of the principle of equality upheld in *Martínez Sala*,[27] the ECJ showed its intention to overcome any vaguely Victorian and explicitly mercantile legacy in the newly born citizenship of the Union,[28] and to 'take seriously' the rights that could be extracted from the joint provisions of Articles 12 and 18 EC (now Articles 18 and 21 TFEU).

All the signs of a break with that compromise are present in *Martínez Sala*, which is in fact remembered as the first precedent in the case law under examination here, even though, strictly speaking, the legal situation decided by the Court could favour a more traditional approach to the case and the judgment. The applicant in the main proceedings, Mrs Martínez Sala, was in fact a Spanish citizen who had lived for a long time in the Federal Republic of Germany. The ECJ did not have sufficient information to judge whether the applicant in the main proceedings could qualify as a worker under Regulations 1612/68 and 1408/71 and referred the issues back to the referring court. The Court was called to judge whether Community law, and rules on European citizenship in particular, preclude a member state from requiring that a formal residence entitlement be produced before granting a child-raising allowance (that could be defined as a social advantage). The reply of the Court was positive and was based on the fundamental consideration that a national of the Union legally residing in a host member state can make use of the principle of equal treatment recognized by the Treaty in all the situations that fall within the scope *ratione materiae* of Community law.[29]

The judgment was innovative from two perspectives. Firstly, the Court made it clear that the notion of legal residence, a prerequisite of Article 12 EC (Article 18 TFEU), could be entirely based upon national law (in this case, connected to international obligations of the member state), and not necessarily on Community law itself. In this way the scope of application of the principle of equal treatment under Article 12 EC (Article 18 TFEU) was, at least partly, disconnected from the provisions on the limitation of the freedom of movement

[25] Dougan, n 18 above, 624. [26] Tomuschat, n 24 above, 457. [27] See n 11 above.

[28] See more recently S. Wernicke, 'Au nom de qui? The European Court of Justice between Member States, civil society and Union citizens' (2007) 13 Eur LJ 380 especially 385.

[29] See para 63 of the judgment.

of economically inactive European citizens set by Community secondary law implementing Article 18 of the EC Treaty (21 TFEU). The apparent dependence of Article 12 EC upon Article 18 EC was subtly but powerfully reversed for the first time, since the application of the first rule was not conditional on the Community citizen meeting the requirements of free movement and residence mentioned in the second rule. In this way of reasoning, 'once the construct of lawful residence becomes disjointed from the requirement to meet the conditions to which the right of residence is subjected, the conditional nature of the right to residence under Art.18 becomes neutralized by the right to equal treatment under Art.12'.[30]

Secondly, the Court—here again with some circularity of reasoning—defined the scope of application *ratione materiae* of Community law for the purposes of Article 12 EC (Article 18 TFEU) in a broad manner. It applied, in fact, the provisions of Regulations 1612/68 and 1408/71 to a situation in which they were, strictly speaking, inapplicable. The applicant in the main proceedings could not be qualified (at least directly) as an employed worker on the basis of the elements of the judgment. The Court used a qualifying proceeding of analytical nature, in which the subsumption in the objective scope of application of the Treaty was made dependent on rules of secondary law, and hence on the existence of a Community competence. However, in *Martínez Sala* the identification of the scope of application *ratione materiae* was made separately from that of the determination of the scope of application *ratione personae*. A trend is already clear: the Court exploits any useful connection to Community law for these purposes, even beyond its formal relevance.

Apart from questionable arguments and the criticism received for straining conventional wisdom regarding the relationship between the 1990 Directive and Article 18 EC (Article 21 TFEU),[31] *Martínez Sala* offered a springboard for further strengthening the rights of economically inactive citizens to move freely and to access welfare systems. A new building block was laid by *Baumbast*,[32] in which the Court affirmed that the right to reside within the territory of member states laid down by Article 18 'is conferred directly on every citizen of the Union by a clear and precise provision of the EC Treaty'.[33]

Affirming the direct effect of Article 18 EC provides a final cover to the daring reversal of the interpretative perspective that had begun with *Martínez Sala*. If the right arises directly from the Treaty, Directive 90/364 turned from being an instrument granting the freedom of movement and residence, as it was considered to be on its approval, into one specifying the limitations and conditions of

[30] Golynker, n 12 above, 120.

[31] For recent harsh criticism on the fragility and circularity of the court's reasoning, see also D. Martin (2006) Eur J of Migration and L 231.

[32] Case C-413/99 *Baumbast R. v Secretary of State for the Home Department* [2002] ECR I-07091.

[33] para 84 of the judgment.

the exercise of the right in the terms allowed by the very Article 18(1) EC (Article 21(1) TFEU).[34] The obvious consequence is that 'the application of the limitations and conditions acknowledged in Article 18(1) EC in respect of the exercise of that right of residence is subject to judicial review'[35]—hence, to the review of the Court in the light of the principle of proportionality. And irrespective of the implications that will be investigated later in the chapter, this implies that any limitations and conditions referring to this right 'do not prevent the provisions of Article 18(1) EC from conferring on individuals rights which are enforceable by them and which the national courts must protect'.[36]

The fact that the right afforded by Article 18 of the EC Treaty (now Article 21 TFEU) can be directly invoked before national courts does not make it unconditional. However, the limitations mentioned in Article 18 are to be applied consistently with the general principles of Community law and, especially, with the proportionality principle. Therefore, even though member states can make the residence right of economically inactive European nationals conditional upon the availability of sufficient resources, these people can benefit from the principle of equal treatment provided that they have legally resided in the host country for a certain period of time, or have a residence entitlement.[37] And if these conditions exist, they can benefit from Article 12 EC (Article 18 TFEU) and be also granted a social benefit such as the Belgian minimum subsistence allowance.

The member state, of course, has the power to ascertain whether those who benefit from social assistance continue to meet the requirements to which their right of residence is subject,[38] and even adopt, if applicable, a measure for

[34] cf Dougan, n 18 above, 615. [35] para 86 of the judgment.

[36] ibid. In the case submitted to the Court, the national measure did not pass the proportionality test. Denying the exercise of the right of residence, under the provisions of Dir 90/364, on the basis that Mr Baumbast's medical insurance would not cover emergency treatment given in the host member state, would amount to a disproportionate interference with the exercise of that right. This statement takes into account the fact that, on the one hand, the interested party had sufficient resources for himself and for his family, and that, on the other hand, even after his work activities in the territory of the UK came to an end, he had not become a burden for the public finances of the host member state.

[37] See Case C-456/02 *Michel Trojani v Centre public d'aide sociale de Bruxelles* [2004] ECR I-07573, confirming—inter alia—the irrelevance of the 'Community' or 'national' nature of the residence entitlement for the purposes of invoking the principle of equal treatment in the territory of the member state in which the applicant legally resides. Advocate General Geelhoed, in the Opinion of 19 February 2004, proposed a much more restrictive solution than that held by the Court. He argued that in a legal situation in which it was obvious that the claimant in the main proceedings does not have the sufficient resources required by the Directive, the claimant could not even enforce a right of residence under Art 18 EC (Art 21 TFEU). The interpretation that the Advocate General suggested to the Court is in line with the position of the governments that intervened in the judgment, and contrasts with the relationships between the Treaty and the Directive, as reconstructed by the ECJ for the purposes of applying the principle of equal treatment on the basis of nationality. Mainly in agreement with the judgment see A. P. van Der Mei, 'Union Citizenship and the "De-nationalisation" of the Territorial Welfare State' (2005) Eur J of Migration and L 203.

[38] Mr Trojani, a French national who was given accommodation in a Salvation Army hotel in Brussels, where, in return for the assistance received, he did minor jobs, had approached the Belgian Competent Authorities with a view to obtaining the *minimex*.

removing them from national territory. However, the removal measure cannot disregard the general principles of Community law: it cannot be an automatic response arising from the citizen of the Union accessing social assistance in the host member state.

Likewise, the requirement to have sufficient resources in the member state of residence is also subjected to the proportionality test. In *Chen,*[39] the Court had the opportunity to specify that Directive 90/364 does not include any condition concerning the origin of the sufficient resources required. Therefore, it cannot be required that these resources come from the person concerned, without him/her using the resources ensured by an accompanying family member.[40]

A last important development of the case law pointed out in this chapter is also relevant for the overall strengthening of free movement of economically inactive citizens. Here, I refer to the principle whereby the freedom contained in Article 18 EC (Article 21 TFEU), like the other fundamental freedoms afforded by the Treaty to economically inactive citizens, prohibits direct and indirect discrimination, but also, in principle, non-discriminatory obstacles posed by member states. The Court reached this major result gradually and perhaps in an ambiguous way,[41] but the approach adopted at the very end is strikingly similar to that concerning the bold interpretation of the other fundamental (economic) freedoms of movement. In this case, however, the path might have been fraught with greater difficulties, given the non unconditional nature of the freedom established in Article 18 EC (Article 21 TFEU).

Yet the Court remained consistent with the radical reading that had begun with *Martínez Sala.* In its latest judgments, it showed that it was ready to extend the rule prohibiting non-discriminatory obstacles to the freedom of movement and residence for citizens of the Union who are economically inactive, since they

[39] Case C-200/02 *Kunquian Catherine Zhu and Man Lavette Chen v Secretary of State for the Home Department* [2004] ECR I-09925.

[40] If anything, the case was very controversial from another perspective: Mrs Chen, of Chinese nationality like her husband, had planned the birth of her daughter Catherine in Belfast for the sole purpose of obtaining the Irish nationality for her daughter under the principle of *ius soli* in force in that country. The return to the UK to accompany the newly-born daughter, the holder of the right under Art 18 of the EC Treaty as citizen of the Union, allowed her mother—as objected by the English Government—to bypass the limitations of the British immigration legislation. See critically T. Ackermann (2005) 42 CML Rev 1121, and B. Kunoy, 'A Union of National Citizens: The Origins of the Court's Lack of Avant-gardisme in the *Chen* Case' (2006) 43 CML Rev 179. The fact that the income from the unmarried partner can be used to meet the resource requirement is finally confirmed by the ECJ in Case C-408/03 *Commission v Belgium* [2006] ECR I-02647.

[41] The first explicit suggestion was addressed to the Court by Advocate General Jacobs in his Opinion delivered on 20 November 2003 in Case C-224/02 *Heikki Antero Pusa v Osuuspankkien Keskinäinen Vakuutusythiö* [2004] ECR I-5763 (see para 15 in particular). See F. Jacobs, 'Citizenship of the European Union—A Legal Analysis' (2007) 13 Eur LJ 591, especially 597, and M. Cousins, 'Citizenship, Residence and Social Security' (2007) 32 ELR 386, especially 391; previously see H. Toner, 'Non-discriminatory Obstacles to the Exercise of Treaty Rights—Articles 39, 43, and 18 EC' (2004) 23 Ybk of Eur L 275.

can be applied indiscriminately.[42] The consequence is that citizens of the Union who exercise their rights to free movement under Article 18(1) EC (Article 21 TFEU) not only enjoy ample protection against discriminations on the basis of nationality under Article 12(1) (Article 18 TFEU), but also in principle against 'all measures which *obstruct* the right of Union citizens to move and reside freely in other Member States, or which otherwise constitute an *obstacle* which might deter Union citizens from exercising this general right to free movement must be assessed by reference to Article 18(1) EC'.[43]

3. Free movement and maintenance assistance for students

In the last decade, the case law developments on the position of students within the broader category of economically inactive migrant citizens have been equally intense. The judgments on the rights of cross-border access to forms of income safety-net for students (student grants, maintenance allowances and welfare benefits) are one of the most striking and significant threads of case law surveyed here.[44]

A flurry of disputes has erupted in this area. They enabled the Court to establish principles broadening the scope of solidarity towards European citizens in host member states. Moreover, the ECJ has recently opened new channels enabling the exportation of benefits that are specifically provided to this category of Community migrants and placing direct responsibility on the students' countries of origin. It is worthwhile examining the Court's case law from both perspectives. On the one hand, a summary will be provided of the existing principles on access to specific forms of income safety-net or social protection in the *host member state.* On the other, we will be analyzing the most recent and innovative threads of cases in which Article 18 EC was used to found an obligation to export within the Community the student grants provided by the *state of origin* to its own citizens.

As regards to the first perspective, the Court's case law may seem less innovative today, but only because it has settled down over time. But here again the Court made a break from past interpretation patterns that is no less significant than that of the case law on the above relationships between Directive 90/364

[42] See in particular Case C-192/05 *K. Tas-Hagen and R. A. Tas v Raadskamer WUBO van Pensioen-en Uitkeringsraad* [2006] ECR I-10451, and case C-152/05 *Commission of the European Communities v Federal Republic of Germany*. Arguably, these cases concern legal situations in which the existence of a residence requirement implies obstacles (indirectly) discriminating the freedom of movement of Community citizens. However, although the Advocates General may not have had to, they explicitly assumed the model of non-discriminatory obstacles as their decision model of the legal situations under examination. And the Court essentially endorsed this approach.

[43] Advocate General Kokott in her Opinion in Case *Tas-Hagen*, n 42 above, point 50.

[44] For a comprehensive critical reconstruction of this case law see M. Dougan, 'Fees, Grants, Loans and Dole Cheques: Who Covers the Costs of Migrant Education within the EU?' (2005) 42 CML Rev 943; A. P. van Der Mei, 'EU Law and Education: Promotion of Student Mobility versus Protection of the Education Systems', in M. Dougan and E. Spaventa (eds) *Social Welfare and EU Law* (Oxford/Portland, Oregon: Hart Publishing, 2005) 219.

and Articles 12 EC and 18 EC (now Articles 18 and 21 TFEU). For the sake of simplification, we might say that on the basis of the joint provisions of Articles 12 and 18 of the EC Treaty, the Court made a dual innovation, which had a great impact on secondary law (Directive 93/96, replaced by Directive 2004/38).

First of all, the Court fully extended to students—as citizens of the Union—the right to cross-border access to the social protection benefits that are directly rooted in Articles 12 and 18 of the EC Treaty (Articles 18 and 21 TFEU). The well-known and demanding principle concerning the obligation of 'financial solidarity' between citizens of EU member states that underlies the provisions on the freedom of movement is owed to the already mentioned *Grzelczyk* judgment.[45] And the same judgment contains another specific statement that is equally significant: 'there is nothing in the amended text of the Treaty to suggest that students who are citizens of the Union, when they move to another Member State to study there, lose the rights which the Treaty confers on citizens of the Union'.[46] Once more, this almost tautological statement serves to somehow protect the applicability of the principle of equal treatment under Article 12 EC (Article 18 TFEU) from the strict conditions (abstractly) attached to the right of residence of students in the territory of another member state under Directive 93/96 (see Article 1).

In a case in which a benefit of social citizenship was applied for, such as the Belgian *minimex*,[47] the above statement was also needed by the Court for ruling out the obligation potentially and specifically deriving from the provisions contained in Directive 93/96 (see Article 3) which, like the provisions now contained in Directive 2004/38, expressly exclude students from the right to maintenance aid for studies in the host member state. Indeed, the Court has argued that even if Community law in express terms does not allow students to claim a right to the payment of maintenance allowances or grants on the basis of the Directive, nothing prevents these European citizens from resorting to social assistance benefits in the host member state under the general principle of equal treatment, Article 12 EC (Article 18 TFEU).[48] This reasoning is undoubtedly compelling from a formal standpoint. However, on the one hand, it might result in an unreasonable differentiation between member states (penalizing those countries whose social protection systems guarantee student support).[49] And, on the other hand, it weakens the relevance of the students' exclusion from the right to forms of maintenance in the host country, thus denying the broad meaning that could

[45] See n 9 above. [46] para 35 of the judgment.

[47] The *minimex*, as a social benefit generally guaranteeing a minimum maintenance allowance, cannot technically be defined as assistance, in the strict reading upheld by the Court of Justice according to Reg 1408/71. Nor can it be defined as social security, in the absence of the prerequisites provided for in Art 4(1) of the same Reg. It is however a social advantage under Reg 1612/68: see Case C-249/83 *Hoeckx* [1983] ECR 973.

[48] See in particular para 39 of the judgment.

[49] See Dougan, n 44 above, at 964–965.

have been reasonably inferred by the Directive linking Article 3 with the resource requirement imposed by Article 1.[50]

The Court took then a second extremely innovative step, which nearly deprived Article 3 of the 1993 Directive of its scope. The occasion was provided by a referral for preliminary ruling proposed by the High Court of Justice (England and Wales), Queens Bench Division. In the proceedings under examination, the English authority had refused the application of Mr Dany Bidar, a French citizen enrolled at the University College of London, for a subsidised student loan to cover his maintenance costs, on the grounds that the applicant could not be considered as having settled status in the UK. The referring court asked the ECJ whether this aid could still be considered as excluded from the scope of application of Community law—as inferable from two 1988 judgements (*Lair* and *Brown*),[51] and from the 1993 Directive—or whether the introduction of Article 18 EC had changed the relevant regulatory framework.

In its reply to the High Court of Justice, the ECJ did not hesitate to revert the approach of the two cases mentioned, concluding that the economic aid granted to students to cover their maintenance costs falls within the scope of Community law, with reference to Article 12 EC (Article 18 TFEU).[52] In redefining the scope of application of the Treaty, the Court abandoned almost completely the analytical care that could still be found in previous case law and adopted a highly functional approach. By this standard, nothing can escape from the scope of application of Community law,[53] if it is a matter of affirming the fully useful effect of a fundamental freedom such as that afforded to the citizens of the Union in Article 18 of the EC (Article 21 TFEU) Treaty.[54] A functional approach requires to extend the principle of equal treatment to any right, benefit and service afforded by a member state that may facilitate the exercise of the free movement of people. Therefore, the exercise of the fundamental freedom becomes the key,[55] irrespective of the

[50] See also J.-P. Lhernould, 'L'accès aux prestations sociales des citoyens de l'Union Européenne' (2001) Droit Social 1103 at 1105, arguing that in this passage of the judgment '*le sens de la directive 93/96 est semble-t-il forcé, voire détourné*'.

[51] Judgments of the Court in Cases 39/86 and 197/86 respectively.

[52] See Case C-209/03 *The Queen on the application of Dany Bidar v London Borough of Ealing and Secretary of State for Education and Skills* [2005] ECR I-02119. On the judgment see the comments by C. Barnard (2005) CML Rev 1465; M. Brand (2005/2006) 12(1) Columbia J of Eur L 293; and O. Golynker, 'Students Loans: the European Concept of Social Justice According to Bidar' (2006) 31 ELR 390.

[53] Here again, a trend seems clear towards a broad—even all-embracing—application of the fundamental freedoms within the scope *ratione materiae*. See I. Kvesko, 'Is There Anything Left Outside the Reach of the European Court of Justice?' (2006) Legal Issues of Economic Integration 405.

[54] See the thorough analysis by A. Epiney, 'The Scope of Article 12 EC: Some Remarks on the Influence of European Citizenship' (2007) 13 Eur LJ 611.

[55] While the cross-border element is thinning, or rather evaporating, it is difficult to think of areas outside the potential incidence of fundamental freedoms. See, for instance, the famous judgment of the ECJ, Case C-60/00 *Carpenter v Secretary of State for the Home Department* [2002] ECR I-06289, on free provision of services, especially para 28. See E. Spaventa, 'From Gebhard to Carpenter: Towards a (Non-) Economic European Constitution' (2004) 41 CML Rev 743.

existence of a Community competence and even in the event that the subject matter obviously falls within the domain of member state competence.[56]

In this case, however, not even the express exclusion in Article 3 of the 1993 Directive—meanwhile reproduced and even extended as qualified derogation to the principle of equal treatment for students by Article 24(2) of Directive 2004/38/EC—troubled the reasoning of the Court. In this functional logic, the derogation provided for in Article 3 of the Directive, in fact, was not enough to exclude the disputed benefit from the scope of application of the Treaty: according to it, as the judgment reads:[57]

> it is indeed the case that students who go to another Member State to start or pursue higher education there and enjoy a right of residence there for that purpose under Directive 93/96 cannot base any right to payment of maintenance assistance on that directive.

However, the Court added:

> Article 3 of Directive 93/96 does not preclude a national of a Member State who, by virtue of Article 18 EC and Directive 90/364, is lawfully resident in the territory of another Member State where he intends to start or pursue higher education from relying during that residence on the fundamental principle of equal treatment enshrined in the first paragraph of Article 12 EC.[58]

The inevitable consequence is that a member state is not allowed to refuse citizens of the Union the right to obtain a benefit covering their maintenance costs as students if the citizens legally reside in its territory and have pursued a significant part of their secondary studies in the host country, thus establishing an actual bond with society in that state.

The sophism is self-evident. The distinction between citizens who go to a member state to start or pursue higher education there, and citizens who move to another member state in their 'residual' capacity of beneficiary of Directive 90/364 and intend to pursue these studies only at a later stage is indeed more artificial than the distinction in *Grzelczyk* admitting the student's right to social assistance without touching on the exclusion of the right to maintenance aid. Nevertheless, that was enough for the Court to keep together the provisions of the Treaty and those of the Directive, in a sort of repealing interpretation resulting in the actual abrogation of the interpreted rule.[59]

Most recently, in *Förster*,[60] the Court has however shown to be ready to endorse a line of reasoning which comes quite close to a retreat to a black-letter interpretation

[56] See again Epiney, n 54 above, 615–616. [57] para 45. [58] para 46.

[59] In legal literature there are those who doubt that the present provision of Art 24(2) of the 2004 Directive is incompatible with Arts 12 and 18 EC (now Arts 18 and 21 TFEU), as interpreted by the Court of Justice. The validity of these provisions may however be admissible following the Court's questionable approach and applying the secondary rule consistently with the principle of proportionality. See Dougan, n 44 above, 968–969.

[60] Case C-158/07 *Jacqueline Förster v Hoofddirectie van de Informatie Beheer Groep*. Grand Chamber Judgment of 18 November 2008.

of the relevant secondary legislation. Ms Förster had challenged the refusal by the competent Netherlands authority to grant her financial assistance covering study and maintenance costs ('study finance') in relation to a period during which she was no longer economically active in the host country, on the grounds that she neither retained the status of Community worker nor fulfilled the requirement of lawful residence in the Netherlands for a continuous period of five years. The Court was indeed explicitly invited 'to refine its *Bidar* case law and, in particular, its finding that it is legitimate for a Member State to grant financial assistance only to students who have demonstrated a certain degree of integration into the society of that State'.[61]

Advocate General Mazák delivered an opinion entirely consistent with the *Bidar* approach, concluding that a member state is precluded by Article 12 of the EC Treaty (now Article 18 TFEU), read in conjunction with the principle of proportionality, from denying study finance such as that at issue to an economically inactive student from another member state who had already been lawfully resident for three years if other factors indicate a substantial degree of integration into the society of the host European country. But the Court, although paying lip-service to its previous case law, went swiftly in the opposite direction, stating that, in the case at issue, such a condition of a five years uninterrupted residence is to be considered both appropriate and proportionate to the legitimate objective pursued by the national law. In the scant reasoning of the Court a decisive ground for reaching this conclusion is the very fact that Directive 2004/38, although not applicable *ratione temporis* to the facts in the main proceedings, expressly provides, in the case of non economically active persons, that the host member state is not obliged to grant maintenance assistance for studies, including vocational training, consisting in students' grants or students' loans, to students who have not acquired the right of permanent residence for not having resided in the host country for a continuous period of five years.

The case law discussed so far extends the rights to social protection (broadly speaking) of European students in the host country.[62] The second thread of the ECJ's case law, instead, bases the right to export student aid and grants (from the beneficiary's state of origin) on Article 18 of the EC Treaty (Article 21 TFEU). Here the perspective is somehow inverted. And the same inversion goes for the distribution of the financial costs of student mobility within the Community.[63] And here again, the use of Article 18 EC is no less incisive, nor less creative.

[61] Point 5 of the Opinion delivered on 10 July 2008 by A. G. Mazák.

[62] See also Case C-413/01 *Franca Ninni-Orasche v Bundesminister für Wissenschaft Verkeher und Kunst* [2003] ECR I-13187.

[63] There is no problem of solidarity upon the host member state here, and therefore there is no problem of balancing the interest of this state in avoiding excessive burdens on public finances. These issues are in fact addressed by the Court by modulating the proportionality test to the residence requirements imposed by the country hosting the migrant for the purposes of welfare access. In the case concerned here, in which the social costs of mobility are incumbent upon the state of origin, the issues have to do with containing the public spending resulting for this state from new opportunities of cross-border access to benefits. And connected to this, there are issues of moral hazard and free-riding (for instance, an undue overlapping of benefits) that might arise from benefits exportability in the absence of Community coordination. See S. Borelli, 'Libertà di circolazione e scelta del sistema di protezione

The most alert commentators had anticipated a similar development.[64] The Court did not fall short of expectations and, on the first suitable occasion, it affirmed that Articles 17 and 18 EC (now Articles 20 and 21 TFEU) preclude the requirement that in order to benefit from aid for studies pursued in a member state other than that of the applicant students, 'those studies must be a continuation of education or training pursued for at least one year in the Member State of origin of those students'.[65] A clause requiring residence in the state paying the benefit, or a condition imposing a minimum period of training in that state is an obstacle to the freedom of movement enjoyed by student citizens under Article 18 EC (Article 21 TFEU). This restriction may be justified provided that it is based on objective considerations of general interest that are independent of citizenship and is proportionate to the legitimate aim of the national provisions. But the Court ruled out this hypothesis in this case, since the requirement of national provisions exceeded what was needed to reach their aim.

In the rich and provocative Opinion of Advocate General Ruiz-Jarabo Colomer—in which the creative role of the Court as 'judge artist' was recognized with palpable satisfaction—explicit reference was made to the analogy between the question submitted to the Court and the well-known issue of the right to access medical treatments in another member state under Article 49 of the EC Treaty (now Article 56 TFEU).[66] Moreover, the Advocate General made an argument for qualifying university education as a service provided against remuneration.[67] However, even though he considered the theoretical possibility of applying Article 49 of the EC Treaty (now Article 56 TFEU) to the case in point, he concluded along the lines that the investigation was unnecessary because the information needed was lacking. At any rate, the application of Article 18 of the EC Treaty (now Article 21 TFEU) would have been sufficient, because, from this perspective, it is functionally equivalent to the rule on free movement of services, as recognized by the Court itself.

4. Cross-border access to welfare systems for jobseekers and unemployed

As *Grzelczyk* and *Bidar* marked a turning point in the area of student rights, the same holds true for the *Collins*[68] judgment on the rights to cross-border social

sociale più vantaggioso' (2006) Rivista del Diritto della Sicurezza Sociale 671, and S. Giubboni, 'Libertà di mercato e cittadinanza sociale europea' (2007) 4 Diritto Immigrazione Cittadinanza 13.

[64] See Dougan, n 44 above, 977–985; Verschueren, n 12 above, 345.

[65] n 5 above.

[66] For a recent summary see G. Orlandini, 'Libera prestazione e servizi sociali. Il caso dell'accesso cross-border alle prestazioni di cura', in S. Sciarra (ed) *Solidarietà, mercato e concorrenza nel welfare italiano. Profili di diritto interno e comunitario* (Bologna: Il Mulino 2007) 171.

[67] See especially points 99 and 100 of the Opinion, n 5 above.

[68] Case C-138/02 *Brian Francis Collins v Secretary of State for Work and Pensions* [2004] ECR I-02703. See eg the comment by H. Oosterom-Staples (2005) 42 CML Rev 205.

security for jobseekers. The case law that developed before the entry into force of provisions on Union citizenship, in fact, ruled out the possibility that Community citizens who were looking for a job in another state could claim rights similar to the social advantages referred to in Article 7 of Regulation 1612/68,[69] even though they enjoy full equality of treatment under Article 39 EC (now Article 45 TFEU) concerning access to labour market and employment services. The 1968 Regulation was clear: those rights should be considered reserved to those having full migrant status due to having already entered the employment market in the host member state. A graduation of the rights of jobseekers, who have a somewhat intermediate status,[70] between economically inactive citizens and workers, but closer to the latter,[71] seemed justifiable from a broader systematic perspective, which the Community provisions on unemployment benefit coordination helped design.

However, by the time the Court had to rule over the *Collins* case, it had dramatically redesigned the contours of the legal landscape in a way in which the old case law would not apply any more. Thus, the solution given to the case—substantially extending the social advantages provided for in Article 7 of Regulation 1612/68 to work seekers—did not surprise many commentators.

The issue was whether a Community citizen who had just gone back to Great Britain to look for a job could claim a right to the unemployment benefits that are intended for those who have insufficient financial resources and are conditional, by law, on habitual residence in the host country (income-based jobseekers' allowance). The Court based its ruling on a new reading of the right to equal treatment under Article 39 of the EC Treaty (now Article 45 TFEU), in the light of the new case law concerning the joint provisions of Articles 12 and 18 EC (Articles 18 and 21 TFEU). The Court stated that this right does not preclude a national rule—such as the English one—making the jobseeker benefit conditional on a residence requirement, *provided that* this requirement—indirectly discriminatory as such—can be justified on the basis of objective grounds, which are independent of citizenship and are proportionate to the aim pursued by national provisions.

The heart of the judgment lies in the make-up of the proportionality test, in particular the consistency between the residence requirement and the legitimate need to establish a genuine tie between the jobseeker and the labour market in the host country. However, an equally important point was to reaffirm the central role acquired by the status of European citizen under Articles 12 and 18 EC

[69] See Case-316/85 *Centre public d'aide sociale des Courcelles v Lebon* [1987] ECR 02811; and Case C-344/95 *Commission of the European Communities v Kingdom of Belgium* [1997] ECR I-01035. For a summary of relevant case law evolution, see M. Cousins, 'Diritti di soggiorno, sicurezza sociale ed il concetto evolutivo di cittadinanza europea' (2008) *Rivista del Diritto della Sicurezza Sociale* 65.

[70] The idea of a '*semi-status*' is discussed by M. Dougan, 'The Court Helps Those Who Help Themselves... The Legal Status of Migrant Work-seekers under Community Law in the Light of the Collins Judgment' (2005) 7 Eur J of Social Security 7 at 12.

[71] The free movement of jobseekers is not conditional on the resource requirement that is provided for economically inactive citizens.

(Articles 18 and 21 TFEU) when rereading the other fundamental freedoms, and specifically the traditional freedom of movement afforded to workers under Article 39 EC (Article 45 TFEU). From this perspective, the status of being a citizen of the Union is a fundamental, a 'founding' status. This ubiquitous condition, as it has been metaphorically described,[72] underlies a new reading of all fundamental freedoms mainly because they share the common foundation of European citizenship. The constitutional force of this status may push towards interpretive results that, theoretically, cannot even be inferred from traditional freedoms, especially when giving a new reading to secondary legislation implementing them, such as Regulations 1612/68 and 1408/71. Therefore, a new reading of Article 39 EC (Article 45 TFEU) in the light of citizenship rules is a key as much as the new case law *acquis*. And it is so even when—in the name of the residual freedom afforded to the citizen of the Union with respect to other forms of free movement—the Court omits to give its opinion on the interpretation of Articles 12, 17 and 18 EC (Articles 18, 20 and 21 TFEU).[73]

This reading also applies, and increasingly so, to the definition of the status of unemployed migrants. Here again, for reasons that are partly similar to those given for jobseekers,[74] secondary legislation is rather strict. In particular, it aims at reconciling the free movement of workers with the need to verify the actual entitlement to the social security benefits to be paid by the competent country.[75]

The most relevant rules are therefore those provided by Regulation 1408/71 on the coordination of social security systems, which are destined to be slightly adjusted with the future entry into force of Regulation 883/2004. The main

[72] O. Golynker, *Ubiquitous Citizens of Europe. The Paradigm of Partial Migration* (Antwerp: Intersentia, 2006).

[73] This is demonstrated by two judgments pronounced by the Court on the tide-over allowances provided by Belgium legislation for young people seeking first employment. The first is rendered under Arts 12 and 18 EC (Arts 18 and 21 TFEU); the second is based—with the same results—on Art 39 EC: see Case C-224/98 *Marie-Nathalie D'Hoop v Office national de l'emploi* [2002] ECR I-06191; Case C-258/04 *Office national de l'emploi v Ioannis Ioannidis* [2005] ECR I-8275. See also, for a different case on a similar line, Case C-76/05 *Herbert Schwarz, Merga Gootjes-Schwarz v Finanzamt Bergisch Gladbach* [2007] ECR-6849.

[74] The two figures overlap in all cases in which workers lose their job in the member state of origin and move to another Community country to look for another job. In these cases, unemployed workers looking for a job in another member state may claim rights there hypothetically under Reg 1408/71. See Verschueren, n 12 above, 335–336, also for interesting speculation on how the Court could (or should) have decided *Collins* if the applicant in the main proceedings had been able to invoke the EC Regs on social security coordination.

[75] As a rule of thumb, the benefit is paid by the competent institution of the member state in which the unemployed worker was lastly employed (Art 70(2) of Reg 1408/71). In the case of a frontier worker who is wholly unemployed, the benefit is exceptionally paid by the institution of the place of residence and provides such benefits at its own expenses (Art 71(1)(a)(ii)). In this latter case, Reg 1408/71 implements a very clear form of cross-border solidarity, since the benefit is paid by the state of residence of the cross-border worker, rather than by the institution of the country of employment in which social security contributions were paid during employment. However, this is an exception to a system that is generally based on an commutative occupational-type of solidarity that lacks any truly pan-European universalistic dimension; see S. Giubboni, 'Free movement of persons and European solidarity' (2007) 13 Eur LJ 360.

limitation established by these rules concerns the limited exportability of unemployment benefits in the state in which the persons receiving the benefits intend to move to seek another job. Article 10 of Regulation 1408/71, which sets the general rule waiving the residence clause for the purposes of the payment of the social security benefits accrued, does not cover unemployment benefits. As a result, the Regulation does not generally prohibit member states from setting residence requirements, nor to suspend payments on the ground that the recipients of the benefit reside in another member state. Moreover, the Regulation provides for two exceptions to the general provision whereby limitations to the export of unemployment benefits are not forbidden. In fact, if we consider the rules in force to date, Article 69 provides for the right to export unemployment benefits to another member state for a period not exceeding three months, provided that the unemployed is registered as a person seeking work. Also, Article 71 provides for the right to unemployment benefits for those who—during their last employment—were residing in the territory of a member state other than the state in which they were insured under social security schemes.

It is clear that following these restrictive rules on the exportability of unemployment benefits—which may limit or hinder the free movement of workers within the internal market—the pressure put by the new trend of case law (just as Articles 17 and 18 EC) has naturally led to overcoming the 'bottlenecks' created by secondary legislation. Moreover, a similar and consistent pressure has begun on another area of regulation marked by a strong compression—or rather exclusion[76]—of exportability, ie the area of special non-contributory benefits.[77]

In *De Cuyper*,[78] the Court was particularly asked to assess the current compatibility of this traditional regulatory system with reference to an unemployment allowance provided for by the Belgian law. In that case the applicant in the main proceeding had obtained an unemployment allowance in 1997, though he was dispensed from the obligation to be available on the labour market on the grounds of his age; however, Mr De Cuyper had moved his residence to the South of France in 1999, thus infringing the obligation upon him that was expressly laid down in the Belgian legal system in order to be eligible for the allowance. Hence, the Belgian court who heard the claim against the measure that withdrew the benefit referred to the Court the question of whether the obligation to reside as a condition to be awarded an unemployment allowance, applied to unemployed persons over fifty years old who enjoy an exemption from the requirement to be available for work, amounted to a fetter on the freedom of movement and residence of all European citizens under Articles 17 and 18 EC (Articles 20 and 21 TFEU), and, if so, whether it could be considered justified.

[76] See Reg 647/2005.

[77] See also for the broad references to the historic case law of the Court of Justice, S. Giubboni, G. Orlandini, *La libera circolazione dei lavoratori. Principi e tendenze* (Bologna: Il Mulino, 2007) 166.

[78] Case C-406/04 *Gérald De Cuyper v Office national de l'emploi* [2006] ECR I-6947.

Aware of the extreme sensitivity of the matter concerned, Advocate General Geelhoed had strongly advocated in his Opinion the perfect compatibility of the contested residence requirement with the Treaty rules on Union citizenship. In fact, the subject of the scrutiny was not only the choice of the Belgian legislature, but also, and possibly in particular, though indirectly, the choice expressed in rules posed by Community secondary law. The Advocate General was fully aware that 'to hold that a residence requirement is an unjustified restriction on the free movement of a citizen of the Union would undermine entirely the purpose of the rules on unemployment benefit in Regulation No 1408/71 and would run counter to Article 10(1) of that regulation'.[79] To accept the approach proposed by *De Cuyper* would essentially mean to question the very function of the social security Regulation and, with it, the underlying principle whereby Community law does not detract from the powers of the member states to organize their respective systems, by coordinating them without jeopardizing their full autonomy. This is the reason why the Advocate General suggested in substance that the Court acknowledge a sort of broadened constitutional coverage to Regulation 1408/71, reshaping it as a measure that, being adopted on the basis of Article 42 EC (now Article 48 TFEU), could have been passed for the purposes of setting the limitations and conditions laid down in Article 18 of the Treaty.[80]

The Court addressed this issue by adopting the *practical* solution suggested by the Advocate General, but it *did not* follow the general approach of his Opinion. Indeed, the Court ruled that the freedom of movement and residence conferred on every citizen of the Union by Article 18 EC (Article 21 TFEU), does not preclude a residence clause, such as that applied in the case in the main proceedings, but it did so only after performing the usual review of proportionality on the mentioned condition. This clearly means that the residence requirements laid down by the member states in the application of the mentioned provisions of Regulation 1408/71 are no longer automatically justified, in a general and abstract way, by referring to Article 42 EC (as suggested by the Advocate General, in combination with Article 18(1)) EC, but they will instead have to be judged case by case, as restrictions on the free movement of Union citizens, in the light of the proportionality principle. Hence, the more or less rigorous standard with which the suitability and the correct appropriateness (ie proportionality) of the national provision vis-à-vis the objective pursued (such as, for instance, the need to exercise effective control over the actual condition of unemployment of the worker concerned) is measured *in practice* will determine whether a measure is legitimate under Community law. Clearly, it is a completely different approach from that suggested by Advocate General Geelhoed, the Court's approach having strong constitutional implications on the distribution of powers between the Court and the (European and national) legislatures, as I will further explain below.

[79] Point 116 of the Opinion delivered on 2 February 2006.
[80] See especially point 112 of the Opinion.

In *Petersen*,[81] the Court offered a bold confirmation of this new interpretative course in the field of unemployment benefits covered by Regulation 1408/71. The residence condition provided for by the Austrian legislation for the advance grant of unemployment benefit at issue in the main proceedings, although in principle authorized by Article 10(1) of Regulation 1408/71, was deemed to be incompatible with Article 39 of the EC Treaty (Article 45 TFEU). Notwithstanding the expressed limitations to the exportability of unemployment benefits *in abstracto* permitted by the social security coordination Regulation, a residence condition such as that at issue had no real chance to pass the stringent review of proportionality 'for the purposes of substantive justice'[82] suggested by Advocate General Colomer and envisaged by the Court according to a proper constitutional reading of Articles 39 and 42 of the EC Treaty. (now Articles 45 and 48 TFEU)

A very similar development took place with reference to the derogations to the exportability provided for in Regulation 1408/71 in the field of special non-contributory benefits. In this case, this development was fostered by the case law that had been claiming the full applicability of Article 7 of the Regulation to frontier workers also, so as to enable them to also enjoy (in practice, to export) those social advantages that the provision grants in their state of residence.[83] Yet, the Court's most recent judgments go beyond that case law.

Recently, in *Hendrix*,[84] by reversing the case law laid down just the previous year,[85] the Court stated that in principle Article 39 EC (Article 45 TFEU) and Article 7 of Regulation 1612/68 must be interpreted as not precluding national legislation which applies Article 4(2a) and Article 10a of Regulation 1408/71 and provides that a special non-contributory benefit[86] may be granted only to persons who are resident in national territory. However, the Court immediately added, with a very ambiguous formula,[87] that 'implementation of that legislation must not entail an infringement of the rights of a person in a situation such as

[81] Case C-228/07 *Jörn Petersen v. Arbeitsmarktservice Niederösterreich* (Judgment 11 September 2008, nyr).

[82] Point 27 of the Opinion of Advocate General Ruiz-Jarabo Colomer on 15 May 2008.

[83] See the famous Cases C-57/96 *Meints* [1997] ECR I-06689, and C-337/97 *Meeusen* [1999] ECR I-03289.

[84] Case C-287/05 *D. P. W. Hendrix v Raad van Bestuur van het Uitvoerringsinstitut Werknemersverzekeringen* [2007] ECR I-6909. For an insightful analysis see O'Brien (2008) 45 CML Rev 499.

[85] Case C-154/05 *J. J. Kersbergen-Lap and D. Dams-Schipper v Raad van Bestuur van het Uitvoeringsinstituut Werknemersverzekeringen* [2006] ECR I-06249. See also Cousins, 'Social Security, Social Assistance and the Special Non Contributory Benefits: the Never-ending Story', (2007) 9 Eur J of Social Security 97.

[86] The case dealt with benefits paid in the Netherlands to disabled young people.

[87] Advocate General Kokott had reached less ambiguous conclusions when she stated, in general terms, that 'a provision of national law which makes the grant or continuation of a benefit conditional on the person concerned being resident in the territory of the Member State *is not always compatible* with Article 39 EC and Article 7(2) of Regulation No 1612/68 *on the ground* that the benefit constitutes a special non-contributory benefit within the meaning of Article 4(2a) of Regulation No 1408/71 which in accordance with Article 10a of that regulation is granted only at the place of residence' (emphasis added).

that of the applicant in the main proceedings which goes beyond what is required to achieve the legitimate objective pursued by the national legislation'.[88] Thus, it will be for the national court—which must apply the provisions of its legal system by interpreting them in conformity with Community law—to take account in particular of the fact that the applicant in the main proceeding, although he moved his residence abroad, has maintained all his economic and social links with the member state of origin.

The formula is ambiguously cryptic: one could almost say that in a sort of refined exercise of 'honest dissimulation' with a seventeenth century flair[89] it substantially overcomes the special system of exemptions to the non-exportability of non-contributory benefits without overtly declaring it. Hence, it is apparent that the prohibition to export benefits always entails a potential infringement of an individual's right to freely move throughout the EU, an infringement that might be justified—*in practical cases*—only by the rule of reason, ie by applying national law in conformity with the principle of proportionality. And in a case such as that in the main proceedings—in which the Court itself reminded the national court that the applicant had maintained very strong links with the country of origin—the residence clause—*though provided for by national law in application of Regulation 1408/71*—may hardly pass the review of proportionality.[90]

Obviously, in other cases the requirement to reside in national territory may continue to be fully justified, but this will depend increasingly more on the assessment of the actual circumstances under the rule of reason and increasingly less on the 'abstract' rules laid down by the Community legislature. And it may well be that a residence requirement laid down by national law for the same benefit might be considered legitimate in one case and disproportionate in another.[91]

5. Tensions between the case law of the European Court of Justice and secondary legislation

The time has come to draw some conclusions from this critical overview of the case law of the Court of Justice. To this end a first aspect that needs to be considered is the often recalled difficulty of reconciling Treaty provisions, that are so boldly construed by the Court, with Community secondary legislation.

[88] para 58 in *Hendrix*.

[89] The reference here is to Torquato Accetto, *Della dissimulazione onesta* (1641), edited by S. S. Nigro (Turin: UTET, 1997).

[90] In fact, Mr Hendrix had moved from the Netherlands to Belgium though he went on working—thanks to the non-contributory benefit awarded to him—in the state of origin.

[91] This is what seems to have happened with reference to the German child-raising allowance, for which the residence requirement in the member state was in practice considered legitimate in Case C-213/05 *Wendy Geven v Land Nordrhein-Westfalen* [2007] ECR I-6347 and, by contrast, illegitimate in the judgment rendered the same day by the Grand Chamber in Case C-212/05 *Gertraud Hartmann v Freistaat Bayern* [2007] ECR I-6303.

Mention has already been made of the tensions originated by Directive 2004/38/EC, with which the Community legislature made a concrete effort to adjust the legislation to the Court's case law by overcoming—at least in its basic approach—the strictly category-based and functional approach that was typical of the previous legislation, as well as its visible link between the right to stay in another member state and the pursuance of an economic activity. Nonetheless, many areas of conflict with the case law of the ECJ have developed in the meantime.

As already mentioned, the most visible one is likely to concern the rules on maintenance aid for studies: Article 24(2), which may be reconciled with some efforts with *Grzelczyk*, can hardly be justified in the light of *Bidar*, unless the letter were to become a sort of repealing interpretation abrogating de facto the provisions of the Directive. This seems exactly to be the course taken, at least until *Förster*,[92] by the Court, which, on the one hand, seems to limit the exclusion laid down by the Directive to the sole cases in which a student moves in this capacity to another member state in order to study there, and, on the other hand, permits in any case a derogation to the principle of equal treatment provided that it is compatible with the proportionality test.[93] But the recent *Förster* ruling clearly indicates a more cautious approach of the Court and a possible move towards a strict interpretation and application of Article 24(2) of the Residence Directive.

Moreover, there is always a visible tension (though not a contradiction) between the *acquis* since *Collins* and the Community rules, with regards to Article 24(2) of Directive 2004/38/EC, in the field of social protection for jobseekers in another member state. In this case also it seems appropriate to conclude that the general rule laid down by the Directive—whereby *jobseekers* are excluded from the right to equal treatment in social assistance matters for the time that they are looking for a job even though it is longer than three months—will be considered legitimate in so far as it passes the proportionality test *in the actual cases in which it is applied*.[94]

A member state may certainly be entitled to lay down a residence condition, that may even be relatively long,[95] but, as in the case of the British habitual residence test, account must always be taken of the fact that the genuine link with the labour market of the host country—which is relevant for jobseekers according to *Collins*—can also be proved by means of other indicators.[96] In fact, already in *Swaddling*[97] the Court clearly ruled that the length of residence cannot be

92 n 60 above.

93 See Lang, Nascimbene, 'L'attuazione in Italia della direttiva 2004/38/CE sulla libera circolazione dei cittadini dell'Unione europea' (2007) 2 Diritto Immigrazione Cittadinanza 43.

94 See in this respect Dougan, n 70 above, 21–24, and see most recently the ruling of 4 June 2009 in Joined Cases C-22/08 and C-23/08 *Athanasios Vatsouras and Josif Koupatantze v Arbeitsgemeinschaft (ARGE) Nürnberg 900*.

95 cf Jacobs, n 41 above, 594.

96 See again Dougan, n 70 above, 27.

97 Case C-90/97 *Robin Swaddling v Adjudication Officer* [1999] ECR I-1075.

considered as the only indicator that the person has established his/her centre of their interests in the host country, as account should always be taken of other facts, such as, for instance, the person's family situation and the reasons which have lead him/her to move.[98]

The exclusion from any entitlement to social assistance, permitted for the first three months of residence in the host member state by Article 24(1) of the 2004 Directive, seems in this respect to be justified, in the same general terms in which it is drafted, by any plausible version of the proportionality test.[99] Hence, more generally, derogations from equal treatment in matters of social assistance or maintenance aid that the Directive allows member states to link with the length of residence do not as such conflict with the Court's case law, but always need to be applied pursuant to the proportionality principle and the circumstances of the individual case. The length of residence—though a key element—cannot however be considered as the exclusive indicator of a person's integration into the host member state society or of the link with the labour market in which a job is sought.

On the other hand, it must be considered that, for compliance with both the residence requirement and the financial self-sufficiency and health cover conditions provided for by the 2004 Directive, help may come from the provisions of Regulation 1408/71 and, in the future, of Regulation 883/2004, which extends the scope of coordination of social security systems to all Union citizens, even if they do not (or have not) carried out any economic activity.[100] In the personal scope of the Regulations it will be certainly necessary to apply the Community notion of residence—as the main centre of a person's interests—which the Court of Justice has already qualified in *Swaddling*. The provisions of the Regulation—in particular those on special non-contributory benefits—may play an important role so as to 'enable EU-citizens moving from one Member State to another to obtain sufficient income in the host State in order to fulfil the subsistence requirement for obtaining a residence right in that host State'.[101] Nor should it be neglected that the same provisions may play a role also in the aggregation of periods of residence completed by an individual in the member state of origin.[102]

Moreover, the reviewed case law shows equally problematic issues with regards to the relations between Article 7(2) of Regulation 1612/1968, read in conjunction with Article 39 EC (Article 45 TFEU), and Regulation 1408/71, with specific reference to those areas of protection which are subjected to strict

[98] For interesting remarks on the notion of normal residence as the permanent centre of interests of the person concerned see ECJ, Case C-392/05 *Georgios Alevizos v Ypourgos Oikonomikon* [2007] ECR I-3505, in particular para 57.

[99] This may be reasonably inferred from the *Trojani* judgment, in particular para 43.

[100] See Art 2 of Reg 883/2004, whose pre-condition is that a Community national is or has been subject to the social security legislation of a member state.

[101] Verschueren, n 12 above, 326.

[102] ibid 323.

restrictions by the same Regulation on the export of benefits. The traditional interpretation of the relations between the two Regulations relied on the express provision of Article 42(2) of the former, under which it did not affect the provisions provided by the latter on the coordination of statutory social security systems.[103] This approach—which is the only one capable of preserving the specific coordination function performed by Regulation 1408/71—has been just recently strongly supported by Advocate General Geelhoed in *De Cuyper*, who not only relied on the technical argument of the natural supremacy of the *lex specialis*, but also tried to ground this interpretation on sounder constitutional foundations, ie on the double reference to Articles 18 and 42 EC (Articles 21 and 48 TFEU).

However, the Court has completely disregarded this argument and ruled that in cases of concurrence/conflict, the provision under Article 7 of the 1968 Regulation takes precedence, and the latter can be relied on so as to obtain social advantages in the beneficiary's state of residence also in situations where Regulation 1408/71 would rule out this option. Hence, the Court has constitutionalized the provision of Article 7 of Regulation 1612/68 as 'the particular expression, in the specific area of the grant of social advantages, of the principle of equal treatment enshrined in Article 39(2) EC'.[104] And in this case also to the cost of an overtly strained interpretation of the letter of secondary legislation: despite the wording of Article 42 of Regulation 1612/68, it was ruled that 'the regulations should apply independently of one another, that is to say, in parallel',[105] and hence their hierarchy is only apparent, not real. Indeed the hierarchy—which should have favoured under all examinations the special system of Regulation 1408/71—has (again) been upset without any concern about resorting to contrived interpretative tricks.

6. A constitutional assessment of the case law of the European Court of Justice

It is indisputably only thanks to the Court's case law that the freedom of movement, from being a simple economic right, has become 'the concrete expression of a real Union citizenship'.[106] The objective anticipated by Advocate General Ruiz-Jarabo Colomer with a prescient phrase has nearly been attained only thanks to this case law:

[103] See A. P. van der Mei, *Free Movement of Persons within the European Community. Cross-Border Access to Public Benefits* (Oxford/Portland, Oregon: Hart Publishing, 2003) 64–65.

[104] So the Court in *Hendrix*, para 53.

[105] So Advocate General Kokott in her Opinion delivered in *Hendrix* (para 54).

[106] Commission (EC), 'The third report from the Commission to the Council and the European Parliament on the application of Dirs 93/96, 90/364, 90/365 on the right of residence for students, economically inactive and retired Union citizens' COM (2006) 56 final, 5 April 2006, 9.

the creation of citizenship of the Union, with the corollary of freedom of movement for citizens throughout the territory of the Member States, represents a considerable qualitative step forward in that it separates that freedom from its functional or instrumental elements (the link with an economic activity or attainment of the internal market) and raises it to the level of a genuinely independent right inherent in the political status of the citizens of the Union'.[107]

Today it is a commonplace that European citizens can exercise their rights of movement and residence—and hence be entitled to access national social protection systems—substantially beyond what is laid down not only in the Directives of the 1990s but also in the 2004 're-codification' Directive. The Luxembourg Court has reversed the logic (and hierarchical) order under which Article 18 may have been considered—in the traditional perspective—with regards to the other Treaty provisions on fundamental freedoms.[108] The outcome of this innovative perspective is that:

secondary legislation adopted pursuant to the Treaty no longer defines the conditions for exercising the Union citizens' rights; it merely identifies the relevant public interests which have to be balanced against the fundamental freedom protected by Article 18 EC, and provides certain criteria which the national authorities should take into account for these purposes, in addition to further criteria identified by the Court itself within the context of the proportionality assessment'.[109]

In this regard, the Court's renewed activism has undoubtedly brought about a change with remarkable constitutional repercussions which need to be investigated in the context of the two most important issues for our purposes: firstly, momentum is (apparently) given to a new paradigm of social solidarity for the EU; secondly, the relations between the Court itself—as a fully-fledged constitutional court—and the Community legislature are undergoing radical changes.

Within the first issue, emphasis should be given to the role of 'social engineering'[110] that the Court intentionally played, in that it made the status of Union citizen, rather than that of individuals entitled to market freedoms under Community law, the engine of new forms of cross-border solidarity. This form of solidarity, though still in its infancy, is new as against the 'mechanic' and 'functional'[111] one that dominated the history of the construction of the integrated market and that was selectively addressed in principle only to the active players in the process of European production and circulation of wealth. In fact, an idea of 'organic solidarity' emerges here, whose vocation is to expand both beyond the

[107] So point 82 of the Opinion delivered in *Morgan*, n 5 above. See also Opinion delivered in Case C-386/02 *Baldinger* [2004] ECR I-08411.

[108] In this regard, see the precise image suggested in the Editorial eloquently entitled 'The Unbearable Heaviness of European Citizenship' (2006) 31 ELR 779.

[109] Dougan, n 70 above, 24.

[110] ibid 18–19.

[111] I use, with a certain freedom, the terminology of Reiner Zoll, *La solidarietà. Eguaglianza e differenza* (Bologna: Il Mulino, 2003), who, in turn, has reworked Durkheim's well-known distinction.

circle of those who take part in market processes (though at a European level), and, at the same time, beyond the boundaries of national communities, within which the welfare state has historically operated. Hence, at least apparently, it is an idea of solidarity that is truly implemented 'among strangers' at a cross-border level.[112] According to Zoll,[113] the mechanic solidarity is achieved within a group or a class of people sharing the same social or market condition and thus not extended beyond the members of a socially homogeneous community. By contrast, organic solidarity extends the bonds of mutual social responsibility outside the borders of such a restricted community.[114]

Between the two circles of European solidarity—the 'mechanic', which is typically addressed to economically active individuals, and the 'organic' one, whose foundations rest on the general and inclusive sphere of the new common *civitas*—there are still outstanding differences, but these are clearly of a more quantitative than qualitative nature, while the gap between the two is gradually closing in any case.[115] Economically inactive nationals can certainly have restrictions imposed on their rights of residence and cross-border access to social protection that are in no way allowed for employed or self-employed persons exercising the relevant freedom of movement. To use a classic social security law terminology, the eligibility criteria for the former are different, and indeed harsher, than those for the latter. It suffices to mention criteria such as habitual residence, sufficient degree of integration into the host country, genuine link with its labour market (for jobseekers), which, according to the Court's case law,[116] lawfully influence access to forms of social protection in the host member state of Union nationals who do not work, but cannot be required from those enjoying the status of workers pursuant to Article 39 EC (Article 45 TFEU).[117] Mention may also be made to the constraint of the 'unreasonable burden' that sets the mobile boundaries to the financial solidarity owed by the member states to European nationals in social need; this limit cannot apply to those who are entitled to the 'mechanic' solidarity pursuant to Article 39 EC (Article 45 TFEU).

But these differences, although important at an abstract level of understanding the two models of solidarity, seem to be loosing their practical relevance once assessed in the light of the proportionality test. It is indeed evident that those persistent differences in the eligibility criteria laid down for inactive European

[112] For this terminology see J. Habermas, *The Postnational Constellation. Political Essays* (Cambridge: Polity Press, 2001).

[113] See now in the same vein, with explicit reference to European cross-border social solidarity, M. Paci, 'Welfare, solidarietà sociale e coesione della società nazionale' (2008) Stato e Mercato 1.

[114] See especially Zoll, n 111 above, 32–33.

[115] See the critical remarks of Advocate General Geelhoed in his Opinion in *Hartmann*, points 34 and 38.

[116] These criteria can be found, for example, in *Bidar* and *Collins*.

[117] With the significant exception of frontier workers: see *Geven*, n 91 above. I am grateful to Charlotte O'Brien for this observation.

citizens tend to be played down within the flexible and 'context sensitive'[118] interplay of the review of proportionality.[119] Mention may be made once again of the limit of the unreasonable burden posed to the social assistance of the host member state: so far the Court has been very cautious in applying it and has rather focused on the requirements of the indebted welfare states' budgets.[120] Yet, everything clearly depends on the actual allocation of the burden of proof with regards to the practical conditions under which the member state concerned may rely on this constraint. In this respect, the Court seems to be requiring more stringent conditions: in fact—though with reference to a case that is rather different from the ones analyzed—it has recently made clear that it is (no longer) satisfied with generic claims on the adverse financial effects that granting benefits to those who are currently excluded from them may have if those claims are not adequately substantiated.[121]

This final consideration brings us back to the other noticeable constitutional innovation operated by the Court's case law. Michael Dougan has convincingly argued that interpreting Articles 12 and 18 of the Treaty the Court has pushed its teleological approach so far as to surpass the functional way of reasoning 'ordinarily applicable to the purely economic Treaty provisions'.[122] This is demonstrated by the fact that the Court—even though through the review of conformity of national implementation measures—carries out an increasingly stringent review of proportionality over Community secondary legislation. As Dougan also remarked, 'the *Baumbast* rule is something of a constitutional novelty: the Court of Justice has chosen to subject Community secondary legislation *indirectly* to a level of judicial scrutiny normally associated with Member State action'.[123] Unlike what has traditionally happened with regards to the economic freedoms of movement in rulings such as *Grzelczyk* and *Baumbast,* the Court has not refrained from carrying out a review of proportionality under Articles 12 and 18 EC over national measures that appeared to fully comply with Community secondary legislation;

And in effect—that is, *indirectly* and through the medium of the Member States—this amounts to *judicial review of that very Community legislation*, not of the privileged sort one would expect as regards questions of competence in the exercise of the Community's own

[118] Dougan, n 18 above, 624.

[119] See also Golynker, n 52 above, 395.

[120] See in this regard S. Besson and A. Utzinger, 'Introduction: Future Challenges of European Citizenship—Facing a Wide-Open Pandora's Box' (2007) 32 Eur LJ, 573, 587; Jacobs, n 41 above, 598.

[121] See joined cases C-396/05, C-419/05 and C-450/05 *Doris Habelt, Martha Möser, Peter Wachter v Deutsche Rentenversicherung Bund* [2007] ECR I-11895, in which the Court ruled that 'the German Government has failed to demonstrate how transfers of residence from Germany such as those which took place in the cases in the main proceedings, are liable to impose a heavier financial burden on the German social security scheme' (para 83).

[122] Dougan, n 18 above, 625.

[123] ibid 614.

legislative powers, but rather of the front line sort one witnesses all the time as regards national provisions restricting free movement under the primary Treaty provisions'.[124]

Guided by the rule of reason and the variable adjustments of the adequacy and proportionality review-tests,[125] the Court of Justice in fact performs an insightful review of constitutionality over the choices made by the Community legislature, and considerably affects the discretion conferred to it when exercising its powers. Rigorous judicial review and restrictions on the European legislature's autonomy are closely interlinked, hence it is self-evident that the review of proportionality performed by the Court poses a problem of competencies and powers.[126] Yet, the topical question does no longer, or better not only, affect the powers that member states exercise under the aegis of Community law, but, though only indirectly, the very powers of the *Community legislature*.[127]

7. Conclusions

The boundaries of membership to the communities of solidarity-based redistribution laid down by the national welfare schemes have certainly become—especially thanks to the case law of the Court of Justice—more open and permeable, and hence more inclusive, at least for European citizens. Union citizenship, from being a complementary and secondary institution as it was considered in the Maastricht's revision, has become the epicentre of deep constitutional transformations and a sound anchor point of new bonds of 'mutual social responsibility'[128] among member states' citizens. The cross-border opening of welfare schemes to economically inactive Community citizens who can prove a certain degree of integration with the society of the host country may rightly be considered as the founding act of a new and more advanced notion of European solidarity.[129]

However, the apparent conquest of this strong social dimension for the European citizenship is not devoid of limits and contradictions. The most blatant limit is that the inclusive and solidarity based approach of the European citizenship is offset by a symmetric closure vis-à-vis of those who are excluded from the membership. If one considers the situation from the point of view of third-country migrants, one must indeed conclude that a 'process of equalisation co-exists with processes of exclusion, and the relativisation of the Member States' borders is accompanied by the reinforcement of the external frontiers of the Union

[124] ibid 620–621.

[125] See Ross, n 14 above, 1067.

[126] See also Besson and Utzinger, n 120 above, 575.

[127] In this sense, the stance illustrated in the Advocate General's Opinion in *Hendrix*, especially point 57, is emblematic.

[128] J. H. H. Weiler, 'To be a European citizen', in *Scritti in onore di Giuseppe Federico Mancini*, Vol. II, *Diritto dell'Unione europea*, Milan, Giuffrè, 1067 at 1095.

[129] See in this regard Ross, n 14 above, 1065.

and the relocation of migration controls in third countries'.[130] On the contrary, it may be observed that whilst a comprehensive de-nationalization and a de-territorialization trend in the welfare systems is currently empowering Union citizens, for third-country migrants the functional status is becoming increasingly significant. And 'it is particularly ironic that whilst union citizenship is transitioning away from the market citizenship model, this is being reconstructed in respect of third country nationals'.[131] The goal of overcoming this limit that is intrinsic to the 'dual'[132] nature of the European citizenship will only be attained by replacing nationality with residence as a prerequisite for cross-border membership, something which is unrealistic today, especially for third-country nationals.[133]

Yet, as I have tried to outline in this critical review, even the area of European solidarity, whose new boundaries have been traced by the Court of Justice, is not exempt from significant constraints and contradictions. Even though, admittedly, (as of today) there is no conclusive empirical evidence, the risk that the erosion of forms of domestic control by member states over the access to welfare schemes may in turn cause a reduction in the supply of social benefits, thus triggering dynamics of 'social levelling-down',[134] cannot be by any means neglected.[135] Indeed, it is an only apparent paradox that the progression of a case law that is inspired by a genuine ethos of integration may bring about negative social disintegration.

Such a risk may be intrinsic to the position that the Court of Justice was forced to adopt, which inevitably is individualistic as it is tailored on the single case heard by the Court.[136] The outstanding prominence acquired by the provisions on Union citizenship actually rests on the same ratio that allowed the Court to model the constituent traits of the European economic constitution on the market freedoms. Yet, an approach based on the rights of individuals—even of Union citizens in need claiming a form of social assistance in the host member state—defies the necessarily collective dimension of solidarity.[137] Financial solidarity among member states' citizens thus becomes the piecemeal, individualistic, atomistic solidarity uprooted from a collective context: the dominant dimension of the European cross-border solidarity sanctioned by the Court of Justice in the individual case examined turns to be the fragmented one which is individually and sometime opportunistically accessed by European citizens who have exercised

[130] Kostakopoulou, n 8 above, 634. [131] Bell, n 2 above, 329.

[132] Lippolis, *La cittadinanza europea*, Bologna, 1994, 61.

[133] cf Besson and Utzinger, n 120 above, 580–581; Epiney, n 54 above, 614, and, notably, for a wider perspective, Davies, '"Any Place I Hang My Hat?" or: Residence Is the New Nationality' (2005) 11 Eur LJ 43.

[134] Besson and Utzinger, n 120 above, 589.

[135] See M. Ferrera and S. Sacchi, 'A More Social EU? In What Areas? In What Forms?' URGE Issue Paper No 1/2007, 5, available on <http://www.urge.it>.

[136] See C. Newdick, 'Citizenship, Free Movement and Health Care: Cementing Individual Rights by Corroding Social Solidarity' (2006) 43 CML Rev 1645.

[137] See also Kostakopoulou, n 8 above, 636–638.

their freedom of movement. From this perspective, a recovery of the truly collective dimension of social solidarity may be traced in those Court's rulings in which, by balancing the state's interest in keeping public spending under control and the individual exercise of a fundamental freedom, the Court emphasizes a limit such as the 'unreasonable burden' that is also considered by the 2004 Directive.

It then becomes hard to identify a collective, political cement for European solidarity in the ECJ's case law: the reference model, if not the market citizen, would in any case remain the rational player who takes advantage of the opportunities offered by the opening, or in any case the easier access to national welfare schemes. A sort of counter-argument supporting *a contrario* this conclusion can be extracted from the very recent case law that de-values the meaning and European potential of the classic form of 'mechanic solidarity' which underlies industrial action at national and transnational level. The infamous *Viking* and *Laval* cases[138] at least demonstrates that the Court of Justice is not (yet) prepared to recognize the constructive potential for the European political project of social solidarity which truly originates from transnational collective action at Community level. By subjecting these forms of collective solidarity to a still dominant market-integration rationale, the judges in Luxembourg, quite apart from a correct balancing exercise between fundamental social rights and market freedom, vividly demonstrate a total absorption within this individualistic and quite paradoxical paradigm of 'European solidarity'. Trade unions are asked to incorporate, in their evaluations of the options at stake for defending the workers' interests, the 'objective' interest of market integration, that is to say the very interests of the counterparts they are acting against. The concrete collective solidarity which is at the core of industrial action (also at transnational level) is *ex ante* limited by this new duty to take into consideration the employers' economic freedom as protected by Articles 43 and 49 of the EC Treaty (Articles 49 and 56 TFEU).[139]

This is why criticism of the Court's excessive activism[140] seems, at least partly, justified. No matter how clever and appropriate the balancing of interests at stake performed by the Court under the principle of proportionality is in practice, there is still an 'ontological' gap between the complexity of the issues raised by the re-modelling of the boundaries of social solidarity in Europe and the—cognitive and legitimacy—resources that the Luxembourg Court has to tackle them. Hence, the Court should rather refrain from excessively interfering with the powers attributed to the legislature (European in the first place) with reference to

[138] Case C-438/05 and Case C-341/05 respectively. See C. Barnard in this volume.

[139] See especially Lord Wedderburn, 'Labour Law 2008: 40 Years On' (2007) 36 ILJ 397, and C. Joerges, 'Democracy and European Integration: A legacy of Tensions, a Re-conceptualisation and Recent True Conflicts', EUI Working Papers Law No 2007/25.

[140] For a new example of this activism see the Judgment of the Court (Grand Chamber) in Case C-352/06 *Brigitte Bosmann v Bundesagentur für Arbeit—Familienkasse Aachen* [2008] ECR I-3827.

the fundamental rules and procedures that are instrumental to the definition of those boundaries.

At the same time, the European legislature should exercise this role with greater awareness and efficacy. For instance, many have voiced the need to return to a more active and far-sighted use of the coordination technique, which has always provided the basis for Community social security law. The relevant regulations—which in the 2004 reformed version already have a general personal scope—should widen their material scope also. For example, it should be of the utmost importance to extend to social assistance and, notably, to the general minimum income schemes that are in force in many Union member states but are nonetheless excluded, as the former, from the substantive scope of Regulation 883/2003, coordination criteria similar to those that have been in force for quite some time for special non-contributory benefits.[141]

Bolder action is needed in the field of export of unemployment benefits, which are still burdened by the constraints of an anachronistic view of the European labour market. And if one wants to avoid the case-by-case approach of the Luxembourg Court to the very sensitive issues raised by the exportability of healthcare benefits and students maintenance aid, the European legislature must clearly lay down appropriate rules even for this matter, which are capable of balancing, on a necessarily general level, considerations of control over public spending (and elimination of forms of free riding) with those of individual freedoms.

However, one must be aware that the institutionalization of a properly European form of social solidarity presses the Community legislature to overcome the mere logic of coordination of national welfare systems. The rooting of a form of 'organic' solidarity 'among strangers' in the enlarged Europe—to take up again the evocative terminology used by Rainer Zoll—requires a minimum core of citizenship social benefits that are governed, and at least in part financed, at the Community level.[142] The idea of a European minimum income,[143] which has been discussed for some time, as that recent notion of 'a civic remuneration in return for social, ecological and cultural services',[144] go exactly in this direction, and yet they point to reform objectives that may be too far away on the Union's horizon. However, the first positive experiences of mobilization of the European Globalization Adjustment Fund (EGF) demonstrate that the Union is now ready to give its practical contribution to the governance of the processes of economic restructuring that are currently under way in Europe and to act as a buffer for their social consequences. The Fund—which does not replace the measures for which companies are competent under national legislation and

[141] See in this respect Verschueren, n 12 above, 342ff.

[142] Of course, these European social rights to a decent level of living should be modelled according to a true universalistic paradigm of 'civic citizenship', encompassing third-country residents. See again Bell, n 2 above.

[143] See Ferrera, Sacchi, n 135 above.

[144] Zoll, n 111 above, 189 (my translation).

collective agreements—has already co-financed customized service packages whose aim is to provide re-training and, hopefully, new jobs to workers who have been dismissed by European companies as a consequence of the delocalization of productive activities, mainly to China. If the scope of the EGF were enlarged, for instance, one may think of an active, truly Community-based protection scheme against unemployment as a first stage of an incremental construction of a 'pan-European welfare scheme',[145] capable of shaping that bond of organic solidarity among member states' citizens that currently only rests on their finances. Also a Community framework legislation on social services of general interest could help strengthen—in this optimistic, wishful picture—a true political dimension of European social solidarity.[146]

Yet, beyond the examples that have already been suggested or that can be imagined, the redefinition of the boundaries of the welfare systems of the 'Old Europe' certainly requires new and suitable *political* answers. As already observed, it is an integral part of a new social question that directly affects the EU and its scope and capability to contribute to steer such complex processes of economic and social restructuring. And it is difficult to imagine that the Court of Justice, inspired as it may be by the best intentions, may alone give the answers that are needed.

[145] Ferrera, Sacchi, n 135 above, 7.

[146] See essentially Ross, n 14 above.

10

Age Discrimination in Law and Policy: How the Equal Treatment Directive Affects National Welfare States

Deborah Mabbett

1. Introduction

This chapter examines how the European Court of Justice (ECJ) has navigated, or sometimes failed to navigate, a knotty problem in the application of equality laws. The problem can be outlined as follows. The principle of non-discrimination finds its legal expression in two main forms. One is ordinary law, directed at economic actors, applying tests for direct and indirect discrimination on a range of grounds which have changed with changes in social norms and social policy. The other is constitutional law, directed at legislatures and governments, applying the principle of equality before the law or 'equal protection'. This is not a static body of law either, but its progress is marked by a different dynamic, because it pertains to the relationship between judicial and political power. Constitutional courts apply tests of reasonableness and proportionality in scrutinizing legal categories, and allow distinctions made in legislation between different groups of people to be justified on a range of grounds relating to public values and public purposes.

The distinction between these two forms of law is readily made in many national legal systems, but not in the EU, where economic law is 'constitutionalized'. Since the ordinary law against discrimination originates in the Treaty, it applies to the legal and regulatory acts of governments, as well as to the market actions of economic entities.[1] However, as befits Europe's 'market constitution', it applies to governments' interventions in the economy, not to non-economic law and policy. This means that governments cannot act (as economic entities themselves) or regulate private economic entities in contravention of EU equality law. However, this standard of review does not extend to areas where the national

[1] A. Stone Sweet, and R. Cichowski 'Sex Equality' in A. Stone Sweet (ed) *The Judicial Construction of Europe* (Oxford: OUP, 2004) 156–157.

government can be found to be acting within its domestic policy competence in reasonable pursuit of legitimate social purposes. The definition of this area of competence has been a source of perpetual difficulty for the ECJ. For example, it would seem normally to include areas of social policy where governments dispose of their own fiscal resources ('budgetary social policy') but this domain is neither fixed nor clearly defined.

The ECJ's struggle to establish the boundary between economic regulation and social policy in the area of sex equality is well documented in the literature and is reviewed in the next section below. Around the turn of the century, the ECJ's task got harder still, as the member states inserted into the Treaty a general clause empowering the Council to legislate against discrimination on a wide range of grounds. This was quickly followed by new directives, including the Framework Equal Treatment Directive (FETD)[2] which is the focus here. The prohibition on discrimination widened to include age and disability, among other grounds.

Why does this extension make the ECJ's knotty problem knottier? Sex equality law carved out a path through employment regulation and social policy which contributed to the removal of many sex-discriminatory measures in social security. This was part of a reform process which, most people would agree, enhanced the adaptation of the welfare state to changing social conditions.[3] This is a hard path for age and disability equality provisions to follow. It is not clear that people with disabilities would be well served by the removal of disability categories from social legislation,[4] while the use of age categories in social policy also has positive attributes. For example, longer working lives might be promoted by the removal of pension entitlements based solely on age, but this could have other perverse consequences due to increased reliance on means-tested benefits.

The more general issue is whether discrimination which is impugned when applied by an employer in market relationships should be subject to the same legal sanction when applied by an elected government in pursuit of social policy objectives. To answer in the affirmative is to imply that a distinction between ordinary and constitutional law should not be maintained: the two could be a seamless whole. But this not only presents a problem for the relationship between the elected government and the judiciary; it is also a problem for our understanding of social policy. If social policy should comply with the same limitations on discrimination that apply in market relationships, this goes against the idea that social policy is in some sense a 'countervailing force' to the market, and works on different principles. For example, we can hold that it is wrong for an employer to

[2] FETD, 2000/78 EC.

[3] D. Mabbett 'Aspirational legalism and the role of the Equality and Human Rights Commission in equality policy' (2008) 79 (1) Political Q 45–52 at 45.

[4] H. Bolderson, and D. Mabbett 'Non-Discriminating Social Policy? Policy scenarios for meeting needs without categorisation' in J. Clasen (ed) *What Future for Social Security? Debates and Reforms in National and Cross-National Perspective* (The Hague: Kluwer, 2001); D. Mabbett 'Why Have Disability Categories in Social Security?' (2003) Vol 11, No 3, Benefits 163–168.

refuse to employ a person with an impairment by applying the principle of equal opportunity (possibly extended by 'reasonable accommodation') to the market sphere. At the same time, we can support an entitlement to a cash benefit arising from that impairment, on the basis of another principle, such as compensation or need. But this entitlement calls for discrimination, in the sense of categorization or distinction-drawing, as social policy administrators have to determine who counts as disabled.

One difficulty in establishing a sphere of social policy in which non-market norms may apply is that large areas of social provision are closely linked to employment. In particular, social insurance is not an autonomous sphere of social policy, as entitlements are largely derived from employment. As the next section shows, in the field of sex discrimination, social policies linked to employment have been made subject to EU sex equality norms. Failure to eliminate sex discrimination in social insurance would have produced anomalies in achieving equal pay, particularly once it was determined that occupational pensions were part of pay. More generally, it seems that social policy can live without direct sex discrimination in the modern age, although indirect discrimination is endemic. Since more women than men are poor and looking after children, social policies which make allocations according to needs and family responsibilities will indirectly discriminate in favour of women. Whereas payment according to needs is nowadays not thought to be an appropriate principle to apply to market relationships (although this was not always so, as the long history of the 'family wage' testifies), it is, of course, a central principle in social policy.

This chapter is structured as follows. In the next section, the ECJ's approach to the relationship between sex equality law and social policy is discussed, followed by an account of recent cases which take up the age discrimination provisions in the FETD. It is shown that the ECJ steered itself into stormy waters in its early decision in *Mangold*,[5] but has since tried to find a way out. In so doing, it might seem to have weakened the potential impact of the FETD, and the fourth section considers whether and why this might be an appropriate outcome in light of the policy objectives of the Directive and the political conditions under which it was promulgated.

2. European sex equality law and social policy

The Treaty of Rome and its successors commit the member states of the EU to integrating their economies by opening their markets to competition and removing rules, standards and practices that discriminate against suppliers from other states. The Treaty provided that men and women should receive equal pay for equal work (Article 119), a measure introduced at the insistence of France,

[5] Case C-144/04 *Mangold v Helm* [2005] ECR I-1549.

which argued that female-dominated industries in countries which maintained discrimination would have an unfair competitive advantage.[6] While this Article is nowadays seen as founding a robust strand of European equality policy, its original rationale was arguably that of ensuring that fair competition could take place in open markets.

Despite the economic orientation of these measures, it has been apparent since the 1970s that they may affect social security and social protection. First and foremost, this is because social protection policy may be conducted through the regulation of employment or through measures closely linked to employment. When, in the 1970s, Article 119 was developed through directives on equal pay and equal treatment, the potential impact on social security was apparent. Member states could in theory have dug in their heels and insisted on the autonomy of their budgetary social security arrangements. However, this would have produced many anomalies, particularly once the Court decided that the scope of directives extended to occupational pension entitlements arising from employment. Most member states maintained state or social insurance schemes that were interlocked with occupational pension provisions. Member states' resistance to reforming their pension systems to achieve sex equality came to focus on issues of timing and transitions, rather than on the principle of equality itself.

Against this background, we can understand why the member states agreed to Directive 79/7 'on the progressive implementation of the principle of equal treatment for men and women in social security'. For many states, the emphasis was on the word *progressive* (ie not immediate): member states allowed themselves six years for implementation. Furthermore, the Directive was confined to social security entitlements linked to employment, thereby apparently preserving states' competence over social policies that were not linked to the labour market. In the numerous cases that have come before it, the ECJ has broadly respected this boundary. It held that benefits paid to people on a low income that were not linked to employment status were not within the scope of the Directive, and that concessionary travel schemes and child-raising allowances were also excluded.[7] Thus the Court endeavoured to maintain a boundary between the market sphere and social policy.

However, there were some decisions which seemed to permeate the boundary. The specified risks covered by the Directive were those normally covered in Europe by contributory social insurance, available to employees but not to those engaged in work in the home. Nonetheless, in the case of *Drake*,[8] the ECJ found that the rule that married women could not receive a non-contributory benefit, the Invalid Care Allowance, was within the scope of the Directive.[9] The Court reasoned that Mrs Drake should be seen as a member of the working population,

[6] C. Barnard, *EC Employment Law* (3rd edn, Oxford: OUP, 2006) 298.

[7] ibid 494–495.

[8] Case 150/85 *Drake v Chief Adjudication Officer* [1986] ECR 1995.

[9] C. Barnard, n 6 above, 493–494.

who had had to interrupt her employment to care for her mother. Through this reasoning, the Court escaped the constraint that the scope of EU law was confined to economic law affecting employment and did not extend into redistributive social policy. In *Teuling* the Court reviewed an arrangement for the payment of dependents' allowances for conformity with the prohibition on discrimination in Directive 79/7.[10] In *Meyers*,[11] the Court found that Family Credit fell within the scope of Directive 76/207 on equal treatment. Family Credit (since replaced by Tax Credits) paid supplements to workers in low income families; the Court found that it might encourage an unemployed worker to seek work, and thereby affected equality of access to the labour market.[12]

While these cases widened the scope for judicial scrutiny of national social policies, the Court nonetheless often showed deference to the social policy aims of the member states. In *Drake*, direct discrimination against married women was held by the ECJ to be contrary to the Directive. In *Meyers*, the judgment as to whether the indirect discrimination that arose from the operation of the rules could be justified was left to the national court, which found that it could not. However, in *Teuling*, the Court indicated that there was justification for the system.[13] Similarly in *Nolte*[14] and *Megner and Scheffel*,[15] where the exclusion of 'minor' (short hours/ low-income) employment from social insurance was scrutinized, the Court held that indirect discrimination could be justified by considerations of national social policy.

In subsequent cases the Court has refined its tests for deference to national social policy considerations without arriving at a settled point. Thus the Court has established that a measure with different indirect effects on men and women may be justified if it 'reflects a legitimate aim of social policy and the aim is unrelated to any discrimination based on sex, and [the member state] could reasonably consider that the means chosen [are] suitable for attaining that aim'[16] quoted in Costello and Davies (2006)[17]. Ellis (2000)[18] suggested that there was a 'hierarchy of tests [for discrimination] ... The weakest rule apparently applies to the justification of a social security provision... Next comes... a statutory employment provision.. The strictest test ... applies to the justification of an employer's practices...'. Six years later, Costello and Davies also noted this hierarchy of review, although member states have not always fared easily in the cases that have recently come before the Court, particularly in those involving indirect

[10] Case 30/85 *Teulin* [1987] ECR 2497.
[11] Case C-116/94 *Meyers* [1995] ECR I-2131.
[12] C. Barnard, n 6 above, 395–396.
[13] ibid 496.
[14] Case C-317/93 *Nolte* [1995] ECR I-4625.
[15] Case C-444/93 *Megner and Scheffel* [1995] ECR I-4741.
[16] Case C-167/97 *Seymour-Smith and Perez* [1999] ECR I-623.
[17] C. Costello, and G. Davies 'The Case Law of the Court of Justice in the Field of Sex Equality Since 2000' (2006) 43 CML Rev 1567–1616 at 1588.
[18] E. Ellis, 'The Recent Jurisprudence of the Court of Justice in the Field of Sex Equality' (2000) 37 CML Rev 1403–1426 at 1410.

discrimination against women arising from differences in social security rules for part-time and full-time workers.

Since this case law concerns the application of directives, it might be thought that the member states could 'correct' decisions of the Court by amending the relevant directive. However, this has rarely happened in any area of EU law, and it is widely held that the Court is empowered by the difficulty of getting unanimous agreement in Council.[19] Also important is the agenda-setting role of the Commission, which has often encouraged the Court to adopt venturesome interpretations of directives. For example, the Commission advocated a 'fluid' definition of the scope of Directive 79/7, to encompass means-tested social assistance as well as employment-related social insurance.[20] On this reading, the principle of equality in employment would spill over beyond insurance to affect access to social benefits more generally.

The position of the Court vis-à-vis the member states is further strengthened when it is able to invoke the Treaty in support of its judgments, as the capacity of member states to revise the Treaty in response to unwanted Court decisions is very limited indeed.[21] One striking example where the Court relied on the Treaty was in *Barber*.[22] Member states had endeavoured to regulate the impact of sex equality law on occupational pensions (ie pensions which are part of remuneration, rather than falling within the sphere of 'a statutory system of social security') in Directive 86/378. On one hand, the Directive listed a number of provisions as discriminatory, including maintaining unequal retirement ages and setting different conditions for the granting of benefits. On the other hand, it listed various derogations by which discrimination would continue to be allowed, including allowing equality in retirement ages in occupational pensions to be deferred in line with its progressive implementation in state social security schemes. In *Barber*, the Court ruled that occupational pensions were part of remuneration and therefore subject to the Treaty provisions on equality. The Council had acted inconsistently with the Treaty in derogating from equality, and part of the Directive was, therefore, invalid.

3. Article 13 and the Framework Equal Treatment Directive

At the 1997 IGC at Amsterdam, the first part of the Treaty on 'citizenship of the Union' was substantially extended. Among the new provisions was Article 13,

[19] See eg A. Stone Sweet, and T. Brunell 'Constructing a Supranational Constitution: Dispute Resolution and Governance in the European Community' (1998) 92 American Political Science Rev 63–81.

[20] T. Hervey 'Sex equality in social protection: New institutionalist perspectives on the allocation of competence' (1998) 4 Eur LJ 196 at 201–202.

[21] K. Alter, 'Who are the "Masters of the Treaty"? European Governments and the European Court of Justice' (1998) 52 Intl Organization 121–147.

[22] Case C-262/88 *Barber* [1990] ECR I-1889.

which enables the Council to take 'appropriate action' to combat discrimination on a wide range of grounds. Soon after, in 2000, the Race Directive (2000/43 EC) and the Framework Equal Treatment Directive (FETD) (2000/78 EC) were agreed unanimously by the Council. The FETD extends the prohibitions on direct and indirect sex discrimination in employment to other grounds: religion and belief, disability, age and sexual orientation. This section examines how these provisions have been tested in the area of age discrimination. The Directive did not put all the discrimination grounds on the same footing. Indirect disability discrimination was not prohibited, but made subject to the requirement that employers provide 'reasonable accommodation' (Article 5). Age discrimination was subject to the derogation that 'Member States may provide that differences of treatment on grounds of age shall not constitute discrimination if, within the context of national law, they are objectively and reasonably justified by a legitimate aim..' (Article 6(1)).

One of the first age discrimination cases to come before the ECJ was *Mangold*.[23] The case concerned a German regulation which prohibited fixed-term contracts except where there were objective reasons for them. The regulation did not apply to contracts with workers aged over 52. The ECJ upheld Mangold's challenge to this rule, based on critical scrutiny of the considerations of German social policy that had led to the adoption of the limit. The Court noted that the case concerned the field of application of the Directive on fixed-term work (1999/70/EC) which seeks to limit the duration of successive fixed-term contracts and to establish that objective reasons for such contracts should normally be provided, so the measure fell within the scope of Community law. In the formulation of the Court, it was therefore appropriate to provide 'criteria for interpretation', based on general principles of Community law, for a measure falling within the scope of a European directive.[24]

The Opinion and the judgment suggested two main criteria for judging whether a measure entailed unacceptable discrimination. One was the disadvantage experienced by the complainant. The Court's evaluation drew attention to the possibility that a person could be employed on successive short-term contracts for 'a substantial part of [his or her] working life', until reaching pensionable age. During this time, an older worker would be 'excluded from the benefit of stable employment, which [...] constitutes a major element in the protection of workers'.[25] The other criterion, put forward by the Advocate General, concerned the 'closeness of fit' between the impugned measure and its social purposes. The Advocate General reviewed the history by which the limit had been lowered from 60 in 1996, to 58 in 2000, to 52 in the Hartz reforms of 2002. The justification cited by the German Government was research which showed that a person over 55 had only a one-in-four chance of re-employment.[26] The Advocate General drew attention to the difference between 55 and 52, suggesting that research did not really support the policy adopted.

[23] Case C-144/04 *Mangold*, n 5 above.

[24] ibid para 75 of the judgment.

[25] ibid para 64.

[26] ibid para 77.

Mangold arose before the FETD came into force in Germany. The Court evaded this problem by finding that non-discrimination was a 'general principle of Community law'. While the FETD developed the application of this principle, its origins lie 'in various international instruments and in the constitutional principles common to the Member States'.[27] This move on the part of the Court has attracted a great deal of legal commentary, much of it critical. It has been questioned whether age equality really is a fundamental principle in international instruments.[28] Furthermore, if it is a general principle of Community law, this still implies that the Court can act only against the most manifest instances of discrimination, invoking the 'hard, legally perfect core, which can be applied as such by a court, without the necessity of further elaboration in directives'.[29] This meant that, if a constitutional principle of equality was being invoked, it should be applied with deference to the German Government's pursuit of its social policy goals. The impugned regulation might not have been well-designed in all its details, but it was also not completely arbitrary and unreasonable.

The judgment in *Mangold* was greeted very critically in Germany.[30] The Federal Labour Court (the Bundesarbeitsgericht) decided subsequently that it should follow *Mangold*,[31] but only after some consideration of whether the ECJ had exceeded its competence. This decision evoked further criticism in the media, and the Constitutional Court is to deliver its own verdict on the status of the *Mangold* judgment in a ruling due in 2009.[32] In the meantime, the offending regulation remains on the statute book, although with small amendments that would possibly now satisfy the Court: the worker offered the short-term contract must have been previously unemployed, and contracts cannot be repeatedly renewed beyond five years.[33]

Since the ruling in *Mangold*, another case, *Bartsch*,[34] also pertaining to the period before the FETD came into force in Germany, has been ruled on by the Grand Chamber. *Bartsch* is notable for an extensive discussion by Advocate General Sharpston of all the possible ways in which 'Mangold and its progeny' might be dealt with by the Court. In the end, the judgment took the simplest route, of deciding that *Bartsch* did not fall within the scope of Community law. The case arose from a claim by a widow for payment of a survivor's benefit under an occupational pension policy. Since there was no relevant EU measure

[27] ibid para 74.

[28] D. Schiek, 'The ECJ decision in *Mangold*: A further twist on effects of directives and constitutional relevance of Community equality legislation' (2006) 35(3) ILJ 329–341.

[29] J. H. Jans 'The effect in national legal systems of the prohibition of discrimination on grounds of age as a general principle of Community law' (2007) 34 (1) Legal Issues of Eur Integration 53–66 at 59.

[30] M. Schmidt, 'The Principle of Non-discrimination in Respect of Age: Dimensions of the ECJ's *Mangold* Judgment' (2005) 7 (5) German LJ 505–524, at 506.

[31] 7 AZR 500/04. [32] 2 BvR 2661/06.

[33] M. Schmidt, 'Germany', in M. Sargeant (ed) *The Law on Age Discrimination in the EU* (Leiden: Kluwer Law International, 2008) 52.

[34] Case C-427/06 *Bartsch* [2008] OJ C301, 6 (judgment Grand Chamber, 23 September 2008).

governing occupational pension entitlements, the Court concluded that there was 'no link with Community law'.[35] This is, it must be said, a temporary escape for the Court, since the FETD does apply to occupational pensions, now that it has come into force. The German courts seem intent on testing the impact of the FETD, with two referrals, *Kücükdeveci*[36] and *Rosenbladt*[37] awaiting decisions at time of writing. *Kücükdeveci* concerns an age limit that affects the period of notice employers are required to observe on termination of service; *Rosenbladt* concerns the legality of compulsory retirement provisions.

Advocate General Sharpston's extensive discussion of *Mangold* in her Opinion touches on a number of issues which are relevant to the central theme of this chapter, concerning the relationship between 'constitutional' discrimination provisions and those contained in ordinary law. Sharpston's own preferred formulation is that 'discrimination on grounds of age has always been precluded by the general principle of equality, and ... Directive 2000/78 ... introduced a specific detailed framework for dealing with, inter alia, that discrimination'.[38] Thus she does not endeavour to establish a sharp boundary between a constitutional principle and an employment regulation based in ordinary law. In the face of very little evidence that the general principle of equality has been applied to age, she argues that equal treatment has always been historically contingent, using a range of constitutional examples (the exclusion of metics, Helots, slaves and women in ancient Greece and Sparta, the exclusion of black slaves in the US). On this account, the FETD represents yet a further development in the evolution of the principle of equality.

The Advocate General is drawn into this approach by her determination to resolve the problem of *Mangold*—a problem which, as she notes, the Court had steadfastly refused to address in four previous cases where Advocates General had discussed the case and endeavoured to distinguish it.[39] The difficulties presented by her proposed solution are highlighted by the case of *Palacios de la Villa*.[40] That case concerned a compulsory retirement provision in Spain, reviewed at a point where the FETD had come into force. The Court concluded that a measure providing for compulsory retirement based on age was 'objectively and reasonably justified in the context of national law by a legitimate aim relating to employment policy and the labour market'.[41] The Court found that compulsory retirement at 65 was justified by policy considerations, and rejected as a technicality the objection that the justification was not clearly stated in the national legislation at issue.[42] It is for the national authorities to 'find the right balance' so long as

[35] ibid para 25 of the judgment.

[36] Case C-555/07 *Kücükdeveci* (Reference for a preliminary ruling from the Landesarbeitsgericht Düsseldorf (Germany) lodged on 13 December 2007).

[37] Case C-45/09 *Rosenbladt* (Reference for a preliminary ruling from the Arbeitsgericht Hamburg (Germany) lodged on 2 February 2009).

[38] Case C-427/06 *Bartsch*, n 34 above, para 34 of the Opinion.

[39] ibid para 37.

[40] Case C-411/05 *Palacios de la Villa* [2007] ECR I-08531.

[41] ibid para 77.

[42] ibid para 56.

they 'do not go beyond what is appropriate and necessary'.[43] However, the court also noted that, since the compulsory retirement measure only applied to workers who were eligible for a pension, their rights were not unduly compromised by virtue of the financial compensation available,[44] suggesting that it was not shy of making its own substantive evaluation of the merits of the measure.

The Court also approved of the 'fine-tuning' of Spanish retirement law, deeming it legitimate that the authorities had removed but then reintroduced compulsory retirement for employment reasons. The national authorities could make their choices 'on the basis of political, economic, social, demographic and/or budgetary considerations'.[45] Since these choices were contingent on the actual situation in the labour market, which can change through time, it was acceptable that the policy also changed. The fact that retirement provisions could readily be adjusted in collective agreements in the light of labour market conditions was also interpreted favourably by the Court, as indicating that the measure was flexible in its application.[46]

The difficulty that *Palacios de la Villa* presents for Advocate General Sharpston is as follows. As she notes, the Court made no mention of a general principle prohibiting age discrimination, as it was able to apply Directive 2000/78. Since the Directive contains explicit provisions spelling out the policy considerations that a member state can take account of to permit the continued use of age distinctions, the application of this specific law led to a wider margin of discretion for the respondent than was applied in *Mangold*, where the Court was supposedly applying a general principle. More generally, it is inconsistent to argue that Community or national legislators should define the scope of the prohibition on age discrimination while at the same time claiming that they are developing a constitutional principle, since a constitutional principle stands above ordinary legislative acts.

One question put by the referring Court in *Bartsch* was whether the general principle of non-discrimination on grounds of age had 'horizontal application' to private as well as state parties. The case in *Bartsch* concerned the rules of an occupational pension scheme, although the rule in question (denying a pension where the survivor was more than 15 years younger than the primary policyholder) was derived from one operating in the statutory pension scheme. In addressing this question, the Advocate General noted the difficulty of setting a borderline between state and private action. For example, 'a private association ... [with] a regulatory function ... could ... perhaps be assimilated to an emanation of the State'.[47] Furthermore, a 'constitutional' challenge to a state regulation could arise out of an action between private parties, as was indeed the case in *Mangold*. Thus the Advocate General concluded that 'a general principle of Community law may, in appropriate circumstances, be applied horizontally'.[48]

[43] ibid para 71. [44] ibid para 73.
[45] ibid para 69. [46] ibid para 74.
[47] Case C-427/06 *Bartsch*, n 34 above, para 84 of the Opinion. [48] ibid para 85.

It might indeed be possible to defend the application of a general 'equal treatment' principle to relations between private parties, especially where the power relationship is asymmetric, as in employment. However, a difficulty arises when it is envisaged that a government can *deviate* from equal treatment on public policy grounds. A private entity cannot be expected to evaluate and apply public policy considerations—in other words, to ask whether the distinction it wants to make is in the public good. Rather, we would expect that a private entity in a market economy is able to act according to its preferences—for example, in pursuit of profit maximization—provided that action is within the law. Put another way, applying a general principle of non-discrimination to private parties could potentially bear harder on them than on the state, as they have no legitimacy to plead 'public purposes'. As Advocate General Sharpston puts it: 'it is not appropriate to expect a private employer to make, without guidance, the social and policy choices that lie behind the Article 6(1) derogation. It is explicitly for the Member State to make those choices and to bear the responsibility for them.'[49] The Advocate General sidestepped this problem by arguing that any application of a general principle must be within a specific Community law framework; this framework (such as the Directive on fixed term work in *Mangold*) fills the gap of setting out the social policy choices that are relevant.

Both the Opinion and the judgment in *Bartsch* propose a re-reading of *Mangold* in which a good deal more weight is put on the existence of the Directive on fixed-term work than is evident from the original judgment. But the approach taken by Advocate General Sharpston finds support in the sex equality cases discussed in the previous section. As noted there, deference to public policy is evident in the application of sex equality norms to social policy provisions. However, in recent cases of indirect discrimination arising from unequal treatment of part-time and full-time workers, the Court has been noticeably lacking in deference. This is because proportionate equality for part-time workers has been brought into the scope of Community law by the Directive on part-time work.[50] Where a clear direction for social policy has been established at the EU level, the principle that member states retain competence over their own welfare states is superseded.

While the Advocate General in *Bartsch* was concerned to find a way of distinguishing *Mangold*, other Advocates have been less circumspect in rejecting the line of argument developed in that case. In *Chacon Navas*,[51] the Court was asked to consider whether the definition of disability should be widened to include sickness. Arguing against widening the discrimination grounds and promoting a general principle of equality, Advocate General Geelhoed pointed out that the question at issue related to the fields of employment and social policy 'where the Community has at best shared, but for the most part complementary powers'. It followed that 'the Court must respect the choices made by the Community legislature' and not use Article 13 'as a lever to correct [...] the decisions made by the

[49] ibid para 90. [50] Dir 97/81. [51] Case C-13/05 *Chacon Navas* [2006] I-06467.

Member States in the exercise of powers which they—still—retain.'[52] It followed that the Court should stay within the boundaries of directives, rather than invoking the Treaty (Article 13) or other sources of 'general principles'.

Finally, a case brought by a pressure group, *Age Concern*,[53] challenged the transposition of Directive 2000/78 into UK law. Age Concern argued that Regulation 30, which set a 'default' retirement age of 65, was in breach of the Directive. More generally, it claimed that the grounds on which age discrimination would continue to be permitted are inadequately specified in the UK regulations. The UK Government argued in response that the contested provision on the retirement age was not covered by the Directive, or, alternatively, that it fell within the defence of justifiability envisaged by Article 6(1). The High Court referred the question of whether the retirement age Regulation was within the scope of the Directive, along with the general issue of adequate specificity in transposition, to the ECJ for a preliminary ruling.

The Court decided, following *Palacios de la Villa*, that the retirement age was within the scope of the Directive. Recital 14 in the Preamble to the Directive states that it shall be 'without prejudice to national provisions laying down retirement ages', but the Court read this provision as referring to the *pension* age, and asserted that the Recital did 'not in any way preclude the application of the directive to national measures governing the conditions for termination of employment contracts where the retirement [pension] age, thus established, has been reached' (*Palacios* Judgment, para 44). UK policy-makers have established a distinction between the pension age and the retirement age (see below) that makes this formulation seem convoluted, if not wrong, but the same distinction does not appear in the practices (and languages) of many other member states.

The Court rejected Age Concern's general claim of inadequate specificity in transposition. Again, the judgment mainly follows *Palacios* in finding that it is not necessary for the national law to spell out its rationale in terms which mirror those of the European Directive. The justifications found in Article 6(1) of the Directive (that the measure is proportionate and necessary for 'legitimate employment policy, labour market and vocational training objectives') do not have to be listed in national law.

The terms of the High Court's reference to the ECJ did not invite the European court to assess the justification for compulsory retirement. Instead, the ECJ's ruling on the first point left it open for the UK court to conduct its own assessment. This restriction of the terms of reference, in effect asking the ECJ to clarify the scope of the law but not evaluate its substantive application, has not been adopted in other cases. For example, in the pending case of *Rosenbladt*,[54] the Arbeitsgericht Hamburg has asked specifically whether compulsory retirement contravenes the Directive. In a recently decided case, *Hütter*,[55] the Oberster

[52] ibid paras 52–54 of the Opinion.

[53] Case C-388/07 *Age Concern* [2009] OJ C102, 6.

[54] Case C-45/09 *Rosenbladt*, n 37 above.

[55] Case C-88/08 *Hütter* [2009] OJ C180, 15.

Gerichtshof (in Austria) asked whether the legislation in question, related to accreditation of previous years of service, was precluded by Articles 1, 2 and 6 of the Directive. (The ECJ decided that it was.) Clearly, the potential for judicial controversy about the application of the Directive is very much affected by these variations in referral practices.

4. Non-discrimination law in social Europe

It is evident that interpretative uncertainty shrouds the scope of the prohibition on age discrimination in the FETD, and that the principle that age distinctions are discriminatory is not generally firmly established. As Advocate General Mazak remarked in *Age Concern*: 'Age is not by its nature a "suspect ground", at least not so much as for example race or sex. Simple in principle to administrate, clear and transparent, age-based differentiations, age-limits and age-related measures are ... widespread in law and in social and employment legislation in particular.'[56] In the light of this, it is salient to ask what the member states might have been trying to achieve when they unanimously agreed to the inclusion of age in the FETD. Can we identify the legislative intent behind the measure, and thereby get a guide to how it should be interpreted?

Article 13 and the FETD can be seen as the result of the conjoining of two processes: the development of the constitutional foundations of the EU and the reform of European welfare states to promote efficiency and competitiveness. These processes are not natural companions. The former finds lawyers speaking the language of fundamental rights; the latter economists and policy-makers speaking of responding to demographic change by promoting flexible labour markets.

The latter group expressed itself at the European level in the late 1990s through communications linked to the Employment Strategy, notably the Commission Communication, 'Towards a Europe for all ages—promoting prosperity and intergenerational solidarity.'[57] The 2000 Joint Employment Report emphasized that older workers were exiting prematurely from the labour market, producing an average employment rate for the EU of only 37 per cent among workers aged 55–64. At Lisbon in 2000, the goal of raising the overall employment rate to 70 per cent and women's employment rate to 60 per cent by 2010 was set. At the Stockholm meeting the following year, more emphasis was put on policy problems arising from population aging, and a target of 50 per cent was set for the employment rate of workers aged 55–64 by 2010.

Action to combat age discrimination is mentioned in successive Employment Reports as a policy instrument to achieve this goal, and it is specifically mentioned in Recital 25 of the FETD, which states that 'the prohibition on age

[56] Case C-388/07, n 53 above, para 74 of the Opinion.

[57] COM (1999) 221 final.

discrimination is an essential part of meeting the aims set out in the Employment Guidelines'. However, the process leading up to the inclusion of Article 13 in the Treaty at Amsterdam had different origins. Its roots can be found in a programme to develop statements of fundamental rights that would bind the Community institutions.[58] The first initiatives were brought forward by the Directorate General (DG) for Justice and Home Affairs to respond to the challenge posed by the German constitutional court as to how Community law, as interpreted by the ECJ, could have supremacy over national constitutional law.[59] This became part of the more general project of building a constitution for Europe.

This project is marked by slippage between developing constitutional principles for the institutions of the EU and introducing new constitutional principles for the member states. As Barnard has observed, 'rights intended to foster a commitment to the *Union* are actually being exercised against the *Member States*'.[60] An example of how this slippage occurs is provided by Geddes and Guiraudon's analysis of the progress of the Race Directive.[61] They show that the election of Jörg Haider in Austria provided other states with an opportunity to make rhetorical statements about the values of the EU. They argue that the French (in particular) backed themselves into a trap 'with their richly symbolic opposition to Haider, making it nearly impossible for them to turn around and veto anti-discrimination measures'.[62] Specifically, the French were trapped with an account of what Europe should stand for, made in a supranationalist frame of reference, which led them to agree to a measure which clearly applied to the member states.

Slippage between the supranational and national frame of reference also helps to explain why, in recent years, directives promulgated under Article 13, in the citizenship chapter of the Treaty, have made more rapid progress through Council than those made under Articles in the Social Policy chapter. This pattern seems particularly anomalous given that the Article 13 directives require unanimity, whereas Qualified Majority Voting (QMV) can be used under some social policy Articles. It is as if the context of 'European citizenship' and the decision-setting of unanimity serves to orient the participants towards supranationalism and to draw a veil over national interests, while QMV highlights national differences and renders them salient for decision-making.

[58] D. Mabbett 'The development of rights-based social policy in the European Union: The example of disability rights' (2005) 43(1) J of Common Market Studies, 95–118, at 104–105.

[59] J. Wieland, 'Germany in the European Union—The Maastricht Decision of the Bundesverfassungsgericht' (1994) 5 Eur J of Intl L 259–266; L. Betten and N. Grief, *EU Law and Human Rights* (Longman European Law Series, 1998); R. Bellamy, and D. Castiglione 'Legitimizing the Euro-"Polity" and its "Regime": The Normative Turn in EU Studies' (2003) 2(1) Eur J of Political Theory 7–34.

[60] C. Barnard 'Article 13: Through the Looking Glass of Union Citizenship' in D. O'Keefe and P. Twomey (eds) *Legal Issues of the Amsterdam Treaty* (Oxford: Hart, 1999) 384, emphasis in original.

[61] A. Geddes, and V. Guiraudon 'Britain, France, and EU Anti-Discrimination Policy: The Emergence of an EU Policy Paradigm' (2004) 27(2) West Eur Politics 334–353.

[62] ibid 348

Furthermore, the governments of the member states may utilize the distinctive character of the supranational venue for their own ends. In particular, national governments can use the EU-level forum in a 'two-level game' of reform politics. Measures which are blocked domestically may be agreed in Europe. In the area of non-discrimination, we can see that politicians with a common concern to 'modernize' their welfare states but faced with opposition from domestic interest groups may see an EU-level measure as a potential reform lever. This may seem to be a high-risk strategy, as they will subsequently find themselves bound by judicial application of the directives. But they may believe that a directive is sufficiently vague to avoid this problem (although, time after time, ECJ decisions show this belief to be wrong). Certainly, the provisions on age in the FETD were so hedged around with caveats that member states may have believed they were gaining a resource which they could use at will, rather than agreeing to a measure that would subsequently bind them.

The idea that a measure might be deliberately vague may offend legal sensibilities, but it is arguable that ambiguous and symbolic declarations are an inevitable, and even useful, part of policy-making. Sunstein's analysis of the 'expressive function of law' draws attention to the way in which laws in areas such as non-discrimination may aim to change social norms and attitudes.[63] While this process has a large capacity for unintended consequences, it remains that the expression of social norms *is* a function of law.

The passage of the Employment Equality (Age) Regulations 2006[64] in the UK gives some insight into the way that the FETD could be used as a reform lever. The government had opened discussions on age discrimination before the passage of the FETD (but after the Amsterdam IGC had included age among the Article 13 grounds). A consultation exercise launched in 1997 focused on raising employment among the 55–64 age group, rather than on the retirement age.[65] The outcome of this exercise was very limited: the Department of Trade and Industry produced a code of practice on age discrimination in employment, but preferred a 'voluntaristic' approach, rather than legislation. The passage of the FETD changed this; transposition would require legislation.

A general consultation on the FETD and the Race Directive took place in 2001. The debate at this stage was dominated by the proposal to establish a single Equality Agency, and the specific issue of age discrimination was not high on the agenda. Taking advantage of the possibility to extend the transposition period for the Directive, the government produced another consultation, specifically on age (*Age Matters*) in 2003. This consultation opened the question of whether compulsory retirement would be allowed under the Directive, drawing on a parallel

[63] C. Sunstein 'On the expressive function of law' (1996) 144 U of Pennsylvania L Rev 2021–2053.

[64] SI 1031/2006.

[65] M. Sargeant, 'The Employment Equality (Age) Regulations 2006: A Legitimisation of Age Discrimination in Employment' (2006) 35 (3) ILJ 209–227 at 212.

report by the Department of Work and Pensions (DWP). This must be seen as a highly strategic move, because, on the face of it, there was little support for the DWP's claim that '[u]nder the Directive, compulsory retirement ages are likely to be unlawful unless employers can show that they are objectively justified'.[66] This went against the statement to the contrary in the 14th Recital to the Directive, and the ECJ had yet to execute the ingenious manoeuvre in *Palacios* that effectively set the 14th Recital aside. It is possible that a DWP lawyer anticipated the ECJ's approach, but it is more likely that the Department saw the Directive as an opportunity to open a question of some political delicacy. If the public reaction turned out to be overwhelmingly hostile, they could pull back and blame 'Europe'.

As it turned out, the response from trade unions to the possibility of ending compulsory retirement was positive. This was by no means a preordained outcome: historically, unions were actively involved in the 'invention' of retirement.[67] However, by 2003 the removal of the retirement age was seen by the unions as an opportunity to extend unfair dismissal and redundancy protection to workers over 65. The DWP was careful to detach the setting of retirement ages from the determination of the *pension* age: in the UK, the state pension is payable at 65 (and still younger for women) regardless of whether the recipient retires from work. This ensured a widely positive response to making retirement voluntary, except from employers, who sought to maintain compulsion. The government's response, which was well-received by employers, was to introduce the concept of a 'default' retirement age, which envisaged the possibility that individual and collective agreements could deviate from that age.

As noted above, the Regulations transposing the Directive were challenged in the High Court, and some questions were referred to the ECJ. While Age Concern's direct challenge to the validity of the Regulations failed, the ECJ confirmed that the provisions on the retirement age fell within the scope of the Directive and could therefore be scrutinized for justification. This part of the judgment was taken up by Age Concern, joined by another campaigning organization, Help the Aged. As well as publicizing the judgment through press releases emphasizing that the justification for compulsory retirement provisions would now be reviewed by the High Court, they seized the political opportunity to make their argument against compulsory retirement at hearings going on at the time before the House of Commons Work and Pensions Committee,[68] ostensibly concerned with disability equality.

The Committee did not disappoint, and inserted into its disability equality report the observation that the default retirement age 'contradicts the Government's

[66] Quoted in ibid 215.

[67] L. Hannah, *Inventing retirement: the development of occupational pensions in Britain* (Cambridge: Cambridge University Press, 1986).

[68] House of Commons Work and Pensions Committee, *The Equality Bill: how disability equality fits within a single Equality Act*, Third Report of Session 2008–2009, HC158–1, 29 April (London: The Stationery Office, 2009).

wider social policy and labour market objectives to raise the average retirement age and allow people to continue to work and save for their retirement and should be removed'.[69] The government responded by bringing forward its planned review of the default retirement age to 2010. This decision fortuitously prevented an adverse ruling by the High Court, which asserted that,[70] in the absence of an imminent review, it might have ruled that setting a default retirement age of 65 would have constituted discrimination disproportionate to its public policy goals.

5. Conclusion

This chapter has documented how the ECJ has restrained its interpretation of the scope of the age discrimination provisions in the FETD after its venturesome decision in *Mangold*. It is clear that the Court risked serious conflict with member states if it kept to the *Mangold* path, but this raises the question of why the member states unanimously agreed to the inclusion of a prohibition on age discrimination in the FETD if they did not intend it to have legal force over their own social policy decisions. Answers to this question can be found in two features of the equality and non-discrimination provisions: the interaction or slippage between measures to regulate the European level of governance and the member state level, and the symbolic and rhetorical properties of equality law. These features help to explain how the FETD came about; they do not, however, provide much guidance to courts on how the measure should be interpreted.

One major problem of interpretation for the ECJ, given the delicate politics of its relationship with the member states, is how to distinguish the application of ordinary law to regulate discrimination by economic actors from the application of constitutional law to the social policy decisions of the member states. The argument for making this distinction requires acceptance that discrimination which we would criticize if applied by an employer in market relationships may be less pernicious when applied by an elected government in pursuit of social policy objectives. However, these are difficult judgments to make. The principle of non-discrimination applied to sex has proved to be a powerful reform lever because its advocates argued that its application to social policy should *not* be different to its application to market relationships. They criticized policy-makers' reliance, in designing social policies, on norms about familial relationships which perpetuated women's dependent relationship to men and their secondary economic status.

By contrast, in the areas of age and disability discrimination, it is possible to hold that people should not lose employment rights at a certain age without also

[69] ibid para 118.

[70] *Age UK v Secretary of State for Business, Innovation and Skills* [2009] EWHC 2336 (Admin), 25 September 2009.

regarding it as wrong that age is a criterion in determining eligibility for a pension or benefit. In the area of disability, we may feel that it is wrong for an employer to refuse to employ a person with an impairment, while at the same time supporting an entitlement to benefits arising from that impairment. But even in these examples, it is clear that economic regulation and social policy design interact. Disability benefits may be supportable, but they could also be seen as entrenching outmoded assumptions about dependency. Age criteria may make for efficient and unobtrusive benefit administration, but they also reinforce expectations about patterns of working life. In the UK debate, this interaction has come to focus on the maintenance of a compulsory or default retirement age.

In the cases discussed here, these basic questions of social policy run alongside equally basic questions about the relationship between judicial and political power. It is questionable whether the ECJ should take a leading role in the dialogue between economic regulation and social policy, by pressing for changes in social policy at the member state level, when other venues are available and have been heavily utilized. Taking the example of the UK, we can see that it has engaged in an extensive policy debate about age discrimination, using the FETD as a reform lever to set an agenda in which the issue of compulsory retirement has been opened up. It is arguable that the FETD has been a judicial failure but a public policy success in the UK, utilized effectively by the government to shift the terms of the debate and change expectations about retirement.

11

Promoting the Multi-Pillar Model? The EU and the Development of Funded Pension Schemes

Karen Anderson

This chapter investigates the ways in which European integration is shaping the development of national pension systems in the EU. EU legislation and European Court of Justice (ECJ) judgments increasingly create constraints and opportunities for national pension systems, as does the deepening of European financial integration. These parallel developments have altered the external context within which national pension systems operate and create incentives for increasing the role of pre-funded supplementary pensions in the member states. To be sure, there remains considerable institutional diversity in pension provision among the member states. However, European developments are pushing national policy in a very specific direction: towards a multi-pillar model based on individual, employment-based pension entitlement. The central features of this emerging pension paradigm are: financially sustainable and adequate public pensions coupled with portable, funded occupational pension schemes that take full advantage of the internal market. To the extent that these principles become institutionalized in national policy, they will have important implications for conceptions of solidarity embedded in national pension arrangements.

The chapter begins with a brief discussion of the variable forms of solidarity embedded in national pension systems. The second section briefly discusses the three core components of the EU's emerging pensions paradigm: the Open Method of Coordination (OMC) process as applied to pensions, the recently adopted occupational pension fund Directive, and the proposed Directive on pension portability. This includes discussion of some of the consequences of EU pension policy in Germany and the Netherlands. The concluding section discusses the implications of the analysis for the future of social solidarity in the EU.

1. Pension systems and solidarity

Social science scholarship on welfare state variations typically focuses on the ways in which the structure of social protection differs along three dimensions: benefits, financing and administration. For social insurance schemes like pensions, this means asking: What is the basis for benefit entitlement (citizen, worker, or dependent?), and how are benefits calculated (flat-rate or earnings-related)? How will benefits and services be financed (general tax revenues, employer/employee contributions, VAT)? Which group or agency will administer the scheme (unions, employers, mutual societies, private actors, or the state)?

Obviously there is a wide range of institutional variation in Europe, depending on how political actors designed the first social insurance schemes and how subsequent sets of actors modified them. In the field of pensions, this diversity is often overwhelming and exceedingly technical because of the extensive coverage and complexity of pension schemes and the large sums of money involved.[1] Even though Esping-Andersen[2] has been explicit about the different kinds of solidarity embedded in national social policies, we still do not know enough about the relationship between solidarity and pension design. Analysts regularly invoke the concept of solidarity in discussing the effects of pension reforms, but this is usually not done systematically; scholars often refer, rather vaguely, to cost-saving pension reforms resulting in 'declining solidarity' without ever really discussing the type of solidarity embedded in the pre-reform pension system and comparing it to the type of solidarity promoted by the reformed pension system. In contrast, Stjernø's analysis of the history of solidarity as an idea demonstrates the complexity of solidarity as a concept.[3] But again, there is little discussion of the relationship between solidarity and policy design.

This section attempts to briefly sketch out what seem to me to be the main ways that different aspects of pension design generate different kinds of solidarity:

(1) universalism v segmentalism;
(2) individual v breadwinner entitlement;
(3) flat-rate v earnings-related entitlement;
(4) intergenerational v intragenerational obligations;
(5) public v private provision.

[1] For two influential typologies see: G. Esping-Andersen, *The Three Worlds of Welfare Capitalism* (Princeton: Princeton University Press, 1990); and G. Bonoli, 'Two Worlds of Pension Reform in Western Europe' (2003) Comparative Politics 35, No 4, 399–416; P. Baldwin, *The Politics of Social Solidarity: Class Bases of the European Welfare State, 1875–1975* (Cambridge: Cambridge University Press, 1990) uses the concept of 'risk category' to distinguish between different kinds of social policy design.

[2] G. Esping-Andersen, *Politics Against Markets* (Princeton: Princeton University Press, 1985); G. Esping-Andersen, *The Three Worlds of Welfare Capitalism,* n 1 above.

[3] S. Stjernø, *Solidarity in Europe. The History of an Idea* (Cambridge: Cambridge University Press, 2005).

The notion of solidarity implies that the members of some defined group are bound by a set of mutual rights and obligations. Thus the first question in terms of pension design is: who will be included in the pension scheme? Universal coverage, as in the Scandinavian countries, means universal solidarity: all residents are entitled to benefits. No group can opt out, and no group has access to a better set of benefits on the basis of group membership. Segmentalist coverage means that different occupational groups are covered by different pension schemes, often with varying levels of benefits and contribution rates. The continental or Bismarckian welfare states exemplify this approach to solidarity. For example, in Germany civil servants, farmers and miners have their own pension schemes. The free professions (lawyers, doctors, pharmacists, etc) have access to separate pension arrangements. Blue and white collar workers in dependent employment (about 80 per cent of the workforce) participate in the statutory pension scheme.[4]

Second, significant differences in benefit entitlement persist among EU member states as well. In the Scandinavian countries, individual entitlement to pensions and other social insurance schemes is the norm, while the continental and liberal (UK and Ireland) rely on both individual and derived rights. ECJ interpretations of EC law prompted the reform of breadwinner-only access to statutory and occupational social security schemes in the 1970s and 1980s.[5] Despite the massive entry of women into the labour force across the EU since the 1970s, many Bismarckian pension schemes retain extensive derived pension rights. This means that an individual worker accrues pension rights not just for him/herself, but also for his/her spouse or partner if he/she dies.[6]

Third, member states differ in terms of whether their statutory pension schemes provide flat-rate benefits, earnings-related benefits, or both. Only the Dutch and Danish pension systems include public flat-rate pensions that are sufficient to prevent old-age poverty. Both schemes pay flat-rate benefit to those who have lived in the country for 50 years.[7] In most EU member states, earnings-related public schemes dominate, and this is usually supplemented by means-tested minimum provision.[8]

Broadly speaking there are two ways to design earnings-related pension benefits: defined contribution (DC) and defined benefit (DB). In its purest form, a DC scheme involves an individual account in which participants save for

[4] B. Ebbinghaus, M. Gronwald, and T. Wiss, 'Germany: Departing from Bismarckian Pensions?' in B. Ebbinghaus (ed) *Occupational Pensions in Europe* (Oxford: OUP, in press); I. Schulze and S. Jochem, 'Germany: Beyond Policy Gridlock.' in E. M. Immergut, K. M. Anderson and I. Schulze (eds) *The Handbook of West European Pension Politics* (Oxford: OUP, 2007) 660–710.

[5] K. Hoskyns, *Integrating Gender. Women, Law and Politics in the European Union* (London: Verso, 1996).

[6] See Sainsbury (1996) on different types of benefit entitlement.

[7] The pension is reduced proportionately by 2% for each missing year. The UK and Irish pension systems include flat-rate pensions, but they are not high enough to prevent old-age poverty.

[8] For details on the balance between public and private benefits in the EU-15 see E. M. Immergut, K. M. Anderson and I. Schulze (eds) *The Handbook of West European Pension Politics* (Oxford: OUP, 2007).

retirement. The contributions are often co-financed or fully financed by employers. The principal and income earned by the investments in the account are then converted to an annuity at retirement or simply withdrawn at regular intervals after retirement.[9] There is no insurance or compensation for bad financial decisions or market turmoil; returns are completely dependent on the level of contributions and investment performance.

In contrast, a DB scheme is based on a promise by the pension scheme sponsor to pay an employee a specific benefit at retirement. These schemes may be pre-funded or paid out of current payroll costs, but the key difference with DC schemes is that the size of the pension benefit is fixed in advance, and contribution levels are adjusted as necessary to finance pension benefits. Typical DB occupational schemes pay some percentage (often 60 per cent) of average earnings or the final salary after 40 years of service. Obviously, the number of years required for a full pension, annual rate of pension accumulation, and the reference salary (final salary, average salary) used to calculate the pension level varies greatly across schemes.

These two 'pure' types obscure the ways in which the DB/DC distinction is really a continuum rather than two mutually exclusive categories. DC schemes may include elements associated with DB schemes, such as guaranteed rates of return. And DB schemes may include features more commonly associated with DC schemes such as making a portion of the pension dependent on investment returns.

Notional defined contribution (NDC) schemes complicate things further because they are based on the same principles as pre-funded DC schemes. NDC schemes are almost always PAYG (pay as you go) statutory schemes (Switzerland is an exception). Earnings-based contributions accrue in individuals' pension accounts and are indexed according to some specified formula for calculating the rate of return, usually wage growth. At retirement, the accumulated notional capital is converted to an annuity. Sweden and Italy have introduced NDC into their statutory schemes, as have many of the new member states (ie Poland).

Fourth, the financing structure of pension schemes involves explicit assumptions about the rights and obligations of different generations. PAYG DB schemes imply an *inter*generational contract whereas PAYGO NDC schemes imply an *intra*generational contract. The very essence of a PAYGO system is that there is little or no funding. Instead, current pension benefits are financed by current tax or contribution revenues. This means that current pensioners depend on current workers to finance their pension payments, and current workers depend on future workers to finance their pension payments when they retire. In contrast, funded DC schemes are individually-based and thus involve few or no intergenerational obligations. In a funded DC scheme, each individual saves for his/her pension in an individual account and there is no pooling of risks. Funded DB

[9] For a detailed discussion see P. Davis, *Pension Funds. Retirement-Income Security and Capital Markets. An International Perspective* (Oxford: Clarendon Press, 1995).

schemes involve a weak form of intergenerational solidarity because current contributions and current benefits are linked. Contributions rise or fall (unless the pension scheme sponsor pays the full cost) depending on the cost of current benefits, so contributors and beneficiaries are mutually dependent in a way that does not apply to DC or NDC schemes.

Finally, the distinction between public and private provision merits discussion. One tends to think of public pension schemes as more redistributive and therefore more solidaristic than privately organized ones, but this impression is often misleading. To be sure, the empirical reality is that most public schemes are more redistributive than private ones, but this need not be so. As the examples discussed above show, the public NDC schemes like those in Italy and Sweden can be actuarially fair and thus involve little redistribution across groups. Similarly, privately organized occupational pension schemes like the funded DB schemes in the Netherlands can promote solidarity within occupational groups. The essential point here is that, at least in theory, the public/private distinction is not as important as other aspects of pension design (PAYG, the basis of entitlement, the actuarial fairness of benefits) in shaping the kinds of solidarities embedded in pension schemes.

What does all of this mean in the real European world of pension provision? At one extreme are the Nordic, liberal (UK and Ireland) and new member state approaches to pension provision in which individual entitlement prevails, and derived rights are weak or non-existent. Among these individually-based systems there are substantial differences in reliance on DB/DC, flat-rate v earnings-related pensions and the mode of financing. Nordic pension provision is based on the principles of universal, individual entitlement based on work and intra-generational solidarity; every generation pays for itself. The Anglo-Irish approach is characterized by weak universal solidarity (the state pension) embedded in a weak intergenerational contract, coupled with the strong segmentalism in the occupational pension system. In the Bismarckian countries, intergenerational segmentalism prevails: universal solidarity is weak or non-existent (weak minimum pension provision) and pension entitlement is often linked to parental status. Parents (almost always mothers) often accrue pension rights for child-rearing, and the childless sometimes pay higher contributions than parents (ie the Riester pension subsidies in Germany). And the PAYG, DB structure of pension provision implies a very strong intergenerational contract. Pension rights accrued today have to be paid for by the future contributions of today's children. This makes a DB, PAYG system sensitive to employment and fertility rates.

The point of this brief overview is to demonstrate that there are multiple solidarities built into European pension systems.[10] While it is true that public

[10] See also M. Ferrera, and A. Hemerijck 'Recalibrating Europe's Welfare Regimes' in J. Zeitlin, and D. Trubek (eds) *Governing Work and Welfare in a New Economy* (Oxford: OUP, 2003), which groups of the member states into four 'social Europes'.

provision still dominates in all but two or three countries (the Netherlands, UK and Denmark), it is certainly *not* true that public provision is characterized by some sort of one-size fits all solidarity that all member states more or less agree on. The reformed Swedish public pension system entails a very different sort of solidarity than the German one even if both systems rely on earnings-related benefits. Most Swedish policy-makers would never dream of rewarding parents with subsidies for occupational pension provision, and it is a cornerstone of public policy that women should be economically independent. This principle is reflected in labour market policy, tax policy and pension policy. In contrast, German principles of solidarity entail that society should be supportive of parents (usually mothers) who stay at home to care for children, so pension credits for child-rearing are financed by the general budget.[11] The existence of multiple solidarities (intergenerational v intragenerational; universal v segmentalist; individual v breadwinner/parents) means that member states are affected differently by the emerging EU approach to pensions policy.

2. The European Union and pension policy

The EU has few explicit competences in the area of pensions. There are considerable institutional obstacles to EU-level social policy-making stemming from the relatively narrow treaty bases (until recently) for social policy initiatives and the multi-level character of EU decision-making. Most analysts point to the strong political salience of social policy in national politics.[12] Welfare states remain primarily nationally organized because the member states intensely value social policy autonomy. Elections are won and lost on social policy issues, and social policy objectives absorb one half to two thirds of public budgets. Moreover, the substantial degree of social policy diversity across the member states means that attempts to Europeanize national social policies will face formidable obstacles.[13] Unlike other public policies, the sunk costs and sheer density of social policies mean that they are difficult to harmonize. There is thus widespread agreement among observers of social policy integration that the member states are reluctant to cede social policy sovereignty to European institutions, and they respond defensively to EU initiatives that fundamentally challenge their welfare state status quo.[14]

[11] The Swedish pension system also awards pension rights for child-rearing, but this arrangement is not nearly as generous as the German one.

[12] S. Leibfried, 'Social Policy' in H. Wallace, W. Wallace, and M. A. Pollack (eds) *Policy-Making in the European Union* (5th edn, Oxford: OUP, 2005); S. Leibfried, and P. Pierson (eds) *European Social Policy. Between Fragmentation and Integration* (Washington DC: The Brookings Institution Press,1995).

[13] F. W. Scharpf, 'The European Social Model. Coping with the Challenges of Diversity' (2002) 40(4) J of Common Market Studies 645–670.

[14] M. Ferrera, and A. Hemerijck (2003), n 10 above; W. Streeck, 'From Market Making to State Building? Reflections on the Political Economy of European Social Policy', in S. Leibfried and

These constraints do not mean that European integration has little impact on national social policies. Pierson and Leibfried argue that multi-level systems like the EU are characterized by three central processes: the importance of constituent units in policy-making, the tendency toward conflictual policy-making and lowest common denominator solutions, and the reconfiguration of the political opportunity structure as actors organize transnationally and the member states lose their monopoly status as the target of interest group activity.[15] These features tend to reinforce the social policy status quo in the EU: the dilemmas associated with shared political authority as well as the institutional barriers to social policy-making militate against radical transfers of policy competences to the EU. Thus Pierson and Leibfried confirm Hooghe and Marks argument that the member states remain key actors but have lost control over important aspects of domestic policy, not only because of the power of supranational institutions such as the ECJ, but also because of the political effects of previous policy commitments.[16] Once European legislation is in place, it is exceedingly difficult to reverse it. On the other hand, issue density and spillovers caused by the internal market create incentives for European social policy initiatives, despite institutional barriers.

In his later work, Leibfried argues that social policy integration is primarily market and court-driven.[17] The process of market-making has led to spill-over and demands for EU social policies concerning labour market issues like gender equality and occupational health and safety. Market-building and judicial activism have, in fact, created somewhat of a social policy vacuum because the member states have lost considerable social policy autonomy in the process of integration while the EU has not gained equivalent competences. In other words, the loss of member state social policy sovereignty has not been matched by a corresponding expansion of competences at EU level.

Streeck[18] and Scharpf[19] share this fundamentally pessimistic view of social policy integration, pointing to the frequent subordination of national social policies to the EU's market-making ambitions and the seemingly permanent policy stalemate in Brussels that prevents substantial positive social policy initiatives.

P. Pierson, *European Social Policy,* n 12 above; W. Streeck, 'Neo-Voluntarism: A New European Social Policy Regime?' in G. Marks, F. Scharpf, P. Schmitter, and W. Streeck (eds) *Governance in the European Union* (London: Sage, 1996) 64–94.

15 P. Pierson and S. Leibfried, 'Multitiered Institutions and the Making of Social Policy.' in S. Leibfried, and P. Pierson (eds) *European Social Policy. Between Fragmentation and Integration* (Washington DC: The Brookings Institution Press, 1995) 1–40.

16 L. Hooghe, and G. Marks, *Multi-Level Governance and European Integration* (Lanham: Rowman and Littlefield, 2001).

17 S. Leibfried, 'Social Policy', in *Policy-Making in the European Union*, n 12 above.

18 W. Streeck, 'From Market Making to State Building?', and 'Neo-Voluntarism', both n 14 above.

19 F. W. Scharpf, 'The European Social Model. Coping with the Challenges of Diversity', n 13 above; ibid in 'Legitimate Diversity: The New Challenge of European Integration', in T. A. Börzel and R. A. Cichowski (eds) *The State of the European Union. Law, Politics, and Society* (Oxford: OUP, 2003) 79–104.

In other words, EU policies, especially the internal market, constrain national policy-making autonomy and hinder many of the Keynesian strategies associated with the post-war welfare state. Fererra makes a similar argument: European integration unleashes a 'new spatial politics of welfare' where member states no longer control the boundaries of social provision.[20] Palier and Pochet[21] take a more optimistic stance, arguing that EU policies constitute 'a distinct European economic and social model' embedded in innovative forms of governance, including the OMC. Although they acknowledge the supply-side bias of EU economic and social policies, Palier and Pochet view the emerging forms of social policy governance as a positive contribution to welfare state development. Even if demand-side policies are less attractive or even impossible, the EU's emerging multi-level social policy governance offers opportunities to strengthen social citizenship, solidarity and social inclusion. Moreover, EU social policies, especially the soft policy coordination aimed at promoting employment, fighting social exclusion and modernizing social protection systems are essential ingredients in the Lisbon strategy.

Ferrera and Hemerijck[22] as well as Zeitlin[23] echo this optimistic view of social policy in the EU, pointing to the considerable expansion of EU social policy competences since the Treaty of Maastricht and the innovative use of new governance instruments in order to overcome policy stalemate. The Maastricht Treaty expanded the EU's social policy remit as part of the internal market process, and the Treaty of Amsterdam incorporated the Social Agreement (previously attached to the Maastricht Treaty as the Social Protocol by all member states except the UK) and established employment and social exclusion as common EU concerns. The OMC, introduced as part of the Lisbon process in 2000, has grown from its initial status as a core component of the European Employment Strategy and has become the basis for EU soft coordination in the areas of public pension sustainability, social exclusion, and health.

Unlike the 'community method' in which EU institutions adopt binding legislation (see chapter three), the OMC relies on benchmarking, the diffusion of best practices and policy learning in order to work toward desired outcomes. As such the OMC represents a dramatically different type of policy-making procedure that gives the member states considerable flexibility in their efforts to reach agreed goals. Proponents of the OMC see in it a viable foundation for

[20] M. Ferrera, *The Boundaries of Welfare. European Integration and the New Spatial Politics of Social Protection* (Oxford: OUP, 2005).

[21] B. Palier, and P. Pochet, 'Toward a European Social Policy—At Last?' in N. Jabko, and C. Parsons (eds) *The State of the European Union. With US or Against US? European Trends in American Perspective* (Oxford: OUP, 2005).

[22] M. Ferrera, and A. Hemerijck, 'Recalibrating Europe's Welfare Regimes', n 10 above.

[23] J. Zeitlin, 'The Open Method of Coordination in Action. Theoretical Promise, Empirical Realities, Reform Strategy' in J. Zeitlin and P. Pochet (eds) *The Open Method of Coordination in Action. The European Employment and Social Inclusion Strategies* (Brussels: Peter Lang, 2005) 447–503.

an acceleration of positive social policy initiatives that preserves member state autonomy and allows for institutional diversity in the pursuit of common goals. Skeptics view the expansion of soft coordination in more social policy areas as a smoke screen for inertia and the re-assertion of member state control over the social policy agenda.

2.1 OMC and pensions

By the late 1990s, EU legislation and jurisprudence had already extended the principles of equal pay and non-discrimination to statutory pensions as well as occupational pensions.[24] With the completion of the European Monetary Union (EMU), however, the fiscal implications of public pension provision came under scrutiny for the first time, and EU institutions took the first steps toward prodding member states to reform their pension systems. In 2000, the European Council decided to apply the OMC to pensions in order to promote pension system modernization as part of the overall strategy of reforming social protection to support the Lisbon strategy.[25]

As Annesley argues, Lisbon re-opened debates about the role and status of a European Social Model (ESM).[26] Pension policy is obviously a core element of the ESM because of the sheer scope of pension provision in the member states. For pensions, as well as other parts of social protection systems, the key issue was how to promote economic modernization and social sustainability at the same time. According to Annesley, the 'emerging' ESM is an Adult Worker Model approach to social provision which is more social democratic than neo-liberal. Consistent with previous EU policy and the Lisbon agenda's focus on activation, the OMC focuses on EU citizens as workers. In contrast to previous EU policy promoting paid employment, the Lisbon strategy explicitly supports the activation of groups that were often inactive in many member states, especially older workers, women and the disabled. Thus, the Lisbon strategy actively pushes all

[24] J. A. Sohrab, 'An Overview of the Equality Directive On Social Security and Its Implementation in Four Social Security Systems' (1994) 4(4) J of Eur Social Policy 263–276; A. Eylenbosch, and K. Verreth 'Equal Treatment for Men and Women in Complementary Pensions: Answers or Unresolved Questions?' (1996) 6 J of Eur Social Policy 123–146.

[25] M. Eckardt, 'The open method of coordination on pensions: an economic analysis of its effects on pension reforms' (2005) 15(3) J of Eur Social Policy 247–267; C. de la Porte, and P. Pochet 'Supple Coordination at EU Level and the Key Actors' Involvement' in P. Pochet and C. de la Porte (eds) *Building Social Europe through the Open Method of Co-ordination* (Brussels: Peter Lang, 2001). The process is now called the 'EU Social Protection and Social Inclusion Process.' According to the DG Employment/Social Affairs website, this process 'coordinates and encourages Member State actions to combat poverty and social exclusion, and to reform their social protection systems on the basis of policy exchanges and mutual learning. As such, it underpins the achievement of the Union's strategic goal of sustained economic growth, more and better jobs, and greater social cohesion by 2010'.

[26] C. Annesley, 'Lisbon and social Europe: towards a European "adult worker model" welfare system' (2007) 17 (3) J of Common Market Studies 195–205.

adults to enter paid employment, and the reform of social protection schemes should support this goal.

Pension provision represents the core of the welfare state; public pensions typically are the largest item in member states' budgets and account for a large share of member states' economies, averaging about 12 per cent of GDP in the EU-25 in 2006 (see figure 1 below). The modernization of social protection schemes, particularly pension schemes, has been an important item on the EU's agenda since 2000, largely because of the well-known financing problems associated with mature public pension schemes like the ones in the EU-15. As noted, PAYG public pension provision dominates in the EU-15. As figure 2 shows, the majority of the member states have comparatively low levels of funded occupational pension provision. Since the 1970s, demographic and economic shifts have undermined the essential preconditions of public PAYG systems. First, low fertility rates and increasing longevity mean a substantial increase in the dependency ratios[27] in the member states. Second, persistently high levels of unemployment in most member states mean that fewer employed persons pay the taxes and contributions that finance current pensions. These trends combine to create extremely unfavourable financial circumstances for PAYG pensions because fewer workers must finance the pensions of increasing numbers of retirees.

These unfavourable trends were particularly alarming in the context of EMU. Given the fairly tough fiscal constraints embedded in the Maastricht Convergence Criteria, the spectre of increasing public pension obligations in an era of seemingly permanent fiscal austerity was a source of concern. Indeed, one of the initial activities of the OMC process in pensions was to gather more systematic data about the nature of the 'pensions crisis' in the member states in order to increase awareness of the future fiscal implications of expanding PAYG pension liabilities. The actors at EU level who pressed for reform hoped that the OMC would stimulate high-spending member states to rein in pension expenditure today in order to prevent budget deficits tomorrow. Adapting pension schemes to changing employment and family patterns is another core concern of the EU's recent approach to pensions policy. The Commission increasingly pointed to the outdated and/or inefficient aspects of member states' pension provision, including their contribution to non-wage labour costs, their negative impact on work incentives, and the ways in which occupational pensions hinder worker mobility.

In 2000, the newly formed Social Protection Committee of the Commission issued the first of several reports concerning pension policy, and these have been instrumental in defining the Commission's agenda. From the beginning, two principles have guided EU policy: promoting both the adequacy and the

[27] The old age dependency ratio is the ratio of the number of persons over the age of 65 per 100 persons of the working age (15 to 64 years old).

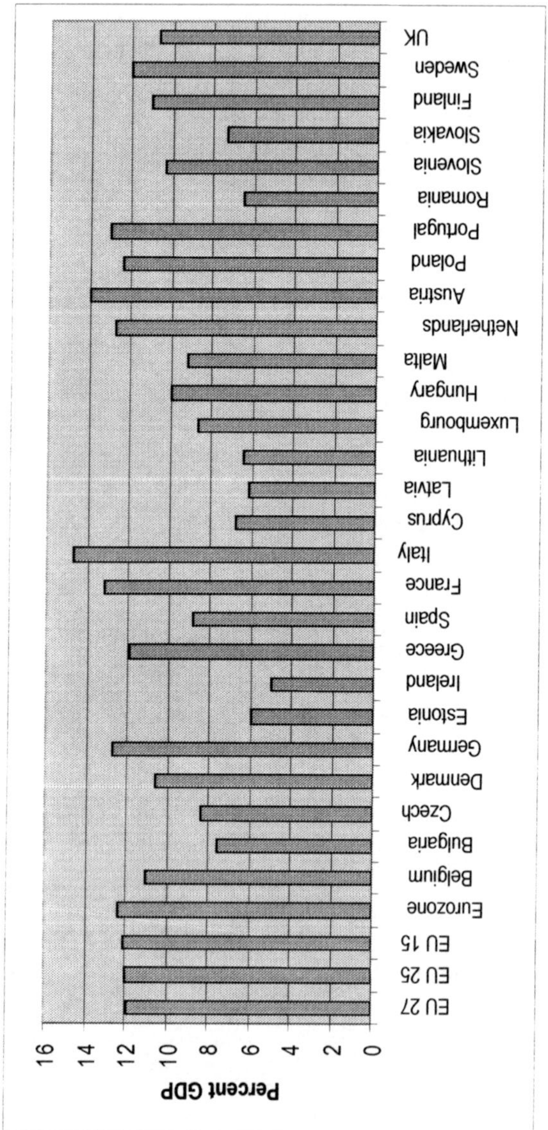

Figure 1. Public Pension Expenditure as per cent of GDP, 2006
Source: Eurostat

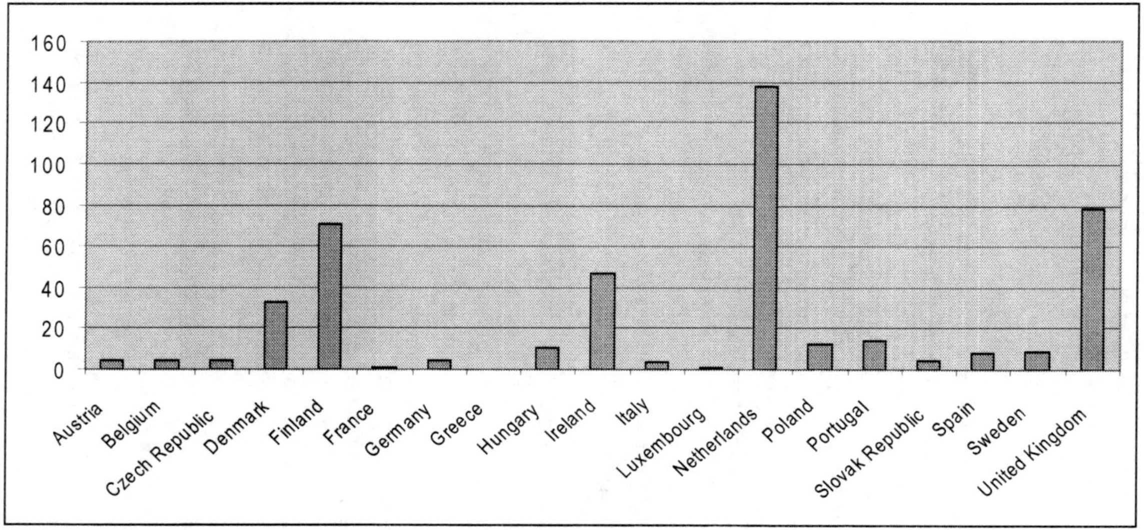

Figure 2. Occupational Pension Assets as per cent of GDP, 2007
Source: OECD

financial sustainability of public pensions.[28] The Commission and Council's 2003 Joint Report on Pensions demonstrates this new orientation.[29] The Joint Report argued that financial sustainability was essential to the future adequacy of public pensions because of population ageing. The Report called on the member states to undertake comprehensive reforms in order to strengthen both financial sustainability and adequacy. The Joint Report identified eleven objectives to guide pension reforms, including improving incentives for older workers to remain longer in the labour market, strengthening the link between contributions and benefits and increasing public and private funding. Since 2000, the OMC in pensions has gone through two cycles, with the member states producing national strategy reports in 2002 and 2005.

The mechanics of the OMC in pensions are well-known and need not be rehearsed here.[30] The point of this brief section is to ask how the principles embedded in the Lisbon strategy and the OMC pensions process affect national systems of pensions provision and the multiple solidarities embedded in them. First, if we return to Annesely's point that the Lisbon strategy represents the promotion of the Adult Worker Model,[31] it seems clear that this principle potentially conflicts with the notions of solidarity embedded in the continental/Bismarckian pension schemes. The EU's approach to pension reform emphasizes the impact of pension schemes on both public finances and labour costs. The continental model of pension provision in which payroll contributions finance earnings-related breadwinner benefits is clearly out of sync with the EU approach. The EU approach to pensions and the principles of the Lisbon strategy push in the direction of increased labour market participation of previously inactive groups, including mothers and spouses.

Second, the OMC's focus on the fiscal sustainability of pensions pushes in the direction of intragenerational solidarity, away from intergenerational solidarity. This has mainly to do with the financing problems associated with mature, PAYG DB schemes prevalent in the member states. As part of the OMC process, the member states have done the maths, and the numbers are devastating for PAYG DB schemes. Barring a surge in either fertility, employment, or both, PAYG schemes will absorb unsustainable levels of public expenditure. Even the countries with what some consider to be a healthy multi-pillar mix (the Netherlands,

[28] Commission (EC), 'Adequate and sustainable pensions. A report by the Social Protection Committee to the Gothenburg European Council on the future evolution of social protection' (2000) June; Commission (EC), 'The future evolution of social protection from a long-term point of view: safe and sustainable pensions' (Communication) COM (2000) 622, adopted on 11 October 2000.

[29] Commission (EC), 'Joint Commission/Council report on adequate and sustainable pensions' (CS 7165/03, 18 March 2003), available at <http://ec.europa.eu/employment_social/spsi/docs/social_protection/2006/rapport_pensions_final_en.pdf>.

[30] See M. Eckardt, 'The open method of coordination on pensions: an economic analysis of its effects on pension reforms', n 25 above; J. Zeitlin, 'The Open Method of Coordination in Action. Theoretical Promise, Empirical Realities, Reform Strategy', n 23 above.

[31] C. Annesley, 'Lisbon and social Europe: towards a European "adult worker model" welfare system', n 26 above.

Denmark, Sweden perhaps) are not completely immune to these same demographic constraints.

Third, the OMC's emphasis on paid employment and fiscal sustainability pushes in the direction of 'actuarial fairness' in pension benefit formulae. Indeed, one of the most common features of pension reform across the EU is the strengthening of links between contributions and benefits. Most member states have increased the number of years required to qualify for a full pension and shifted the benefit reference period from a 'best' number of years to career average earnings.

To be sure, the Lisbon strategy and the OMC process in pensions cannot force any member state to reform pension provision in the direction of intragenerational solidarity, individual entitlement, and employment-based benefits. The OMC only offers incentives and a forum for mutual learning that provide the context for national-level debates and decisions concerning pension reform. But given that pension reform will occupy national political agendas for many years, it would be unwise to ignore the normative force and specific content of the OMC pension agenda.

2.2 The Occupational Pension Fund Directive

One of the elements of the OMC pension process is the increased importance of supplementary and private pension provision to compensate for decreases in public provision. Only three member states have occupational pension sectors that cover at least 90 per cent of the workforce: the Netherlands, Denmark and Sweden. Despite the very large size of the UK occupational pension sector, coverage is far below 90 per cent.[32] There is also considerable variation across the member states in the organization of occupational pensions. In Denmark and Sweden occupational pensions are mainly organized according to life insurance principles. In the Netherlands and the UK, a pension fund arrangement is much more common. Life insurance contracts require full funding, whereas pension funds can be either partially or fully funded depending on national regulations. Book reserve schemes, common in Germany, are occupational pension schemes in which pension liabilities are entered on a firm's balance sheet. As figure 2 (above) shows, only the Netherlands and the UK have significant funded occupational pension sectors.

Before 2003, there was no EU legislation covering pension funds whereas life insurance has been regulated for more than two decades. The completion of the internal market and the emergence of funded pension provision (as a component of pension reform) meant that occupational pension regulation took on new salience in the EU, and the Commission initiated pension fund legislation in the 1990s. Haverland[33] traces the decision-making process concerning the pension

[32] Commission (EC), 'Adequate and Sustainable Pensions' (Synthesis Report, 2006) 77–78, available at <http://ec.europa.eu/employment_social/social_protection/docs/2006/rapport_pensions_final_en.pdf>.

[33] M. Haverland, 'When the Welfare State Meets the Regulatory State: EU Occupational Pension Policy' (2007) 14 (6) J of Eur Public Policy, 886–904.

fund Directive.[34] The Commission adopted the proposal in October 2000.[35] The proposal was made under the provisions of the single market. The Directive continued the process of financial market liberalization because it would grant pension funds (IORPs, Institutions for Occupational Retirement Provision) the freedom to operate cross-border, something that other financial institutions could already do. The proposal included regulations concerning investment mix, financial oversight, and the definition of full funding (sufficient assets to cover current and future liabilities). Book reserve schemes were excluded from the Directive, and there was no mention of biometric risks.

The Directive was adopted in 2003 and the deadline for transposition was October 2005. Even though it was only recently adopted, the effects of the Directive are becoming clear. First, the Directive creates incentives for member states to compete to be the domicile of choice for pension funds by implementing a more lenient regulatory regime. Belgium, Ireland and Luxembourg have already taken steps to increase their attractiveness as domiciles. The Netherlands joined this group later. Second, national transposition of the Directive will consolidate and hasten the expansion of funded second pillar provision in member states that recently took steps to expand the second pillar.

Germany is a good example of the latter process. Book reserves (*Direktzusage*)[36] comprise about 60 per cent of German occupational pension assets.[37] Germany's transposition legislation loosened rules for its two types of pension funds, *Pensionskassen* and *Pensionfonds* which account for 20 per cent of the 367 billion euros in German occupational pension assets.[38] *Pensionfonds* were created as part of the Riester reform in 2001. Unlike *pensionskassen*, they operate according to the prudent person principle. *Pensionskassen* are subject to quantitative investment restrictions (maximum 35 per cent of assets in shares and 5 per cent in hedge funds) because they guarantee a minimum rate of return. German implementing legislation also included changes in the discount rate used to value liabilities (*Rechnungszins*) for *pensionfonds*. This will create incentives for pension schemes set up as book reserves to switch to the *pensionfonds* model. As noted, *pensionfonds* are not as restrictive as pensionskassen which means that they offer a potentially cheaper route than *pensionskassen* for employers who want to switch from book reserves to funding.

The Directive coincides with developments in international accounting standards that create incentives for firms to shift book reserves to pension funds.

[34] Commission (EC), 'Adequate and Sustainable Pensions', n 32 above, 77–78.

[35] 2001/C 96 E/06, 'Proposal for a Directive of the European Parliament and of the Council on the activities of institutions for occupational retirement provision (COM (2000) 507 final—2000 /0260(COD)) (1). Procedure was co-decision.

[36] Book reserves are pension liabilities recorded on a firm's balance sheet. There are no assets held outside the firm as there are in autonomous pension funds like those in the Netherlands.

[37] J. Wagner, 'Germany implements pension fund directive' (2005) <http://www.ipe.com>, 12 July 2005.

[38] ibid.

Table 1. Occupational Pension Assets as per cent of GDP in Germany, 2001–2007

2001	2002	2003	2004	2005	2006	2007
3.442	3.489	3.636	3.791	4.036	4.213	4.11

Source: OECD

German DAX companies have already started to shift to funding, so the implementation of the Directive provides them with another, perhaps more attractive option, for shifting to funded schemes. International accounting standards (IAS 19) requires adjustments to the ways in which liabilities are included on a firm's balance sheet.[39] This makes book reserves unattractive because they are basically unfunded pension liabilities. Bosch, as well as many other German multinationals have shifted from book reserves to either *Pensionfonds*, *Pensionskassen* or contractual trust arrangements.[40]

The size of the funded occupational sector in Germany has grown significantly since the Riester reform of 2001, and the occupational pension Directive has contributed to this development. As table 1 shows, the size of the occupational pension sector has grown from 3.442 per cent of GDP in 2001 to 4.11 per cent of GDP in 2007.

2.3 Occupational pension portability: Netherlands and Germany

Efforts to adopt a directive on occupational pension portability have until now been unsuccessful. Increasing the portability of occupational pensions has been on the Commission agenda for several years and took on new importance in the 2000s as part of the Lisbon strategy's goal to increase employment, among other things by promoting worker mobility. The proposed Directive announced in October 2005 has been extremely controversial, especially in the Netherlands and Germany. The core of the proposal would permit workers to take accrued pension rights with them to a new job after a vesting period of two years. Another important aspect of the proposed Directive is the requirement for pension providers to index the value of dormant pension rights.

The Directive sparked the most opposition from the member states with the largest funded and unfunded occupational pension sectors: the Netherlands and Germany. The Dutch threatened to veto the Directive (which they have never done before as EU members) because it would result in the transfer of pension assets

[39] IAS 19 lays out the rules for the accounting and disclosure of employee benefits and requires that the cost of employee benefits be recorded for the period in which the employee accrues the benefit rather than when it is paid.

[40] J. Wagner, 'German firms plan "pan-European pensions"' (2006) <http://www.ipe.com>, 23 March 2006.

out of the Netherlands. As figure 2 above shows, the Netherlands has the largest funded occupational sector in the EU, with assets totalling more than 100 per cent of GDP. Given that pension contributions are exempt from tax, Dutch policy-makers saw pension portability as the potential exit of untaxed assets and lost tax revenues. German concerns were based on the widespread use of book reserves in their relatively small occupational pension sector. In contrast to the Netherlands where the size of the public pension and private occupational pension sectors are roughly equal (measured in terms of benefit pay-outs), German pension provision is dominated by the statutory, earnings-related pillar. German occupational pension providers criticized the provision requiring pension schemes to guarantee portability by capitalizing assets held as book reserves when a worker changed jobs and pension scheme. German employers lobbied for the exclusion of book reserves and PAYG schemes[41] because capitalizing accrued benefits would be too costly.

Dutch employers as well as the government opposed the proposal's provisions concerning the indexation of pension accrual.[42] Current Dutch legislation does not require the indexation of pension accrual nor of dormant pension rights. In the wake of the 2000/2001 stock market downturn and heavy investment losses, the indexation of pension accrual, dormant rights, and pension payouts were made dependent on pension fund solvency. This is one of the prime policy instruments for keeping DB pensions in the Netherlands solvent.[43]

Because of member state opposition, the pensions portability Directive is now stalled in Council. The Commission proposed an amended Directive with watered-down provisions in 2007, but the proposal's fate remains uncertain. Despite these obstacles, enhancing worker mobility remains high on the EU's agenda as part of the Lisbon strategy, so it is reasonable to expect some sort of portability legislation to be adopted in the near future. One option in circulation is to integrate rules on portability with a revision of the Occupational Pension Fund Directive.

3. Conclusion

Both the ongoing OMC process embedded in the Lisbon strategy and European legislation concerning occupational pension funds are premised on a conception of solidarity that in many ways is at odds with prevailing notions of solidarity embedded in national systems of pension provision. Both the OMC and the pension fund Directive push the member states in a multi-pillar direction by creating

[41] J. Wagner, D. Brooksbank and B. Evans-Pritchard, 'New pensions portability plan facing criticism' (2005) <http://www.ipe.com>, 21 October 2005.

[42] C. Widdershoven (2006) 'Dutch Government critical of portability directive' (2006) <http://www.ipe.com>, 24 March 2006.

[43] K. M. Anderson, 'The Netherlands: Political Competition in a Proportional System' in E. M. Immergut, K. M. Anderson, and I. Schulze (eds) *The Handbook of West European Pension Politics* (Oxford: OUP, 2007).

the normative and legal foundations for the recalibration of public provision, the expansion of funded occupational provision, and the strengthening of individual, employment-based pension entitlement. The type of solidarity that is most congruent with this emerging pension paradigm is intragenerational, and it is based on the individual's obligation to work. And a range of public policies and services support employment and the reconciliation of work and family. To be sure, the OMC process also promotes the principle of pension adequacy by encouraging member states to improve policies that guarantee a minimum income in old age, but the overall tendency in the EU's policy initiatives emphasizes financial sustainability.

To those familiar with the Nordic models of social protection, these norms will look familiar. One of the pillars of the Nordic model is the 'work line', or the idea that work always comes before welfare. Cash benefits were a last resort, to be drawn when retraining, rehabilitation and other measures were exhausted. Sweden, Denmark and Finland each experienced deep economic recessions in the 1980s and 1990s. Each country adopted a series of welfare state reforms that corrected deviations from the 'work line'. Pension reform was a centrepiece of these reform processes. Sweden transformed its PAYG defined benefit public scheme into a PAYG notional defined contribution scheme with obligatory funded individual accounts in 1998. In other words, Sweden shifted from intergenerational solidarity to intragenerational solidarity. Denmark did more or less the same thing, but a bit earlier. Denmark never legislated public earnings-related pensions in the 1950s as Sweden and many other European countries did. Instead, the flat-rate state pension was the main source of income for low-wage workers, while many middle class wage earners were covered by occupational pensions. Coverage was less than 60 per cent until the late 1980s, however, until blue collar unions and employers agreed on the extension of occupational pensions to these groups. By the early 1990s coverage had reached more than 90 per cent of the labour force.

Thus the Danish, Swedish and Finnish public pension systems rest on principles of individual entitlement within a collective scheme based on intragenerational solidarity. The size of the funded occupational pension pillar differs across these three countries, but the underlying principle is fairly clear: portable defined contribution benefits.[44]

This set of first and second pillar pension institutions is most compatible with the types of solidarity implied by the OMC pensions process and the direction of EU legislation concerning occupational pensions and pension portability. The norms of solidarity embedded in the Bismarckian/continental pension systems are very different because they rely much more on intergenerational rights and obligations as well as family-based rights and obligations. Moreover, the fragmentation of pensions along occupational lines in many Bismarckian countries has

[44] Some second pillar schemes in Sweden are still DB, but the trend is towards DC.

created multiple, competing solidarities which are hard to undo. These aspects of Bismarckian pension provision thus create a situation in which current pension institutions collide with the principles embedded in the EU's emerging pension paradigm. At the same time, the stickiness of Bismarckian pension institutions means that they are difficult to reform.

The 2008/2009 financial crisis complicates the EU's pension reform agenda because of the massive losses sustained by funded pension schemes across the developed world. In the Netherlands, most pension funds lost 20–30 per cent of their assets in the last year. If the 2001/2002 downturn is any indication, the pension schemes will recover within five to ten years, but it would be wrong to underestimate the damage done to the legitimacy of funded pension provision as a normative principle underlying pension reform. If anything, the current financial crisis shows how vulnerable funded schemes are, at least in their current form. Thus the EU is promoting a multi-pillar model of pension provision that has proven to be unstable, at least in the short term.

12

How to Govern for Solidarity? An Introduction to Policy Learning in the Context of Open Methods of Coordinating Education Policies in the European Union

*Bettina Lange and Nafsika Alexiadou**

1. Introduction: governing for solidarity through education policies in the EU?

Poverty and educational attainment are related, therefore education policies are a key aspect of building welfare states. Poverty is limited in the Nordic and Continental welfare states where 75 per cent and 67 per cent of the population between the ages of 25 and 64 have at least upper secondary education. This contrasts with the Anglo-Saxon and Mediterranean welfare states where only 60 per cent and 39 per cent of the population between the ages of 25 and 64 have at least upper secondary education. Here, significant levels of poverty and inequality in income distribution exist.[1]

The European Commission is now developing, through Open Method of Coordination (OMC) processes, an EU dimension in national education policies. Does this contribute to the construction of a European social welfare state? Some argue that—for various reasons—the political institutional basis for solidarity remains firmly national. First, neo-corporatist bargaining regimes which have been central to the development of welfare states at the national level do not seem to be replicated at the EU level. The organization of social interests,

* This chapter draws on qualitative data derived from semi-structured interviews with officials from the Directorate General for Education and Culture in the European Commission (DG EAC) and on official EU documents generated during policy learning activities. We would like to acknowledge the participation of staff from the DG EAC, who gave their time generously for interviews in the research project. The views expressed in this chapter are those of the authors and should not be taken to be the view of the DG EAC or its staff.

[1] A. Giddens, 'A Social Model for Europe?' in A. Giddens, P. Diamond, and R. Liddle (eds) *Global Europe, Social Europe* (Cambridge: Polity Press, 2006) 25.

in particular those of labour—also linked to education policies—still occurs mainly on a national level.[2] There is also no great drive from employers' organizations for EU interest representation, since they are often opposed to the development of an interventionist EU social policy. Second, *national* social policies are an important source of legitimacy for national governments and hence a cornerstone of national democracy. National governments are therefore reluctant to transfer social policy competencies to the EU level. Nationalism and a neo-liberal approach towards social welfare in the EU polity are linked.[3] Third, the functionalist argument that there is a 'spillover' from EU market integration to supranational state formation and hence to common political and social citizenship in the EU has been questioned.[4] Fourth, some commentators are sceptical about the possibility of developing a transnational EU solidarity given that, in the past, solidarity has emerged from a tight link between 'social sharing, political participation and cultural identity'.[5] At least traditional conceptions of political participation and cultural identity are called into question by EU governance and thus may not be a possible basis for EU wide solidarity.

But even if we recognize that substantial political capacity for social policy remains at the national level it is nevertheless important to acknowledge that there is a movement towards a common EU social policy to which greater convergence among national education policies contributes. A functionalist perspective and evidence of new EU initiatives support this view. After intensified integration of the member states' economies, through the European Economic and Monetary Union (EMU), the EU is now tackling linked, but politically sensitive issues, such as employment, education, social exclusion and pensions.[6]

Such developments of common EU social policies may, however, not amount to the construction of a European welfare state, especially in the light of ambitious definitions of the latter. Social policy that builds welfare states is interventionist and seeks to realize equality of opportunity for all and some equality in actual outcomes. Hence, social policy that underpins welfare states needs to have a distinct identity and build on its own values, such as solidarity between

[2] W. Streeck, 'Neo-Voluntarism: A New European Social Policy Regime?' in G. Marks, F. Scharpf, P. Schmitter, and W. Streeck (eds) *Governance in the European Union* (London: Sage Publications, 1996) 64–94; J. Zeitlin, 'Social Europe and Experimentalist Governance: Towards a New Constitutional Compromise?' in de Búrca (ed) *EU Law and the Welfare State* (Oxford: OUP, 2005) 225. For empirical evidence of limited involvement of the social partners in the European Employment Strategy see C. de La Porte and P. Nanz, 'The OMC—a Deliberative-Democratic Mode of Governance? The cases of employment and pensions,' (2004) 11 (2) J of Eur Public Policy 267–288.

[3] Streeck, n 2 above. [4] Streeck, n 2 above, 64.

[5] B. Kohler-Koch, 'European Governance and System Integration' in E. Oddvar, C. Jörges and F. Rödl (eds) *Law and Democracy in the Post-National Union* (ARENA: Centre for European Studies, Oslo, 2006) 93.

[6] C. de La Porte and P. Pochet, *Building Social Europe Through the Open Method of Co-Ordination* (Brussels: Peter Lang Publishing, 2002) 13.

all citizens.[7] Social policies that mainly make or accommodate markets do not occupy such a distinct policy space.[8] But even if at the EU level such a distinct policy space is difficult to detect, there is a movement towards a European Social Model (ESM) which in fact involves—at two levels—a number of models, one at the EU level and various conceptions of welfare at the national level in the different member states.[9] The social construction of welfare, and the establishment of a governance architecture that may eventually be called a European welfare state therefore involves complex interactions between national and EU levels with both national and EU level policies transforming each other in the context of education.[10]

This chapter focuses on policy learning, one specific aspect of the governance process that contributes to the building of an ESM. It starts from the assumption that if we want to understand what forms of solidarity develop in the EU it is important, first of all, to understand the governance processes through which a social dimension of the EU is established. This chapter thereby contributes to an analysis of the 'expressive' dimension of solidarity in the EU.[11] While this dimension is often analysed through the lens of constitutional legal provisions the functioning of the European Unions, such as Articles 2 and 3 of the Treaty or fundamental rights, this chapter examines the soft law architecture of solidarity building. Procedures for governing and outcomes are, however, linked. Some associate the OMC with the pursuit of 'third way' politics in the EU.[12] More specifically, it has been argued that OMC processes involve a shift from traditional concepts of protective and redistributive solidarity to competitive and productive solidarity. Northern and Continental European national welfare states developed, in the 1970s, protective and redistributive solidarity under the leadership of social democratic governments. Competitive and productive solidarity emerged in the 1980s. It no longer seeks to correct market outcomes but merely aims to better equip individuals to compete for jobs and it involves partly privately provided welfare in market economies. The aim of social policy is not primarily redistribution of wealth but to enhance the productive capacity of individuals in order to stimulate economic growth.

[7] Whether such a policy space will develop in the EU is, however, questionable given the European Commission's emphasis on flexicurity, ie the combination of flexibility and security in its Employment Strategy and the renewed Lisbon agenda. Flexicurity seeks to reconcile economic and social objectives and turn social policy even into a productive factor (M. Keune and M. Jepsen (eds) 'Not balanced and hardly new: The European Commission's quest for flexicurity', European Trade Union Institute for Research, Education and Health and Safety, Working Paper 2007.01, 11 at <http://www.etui.org/research/activities/Employment-and-social-policies/Reports-and-working-papers/WP-2007.01> (last visited 31 July 2009).

[8] Streeck, n 2 above, 71.

[9] M. Ferrera, *European Integration and National Social Citizenship: Changing Boundaries, New Structuring*, Working Paper C 11 p. 3, (U of California at Berkeley, Centre for German and Eur Studies, 2001 27–35).

[10] Kohler-Koch, n 5 above, 92.

[11] M. Ross in this volume, ch 2, Fig 2.

[12] M. Büchs, *New Governance in European Social Policy: The Open Method of Coordination* (Basingstoke: Palgrave Macmillan, 2007).

But this perception of a 'deregulatory' tendency of OMC processes in social policy-making can be questioned. The devolution of public policy-making to lower levels—one aspect of OMC processes—for instance through peer learning activities (further discussed below) may actually provide an inroad for traditional social welfare state interests into the policy-making process.[13] The classic community method for EU public policy-making—also involving *interstate* bargaining—may be ill-suited to the consideration of *social* interests and redistributive social policy-making.[14] More importantly, the concern that the OMC promotes limited conceptions of solidarity which sideline the social ties that build collectives, seems to rest on the assumption that OMC processes actually do have an influence on policy outcomes and national policy-making structures. In the field of education, however, such impacts may be limited. Objectives agreed upon through the OMC may simply be general aspirational objectives towards which member states work.[15] The question then arises whether 'deregulatory' tendencies can really be attributed to EU OMC processes rather than to neo-liberal education policy ideas which have originated in some of the member states.

This chapter traces how the construction of discourses about policy learning within institutional frameworks comes to govern education in the EU. The chapter argues, firstly, that policy learning contributes to EU governance in education through four distinct policy learning styles: mutual, competitive, surface and imperialistic learning. Secondly, the chapter suggests that policy learning contributes to governance because it is not a separate and discrete strategy but is embedded in already established governance regimes, such as the use of expert knowledge.

In order to understand how governance processes contribute to the building of an education dimension to the European Social Model the next section introduces the focus of our chapter: policy learning as one element of education OMC processes.

2. Policy learning as one element of open methods of coordination for education in the EU

OMC processes are a new phenomenon in the history of EU social policy.[16] They were first applied to economic integration, then invoked in the European Employment Strategy (EES) and are now harnessed for policies, such as pensions, healthcare, social inclusion and education. The conclusions of the Lisbon European Council of 24 March 2000 referred for the first time to the OMC, a soft and potentially new mode of EU governance, as now also applying to education

[13] De La Porte and Pochet, n 6 above. [14] Streeck, n 2 above, 75.

[15] N. Alexiadou, 'The Europeanisation of Education Policy: Researching Changing Governance and "New" Modes of Coordination' (2007) 2 (2) Research in Comparative and Intl Education, 102.

[16] De La Porte and Pochet, n 6 above, 13.

policies in the EU.[17] This is a significant step forward in efforts to achieve greater convergence among member states' education systems as under Article 165 Treaty on the Functioning of the European Union, the European Community has no powers to pass formal legislation in the field of education. OMC processes seek to strengthen an EU dimension in member states' policies through four main strategies:[18] (1) the fixing of European guidelines to which timetables for achieving specific goals are attached; (2) The translation of these guidelines into national and regional policies associated with specific targets; (3) The development of quantitative and qualitative indicators and benchmarks in order to compare best practice among member states; (4) The periodic monitoring, evaluation, and peer review of member states' practices organized as mutual learning processes.[19]

The European Commission has seized the opportunity to influence member states' education policies through OMC processes by developing *three major goals* (quality, access, and openness to the world) and *13 specific objectives* for education and training systems in the EU. These were adopted by the European Council in March 2001. The Education and Training Work Programme 2010[20] further fleshes out how these three strategic goals and 13 objectives should be achieved. This programme is considered by some officials of the Directorate General for Education and Culture (DG EAC) to be the core of OMC processes for education. The Education and Training Work Programme 2010 sets out quite detailed results for member states to accomplish. For instance, in relation to the first major goal of improving the quality of education and training systems, a number of issues are identified, such as teacher training, making the best use of resources, and further equipping pupils with basic literacy, numeracy and IT skills. In relation to these issues, specific results should be achieved, such as that all education and training systems in the EU shall have access to internet and multimedia resources by the end of 2010 and that there should be substantial increases in per capita investment in human resources for education and training systems every year. Policy learning is one of the governance strategies through which this comprehensive Education and Training Work Programme 2010 is implemented.

This chapter starts to address the questions what policy learning *is* and how it contributes to the governance of education in the EU.[21] How can a potentially

[17] European Council, *Presidency Conclusions*. Lisbon, 23–24 March, DOC/00/8, paras 25–27.

[18] B. Lange and N. Alexiadou, 'New Forms of European Union Governance in the Education Sector? A Preliminary Analysis of the Open Method of Co-Ordination' (2007) 6 (4) Eur Educational Research J, 321.

[19] European Council, n 17 above, para 37.

[20] European Council, 'Detailed work Program on the follow-up of the objectives of Education and training systems in Europe' [2002] OJ C142/1. Now further developed through the strategic framework for European cooperation in education and training (ET 2020). See Council Conclusions of 12 May 2009 on a strategic framework for European cooperation in education and training ('ET 2020'), [2009] OJ C119/02.

[21] We focus on education policies in the EU because in comparison to other policy fields in which the OMC is used such as employment, economic policies, social inclusion and environmental protection, education has been less well researched (for exceptions see A. Gornitzka, 'Coordinating

very soft and informal process such as learning about the education policies of other EU member states, turn into a strategy for exercising power and influence and finally contribute to change in the education practices and systems of EU member states? How does learning become transformed when it is employed as a strategy for governance and how does governance change when it relies on learning? The chapter examines small-scale social processes of education policy learning and governance through qualitative empirical data. These were obtained through 14 semi-structured interviews conducted in spring 2007 with officials in the DG EAC, including seven of the eight coordinators of so-called clusters through which peer learning activities that pertain to education are organized. The analysis also draws on official European Commission documents, such as reports that summarize various peer learning activities and general Commission guidance notes on peer learning.

Our empirical focus on small-scale social processes of policy learning and governance is intended to complement existing perspectives in the OMC literature. Some of this literature examines the exercise of power through OMCs with reference to *theories* of experimentalist democracy.[22] New modes of EU governance, such as the OMC, are perceived as an opportunity to address the democratic deficits of 'old' modes of EU governance which embody limited versions of liberal representative democracy. Experimentalist democracy shares features with deliberative democracy but goes further by building on direct and open debates among citizens and local actors who are granted significant autonomy in order to

Policies for a 'Europe of knowledge': Emerging Practices of the "Open Method of Coordination" in education and research' (2005) Working Paper No 16. Oslo: Arena Centre for Eur Studies, U of Oslo, at <http://www.arena.uio.no/publications/working-papers2005> (last visited 31 July 2009); A. Gornitzka, The Open Method of Co-Ordination as Practice: A Watershed in European Education Policy? (2006) Working Paper No 16, Oslo: Arena Centre for Eur Studies, U of Oslo, at <http://www.arena.uio.no/publications/working-papers2005> (last visited 31 July 2009); A. J. Hingel, *Education Policies and European Governance: Contribution to the Interservice Groups on European Governance* (2001) Development of Educational Policies, March, DG EAC/A/1. Brussels: European Commission Directorate-General for Education and Culture. <http://europa.eu/governance/areas/group12/contribution_education_en.pdf> (last visited 31 July 2009). M. Souto-Otero, T. Fleckenstein, R. Dacombe, 'Filling in the Gaps: European Governance, the Open Method of Co-ordination and the European Commission' (2008) 23(3) J of Education Policy, 231–249. Moreover, the question whether a 'soft' tool such as policy learning can contribute to EU governance is raised particularly sharply in the case of education as the education OMC is one of the least formalized and prescriptive OMCs. In contrast to the OMCs in the context of the EES and EMU the education OMC does not have a basis in the EC Treaty. It came into existence merely through the political agreement of the conclusions of the Lisbon Council in March 2000. It is also less prescriptive than the OMCs for the EES, EMU and social inclusion because it does not provide guidelines or national reform/action plans (D. Mabbett, 'Learning by Numbers? The Use of Indicators in the Co-Ordination of Social Inclusion Policies in Europe' (2007) 14 (1) J of Eur Public Policy, 78).

[22] O. Gerstenberg and C. F. Sabel, 'Directly Deliberative Polyarchy: An Institutional Ideal for Europe?' in C. Joerges and R. Dehousse (eds) *Good Governance in Europe's Integrated Market* (Oxford: OUP, 2002) 289; C. F. Sabel and J. Zeitlin 'Learning from Difference: The New Architecture of Experimentalist Governance in the EU' (2008) 14 (3) European Law Journal, 271–327.

find solutions that are tailored to specific problems of governance.[23] In contrast to these theoretical issues, our *empirical* research traces the operation of power on a micro-level by examining how education policy learning contributes to the governance of education in the EU. Moreover, some contributions to the literature on new modes of EU governance adopt a *normative perspective.* Also, with reference to constitutional principles, they seek to develop better procedures for remedying the potentially limited legitimacy and accountability of new modes of EU governance.[24] For instance, soft law can not be challenged through judicial review proceedings before courts. In addition, policy learning gives rise to new networks of policy-makers which can bypass traditional institutions that provide for the democratic legitimacy and accountability of EU policy-making. For example, the European Commission developed OMC initiatives in education without involving the European Parliament. Scrutiny of the outcomes of policy learning may be impaired where there is limited transparency of the results of policy learning.[25] In contrast to these normative perspectives our main aim is analytical. We examine what education policy learning actually involves and how it contributes to the governance of education in the EU in three sections. First, we sketch the theoretical framework for our empirical research. We draw on discourse analytical and institutionalist perspectives in order to examine links between words and action in governing through policy learning. Second, we discuss how discourses and institutions contribute to the governance of education policies in the EU, in particular through a differentiation of policy learning into four distinct policy learning styles: mutual, competitive, imperialistic and surface policy learning. Third, we examine attempts to improve the capacity for governance that is yielded by learning about policy by linking education policy learning to already existing strategies for governance, such as the mobilization of expertise.

3. A discourse analytical and institutionalist perspective of governing through policy learning

3.1 Defining governance and policy learning

We use the term 'governance' in order to draw attention to the exercise of power through networks that are composed of both traditional public institutional

[23] Gerstenberg and Sabel, n 22 above, 291.

[24] G. de Burca and J. Scott, 'Introduction: New Governance, Law and Constitutionalism' in G. de Burca, and J. Scott (eds) *Law and New Governance in the EU and the US* (Oxford: Hart Publishing, 2006) 8. See also the questions about the legitimacy of diversity in Social Europe by W. Lamping in this volume, ch 3.

[25] Where the empirical research was conducted in spring 2007, only some of the papers and reports produced by the new networks set up by the European Commission for policy learning, so-called clusters, were actually published or referred to on the DG EAC's website. Now more of these documents are available through the DG EAC's website.

actors, such as the European Commission, and the Council of Ministers and member states, as well as private individuals, such as businesses, teachers, parents, school pupils, students and academics involved in the making of education policy in the EU.[26] Second, the term 'governance', in particular in its multi-level variety, captures the idea that not only national governments, but also international, regional and local actors are involved in the development of education policy in the EU.[27]

We consider policy learning to be a reflexive, iterative process as policy-makers seek out information about the feasibility, appropriateness and effectiveness of a policy and the various circumstances that influence how a policy will actually work in practice.[28] We depart from views of policy learning that require that a policy be transplanted into another institutional context, often across national borders.[29] Our research concerns policy learning at the EU level. Hence, our data does not address the issue of whether education practices have, in fact, changed in the member states. Moreover, with reference to the perspectives of some DG EAC staff, we also depart from views of policy learning that consider it to be a particular type of *policy making*.[30] We consider policy learning to be an initial step in the policy-making process that—being an aspect of 'cognitive convergence'—can still advance EU integration.[31] Most importantly, we consider policy learning to be a political process, not a technical, neutral method of governance that relies on 'objective' data.[32]

3.2 A discourse analytical and institutionalist perspective

Policy learning relies significantly on talk and text and hence involves the production of discourses. Discourses represent knowledge about 'a topic at a

[26] P. Cort, 'The Open Method of Coordination in Vocational Education and Training—A Triangle of EU Governance' (2007) Aarhus U, School of Education, Dept for Curriculum Research (draft paper, manuscript with authors) 11–15.

[27] M. Telo, 'Governance and Government in the European Union: The Open Method of Coordination' in M. J. Rodrigues (ed) *The New Knowledge Economy in Europe* (Cheltenham: Edward Elgar, 2002) 249.

[28] S. Cropper and M. Goodwin, 'Policy Experiments: Policy Making, Implementation and Learning' in S. Cropper, A. Porter, G. Williams, S. Carlisle, R. Moore, M. O'Neill, C. Roberts and H. Snooks (eds) *Community Health and Wellbeing: Action Research on Health Inequalities* (Bristol: Policy Press, 2007) 46–48.

[29] C. Bennett, and M. Howlett, 'The Lessons of Learning: Reconciling Theories of Policy Learning and Policy Change' (1992) 25 Policy Sciences 285.

[30] ibid 287.

[31] R. Dehousse, 'The Open Method of Coordination: A New Policy Paradigm?' Paper presented at the First Pan-European Conference on European Union Politics: *The Politics of European Integration: Academic Acquis and Future Challenges* (2002) Bordeaux, 26–28 September 2002, 10 at <http://eucenter.wisc.edu/OMC/Papers/Dehousse.pdf> (last visited 31 July 2009).

[32] C. Radaelli, 'Who Learns What? Policy Learning and the Open Method of Coordination', Paper prepared for the ESRC seminar series: 'Implementing the Lisbon Strategy: Policy Learning Inside and Outside the Open Method', Eur Research Institute, U of Birmingham (2004), 26 November 2004, at <http://eric.ex.ac.uk/exeter/bitstream/10036/23652/1/RadaelliPolicy Learning.pdf> (last visited 31 July 2009). Telo, n 27 above, 263.

particular historical moment'.[33] Discourse, however, also constitutes social action.[34] For instance, paragraph 27 of the conclusions of the Lisbon Council 2000 provides a mandate for member states to develop initiatives only in the field of education. But in a 2001 report by the DG EAC on the concrete future objectives of education *and training systems,* the term 'training' was added, which significantly expanded the scope of OMC processes and thereby policy learning. Discourses do not occur in a vacuum. They are often shaped by and mobilized through institutions.[35] In fact it has been argued that education OMC processes are becoming institutionalized.[36] Discourses and institutions can be perceived as situated on a continuum where discourses can develop into institutional structures.[37] Attention to discourses can also help one to understand how the 'cognitive' dimensions of institutions are constructed and how they shape social actors' behaviour. Discourses contribute to the construction of logics of appropriate behaviour within institutions. We draw on the sociological perspective of institutionalism which emphasizes the significance of institutions for explaining organizational change—including the development of particular policies, practices and individual action—by providing incentives and constraints that can influence the behaviour of groups and individuals within them.[38] Institutionalism also seems to be particularly relevant because it seeks to explain organizational change not just with reference to 'coercion' but also through 'normative pressures' and 'imitation', soft methods of governance also utilized in policy learning.[39] Yet what are the institutional frameworks that shape EU education policy learning?

3.3 Institutional frameworks of EU education policy learning

The conclusions of the Lisbon Council 2000 challenged EU member states to develop OMC processes in the field of education. In response to this, the European Commission set up working groups on specific topics in education, such as 'key competences', 'language learning' and 'measuring progress through indicators and benchmarks'. These working groups comprised representatives from each member state. They proved, however, to be slow and inefficient in promoting the coordination of education policies. In addition, incentives for active

[33] S. Hall, referring to Foucault, 'Foucault: Power, Knowledge and Discourse', in M. Wetherell et al (eds) *Discourse Theory and Practice: A Reader* (London: Sage Publications, reprint 2002, original edition 2001) 72.

[34] M. Wetherell, 'Themes in Discourse Research: The Case of Diana' in M. Wetherell et al (eds) *Discourse Theory and Practices: A Reader* (London: Sage Publications, reprint 2002, original edition 2001) 15.

[35] N. Alexiadou, n 15 above, 109.

[36] Gornitzka, 2005, n 21 above, 28.

[37] T. Christiansen, K. E. Jørgensen, and A. Wiener 'The Social Construction of Europe' (1999) 6 (4) J of Eur Public Policy 528, 538.

[38] P. J. DiMaggio and W. Powell, *The New Institutionalism in Organizational Analysis* (Chicago: University of Chicago Press, 1991).

[39] Alexiadou, referring to DiMaggio and Powell, n 15 above, 108.

participation in the working groups were limited because it was unclear what the groups' tangible outcomes would be. The working groups were finally disbanded and in 2006 the European Commission set up eight so-called clusters.[40] The clusters nearly replicate the themes of the working groups. Their topics were selected through a hybrid 'bottom-up' and 'top-down' approach.[41] They are intended to correspond to national priorities regarding education policy *and* the key areas of work identified in the EU's Education and Training 2010 Work Programme.[42] Each cluster is coordinated by a member of staff from the DG EAC and participation is voluntary which should facilitate more active participation and engaged discussions. Ten to twenty five member states participate in cluster work. Clusters are considered to be the second, implementation phase of the work started by the working groups.[43]

One of the main tasks of the clusters is to organize so-called peer learning activities (PLAs).[44] Member states can opt into those PLAs in which they are interested. Usually two people per country participate: a policy-making representative, who is often a civil servant working in a national education ministry, and a representative from a more operational level who can talk about issues of policy implementation. Peer *learning* is different from peer *review* of education policies, as practised for instance by the Organisation for Economic Co-operation and Development (OECD), because it does not involve an evaluation of member states' performance. Instead PLAs aim to develop *mutual* learning and to facilitate the exchange of good practice between countries that share similar interests and concerns. PLAs should help to identify those factors that improve the development of education policies and that ensure the successful implementation

[40] Clusters of member states had already started to form on an ad hoc basis in 2005. Countries that shared a common interest in a particular education topic came together and conducted so-called peer learning activities (European Commission, 'Note to the attention of the education and training 2010 Co-ordination group', subject: '2006–2007 framework of activities in the context of Education and Training 2010 Work Program: clusters and other main measures', 1, Brussels, 10 March, 2006, EAC A1 SV D(2006).

[41] M. Citi and M. Rhodes, 'New Modes of Governance in the EU: Common Objectives vs National Preferences' European Governance Papers (EUROGOV) No N–07–01 (2007), 21 at <http://www.connex-network.org/eurogov/pdf/egp-newgov-N-07–01.pdf> (last visited 31 July 2009).

[42] European Council, 'Detailed work Program on the follow-up of the objectives of Education and training systems in Europe' [2002] OJ C142/01.

[43] The European Commission has started in 2009 to revise again the organizational structure for peer learning and the clusters will be modified.

[44] Clusters also use other working methods such as the organization of seminars, conferences, networks of experts and networks on particular themes, the commissioning of studies and research, and the setting up of expert groups. They receive support from existing EU institutions in the field of education and training, such as the Cedefop, the ETF and Eurydice, an information network on education in Europe. For instance, the cluster on 'Access and Social Inclusion in Lifelong Learning' organized a symposium in Brussels 'On the Future Perspectives of Education and Training for Growth, Jobs and Social Cohesion', 19–20 June 2007.

of education reforms.[45] PLAs are focused on quite specific topics of education policy, such as 'university-business partnerships', which was a PLA organized by the cluster on 'modernizing higher education'. Member states (sometimes also called 'donor countries') volunteer to host PLAs on topics on which they can present particular expertise and experiences of value to other member states. They are sometimes assisted in the organization and running of PLAs by educational consultants appointed by the European Commission. DG EAC has drawn up a basic template for the organization of PLAs[46] that leaves significant flexibility for the organization of each individual PLA. For instance, in relation to the involvement of stakeholders it suggests: 'the host countries should, where relevant, invite social partners and other relevant stakeholders at national level to participate in the PLAs'. The actual participation of stakeholders varies between PLAs. PLAs usually conclude with soft, non-prescriptive 'recommendations', 'conclusions' or 'policy messages'. If the conclusions are considered to be important they may form the basis for European Commission Draft Recommendations, Recommendations or Communications.

4. How do discourses and institutions of public policy learning contribute to the governance of education in the EU?

4.1 From discourses to small-scale institutional structures to cooperation between member states

Discourses that are generated during education policy learning can become embodied in various types of documents. These texts build 'from the bottom up' at two levels the small-scale institutional architecture that facilitates governing through policy learning. At the first level, policy learning discourses can be structured into *concept papers*. These are written in preparation for PLAs and member states that participate in PLAs will formally respond to them.[47] Policy learning discourses can be further condensed into *principles* or tentative *guidelines* which are not yet models of effective practice. For instance, a PLA on the 'validation of non-formal and informal learning' started from a set of common European

[45] DG EAC, Educonsult, 'Report of the PLA focusing on the Dutch Delta Plan, Science and Technology' (2006) Educonsult, for the Pôle Universitaire Européen de Nancy (draft report, version 1/12/06, manuscript with authors) 9.

[46] European Commission, 'Operational Guide for Clusters and Peer Learning Activities in the Context of the Education and Training 2010 Work Programme' (2006).

[47] 'The Shift to Learning Outcomes and National Qualifications Frameworks', 14 March 2007, 2. Document for the cluster 'recognition of learning outcomes' without attribution, manuscript with authors. Concept papers for a PLA on the recognition of outcomes of informal learning addressed such topics as 'the linkage between the European Qualifications Framework and national qualifications frameworks' and 'the ongoing administration and maintenance of a national qualifications framework'.

principles for identifying and validating informal learning that were adopted by the European Council in May 2004.[48] In this PLA, very pragmatic, unstructured and detailed policy learning discourses were distilled into guidelines whose acceptance by member states is voluntary. The guidelines developed in greater detail the European principles on the recognition of informal learning. They addressed such matters as the roles and functions of validation bodies, methodologies for recognizing informal learning and requirements for experts who become involved in the validation of informal learning.[49] The guidelines were also described as a *summary document* which means that they are more specific than general EU perspectives on a particular issue of education policy, but less specific than a description of detailed national practices.[50] Hence, through the development of various text formats, such as concept papers, principles, guidelines and summary documents, small-scale institutional structures are built up that can generate more enduring effects than simply an oral exchange of knowledge in PLAs.

These documents contribute to governance in various ways. On a procedural level, drafting them is considered to promote mutual trust among the different member states that participate in the PLA.[51] The drafting of these documents also helps the development of new networks for education policy-making. On the level of substantive content, the drafting of these documents advances the identification and development of common ground among the participating member states. For instance, the drafting of the guidelines for the recognition of informal learning distils common factors that can promote greater convergence between different national validation schemes without imposing uniformity. The compatibility and comparability of national validation systems should be enhanced through the development of methodologies for recognizing outcomes of informal learning. These methods should not be too prescriptive which will facilitate their application across the EU. They have to take into account that, by definition, informal learning is very diverse across the EU. Portfolios, observation and simulation were therefore recommended as methods for testing informal learning rather than written examinations.[52] The drafting of these various documents in PLAs helps to manage the key tension between uniformity and flexibility in EU education measures across the EU and thus paves the way for EU education governance.

[48] European Commission, 'Conclusions of the Council and of the representatives of the Governments of the Member States meeting within the Council on Common European Principles for the identification and validation of non-formal and informal learning' (2004) 9600/04 EDUC 118 SOC 253, 18 May.

[49] Cedefop and DG EAC (2007) 'Discussion Note Peer Learning Activity, Validation of Non-Formal and Informal Learning, Cluster on "Recognition of Learning Outcomes"', 2–4, Paris, July 2007.

[50] Consultancy Report, 'Recognition of Learning Outcomes, Peer Learning Activity', Brussels, 30 January–1 February 2007, Summary of the PLA, 5.

[51] Cedefop and DG EAC, n 49 above, 2.

[52] Consultancy Report, n 50 above, 6.

At a second, more advanced level, discourses generated during policy learning may be turned into official EU policy documents. Discourses about education measures can become formalized in Draft Recommendations, Recommendations, Communications and Commission Staff Working Papers[53] issued by the European Commission, as well as joint Commission and Council work programmes and Council Resolutions. These documents vary in authority and status and thus form a hierarchy of official EU documents. Commission Recommendations seek to provide specific direction for EU education policy learning. They can set the goal-posts for future action and frame the agenda of discussion with the education Council and directly with education policy actors in the member states. Commission Staff Working Papers mainly publicize, for further discussion, DG EAC's ideas for education measures in the EU. The discourses that are embodied in these documents have the potential to steer thinking regarding education policies in the EU and therefore contribute to the governance of education. They also promote specific interactions between the different institutional actors who are involved in policy learning. For instance, joint Commission and Council Work Programmes develop a cooperative relationship between the Commission and the member states that is crucial to the governance of education in the EU. The Commission can only maintain and increase its sphere of influence if it keeps the member states informed of its initiatives and binds them together through its activities.

Moreover, documents contribute to EU governance of education because they are central to specific obligations regarding reporting and supervision. In the spring of every odd-numbered year, member states have to submit reports to the European Commission that detail their progress towards achieving the targets of the Education and Training 2010 Work Programme. The Commission then analyzes these national reports and writes a cross-country report, which is an extensive Staff Working Paper. On the basis of this report the European Commission and the Council write a draft joint report. This is then sent in the even-numbered years to the European Council as one of the inputs to the European Council reporting process, which deals with the implementation of the entire Lisbon agenda. On the basis of these reports the European Council supervises the activities of member states. It can issue recommendations to individual member states in order to improve their implementation of the Lisbon agenda. In the recommendations that were issued to member states in 2006, education and training featured more prominently than previously. Some of the recommendations focused on the development of school education in member states in order to address the development of skills for labour markets. In addition, member states have to report annually to the Commission on their progress towards the implementation of the economic and employment aspects —the core—of the reformulated Lisbon agenda.

[53] Commission Staff Working Papers are detailed reports that can contribute to, eg the preparation of joint Communications by the European Commission and the Education Council.

Table 1. Key characteristics of different policy learning styles in open methods of coordination for education

Characteristics	Mutual learning	Competitive learning	Imperialistic learning	Surface learning
Aims	Construction of new knowledge, cognitive gain	'Looking good' in interstate competition	Expansion of member state's influence and power	Maintenance of existing distribution of power between member states
Incentives	Voluntary, finding solutions to national education problems	Semi-voluntary, reputational pressures, comparative advantage	Imposed	Preserving member state sovereignty as victory in national politics
Key question	What constitutes good education policies and practices worth learning about?	Who is best?	How can we get other countries to adopt our education policies?	How can we avoid undue EU influence on our national education policies?
Type of knowledge	Wide knowledge base, construction of new empirical knowledge, inductive, learning, acknowledging gaps in knowledge, sharing information of successful and unsuccessful experiences, learning from all countries participating in the PLA, not just the host country	Wide knowledge base in terms of number of member states about which information is collated, but reliance on a particular type of knowledge, in particular quantitative data Learning on the basis of 'objective data'	Narrow knowledge base, strategic presentation of knowledge to maximize influence, knowledge for advocacy, 'knowledge is power', 'we already know it all'	Narrow knowledge base, existing 'old' knowledge is sufficient, 'we already know it all'
Organizational framework	Clusters and PLAs, flexibility in the working methods of clusters and PLAs: clusters choose working method suited to the topic Mixed 'bottom up' from the member states and 'top down' approach reflecting EU Commission's initiatives	Development of benchmarks and indicators by the EU Commission Fixed benchmarks and indicators that measure specific aspects of education practices across all different member states	Intergovernmental negotiation Drawing on established claims of influence over other member states	Working groups, National reporting on education measures which presents existing national practices as responses to European initiatives
Outcomes	Context dependent, can accommodate diversity key conclusions which can be fed into policy-making at EU national, regional and local level	Seeks to impose uniformity, adaptation of member states to the practices of 'the best'	Seeks to impose uniformity, policy export from one country or group of countries to others	Seeks to preserve existing diversity continuing with existing national practices or national autonomy over any possible changes
Governance style	Co-operative, democratic, negotiated, based on consensus	Creating leaders and followers, based on objective knowledge of what is 'best'	Hierarchical, authoritarian, based on power position	Limited EU governance, preserving existing governance structures in MS

Member states then report on guidelines 23, 'expand and improve investment in human capital' and 24, 'adapt education and training systems in response to new competence requirements' which were developed by the Commission and address those aspects of employment that pertain to education and skills.

To conclude, policy learning discourses start to acquire structural properties when talk about education measures in PLAs becomes transformed into various types of documents, including official EU policy documents that seek to construct cooperative relationships between the European Commission, the Council and the makers of education policy in the member states. Member states' annual and bi-annual reports on the implementation of the Lisbon agenda and the Education and Training Work Programme 2010 further develop governance by supervising the activities of member states. Hence, policy learning can contribute to the governance of education. However, seeking to govern through learning also transforms learning about policy. We suggest that policy learning becomes differentiated into four different styles: mutual, competitive, imperialistic and surface learning.

4.2 Mutual policy learning

Mutual learning is a key policy learning style supported through the institutional framework of the clusters and their peer learning activities. It seeks to construct new knowledge about education practices in the 27 member states. Due to the fact that the EU's active involvement in education has until quite recently been limited mainly to financing various mobility programmes for teachers and learners there is a significant lack of knowledge about education policies and practices in the different member states. However, such knowledge is a pre-condition for any development of education measures by the European Commission. Participation in mutual learning is voluntary. The opportunity to obtain knowledge that can help to solve problems of national education policy can be an incentive to participate in mutual learning. For smaller member states mutual learning can be a source of cheap consultancy.[54] What it is worthwhile to inquire into and learn about is constructed differently in the various styles of policy learning. Mutual learning asks what constitute good education practices and what and how other member states can learn from such practices. As one interview respondent put it:

> Ireland won't know what makes its particular policy work well, it's only from exchanging info with other countries that this could possibly be understood.[55]

In contrast to this in imperialistic learning, what is worth learning is defined *a priori* as the policies of the member state or group of member states that seek to influence education policies and practice in the EU. In competitive learning the answer to what is worth learning is found through an 'objective' process of comparing 'performance'. A broad knowledge base is necessary to answer the

[54] Interview no 7. [55] Extract from interview no 2.

more open-ended questions that are tackled in mutual learning. Hence, member states learn in the PLAs not just from the state that hosts the PLA, but also from the other participating member states that contribute reports on the particular topic of the PLA. Member states seek to learn not just from others' successes but also their failures. Knowledge is generated inductively through critical reflection upon knowledge of specific local education practices by a range of local actors who are involved in making education policy, such as teachers, pupils, public education authorities and businesses where relevant. As an inductive, 'bottom-up' form of learning, mutual learning varies from cluster to cluster and PLA to PLA. This heterogeneity is increased by the limited communication and coordination between the activities of the various clusters. Moreover, mutual learning recognizes that knowledge that underpins policy-making will always be limited. First, it is difficult to know exactly why a particular education policy is successful in one country and whether this policy could also be made to work in other EU member states and hence in different economic, social and political contexts that may influence the implementation of the education policy. Second, PLAs should also promote the exchange of 'good practices' in education among EU member states.[56] However, as one cluster coordinator suggested,[57] in the absence of agreement on criteria for defining 'good', let alone best practices, PLAs involve exchanges of education practices that have not been necessarily evaluated through either a political process or research.

Mutual learning constructs particular interactions among member states. It defines education issues as *common* challenges.[58] PLA reports use the following terms in order to engender closer interactions between member states: 'building trust, dialogue and reflection'.[59] Mutual policy learning seeks to accommodate diversity among education policies and practices in the EU. PLA reports, for instance, acknowledge dissenting views where member states have not been able to agree on specific points and recommendations. Mutual policy learning seeks to contribute to democratic governance of education that aims for consensus where possible. A second, but different key policy learning style is competitive learning.

4.3 Competitive policy learning

Competitive learning is another key style of learning about policy. Significant EU resources are spent on competitive learning through the financing of

[56] Commission (EC), 'Operational Guide for Clusters and Peer Learning Activities in the Context of the Education and Training 2010 Work Programme' (2006), 2.

[57] Interview no 2. [58] Educonsult, n 45 above, 30.

[59] See for instance, the following quotation from a preparatory document for work in the cluster 'recognition of learning outcomes': 'peer learning here should not be a framework for allowing some countries that already gained significant experience in the field to teach other countries, rather peer learning should promote *reflection* about the initiatives and potential dilemmas of "newcomers" to a particular education policy issue' (emphasis added, unattributed, n 46 above, 1).

various staff in the DG EAC, Eurydice, Eurostat, the European Centre for the Development of Vocational Training (Cedefop) and the European Training Foundation (ETF), who develop benchmarks and indicators as well as collate surveys and other statistical data on education practices in the EU. Competitive learning starts from specific assumptions. First, indicators of specific educational practices limit the discussion to a selected range of problematic and/or important issues regarding education in the EU. Examples of these are the percentage of graduates in mathematics, science and technology or the percentage of early school leavers in a member state. Second, competitive learning seeks to encourage 'laggards' to learn from and imitate the 'leaders'. This is based on the assumption that best practices should and can be transferred from one or several member states to others. Hence competitive policy learning strives for some harmonization of member states' education practices.

While the rhetoric of mutual learning is concerned with 'deep' learning which invites member states to reflect critically upon their own traditions in education, competitive learning is also concerned with presentation. It is one of the goals of competitive learning 'to look good' in international competition. Competitive learning enables member states to gain status in league tables. This presentational element in competitive learning was also highlighted by one of our interview respondents.[60] He drew attention to potential discrepancies between the surface and actual meaning of benchmarks and indicators when comparing education performance across different EU member states. For instance, indicators, such as the percentage of early school leavers[61] in a member state, fail to capture what these figures actually mean for the individual student and their societies. In highly structured and disciplined Northern European societies leaving school early without entering training is considered as a significant failure and leads to loss of status for the individual young person concerned. Early school leaving also signals a failure of society as a whole because a dense institutional welfare state safety net should have prevented individuals from disappearing from organized and supervised activities which would finally lead to productive employment. In contrast to this, in some Mediterranean countries, leaving school early can be less of a social failure for the individual young person concerned and society as a whole. Dense, informal, private, often extended family networks can provide financial support and routes into local employment. Hence, early school leaving may carry with it limited social stigma. Yet there is no explicit discussion of the different meaning of indicators in different countries in competitive policy learning. Competitive policy learning based on benchmarks, indicators and targets seeks to portray policy learning as a neutral activity that is based on

[60] Interview no 4.

[61] ie those who leave school before the age until which the member state provides compulsory schooling and/or leave school with limited or no formal qualifications and do not enter further training.

objective knowledge derived from quantitative data that measure performance of all member states in specific areas of education. The incentives for member states to participate in competitive policy learning are comparative economic advantages where better performance in some areas of education is associated with improved competitiveness of a member state's economy both in the EU and the international context. Moreover, competitive policy learning relies on pressure on member states to maintain their reputation for enhancing coordination between them. Such pressure can be particularly effective when it is amplified through 'naming' and 'shaming' campaigns in the national media.

Finally, competitive policy learning engenders a style of governance that has some democratic elements. Competitive policy learning has less 'bottom up' involvement of local actors than mutual policy learning because benchmarks and indicators are developed to a significant extent by European Commission and specialist agency staff. However, competitive learning can also open up new channels of influence for those member states who can demonstrate leadership in the comparisons that are based on benchmarks and indicators. Some of the newer member states who lack a tradition of being key players in EU policy-making look particularly good in measurements of some education practices. For instance, there are five eastern and central European countries among the ten European countries that have already achieved the EU benchmark of 'less than ten per cent of early school leavers before 2010'. None of the new eastern or central European member states have rates of early school leaving greater than 25 per cent, while some of the older member states fall into this latter category.[62] While competitive policy learning—through its reliance on 'objective' data—seeks to move away from high politics in the governance of education in the EU, imperialistic learning is explicitly concerned with the exercise of power.

4.4 Imperialistic policy learning

Imperialistic policy learning seeks to impose on other countries what a powerful member state or group of member states has decreed to be the best education practice. In imperialistic learning not all learners are equal:

> Big countries think they know it all, and they have enough resources to know very much more than the small countries. They have more research, they have more evaluation, they have more data, they have more going on in their own systems.[63]

It is, however, not just the traditional 'big' countries, such as France, the UK and Germany, that are candidates for exerting significant influence on EU education

[62] DG EAC, GHK, 'Study on Access to Education and Training: Basic Skills and Early School Leavers (Ref DG EAC 38/04), Lot 3: Early School Leavers, Final Report, A report submitted by GHK, September 2005, 7, at <http://ec.europa.eu/education/doc/reports/doc/earlyleave.pdf> (last visited 31 July 2009).

[63] Extract from interview no 1.

policy learning. Whether a member state can avail itself of imperialistic learning also depends on whether it can present a unified front in EU level discussions. Some of the larger countries, such as Germany, Spain and the UK have diverse regional education systems due to a federal political structure or devolved education systems. Hence, these countries do not always present a single national voice in EU discourse on learning about education policy. Table 2 lists the total of 41 peer learning activities that were organized by the clusters in the time period from 2005 to 2009. The table provides an illustration of who 'leads' policy learning in PLAs. It points to patterns of influence and possible imperialistic learning in the EU. It shows that 56 per cent (23) of PLAs were hosted by northern, western, old member states, while only 29 per cent (12) of PLAs were hosted by a theoretically much larger number of either southern or new eastern or central European member states.[64] The number of new member states is further limited with Hungary hosting four PLAs. Hence, the table suggests that policy learning at the EU level can be an opportunity for member states to consolidate, and further expand, established spheres of influence now also in the field of education.

4.5 Surface policy learning

In contrast to imperialistic learning, the central issue in surface policy learning is how undue influence of other member states and the EU supranational institutions—an infringement of national sovereignty—can be limited. In surface policy learning the participation of member states in learning is superficial. There is little real engagement with, and interest in, changing national education practices in response to 'lessons learnt' by other member states. Heads of state, not national education ministers, had agreed in Lisbon to the development of OMC processes in education. The education ministers of some member states were opposed to further EU cooperation in education. Some interview respondents associated the initial organizational framework of working groups with surface learning because various member states participated rather reluctantly. In some working groups only about a third of representatives in a meeting actually spoke and thus participated actively.[65] Delegates for a number of member states were passive observers of the proceedings who would report back to national administrations in case EU initiatives were perceived as infringing upon national prerogatives of education policy. Surface learning can also occur in the clusters and their PLAs. It is up to member states to opt in to PLAs and some do not participate much. Evidence of surface learning can also be found in national reporting on progress regarding the implementation of the Education and Training Work Programme 2010. According to some DG EAC officials, the bi-annual reports that member states have to deliver

[64] Four PLAs were organized by Norway and two by Iceland (15%).
[65] Interview no 8.

Table 2. Who leads education policy learning in the EU?

Cluster	Modernising Higher Education	Teachers and Trainers	Making Best Use of Resources	Maths, Science and Technology	Access and Social Inclusion in Lifelong Learnings	Key Competences	Information and Communication Technologies	Recognition of Learning Outcomes
Country where Peer Learning Activity (PLA) is being held and topic of the PLA	Norway, Oslo: 'Planning and Implementing Curricular Innovation: Structure, Content and Incentives' 9–11 October 2006	Ireland, Dublin: 'CPD for Teachers and Trainers' 26–29 September 2005	Netherlands, The Hague: 'Evidence Based Policy and Practice' 30 May–01 June 2007	Netherlands, Amsterdam: 'The Dutch Delta Plan' 13–17 November 2006	Belgium, Brussels: 'School Integration of Immigrant Children, Positive Discrimination Measures, Support to School Drop Outs' 9–11 October 2006	Belgium, Flanders: 'Key Competences for Life Long Learning' 29–31 January 2007	Finland, Helsinki: 'Finnish Digital Content Production and Use' 25–27 January 2006	France, Paris: 'Validation of Non-Formal and Informal Learning' 9–11 July 2007
	United Kingdom, Birmingham: 'University-Business Partnerships' 23–25 October 2006	Netherlands, The Hague: 'Schools as Learning Communities for Their Teachers' 28 May–01 June 2006	Portugal, Lisbon: 'Schemes for Supporting Students in Higher Education' 13–16 July 2005	Sweden, Gothenburg: 'Maths Education' 21-24 May 2007	Ireland, Dublin: 'Preventative and Compensatory Measures to Reduce Early School Leaving' 31 January–2 February 2007	Hungary, Budapest and Veszprém: 'The Supporting System for Curricular Reform' 17–19 September 2007	Luxembourg 'Portals and Collaboration' 27–29 September 2006	Belgium, Brussels: 'Quality Assurance Procedures in the Recognition of Non-Formal and Informal Learning' 30 January–1 February 2007

The Netherlands, The Hague: 'Using Financial Instruments for Steering System Performance' 7–9 March 2007	Norway, Oslo: 'How can Teacher Education and Training Policies Prepare Teachers to Teach Effectively in Culturally Diverse Settings' 20–24 May 2007	Denmark, Copenhagen: 'University Governance: Autonomy and Accountability 19–21 April 2006	France, Sèvres and Paris: 'Renovation in Science Education: An Inquiry-Based Approach' 8–12 October 2007	Hungary, Budapest: '(De)Segregation in Education' 25–27 April 2007	Greece, Athens: 'Key Competences for Life Long Learning' 9–13 December 2007	Norway, Oslo: 'Learning Networks' 21–23 September 2005	Hungary, Budapest: 'The Development of National Qualifications Frameworks' 8–10 October 2007
Bulgaria, Sofia: 'Implementing EQF/NQF in Higher Eduation' 8–10 October 2007	Denmark, Copenhagen: 'Relationships between Teacher Education Institutions and Schools' 7–11 October 2007		Norway, Oslo: 'Increased Recruitment and Better Quality Instruction in MST—A Joint Promotion of MST in Norway'	France, Paris: 'Fight Against Failure at School and Inequality in Education' 12–15 November 2007	Austria, Vienna: 'Fostering Cross-Curricular Key Competences for Creativity in Innovation' 10–12 November 2008	UK, Birmingham: 'Leadership in ICT and Parental Involvement' 4–5 October 2007	UK, London: 'Added Value of NQFs as Tools to Support Life Long Learning' 20–21 October 2008
Iceland, Reykjavik: 'Circling the Knowledge Triangle from the Perspective of Education: the Added Value in Better Connecting Higher Education to Research and Innovation' 25–27 June 2008	Estonia, Tallinn: 'Policies on the Induction of New Teachers' 26–30 October 2008		Portugal, Vila do Conde: 'The Action Plan for Mathematics, the Action Plan for Science and the Promotion of Scientific Culture in Portugal' 13–16 October 2008	Spain, Bilbao: 'Schools as Learning Communities' 8–10 October 2008		Greece, Thessaloniki: 'E-Skills in Digital Literacy and Partnerships for Life Long Learning' 8 October 2008	Iceland, Reykjavik: 'Costs and Benefits of Validation of Non-Formal and Informal Learning' 12–13 February 2009

Table 2. (continued)

Cluster	Modernising Higher Education	Teachers and Trainers	Making Best Use of Resources	Maths, Science and Technology	Access and Social Inclusion in Lifelong Learnings	Key Competences	Information and Communication Technologies	Recognition of Learning Outcomes
	Spain, Alicante: 'Ways to Increase Mobility: Funding Models Examined' 29–31 October 2008				Sweden, Stockholm: 'Preschool Education in Sweden and the Connection Between Pre-Schooling, School-Age Childcare and Compulsory School in the Light of Life-Long Learning' 3–5 December 2008		Austria, Vienna: 'E-Inclusion in Digital Competences' 30 November 2008–1 January 2009	Poland, Niepolmice: 'Development of National Qualifications Frameworks' 11–12 June 2006

The research was conducted before the European Commission also established a 'Working Group on the Adult Learning Action Plan' and a sub-cluster on 'Teachers and Trainers in Vocational Education and Training'.

to the European Commission may contain 'propaganda'. Sometimes, member states simply describe their own national education policies and then add the assertion that national targets reflect EU benchmarks or, in some cases, are more challenging, or involve different time lines or a different scope.[66]

Imperialistic, surface, competitive and mutual learning are distinct policy learning styles. Because they share institutional frameworks, however, they can also overlap. For instance, while PLAs organized through the clusters are closely associated with mutual learning, they can also involve imperialistic learning. Initially member states that hosted PLAs were referred to as 'donor' countries while those that learn from host countries were considered to be recipient countries. This terminology suggests a distribution of power which is more closely associated with imperialistic rather than mutual learning where all participants are considered to participate as learners on an equal footing. Moreover, boundaries between different policy learning styles can be fluid. For instance, where peer learning activities also involve elements of peer *review* and hence an evaluation of the 'best performers' it becomes more akin to competitive learning. In addition, sharp differentiations between different policy learning styles fade where they build upon each other. In some clusters PLAs which are associated with mutual learning begin by addressing the issue of how the specific benchmarks that have been set in the Education and Training Program 2010, which are expressions of competitive learning, can be achieved in the different member states.[67] Our identification of four different styles of policy learning complements literature accounts in particular through reference to imperialistic and surface learning. Both imperialistic and surface learning foreground the exercise of power in learning activities. Hence, we suggest that policy learning does not occur in a vacuum but can also reflect pre-existing patterns of interaction and influence between member states. Competitive and cooperative forms of policy learning, which are referred to in the field of education as 'mutual' learning, have been discussed as features of OMC processes more generally.[68] The next section discusses how policy learning becomes embedded in a range of pre-existing governance strategies which have the potential to enhance the capacity for governance of policy learning. Our interview respondents suggested that reliance on expert knowledge

[66] Alexiadou, n 15 above, 112.

[67] For instance, the benchmark to increase by 15% the number of tertiary graduates in mathematics, science, and technology by 2010 was the starting point for some of the PLAs in the MST cluster. Our interview respondents suggested that in practice there are limited links between PLAs and the work on benchmarks and indicators. It is unusual for cluster coordinators to start with the reports on member states' relative performance in relation to the benchmarks and indicators and to define their agenda for peer learning activities accordingly.

[68] C. Radaelli, n 32 above, 14.

is particularly significant. This chimes with the insight of the governmentality literature which has emphasized the significance of 'mentalities of rules', 'forms of truth telling' and 'procedures of expertise' in advanced liberal welfare governance beyond the nation state.[69]

5. Drawing on expert knowledge in education policy learning

EU education policy learning involves representatives of member states' education administrations, European Commission officials and sometimes civil society stakeholders. They collate existing knowledge and generate new knowledge relating to education policies and practices, exchange this knowledge and thereby learn about other EU member states' education measures. Yet much more is involved. Distinct expert discourses become mobilized and hence policy learning becomes professionalized. Participation in EU education policy learning is no longer restricted to just politicians or civil servants but is extended to members of the professional community of education specialists. EU education policy learning seeks to be influential by involving experts and disseminating their knowledge. Hence, when education policy learning is employed as a strategy for governance it mobilizes power, not just by placing new restraints on national education policy-making, but also by harnessing the constitutive effects of power.[70]

Expert knowledge is already being used as a distinct strategy for EU governance. Using expert knowledge in policy learning is therefore different from simply a policy learning process becoming more expert. In the 2001 European Commission White Paper on governance the importance of using expert knowledge in policy-making was referred to in the following terms:

> Scientific and other experts play an increasingly significant role in preparing and monitoring decisions. From human and animal health to social legislation, the institutions rely on specialist expertise to anticipate and identify the nature of problems and uncertainties that the Union faces, to take decisions and to ensure risks can be explained clearly and simply to the public.[71]

Using expert knowledge fits well with evidence-based policy-making which is an already existing strategy for governance. In the UK it has a long history starting in the nineteenth century and being rediscovered in the late 1990s when 'third way' politics left behind the inspiration of grand ideological ideas and

[69] N. Rose, 'Government, Authority and Expertise in Advanced Liberalism' (1993) 22 (3) Economy and Society 283.

[70] M. Foucault, 'Power/Knowledge: Selected Interviews and other Writings' in C. Gordon (ed) *Power/Knowledge: Selected Interviews and other Writings* (Harlow: Longman and Pearson Education, 1980) 156.

[71] Commission (EC), 'European Governance: A White Paper' COM (2001) 428 final, 19, 25 July 2001, Brussels.

instead sought to develop pragmatic public policies 'that work'.[72] Evidence-based policy-making is now also a key paradigm for OMC processes in relation to education. It was the topic of the first PLA for the cluster 'making best use of resources' and the European Commission recently drafted a Recommendation on this. In addition, at the EU level, there is a long history of relying on expert knowledge for preparing legislation in the context of the 'classic community method' of integration, in particular in fields of technical regulation, such as legislation concerning the environment or telecommunications.[73]

Mobilizing expert knowledge is also perceived as a strategy for governance that is distinct from mere political negotiation between member states.[74] In fact, maintaining a certain distance from the high politics of negotiating education matters in the Council and Parliament is considered to enhance the potential for governance of learning relating to education policies. Moving learning relating to education policy onto a more technical footing through the use of expert discourses can help the Commission to secure agreement among representatives of member states on education measures. For instance, a group of education experts developed a matrix for the European Qualifications Framework that was then presented to the member states for consultation. The member states considered the proposals in a political debate and finally asked the experts to simplify the proposed matrix. The distinction between the technical detail of the European Qualifications Framework which was left to experts and the outline political consensus for it from the high level politicians helped to avoid a re-opening of the debate about the Framework. The member states also recognized that requests for changes would require further adjustments, due to the diversity of national frameworks for qualifications in the different member states.[75] Hence, the use of expert knowledge seeks to expand the Commission's and other participants' influence in the politically sensitive field of education policy by appealing to authoritative argument.

There are three main institutional frameworks through which expert discourses become mobilized in EU education policy learning. First, the Commission has established networks of education researchers, comprising an EU wide network of economists of education set up in 2004[76] and a network of other social science education researchers set up in 2006. These networks advise the European Commission on economic and social aspects of education. Experts from these networks also conduct reviews of the literature on particular aspects of education policies that feed into the work of the clusters and participate as 'expert speakers' in

[72] M. Rowe and M. Taylor, 'Community-Led Regeneration: Learning Loops or Reinvented Wheels?' in D. Taylor and S. Balloch (eds) *The Politics of Evaluation: Participation and Policy Implementation* (Bristol: The Policy Press, 2005); S. Nutley and J. Webb, 'Evidence in the Policy Process', in H. Davies, S. Nutley, and P. Smith (eds) *What Works? Evidence Based Policy and Practice in Public Services* (Bristol: The Policy Press, 2000) 20.

[73] Interview no 5. [74] ibid. [75] ibid.

[76] This is EENEE, the European Expert Network on Economists of Education at <http://www.education-economics.org>.

cluster work. For instance, the network of social scientists researching education has also contributed to the work of the cluster on 'access and social inclusion in lifelong learning' by providing studies on early school leaving. Members of these expert networks also advise DG EAC on specific questions on a more ad hoc basis and contribute to the drafting of Commission communications.

Second, expert knowledge is used in the clusters through the involvement of external consultants. These consultants have often previously worked or are still working in universities or research institutes as education academics. Consultants shape PLAs by drawing up their agenda in consultation with PLA participants, including the DG EAC official who is coordinating the cluster. Some interview respondents[77] described consultants as 'stage setting' experts who act independently of member states' perspectives.[78] Sometimes consultants open PLAs by presenting a paper that informs participants of the present state of knowledge about the education matters under discussion. Consultants contribute to the professionalization of policy learning, in that all PLA participants are encouraged to 'establish credibility in the eyes of experts'.[79] Cluster coordinators emphasized the importance of having 'the right' participants in the cluster and PLAs in order to ensure successful work. These were delegates who had significant knowledge in the particular subject area under discussion in contrast to delegates from the education civil service who did not have specific subject knowledge. Hence, mobilizing expert discourses supports the development of informal normative controls deployed within professional groups, in particular the social pressures associated with reputation building.[80]

Third, policy learning through the benchmarks and indicators draws on expert discourses. According to one interview respondent[81] about 500 people are involved in research and discussion about the development of benchmarks and indicators for measuring individual member states' performance and progress in particular areas of education. They are drawn from the DG EAC itself and the specialist agencies of Cedefop, Eurostat, Eurydice, the Standing Group on Benchmarks and Indicators and the European Training Foundation (ETF).

6. Conclusion: developing solidarity by stealth?

This chapter has started to address the question how European Commission coordination of member states' learning about their education policies contributes to social governance in the EU. Policy learning is associated with the development of small-scale institutional structures, such as the drafting of policy documents. Learning about education policy also results in new interactions among member states as well as between member states and the EU supranational

[77] Interview no 4. [78] Interview no 8. [79] Dehousse, n 31 above, 11.
[80] Alexiadou, n 15 above, 104. [81] Interview no 7.

institutions. These interactions vary in their intensity, outcomes and the extent to which they reflect established patterns of influence in EU integration. Moreover, the governance capacity of policy learning in the education OMC is enhanced by being embedded in established governance regimes, such as the mobilization of expert knowledge. This confirms accounts which have emphasized flexibility as key characteristics of new modes of EU governance and which have pointed to continuities between 'old' and 'new' modes of EU governance, despite the fact that policy learning is considered as the key innovation of the OMC.[82] But our account provides a critical gloss on perspectives which perceive policy learning as an *alternative* governance tool by distinguishing it clearly from 'hierarchy' and the use of the authority of law.[83]

So how do OMC processes contribute then to emerging conceptions of solidarity in the EU? The chapter started off by questioning a 'deregulatory' perception of the OMC. Two further points support this. First, bonds of solidarity develop where spaces for democratic contestation of social policies are opened up.[84] PLAs may provide such spaces. It is currently up to PLA organizers to decide whom to include in the discussions and whether to involve all the social partners. PLAs are a new mode of operating for DG EAC and there has so far been limited experience in employing this policy learning process. Further systematic research is needed in order to examine what specific conceptions of solidarity are generated in education PLAs. Second, policy learning may facilitate the emergence of progressive and substantial conceptions of solidarity. Whether this will actually happen may be just as much up to the member states than the EU supranational actors. More research is needed on how education measures developed through OMC processes are received in the EU member states in order to answer the question whether primary, secondary and tertiary education policies provide only a limited conception of competitive solidarity or whether they actually strengthen the bonds of solidarity between EU citizens, regardless of market values and nationality. But it also needs to be acknowledged that where OMC derived education policies in the EU mainly equip people for more intense competition in flexible labour markets, without clear chances of actual employment, insecurity, rather than solidarity, is promoted.

[82] Zeitlin, n 2 above, 232.

[83] Radaelli, n 32 above, 2.

[84] See M. Ross in this volume, ch 2.

13

Relating Territorial Cohesion, Solidarity, and Spatial Justice

*Jane Holder and Antonia Layard**

1. Introduction

Courtesy of the Treaty of Lisbon, the EU Treaty will soon be laced with references to solidarity, accommodating several different contexts—solidarity between the sexes,[1] between the generations,[2] between member states,[3] and 'among peoples',[4] aspects of which form the basis of several other chapters in this volume. But in addition, the Treaty of Lisbon may also provide a firm legal platform for the relatively new policy area of territorial cohesion. Initially described as 'the new buzzword for spatial planning',[5] territorial cohesion now commands a key position in the EU Treaty, describing a main task: '[The Union] shall promote economic, social and territorial cohesion, and solidarity among Member States',[6] as well as providing a legal base for action 'leading to the strengthening of [the EU's] economic, social and territorial cohesion'.[7]

It is exciting to witness the beginning of these new policy directions and ideas in the EU, especially the potential for an alliance, or cross-fertilization, of territorial cohesion and solidarity, creating the conditions for the future development, at the EU level, of a concept of *territorial* solidarity. Our excitement, though, is matched equally by a concern that the (possible) addition to the EU Treaty of territorial cohesion as a third dimension of cohesion policy pursues a certain idea of territorial development in the EU which in terms of spatial impacts is historically driven by and aligned to economic goals and concerns rather than forms of

* Our grateful thanks go to Chris Hilson, Angela Williams, Donald McGillivray and Malcolm Ross for reading drafts of this chapter.

1 Art 2 Treaty Establishing the European Union, as amended by the Treaty of Lisbon (TEU).

2 Art 3(3) TEU 3 ibid. 4 Preamble and Art 3(5) TEU.

5 P. Schon, 'Territorial Cohesion in Europe' (2005) 6(3) Planning Theory and Practice 389.

6 Art 3(3) TEU. 7 Art 174 Treaty on the Functioning of the EU.

justice and fairness in the development of land, the use of resources and the distribution of the impact of environmental harms.

Territorial cohesion forms the subject of a recent Action Programme[8] and a Green Paper,[9] and has been referred to in the European courts.[10] More generally, the concept has been steadily gaining momentum and legitimacy in European policy circles for many years (first appearing in the EC Treaty via the Treaty of Amsterdam in 1997[11]). However, its exact meaning remains unclear. It has been suggested that this uncertain character is one reason for its success in legislative and policy terms, being so easy to sign up to and providing opportunities for local and regional interpretations based on specific historical and cultural characteristics.[12] One simple (and relatively uncontroversial) understanding of territorial cohesion is that it means 'incorporating a spatial planning perspective into decisions that are now made primarily on economic and social grounds',[13] placing the concept firmly within the EU's pantheon of integrated policy-making and new governance approaches to decision-making (with much debate about the appropriateness of the Open Method of Coordination (OMC) as a vehicle for spatial planning) as well as in line with the principle of sustainable development. A reductionist approach to the concept, advanced recently by the Commission, is the lessening of 'territorial concentrations of EU-27 GDP in the traditional core of Europe'.[14] A more far-reaching and contentious interpretation is that territorial cohesion aims at 'spatial justice'.[15]

In this chapter we address these various meanings of territorial cohesion. Section two tracks the various paths which have led to the ascendancy of territorial cohesion in EU law and policy. In section three we discuss the nature of its linkage with the concept of solidarity using four policy directions seemingly being pursued (sometimes simultaneously) by those advancing territorial cohesion as a byword for European spatial planning, but also more broadly as an important aim of the EU: (i) cohesion/competitiveness; (ii) solidarity/diversity;

[8] Portuguese Presidency 'First Action Programme for the Implementation of the Territorial Agenda of the EU' (2007) signed 23 November 2007, Ponta Delgada, Azores. For first stages of implementation of the Action Programme, see 'Slovenian Presidency Report on Activities in the Field of Territorial Cohesion and Urban Development 2008'.

[9] Commission (EC) 'Green Paper on Territorial Cohesion: Turning Territorial Diversity into Strength' COM (2008) 616 final.

[10] Case E-9/04 *The Bankers' and Securities' Dealers Association v EFTA Surveillance Authority* [2006] 2 CMLR 50, para 56; and Joined Cases C-147/97 and C-148/97 *Deutsche Post AG v Gesellschaft Für Zahlungssysteme mbH (GZS) and Citicorp Kartenservice GmbH* [2000] 4 CMLR 838, at n 51.

[11] Art 16 EC in relation to services of general economic interest.

[12] S. Davoudi, 'Understanding Territorial Cohesion' (2005) 20(4) Planning, Practice and Research, 433, 433 and D. Evers, 'Reflections on Territorial Cohesion and European Spatial Planning' (2008) 99(3) Tijdschriftvoor Economische en Sociale Geografie 303, 303.

[13] M.Sint, (2004) 8 Shared Spaces, 4, cited by S. Davoudi, n 12 above, at 433, 434.

[14] Commission (EC), 'Growing Regions, Growing Europe' (2007), xii.

[15] P. Doucet, 'Territorial Cohesion of Tomorrow: A Path to Cooperation or Competition?' (2006) 14(10) Eur Planning Studies 1473, 1473.

(iii) spatializing the European social model; and (iv) sustainable development. In analyzing these various policy directions, my focus is on the foundation of territorial cohesion in broader European spatial policy, and the taking and shaping by the EU of the political idea of 'territorial solidarity'. Referring originally to national autonomy and integrity, I discuss the extent to which this idea now pursues some greater sense of *European* identity, and whether indeed we might talk about 'territorial solidarity' as a specific variant of a broader solidarity concept.

To date, much of the work on territorial cohesion has been carried out by researchers in political science and critical geography, but there is much to be gained from legal analysis of the relationship between law and policy on territorial cohesion and its relationship to solidarity, including examining the development of a constitutional basis for these concepts and how such a basis might be capable of (re)structuring decision-making and influencing the instruments and styles of EU governance. The main insight from a legal perspective, though, is likely to come from questioning the *justice* content of territorial cohesion and solidarity, particularly by analyzing the assertion that territorial cohesion is not only rooted in the European model of society, but that it also extends its affiliation with social protection to incorporate concerns about *spatial* protection.[16] In section four we put forward spatial justice as the missing element of these concepts and consider how several governance approaches and instruments might help to contribute to a broader sense of territorial cohesion and solidarity, so that currently latent justice issues come to the fore in the shaping of European spatial policies.

Our main argument is that, as currently conceived in EU policy, the linking of territorial cohesion and solidarity—the joining of social and spatial protection—is capable of masking the 'bads' (ecological degradation, loss of community and a sense of place) by a focus on the 'goods', as conceived by the EU (prosperity, regional development, global competitiveness). Here, my concern extends beyond a narrow distributive justice approach (the fair allocation of impacts of environmental harms), to take in a broader range of ideals, which might loosely be labelled 'environmental'—the conservation of nature, the protection of public health, ecological and social diversity, and a better quality of life. The success of these and other ideals is dependent upon a radical reorientation of values currently underlying EU spatial policy (and thus a reconfiguring of the 'goods'/'bads' axis) in the hope that, ultimately, these are more likely to contribute to a richer sense of EU identity and also the well-being of EU citizens, and to resonate at a global level, than the more singular pursuit of economic competitiveness. The key question is the extent to which concepts of territorial cohesion and solidarity, and the legal expression of these, might yet contribute to such a reorientation of values.

[16] Davoudi, n 12 above; see generally the project on territorial cohesion and the European Model of Society, discussed below.

2. Advancing territorial cohesion

2.1 Finding a legal base

The story of territorial cohesion properly begins with the development of a European spatial planning agenda in the late 1980s.[17] At this time the EU had no dedicated spatial policy and in many cases the objectives of its policies—at least as defined in the Treaties —had no explicitly spatial character. And yet, it was becoming clear that many of the EU's key policies were having profound (and adverse) impacts on land use patterns and landscapes in the member states—agricultural policy, environmental policy, transport policy, regional policy and energy policy being the main examples. Recognition of the need to better coordinate policies having spatial impacts began a process of negotiations and meetings, led by a Committee on Spatial Development. This process culminated in the European Spatial Development Perspective (ESDP),[18] the 'grand narrative'[19] of European spatial planners. The ESDP represented the EU's first attempt to coordinate and integrate social, economic and environmental policies from a spatial perspective and under a sustainable development 'banner', for example by incorporating European spatial principles in regional funding decisions and more specifically but indirectly by trying to influence the thinking (or 'spatial positioning') of planners and policy-makers in the member states when drawing up development plans, applying for financial assistance from the EU or giving consent for individual housing, transport, commercial or energy projects.[20] In practice it provided a 'mental map', or European reference point.

The main idea driving forward the ESDP project was that the integration of spatial factors into the implementation of Community policy at an early stage would help avoid regional disparities and additionally realign economic growth away from the core of commercial activity, producing a more even geographical distribution of growth. A key means by which the last goal was to be achieved was via 'polycentric' development, the spatially balanced distribution of economically active areas capable of contributing to the global economy.[21] Such a

[17] There had been several spatial planning experiments on a European scale beforehand, such as the Council of Europe's 'European Regional/Spatial Planning Charter' (the Torremolinos Charter) (CEMAT, 1983).

[18] Commission (EC), 'European Spatial Development Perspective: Towards Balanced and Sustainable Development of the Territory of the European Union (ESDP)' (Brussels, 1999).

[19] P. Schon, 'Territorial Cohesion in Europe' (2005) 6(3) Planning Theory and Practice 389, 389.

[20] Committee on Spatial Development, 'European Spatial Development Perspective—Towards Balanced and Sustainable Development of the Territory of the European Union (ESDP)', Presented at the Informal Meeting of Ministers Responsible for Spatial Planning of the Member States of the EU, Potsdam, 10/11 May 1999 (CSD, 1999) 11. This forms the subject of 'Building Spatial Europe: An Environmental Justice Perspective', in J. Scott (ed) *Environmental Protection: EU Law and Governance* (Oxford: OUP, 2009).

[21] Polycentricity is represented in the ESDP by the metaphor of a 'bunch of grapes', replacing, variously, the 'blue banana', the 'Dorsale Europeene' (the backbone of Europe) and, most recently, the 'pentagon', all graphic representations of concentrated economic activity at the 'core' of the EU.

pattern of development was to be facilitated by high levels of 'frictionless' mobility (of people, goods and services), brought about by the completion of the trans-European transport network (TEN-T), involving particularly high speed railways, expansion of road infrastructure and regional airports.[22] Such promotion of mobility heralds a shift from a 'Europe of regions', emphasizing locality, identity and the significance of place, to a 'Europe of "flows"', the term adopted by Hajer to describe the increasing reliance on low cost movement of goods by road, resulting in ruined landscapes and habitats and the dissection of urban and rural communities.[23]

Taking a long view of European spatial policy, strategic planning in urban areas has been widespread since the 1960s, when it was initiated by the state in an attempt to manage urban growth, promote welfare objectives such as housing, and encourage business efficiency.[24] By the early 1980s planned regulatory approaches to development had given way to 'project-led' planning, letting loose entrepreneurial and market forces in urban areas and creating ad hoc planning initiatives such as planning 'holidays', in which planning regulations were relaxed. Healey has examined how this shift advanced the acceptability of business concepts in planning, replacing a welfarist approach of planned space in the 1960s with a '... strategic promotion of place as a product in an external marketplace of investors, business relocators and tourists'.[25] In summary, spatial planning in Europe has its roots in state-led movements for welfare and social justice. In the EU, the ESDP grew from major, but individual, practical initiatives in regional development, transport and the completion of the internal market, all of which were directed towards firmly locating Europe at the heart of the global economy. This early step towards a European spatial policy might be mistaken as a step away from a liberal market territorial integration paradigm towards a market correcting planning approach, but the formative shape of European level spatial planning policy, represented by the ESDP, far from replicated the standards of national welfare spatial policies—'[O]n the contrary, they are constrained by the dilemmas and ambiguities of the global European construction process'.[26]

Although an undeniably significant step, without a legal base in the EU Treaties the ESDP failed to enjoy the status of law or policy. The methods by which it sought to influence decision-making are therefore particularly

[22] For further discussion of key elements of the ESDP, see J. Holder, 'Building Spatial Europe: An Environmental Justice Perspective' in J. Scott (ed) *Environmental Protection: EU Law and Governance* (Oxford: OUP, 2009).

[23] J. Hajer, 'Transnational Networks as Transnational Policy Discourse: Some Observations on the Politics of Spatial Development in Europe', in A. Faludi and W. Salet (eds) *The Revival of Strategic Planning* (London: Kluwer, 2000)

[24] P. Healey, 'The Place of "Europe" in Contemporary Spatial Strategy Making' (1998) 5 Eur Urban and Regional Studies 139, 139.

[25] ibid 140.

[26] G. Giannakourou, 'Towards a European Spatial Planning Policy: Theoretical Dilemmas and Institutional Implications' (1996) 4(5) Eur Planning Studies 595, 602.

interesting, invoking indirect methods such as mutual learning and the establishment of networks[27] in order to generate a sense of 'European positioning', the last suggesting an important role for the ESDP in the creation of a European identity. Notwithstanding the various roles performed by the ESDP and its apparent success as a means of indirectly influencing decision-making,[28] the dismantling of the key institution working for European spatial development policy (the Committee on Spatial Development) and the consequential moving of the spatial planning agenda to the work of the EU structural funds committee, arguably led to a focus on narrowly defined financial concerns,[29] and cleared the way for the emergence of an alliance between policy agendas on spatial planning and cohesion.

From this broad spatial development planning agenda, the high point of which was the ESDP, arose the territorial cohesion concept, the result of a series of esoteric decision-making processes. As described by Faludi, the concept was the idea of Jacques Delors, former President of the European Commission and Michelle Barnier, former EU Regional Commissioner, although it has also been attributed to members of the Assembly of European Regions, with the phrase being mentioned for the first time in one of their reports.[30] Following lobbying by the Assembly, an albeit brief appearance of territorial cohesion in the Amsterdam Treaty in 1997[31] sent an important signal of its potential significance, and the concept was duly included in several subsequent Commission reports on the state of cohesion in the Union. In its second report on economic and social cohesion, 'Unity, Solidarity, Diversity for Europe, its People and its Territory (2001)', territorial cohesion was used to describe the undesirable nature of uneven development in the EU particularly the concentration of population and economic activity at its 'core',[32] against the backdrop of the EU's enlargement. In an associated progress report, the Commission mentions territorial cohesion as an explicit objective of cohesion policy, at the root of which is the promotion of sustainable development,[33] but fails to elaborate as to its meaning. However, in its third report on the subject, 'A New Partnership for Cohesion: Convergence, Competitiveness and Cooperation (2004)', territorial cohesion was given an expansive definition:

27 Most notably, ESPON (European Spatial Planning Observatory Network).

28 A. Faludi, 'The Application of the European Spatial Development Perspective' (2003) 74(1) Town Planning Rev 1.

29 K. Bohme, 'Territorial Cohesion: A Policy Phenomenon in Europe or a Global Issue?' (2005) 6(3) Planning Theory and Practice 387, 390.

30 Assembly of European Regions, 'Regions and Territories in Europe' (Limousin Regional Council, 1995).

31 Inserting what became Art 16 EC.

32 Commission (EC), Third Report on Economic and Social Cohesion: 'A New Partnership for Cohesion: Convergence, Competitiveness and Cooperation' (2004). See Davoudi, n 12 above.

33 Commission (EC), 'First Progress Report on Economic and Social Cohesion' COM (2002) 46 final, 4.

[T]he concept...extends beyond the notion of economic and social cohesion by both adding to this and reinforcing it. In policy terms, the objective is to help achieve a more balanced development by reducing existing disparities, preventing territorial imbalances and by making both sectoral policies which have a spatial impact and regional policy more coherent. The concern is also to improve territorial integration and encourage cooperation between regions.[34]

More strikingly, in this report the Commission stated the rationale for territorial cohesion to be that 'people should not be disadvantaged by wherever they happen to live or work in the Union'.[35]

By the fourth report, 'Growing Regions, Growing Europe (2007)', the Commission presented a narrowly conceived version of territorial cohesion, with the concept taken to mean the lessening of 'territorial concentrations of EU-27 GDP in the traditional core of Europe'.[36] Further examples of a strongly economic interpretation of the concept are found throughout the report. For example the Commission identified access to services of 'general economic interest' as 'of major importance in achieving economic, social and territorial cohesion'.[37] A further challenge was 'to combine high productivity with high levels of employment – to avoid sacrificing one for the other – and to do so throughout a city or region so as to maintain territorial cohesion'.[38] Finally, the achievement of territorial cohesion was seen as dependent upon improving transport infrastructure. Such statements bring to mind Healey's description of the shift towards the 'promotion of place as a product in an external marketplace',[39] capable of overriding the relationships between biological and social diversity and cultural identity.

The need to prepare for a new period for structural funds, running from 2007 to 2013, led to a reconsideration of European spatial development policy. This was combined with a growing sense of the need for a territorially more integrated approach if the goals of structural innovation and sustainable economic growth, identified following the Lisbon and Gothenburg meetings of the European Council, were to be achieved. These events brought the topic of strategic European spatial development policy back onto the political agenda and revived communication between spatial planning ministers.[40] The resulting 'Strategic Guidelines for Cohesion Policy (2005)' stressed that 'the territorial dimension of Cohesion Policy' should be taken into account, with the objective of the concept described as being 'to help achieve a more balanced development, to build sustainable communities in urban and rural areas and to seek greater consistency with other sectoral policies which have a spatial impact'.[41]

[34] Commission (EC), 'A New Partnership for Cohesion: Convergence, Competitiveness and Cooperation—Third Report on Economic and Social Cohesion' (2004) 27.

[35] ibid. [36] Commission (EC), 'Growing Regions, Growing Europe' (2007) xii.

[37] ibid 60. [38] ibid 14. [39] Healey, n 24 above, 140.

[40] Schon, n 19 above, 390.

[41] Commission (EC), 'Strategic Guidelines for Cohesion Policy' (2005) 27.

This understanding of the concept as the third dimension of cohesion policy was then included in the Draft Constitutional Treaty, Articles I–3 of which proposed that the 'Union shall promote economic, social and territorial cohesion, and solidarity among Member States'. The Conference of the Representatives described this 'strengthening of economic, social and territorial cohesion' as aimed at 'reducing disparities between the levels of development of the various regions and the backwardness of the least favoured regions'.[42] However, in this context, territorial cohesion carried an explicitly economic meaning, albeit one mediated by sustainable development, as suggested by the Rotterdam principles: 'the incorporation of the territorial dimension, as well as the concept of territorial cohesion can add value to the implementation of the Lisbon and Gothenburg strategy by promoting structured and sustainable economic growth'.[43]

The territorial cohesion agenda continued to be advanced after the failure of the Draft Constitutional Treaty, particularly by the German Presidency which delivered the 'Territorial Agenda of the European Union: Towards a More Competitive and Sustainable Europe of Diverse Regions' in 2007.[44] This 'action-oriented political framework for our future cooperation'[45] remains remarkably faithful to many of the interpretations and aims of the ESDP, but additionally commits European spatial planning ministers to further strengthen territorial cohesion in order to achieve both greater competitiveness and sustainable development. Territorial cohesion is not defined by the *Agenda*, but seems to encompass several elements: *Integration*—furthering 'territorial integration of places where people live,'[46] including making better use of available resources in European regions;[47] *Cooperation*— encouraging cooperation 'involving the various actors and stakeholders of territorial development at political, administrative and technical levels',[48] to be achieved through 'an intensive and continuous dialogue between stakeholders of territorial development', a process labelled 'territorial governance';[49] and *Coherence*—promoting the coherence of EU policies with a territorial impact, both horizontally and vertically, so that they support sustainable development at national and regional level.

In this context of territorial cohesion policy, the 'Territorial Agenda' sets several priorities for the development of the EU: strengthening polycentric development and innovation through networking of city regions and cities; encouraging

[42] Conference of the Representatives of the Member States, 2004.

[43] EU Informal Ministerial Meeting (2004) Rotterdam, 29/11/2005, cited by Davoudi, n 12 above, 434.

[44] German Presidency, 'Territorial Agenda of the European Union: Towards a More Competitive and Sustainable Europe of Diverse Regions' (2007) <http://www.bmvbs.de/Anlage/original_1005295/Territorial-Agenda-of-the-European-Union-Agreed-on-25-May-2007-accessible.pdf> based upon German Presidency, 'Territorial State and Perspectives of the European Union: Towards a Stronger Territorial Cohesion in the Light of the Lisbon and Gothenburg Ambitions' (2007) <http://www.bmvbs.de/Anlage/original_1005296/The-Territorial-State-and-Perspectives-of-the-European-Union.pdf>.

[45] 'Territorial Agenda', para 2. [46] ibid para 3. [47] ibid. [48] ibid para 4.

[49] ibid para 5.

partnership and territorial governance between rural and urban areas; promoting regional clusters of 'competition and innovation' in Europe (including strengthening their international identity and specialization as a way of becoming more attractive for investment); supporting the strengthening and extension of trans-European networks; promoting trans-European risk management including assessing the impacts of climate change; and strengthening ecological structure and cultural resources as 'the added value for development'.

A 'First Action Programme for the Implementation of the Territorial Agenda' (2007), drawn up by the Portuguese Presidency, was intended to firm up this list of priorities, 'encouraging a structured but flexible process of cooperation' on territorial cohesion.[50] A tightly written document, with clearly set out lines of action and responsibility, a main aim of the Action Programme is to ensure that the territorial dimension is adequately taken into account when reviewing current policies and designing the future policies of the EU.[51] Ministers responsible for spatial planning have thereby committed themselves to reviewing key EU dossiers, notably on climate change, sustainable development, rural development policy, the Lisbon Agenda, transport policy and cohesion policy. The overall aim of the Action Programme is the Europeanization of spatial policy, to achieve 'better coordination between the spatial policies of the Member States by introducing a European dimension and defining and implementing common priorities'.[52] As discussed further below, the Action Programme engages solidarity as a principle, to 'inspire political action and to orientate the individual and shared implementation of the Territorial Agenda',[53] particularly when reviewing key dossiers.

More recently, the Commission's 'Green Paper on Territorial Cohesion: Turning Territorial Diversity into Strength'[54] called for a European-wide discussion on the meaning of territorial cohesion. It offers its own, somewhat inconclusive, definition of the concept, beginning with a flowery description of the diversity of the EU territory and settlement patterns ('From the frozen tundra in the Arctic Circle to the tropical rainforests of Guyane, from the Alps to the Greek Islands, from the global cities of London and Paris to small towns and villages dating back centuries...') and continuing, '[T]erritorial cohesion is about ensuring the harmonious development of all these places and about making sure that their citizens are able to make the most of inherent features of these territories. As such, it is a means of transforming diversity into an asset that contributes to sustainable development of the entire EU'.[55]

The ratification of the Treaty of Lisbon now affirms the place of territorial cohesion as the third dimension of cohesion policy, and provides a legal base for

[50] Portuguese Presidency, 'First Action Programme', 2. [51] ibid 3. [52] ibid 15.

[53] ibid 2.

[54] Commission (EC), 'Green Paper on Territorial Cohesion: Turning Territorial Diversity into Strength' COM (2008) 616 final.

[55] ibid 4.

action in this policy area. As with the Draft Constitution, the Lisbon Treaty also implicitly relates these forms of cohesion to the concept of solidarity. This represents a consistent repackaging or re-labelling of EU spatial policy, but in the more limited form of an 'added dimension' to the existing and well-established cohesion policy. As a result of the Lisbon Treaty, territorial cohesion becomes a shared competence between the EU and the member states.[56]

2.2 Scope

The discussion above suggests to some extent that European spatial planning policy and territorial cohesion are interchangeable, with the latter concept proving more acceptable to member states in both policy and legislative terms. However, more accurately, territorial cohesion and spatial planning should be viewed as distinct because of their different terms of reference. Schon, for example, explains that 'space' and 'territory' are two related but not identical concepts: '[S]pace is a more general, abstract concept, while territory is an important sub-concept of space'.[57] He elaborates that territories are clearly defined spatial units, usually formed as political and administrative entities, but that in the European context, territory is used in a wider sense, to include cities and regions, as well as larger unions or cooperative areas.[58] Analytically, Schon considers that the concept of territory mainly relates to a concern with regional impacts and incidences of policies and the question of how specific local and regional entities (territories) are affected by, in this case, EU policies.[59] So, in referring to territorial policies, territorial cohesion does not cover fully the wider subject of European spatial development policy.[60] But opinions differ. For example, rather than understanding territorial cohesion as of more marginal scope than spatial development policy, Bohme sees it as 'embodying a more comprehensive approach to the preparation and implementation of spatial development policy'. It is 'not just about territories and the interrelationships between territories at all geographical scales but the impacts of sectoral policies in specific places and territories'.[61] Hamez urges a similarly expansive definition of territorial cohesion, so that it is not reduced to a concern for the regions facing economic weaknesses or specific handicaps, such as islands, mountainous areas or peripheral zones (the terms set out in the Draft Constitutional Treaty[62]), but rather is understood to encompass several dimensions—a 'multi-sectoral dimension' in terms of the promotion of social and environmental cohesion as well as economic cohesion; a 'territorial dimension' in terms of different spatial levels from the EU to the local level and concerning both disparities and accessibility to services (the subject of the Third

[56] Art 4 TEU. [57] Schon, n 19 above, 391. [58] ibid. [59] ibid.

[60] ibid 392.

[61] Bohme, 'Territorial Cohesion: A Policy Phenomenon in Europe or a Global Issue?', n 29 above, 387.

[62] Arts III–220.

Cohesion report); and, interestingly, a third, 'temporal dimension', embracing not just present disparities but also those reaching into the future.[63] But, for all this, he concludes that territorial cohesion will be defined as much through the methodologies which are devised and engaged to measure its nature and extent.[64] As a policy concept, then, territorial cohesion will only gain meaning and prove effective through a process of 'appropriation and enactment by local-regional governance actors'.[65] The various levels at which territorial cohesion might be understood therefore becomes particularly important.

2.3 Scales of understanding

The 'Green Paper on Territorial Cohesion' (2008) asks as a question for debate '[What] is the most appropriate definition of territorial cohesion?'[66] As mentioned above, there are strikingly few definitions of the concept. According to Gualini, the lack of a precise definition is just as it should be, because as a concept it is specifically directed towards making cohesion policy more responsive to the diverse territorial needs and characteristics, geographical challenges and opportunities of European regions and cities. This means that 'in principle, there is no effective and legitimate "common understanding" of "territorial cohesion" based on knowledge and expertise at the EU level'.[67] Instead, he suggests, 'there are only effective and legitimate "local" understandings of "territorial cohesion"... the knowledge and expertise applicable to "territorial cohesion" at the EU level is only a framework for legitimate "local" interpretations'.[68] He elaborates:

> [Territorial cohesion] should be interpreted as a framework for enacting innovative forms of regional governance, for promoting collective action at the level of regions and localities – at the region, that is, where the actual mobilization of knowledge and resources and the activation of capacities for policy implementation occur, and where it can be justified and made accountable in democratic terms.[69]

Against such an interpretation of territorial cohesion as an 'appropriable concept', providing supporting frameworks and principles for regional and local interpretations, its increasing elaboration and reworking at the intergovernmental level, signals a 'creeping renationalization of the territorial cohesion discourse', as indicated by the final version of the 'Territorial Agenda':

> We see the future task 'Territorial Cohesion' as a permanent and cooperative process involving the various actors and stakeholders of territorial development at political,

[63] G. Hamez, 'Territorial Cohesion: How to Operationalize and Measure the Concept?' (2005) Planning Theory and Practice 400, 401.
[64] ibid 401.
[65] E. Gualini, '"Territorial Cohesion" as a Category of Agency: the Missing Dimension in the EU Spatial Policy Debate' (2008) 28 Eur J of Spatial Development, 14.
[66] p 17. [67] Gualini, n 65 above, 14. [68] ibid. [69] ibid.

administrative and technical levels. This cooperation is characterised by the history, culture and institutional arrangements in each Member State.[70]

The key point made by Gualini is that territorial cohesion should not be restricted to a purely intergovernmental process, albeit that this might be 'enriched' by stakeholders, but rather that it should properly reach beyond national states and extend to local and regional governance arenas. Thus the meaning of territorial cohesion should be addressed as a category of agency, as 'the expression of concrete patterns of spatially contingent interests, interactions and practices of governance' at local and regional levels.[71] The key difficulty, however, is how to give expression to local and regional understandings of territorial cohesion, whilst remaining responsive to the EU's overarching aims of balanced and sustainable development, and operating within cohesion policy set at the EU level.

3. Policy directions

The above account of the development of the territorial cohesion concept makes clear that it has occurred in a variety of contexts—treaties, guidelines, reports, policy agendas and action programmes—and for wholly different purposes. Doucet identifies within current political debate on territorial cohesion two broadly different policy approaches. The first approach tends to equate territorial cohesion to a range of positive discrimination steps in favour of penalized areas, and has therefore been taken up enthusiastically by lobbies for particular regions. Within regional policy, Doucet explains, this approach embodies neo-corporatism, inspired by financial considerations and a competitive zero-sum game in which certain regions increase their share of funding at the expense of others. In contrast, an alternative approach to territorial cohesion places a greater emphasis on the need for integrated territorial planning strategies and the integration of EU policies. Its proponents are described as the heirs of the post-war urban and regional planning tradition striving to revive a politicized and rationalist ideology based on the notion of the public interest and advocating a cooperative approach focusing on issues of transnational relevance, win-win situations, and, notably, solidarity.[72] Possibly the more idealistic of the two approaches, this cooperation model is, according to Doucet, considerably less influential than its rival.

Doucet accepts that whilst this schema offers a useful depiction of ideal types, or opposing sides in the political debate on territorial cohesion, in practice the picture is far more complex. Accordingly, we draw out below four particular examples of policy directions being pursued by the concept of territorial cohesion, and having relevance to the relationship between territorial cohesion and

[70] ibid. [71] ibid 2. [72] Doucet, n 15 above, 1480.

solidarity, highlighting the existence of conflicting strains within the concept, as well as tension between these categories and over time.

3.1 Cohesion/competitiveness

Territorial cohesion has been described as the 'latest offshoot' of the EU's cohesion policy, which seeks to compensate 'least favoured' regions and member states for disadvantages suffered from the widening and deepening of the EU, thus seeking to promote socio-economic equality across the European territory, and reduce disparities. From this understanding of cohesion policy comes the idea that territorial cohesion is 'about a just distribution of opportunities of space'.[73] The close relation of territorial cohesion with the cohesion-oriented goals of the EU's regional policy was strongly advanced by the Commission in its Third and Fourth Cohesion reports. This relation is now formalized by the Lisbon Treaty's identification of the concept as a 'third dimension' of cohesion policy, representing an attempt to make cohesion policy more responsive to territorial conditions.[74] This legislative context, as well as the roots of the concept, suggests the strength of cohesion as a justification and aim of territorial cohesion.[75] But, in the domain of policy, the aim of advancing territorial cohesion is also allied closely to competitiveness. In the third report on cohesion, for example, the Commission stresses that the ambition for territorial cohesion is not only balanced development and equity, but also competitiveness and sustainability.[76] The 'Territorial Agenda' further highlights as a task of territorial cohesion the need to 'strengthen the global competitiveness and sustainability of all regions of Europe'.[77] This approach is derived from a scoping document which framed debate in this area, 'Territorial State and Perspectives of the European Union—Toward a Stronger Cohesion in the Light of the Lisbon and Gothenburg Ambitions' (2005) and is the product of evidence about territorial development in the EU and the spatial impact of Community policies. This states that as part of the policy to increase Europe's competitiveness, territorial development policies should help areas identify and enhance their 'territorial capital',[78] a term originating in the OECD and elaborated in the final 'Territorial State and Perspectives' report:

> A region's territorial capital is 'distinct from other areas and is determined by many factors [which] ...may include...geographical location, size, factor of production endowment, climate, traditions, natural resources, quality of life or the agglomeration

[73] A. Faludi, 'Territorial Cohesion Policy and the European Model of Society' (2007) 15(4) Eur Planning Studies 567, 568.

[74] Art 3(3) TEU.

[75] See interpretation by Evers, n 12 above, 304.

[76] Commission (EC), Third Report. See interpretation of this by Faludi, n 73 above, 570.

[77] 'Territorial Agenda', para 9.

[78] Luxembourg Presidency, 'Scoping Document and Summary of Political Messages for an Assessment of the Territorial State and Perspectives of the European Union—Towards a Stronger Cohesion in the Light of the Lisbon and Gothenburg Ambitions' (2005) <http://www.eu2005.lu/en/actualites/documents_travail/2005/05/20regio/Min_Doc_1_fin.pdf>.

economies provided by its cities ... Other factors may be 'untraded interdependencies' such as understandings, customs and informal rules that enable economic actors to work together under conditions of certainty, or the solidarity, mutual assistance and co-opting of ideas that often develop in small and medium sized enterprises working in the same sector (social capital). Lastly there is an intangible factor, 'something in the air', called 'the environment' and which is the outcome of a combination of institutions, rules, practices, producers, researchers and policy-makers, that make a certain creativity and innovation possible. This 'Territorial Capital' generates a higher return for certain kinds of investments than for others, since they are better suited to the area and use its assets and potential more effectively.[79]

The EU's 'Territorial State and Perspectives' report goes on to describe the exploitation of territorial capital 'as an important prerequisite for improving the global competitiveness of the whole EU territory'.[80] Spatial positioning is the key to achieving this: under the heading 'Strengthening Territorial Identity, Specialization and Positioning in Europe', regions are urged to 'identify within their territorial development policies their specific territorial advantages in an EU perspective'.[81] Cleverly, through the use of the territorial capital concept, the uniqueness and diverse character of areas is given an economic value, and also described in such terms. This policy direction and prescription for realizing development potential is maintained in the Commission's Green Paper (2008), with competitiveness described as a key objective of territorial cohesion:

Increasingly, competitiveness and prosperity depend on the capacity of the people and businesses located there to make the best use of all *territorial assets* ... Cooperation along with the flow of technology and ideas as well as goods, services and capital is becoming an ever more vital aspect of *territorial development* and a key factor underpinning the long-term and sustainable growth performance of the EU as a whole.[82]

The Green Paper goes on to cite with approval 'Community Strategic Guidelines on Cohesion' (2006) which state that 'promoting territorial cohesion should be part of the effort to ensure that all of Europe's territory has the opportunity to contribute to the growth and jobs agenda'.[83] The idea here is neatly summed up by Allen: '[T]he logic assumes that economic convergence among countries and regions will deliver cohesion, which in turn will deliver growth, competitiveness, employment and sustainable development, and thus the Lisbon and Gothenburg objectives'.[84]

Such an emphasis on competitiveness, as apparent in many of the meanings attributed to territorial cohesion, has been seen as corresponding to a 'shift in paradigm in European regional policy from the traditional focus on structurally

[79] OECD, 'Territorial Outlook' (OECD, 2001) p 1.
[80] 'Territorial State and Perspectives', p 3. [81] ibid 73.
[82] 'Green Paper on Territorial Cohesion', 4. [83] ibid 6.
[84] D. Allen, 'Cohesion and the Structural Funds: Competing Pressures for Reform?' in H. Wallace, W. Wallace and M. A. Pollack (eds) *Policy-Making in the European Union* (5th edn, Oxford: OUP, 2005) 238, cited by Faludi, n 73 above, 568.

weak and disadvantaged regions to strategies aiming at the development of the potential of and opportunities in all regions.'[85] Territorial cohesion appears to have an important part to play in making sense of such a shift, given that its rationale, that 'people should not be disadvantaged by where they happen to live or work in the Union', is by its very nature broadly applicable to the whole territory of the EU. In summary, territorial cohesion is rooted in the EU's cohesion policy, but has increasingly been used to support a policy agenda of competitiveness of all regions, not just those economically weaker areas, and this is indicative of a broader shift taking place in cohesion policy itself.

3.2 Solidarity/diversity

So far, I have explained that at a very simple level the territorial cohesion concept expresses a desire to introduce a territorial element into EU policy-making. Whilst apparently falling short of the EU's original spatial development 'perspective' (which, perhaps erroneously, seemed too much of a threat to member states in terms of European 'control' of their territories), the Treaty of Lisbon grants territorial cohesion a firm legal basis, offering greater opportunities for concrete policy-making. An important, parallel, development is the political and legal use made of the concept of solidarity. As mentioned, the Treaty of Lisbon relates territorial cohesion and solidarity, whilst not explicitly linking them, in the description of the Union's main tasks: '[The Union] shall promote economic, social and territorial cohesion, and solidarity among Member States'.[86] Such an association is familiar in this context. For example, the Commission has previously described cohesion policy as 'the way the European Union expresses solidarity and shows that it is not just a large market but also the guardian of a particular [European] model of society'.[87] In this sense, solidarity is considered an inherent part of cohesion, and by extension, territorial cohesion. In attempting to further intergovernmental cooperation in this area, the 'Territorial Agenda' (2007) similarly relates territorial cohesion and solidarity:

> Through the Territorial Agenda we will help – *in terms of territorial solidarity* – to secure better living conditions and quality of life with equal opportunities, oriented towards regional and local potentials, irrespective of where people live.[88]
>
> . . . we firmly believe that territorial cohesion of the EU is a prerequisite for achieving sustainable economic growth and implementing social and economic cohesion – a European social model. In this context we regard it as an essential task and *act of solidarity* to

[85] European Parliament Committee on Regional Development, 'Follow-up of the Territorial Agenda and the Leipzig Charter: Towards a European Action Programme for Spatial Development and Territorial Cohesion: Ad-hoc Note' (European Parliament, 2007).

[86] Art 3(3) TEU.

[87] 'First Progress Report on Economic and Social Cohesion', 17.

[88] 'Territorial Agenda', para 3 (emphasis added).

develop preconditions in all regions to enable equal opportunities for its citizens and development perspectives for entrepreneurship.[89]

Here the 'Territorial Agenda' appears to give the equity content of cohesion policy the label 'territorial solidarity'. Although this phrase is not defined, the context in which it is placed, and the reference to 'development perspectives for entrepreneurship', suggests that it primarily describes opportunities to participate *equally* in economic life.

This economically oriented nature suggests that in this context at least territorial solidarity carries with it more of a concern with the balanced provision of services and freedom of movement than with social redistribution and the reconstitution of social rights at an EU level. Such a limited approach to spatial development issues has been the subject of sharp criticism. For example, writing on early spatial planning policy, Giannakourou states:

Compared to national state welfarism, actual European-style spatial fairness follows a different conceptualization. In particular, while the former promises the redistribution of resources, services and incomes among the different areas of the national territory and, thus, the equalization of their developing conditions, the latter relies exclusively on the idea of equality of chances through the diffusion of information and knowledge on spatial questions to the national authorities and the market participants. Hence, what is attempted to be redistributed through the new European spatial strategy is not economic prosperity per se but just the chances to access economic prosperity and a better quality of life; in other words, the redistribution of competitiveness opportunities among European areas.[90]

Such analysis of the idea of 'equality of chances' and the 'redistribution of competitiveness opportunities' supports a characterization of the EU's development of a spatial (and now territorial) perspective as a market-accommodating policy, aimed at increasing mobility and competition among the European regions,[91] rather than as previously portrayed, a market-correcting policy concerned with the redistribution of public services and spatial justice in the European territory.[92] This marks a dilution of the concept of territorial solidarity from a thicker version developed in nation states, particularly that in which the 'formal solidarity of citizenship' is expressed by the welfare state.[93] Indeed, at the sub-state level, Beland and Lecours have looked closely at the emergence of territorial solidarity and nationalist movements, finding that 'the processes of

[89] ibid para 8 (emphasis added).

[90] Giannakourou, 'Towards a European Spatial Planning Policy', 607.

[91] ibid.

[92] J. Delors, 'The Social Policy of Europe', Communication to the European Conference of Brussels organized by the European Commission and the Department of European Law of the Catholic University of Louvain, May 1994, cited by Giannakourou, 'Towards a European Spatial Planning Policy', 607.

[93] D. Beland and A. Lecours, 'The Politics of Territorial Solidarity: Nationalism and Social Policy Reform in Canada, the United Kingdom and Belgium' (2005) 38(6) Comparative Political Studies 676.

identity formation/consolidation and territorial mobilization inherent to substate nationalism often involve a social policy dimension'.[94] The important contrast here is with the EU's form of territorial solidarity, which is currently shaped and defined by a notion of equality of economic opportunity, albeit accompanied by attempts to introduce a social reform element by seeking to make apparent and promote links with the European social model, discussed further below.

Notwithstanding such a diluted version of territorial solidarity, an important development remains the elevation of solidarity as a principle guiding the realization of territorial cohesion. Most notably, the 'First Action Programme on the Implementation of the Territorial Agenda', a product of intergovernmental activity, is described as being led by five guiding principles: (i) solidarity between regions and territories; (ii) multi-level governance; (iii) integration of policies; (iv) cooperation on territorial matters and (v) subsidiarity. The adoption of the first principle 'reinforces solidarity between States and regions and expresses the commitment to apply a cohesive and integrated approach adapted to territorial diversity when influencing or deciding on the priorities and funding of territorial and urban development policies at European Union, regional and local levels'.[95] In commenting on the 'next steps' towards territorial cohesion, Michal describes solidarity as a guiding principle in a similar fashion, but this time flanked by the principles of equity and efficiency:

- Equity: one should not be penalized by the location of his (her) employment or home;
- Solidarity: to make so that the territories which have less favourable conditions or which are handicapped by their geography can benefit from a redistribution and equalization of the financial resources;
- Efficiency: to connect the territories so that they are positioned better in the worldwide competition.[96]

Examples such as these suggest a role for solidarity as a guiding principle, reflecting a common value with historical resonance in the EU.[97] This is particularly important given that the EU obviously lacks a (national) identity, a welfare state, and common culture and language, all of which are typically framed by reference to the idea of solidarity.[98]

However, an apparently opposing and emerging strain in policy debates about territorial cohesion is diversity. The 'Green Paper on Territorial Cohesion' (2008), for example, makes no reference to solidarity—territorial or otherwise. Instead, as its subtitle instructs, its emphasis is on 'turning diversity into strength'.[99]

[94] ibid 677. [95] 'First Action Programme', 8.

[96] D. Michal, 'Perspectives and Next Steps Towards Territorial Cohesion', ESPON Seminar, Portoroz, 2 June 2008.

[97] See also Commission (EC), 'European Values in the Globalised World' COM (2005) 525, 4.

[98] D. Beland and A. Lecours, n 93 above, 679.

[99] O. Sykes, 'Strength From Diversity' (2008) Town and Country Planning 430.

The term 'territorial diversity' has been taken to denote the diversity that exists between different geographical areas of a political entity (such as the EU) typically as a result of incorporating territories in which people have developed distinctive cultures, mainly through their language.[100] In the Green Paper, however, the Commission uses it more simplistically, to describe the impressive range of geographical and settlement patterns which are found within the land mass of the EU. The message of the Green Paper is that such diversity can be turned into a 'territorial asset',[101] in a manner reminiscent of the identification of 'territorial capital' in the 'Territorial State and Perspectives' report of 2007.

3.3 'Spatializing' the European social model

Territorial cohesion has been positioned within a wider debate about the European social model, which is itself a matter of debate and dispute but broadly has been taken to stand for the moderation of economic growth and a concern with social welfare and equity, sustainability and good governance.[102] The key argument is that territorial cohesion is not only rooted in this model, but that it also extends the model's affiliation with *social* protection to incorporate concerns about *spatial* protection because the concept expresses concerns about 'a just distribution of opportunities in space'.[103]

Whilst there is certainly evidence that a relationship is recognized at the policy level, with the 'Territorial Agenda' (2007) referring to territorial cohesion as a prerequisite for achieving sustainable economic growth and implementing social and economic cohesion along the lines of a European social model,[104] some caution might also be exercised when signing up to this argument. Gualini, for example, views sceptically the idea that territorial cohesion is consistent with, and furthermore advances, a 'European Model of Society', as one effect of the political stalling of the spatial policy agenda (along with the failure of the Draft Constitution) and the resulting attempt to recast its prospects in the light of an allegedly more persistent 'European social model'. The idea here is that this model provides a convenient hook on which to hang territorial cohesion, offering as it does an existing and well worked policy and theoretical framework,[105] in other words, that reference to the European model might strengthen the hands of those concerned with territorial cohesion. Gualini is particularly scathing of 'erstwhile interpreters' of territorial cohesion as an expression of the European social model who, in his view, have failed to analyze precisely how territorial cohesion and other related policy developments have affected *practices* of the 'public production of space'.[106] Rather, he identifies an ideological 'bent' in the argument: '... reference to the "European

[100] P. van Parijs, *Cultural Diversity Versus Economic Solidarity* (De Broeck U, 2003) 386.
[101] 'Green Paper on Territorial Cohesion', 4.
[102] Faludi, n 73 above, 567. [103] ibid 568. [104] 'Territorial Agenda', para 8.
[105] Gualini, n 65 above, 4. [106] ibid.

social model" tends to become ideological as it attempts to justify, by putting it on a "progressive" background, any development in the *Realpolitik* of European spatial development.'[107] In place of an avowed alliance with the European model of society, Gualini sees the current political-institutional discourse on spatial policy and territorial cohesion as more accurately reflecting a set of unresolved contradictions about how the EU might become more '"effective and democratic" in combining *common concerns* with *growing diversity*'.[108]

All that accepted, the attempted alignment of territorial cohesion with the European model of society offers a useful basis for thinking about a relationship between territorial cohesion and solidarity. Davoudi, for example, argues that territorial cohesion (as with social and economic cohesion) conveys a strong normative dimension, calling for a specific type of social model which puts an emphasis upon reducing disparities, inequalities and injustices:

> [Territorial cohesion] calls for an extension of the underlying principles of the European model from *individuals* to *places* and territories. It calls for solidarity not only amongst European *citizens* but also amongst European *territories*. It extends the call for work-based *social protection* to place-based *territorial-protection*.[109]

Thus, Davoudi considers, the concept not only has the potential to replace the notion of 'spatial planning' within EU arenas, but also to reconceptualize it, by adding an emphasis on spatial justice and equity in territorial development.[110] Faludi, similarly, identifies commonalities between EU territorial cohesion policy and the European model of society. The premise of these commonalities is that conceptualizing certain spatial configurations, spatial structures and territories is an essential part of what territorial cohesion is about. Whereas the European model tends to disregard the concrete shape of the territory to which it applies and is thus a more abstract conceptual entity, for Faludi, '[T]erritorial cohesion policy is one of the ways of rendering it more concrete'.[111] He argues further that the European model of society and territorial cohesion both stand for the 'decommodification' of certain policy objects, being animated by the conviction that 'the market is not everything; that there are values beyond growth', of which one such value is solidarity.

Furthermore, as Faludi explains, territorial cohesion should also include a visionary element. Such spatial visions 'must conceive of towns and cities and regions, indeed of the territory of the EU as a whole, as more than places of production'.[112] He continues, '[T]erritories need to be conceptualized as cohesive. ... People should want to attach themselves to territories. Indeed where the process is conducted in transparent fashion, the very act of visioning territories

[107] ibid.

[108] ibid, citing F. W. Scharpf, 'European Governance: Common Concerns vs. the Challenge of Diversity', MPIfG Working Paper 01/6 (Max-Planck-Institute fur Gesellschaftsforschung, 2001).

[109] Davoudi, n 12 above, 437 (emphasis in original).

[110] ibid.

[111] Faludi, n 73 above, 580.

[112] ibid 580.

and their futures can contribute to this feeling of attachment'.[113] What Faludi is referring to might be described as a type of territorial solidarity, with a sense of identity with a territory being forged by the very process of being involved in deliberation about its future structure, linkages and shape.

Of course, this line of argument, that connections of mutual benefit can and should be drawn between territorial cohesion and the European social model, is possibly over-reliant upon a certain idea of territorial cohesion, one that stresses social and spatial cohesion, shared visions and identity. Such an interpretation of territorial cohesion is tenable, though arguably not so much with current manifestations of the concept which tend to emphasize the economic commodification of land and territory, for example through use of such phrases as 'territorial assets',[114] 'territorial development'[115] and 'territorial potentials'.[116]

3.4 Sustainable development

The principle of sustainable development, originating in international environmental law and, ideally, offering a carefully structured balance between economic, social and environmental factors, has been described as implicit in the notion of territorial cohesion.[117] In turn, territorial cohesion has been seen as capable of promoting sustainable development. The 'Green Paper on Territorial Cohesion' draws upon this apparent affinity:

> Many of the problems faced by territories cut across sectors and effective solutions require an integrated approach and cooperation between the various authorities and stakeholders involved. In this respect, the concept of territorial cohesion builds bridges between economic effectiveness, social cohesion and ecological balance, putting sustainable development at the heart of policy design.[118]

As this statement suggests, the concept of territorial cohesion looks at first like an expanded form of sustainable development, so that the intergenerational or temporal elements of sustainable development are extended and reinforced by the acknowledgment of existing spatial disparities and the wish to alleviate these, found in territorial cohesion. But, whilst providing a strong intellectual and policy impetus for territorial cohesion, as well as placing strong markers towards new governance methods, the form of sustainable development advanced by the EU in relation to debate and dialogue about territorial cohesion is one centred almost exclusively upon a polycentric urban system, linked by transnational infrastructure networks, with a focus on the development of economic growth zones. The 'Territorial State and Perspectives' report, which set the agenda for the 'Territorial Agenda', represents intergovernmental thinking on this point, highlighting in particular the economic dimension of sustainable development:

[113] ibid 581. [114] 'Green Paper on Territorial Cohesion', 4. [115] ibid.
[116] 'Territorial Agenda', para 9. [117] 'Green Paper on Territorial Cohesion', 8.
[118] ibid 6.

The key political challenge for the Union at this moment is to become economically more competitive and dynamic. Urgent action is needed if Europe wants to keep up its model for sustainable development. This requires a stronger focus on growth and employment whilst also taking proper account of social and environmental issues.[119]

The 'Territorial Agenda' took up this message, using as shorthand for such intentions the phrase 'sustainable growth'.[120] This is a subtle but significant change in emphasis, with 'sustainable development' being added to Article 2, with its allusion to forms of development other than economic, alongside a reference to 'sustainable and non-inflationary growth'.[121] Working within a discourse of ecological modernization, such statements uphold the idea that growth can be accommodated within existing social structures and environmental conditions and that there is no need to impose any limits on growth. The form of sustainable development being advanced in the policy context of territorial cohesion is therefore not only permissive of economic development, but is also narrowly focused, with little or no reference to the impacts of the EU's development patterns on the rest of the world. In sum, this pattern of sustainable development cohesion accommodates (and upholds) the status quo, rather than agitating for the transformation of social and economic systems.

A quite different conception arises when one considers sustainable development working alongside a principle of solidarity. Williams, for example, considers both to represent 'value-based concepts aspiring to goals of social justice and equity'.[122] She further identifies that the possible inclusion of the requirement in the EU Treaty to promote 'solidarity between generations'[123] carries with it a commitment to intergenerational justice, and that this is perhaps most clearly exemplified by attempts to prevent and alleviate the effects of climate change. Below, we consider how relating concepts of territorial cohesion, sustainable development and solidarity may forcefully combine in favour of spatial justice within and across communities.

4. Moving towards spatial justice?

In Section three we outlined several policy directions for territorial cohesion, some of which are clearly in competition, but out of which one can begin to see a move towards a conception of territorial solidarity. This political idea, originally (as with citizenship) belonging to the nation state and sub-national movements, has been reshaped and extrapolated to apply to the EU so that it describes the

[119] 'Territorial State and Perspectives', 7. [120] ibid 3ff. [121] Art 2 EC.

[122] A. Williams, 'Sustainable Development and Solidarity in Europe', unpublished paper presented at the workshop, 'Seeking Solidarity in the European Union—Towards Social Citizenship and a European Welfare State?', U of Sussex, May 2008.

[123] Art 3(3) TEU.

equal opportunity to participate in economic and entrepreneurial activity, but has lost any redistributive agenda along the way. Similarly, sustainable development and territorial cohesion, as key planks of the EU's spatial policy, are currently dominated by an economic agenda, both in terms of the values expressed and the use of economic methodologies, as illustrated by the adoption of the concepts of 'territorial capital', 'territorial assets', and 'territorial development'. The important consequence is that there currently exists only a notional recognition of equality and justice issues in planning and development from an EU perspective (unless one counts attempts to align territorial cohesion with the European social model).

In discussing the loss of some sense of spatial justice in development planning, the concern should not be so much with the fair distribution of 'goods', perceived by the 'Territorial Agenda' to be accessibility and mobility, in sum the products of 'sustainable economic growth', but rather with the distribution of the related 'bads', or damaging products of the EU's development path—motorways, bridges, high speed railways, and networks of regional airports, the development and use of which tend to disproportionately affect poor and ethnic minority communities.[124] As Schwarte and Adebowale report, in many areas of Europe, but especially in central and eastern Europe, there are widespread environmental inequalities.[125] The Coalition for Environmental Justice, a network of NGOs in CEE, found that a disproportionate number of settlements of Romani people are sited near hazardous waste sites, large infrastructure development and former mines.[126] More generally the European Environment Agency reports that the environment-related share of the burden of disease is higher in lower-income countries and that climate change particularly affects vulnerable groups.[127] Still, Schwarte and Adebowale note, 'there is no systematic attempt within the EU to link social status, race or ethnicity to environmental risk exposure'.[128] That the environmental or spatial justice element of sustainable development is lacking in its current manifestations is particularly marked when compared to the position in the United States in which the recognition of spatial differences in treatment formed part of a radical agenda for civil rights.[129] At this point, an important link should be made with territorial cohesion, the idea being that territorial cohesion should not primarily be concerned with the just, or balanced, distribution

[124] See generally O. Jensen and T. Richardson, *Making European Space: Mobility, Power and Territorial Identity* (London: Routledge, 2004).

[125] C. Schwarte and M. Adebowale, 'Environmental Justice and Race Equality in the European Union' (London: Capacity Global, 2007) 16.

[126] See <http://www.cepl.ceu.hu>.

[127] European Environment Agency, Environment and Health, available at <http://reports.eea.europa.eu/eea_report_2005_10/en/EEA_report_10_2005.pdf> See also C. Varga, I. Kiss and I. Ember, 'The Lack of Environmental Justice in Central and Eastern Europe' (2002) 11 Environmental Health Perspectives 110.

[128] C. Schwarte and M. Adebowale, n 125 above.

[129] See Holder, n 22 above.

of economic opportunities in space (the lessening of concentrations of GDP) but that it might also refer to a fair distribution of environmental harms—pollution, waste sites, and denuded landscapes—which result from the creation or realization of these opportunities. This suggests the need for an expanded or amended version of the meanings attributed to territorial cohesion. And, to return to Guilani's point about scales of understanding, such meanings should be framed, justified and interpreted locally, and made accountable in democratic terms, in the expectation that under these circumstances social and environmental justice elements will feature more strongly.[130]

At the EU level, the replacement of welfarist or justice elements of national spatial planning by a form of competitive spatial fairness, with its associated compromises and constraints, may be the inevitable product of intergovernmental and Union activity in this area. However, to accept this replacement uncritically is to ignore the apparent misreading of sustainable development which the current treatment of the principle in these contexts suggests, particularly the connections which can, and should, be made between intergenerational justice (responsibility towards future generations) and distributive justice in the present generation in relation to environmental degradation. In trying to work out the nature of the relationship between sustainable development and justice, Barry focuses on the desirability of democratizing definitions of 'social development' and 'progress'.[131] He first describes that environmentalists tend not to be 'against "development" and the improvement of the human condition, but rather against certain forms of industrial, undifferentiated economic growth and "modernization" which is equated with "progress"'.[132] A central task in redirecting this idea of progress towards a more social form is to democratize 'the capacity and power to choose one's development, and to socially define what development is'.[133] In other words, 'for development and preservation to be integrated, the process of defining development itself and not just its implementation needs to be democratized'.[134] For Barry the importance of analyzing our understanding of progress is to grasp *what* it is we owe future generations, according to the concept of sustainable development, as well as identifying our responsibility to current generations. However, as he and others have also made clear, the responsibility for environmental damage and destruction which is held as constituting an injustice to future generations should not be evenly attributed (the rich tending to be more responsible for the environmental crisis than the poor), and it is here that the issue of environmental and social justice for current generations becomes pertinent. As Barry states:

> The debate about intergenerational justice will remain politically impotent unless the intimate connection between it and distributive justice within the present generation

[130] Gualini, n 65 above.

[131] J. Barry, 'Green Politics and Intergenerational Justice: Posterity, Progress and the Environment', in B. Fairweather et al (eds) *Environmental Futures* (Aldershot: Avebury, 1999).

[132] ibid 67. [133] ibid. [134] ibid.

in relation to environmental degradation is established. ... Ultimately, the best way to ensure justice for future generations is to create the conditions of social justice for the present generation, a central aspect of which is the democratic determination of progress and development.[135]

The priority here is with the need to secure *intra*generational justice, as between the developed and developing world, but the argument works equally well when applied to a range of spatial scales, so that environmental and social justice should also prevail within local communities, cities, regions, and 'super-regions'.

It is at this point in discussing how to secure intragenerational justice and to allocate shared responsibility for environmental harm at these levels of governance that the concept of solidarity should be invoked as a way of recognizing and acting upon the linkages which can be identified between social inequality and spatial inequality. To date, these have not been fully integrated in the context of the EU's vision of spatial planning, although there is some recognition of the issue. For example, ESPON (the European Spatial Planning Observatory Network) included equity, justice and socio-economic segregation of communities as matters for debate in its 2007 'Scenarios' report. But there is still little which acknowledges how adverse environmental impacts might affect such segregated communities, beyond a recommendation that risk assessments of local and regional climate hazards should be carried out to target investment in adaptation measures (for example water saving techniques in southern Europe and flood prevention measures in northern Europe).[136] In this context, it is also worth noting that the recent 'Green Paper on Territorial Cohesion' omits references to territorial solidarity made in previous documents, such as the 'Territorial Agenda', in favour of an economic interpretation of diversity, leaving little room to advance the intragenerational justice element of sustainable development. In contrast, working with the idea of solidarity suggests the need for environmental protection and the fight against racial and ethnic discrimination to be considered within an integrated framework.[137] Highlighting the current absence from the EU policy agenda of the distributive aspects of environmental justice,[138] Schwarte and Adebowale advise using antidiscrimination legislation to challenge decisions and activities which create negative environmental impacts and neglect the interests of black, Asian and minority ethnic groups.[139]

A movement in the right direction, in terms of seeking to make apparent the true costs of EU funded developmental activities, is the creation of a framework for *ex post* evaluation of the negative effects of structural and cohesion funding on the environment, a process embarked upon by the EEA and the European

[135] ibid 70. [136] ESPON, 'Scenarios on the Territorial Future of Europe', 61.

[137] Schwarte and Adebowale, n 125 above, 4.

[138] ibid. See also M. Adebowale, *Using the Law: Barriers and Opportunities for Environmental Justice* (London: Capacity Global, 2007).

[139] M. Adebowale, *BAMEs Tackling Social and Environmental Justice* (London: Capacity Global, 2005) <http://www.capacity.org.uk/resourcecentre/reports.html>.

Network of Environmental Authorities (ENEA).[140] The framework is still being designed, but the key foci are in place—waste water treatment and sewerage, biodiversity, and energy. Of these, investment in biodiversity has been singled out as leading to 'increased territorial cohesion, economic and social benefits',[141] and flood management as contributing to 'territorial cohesion and competitiveness'.[142] Initiatives such as this have arisen from the need to assess spending in the light of the EU's Sustainable Development Strategy,[143] for example by shifting funds away from road building and towards rail projects, and promoting renewable energy and energy efficiency projects (although, as the EEA note, 'road projects across the EU continue to receive billions of Euros').[144] The overall focus of this evaluation framework will be the environment. The outstanding and vital issue is how to interrelate such evaluations with socio-economic criteria such as 'quality of life' or a 'decent standard of living'[145] so that for example enhancing biodiversity may be recognized as one means of fostering a positive sense of identity with a place, or that visions of that place in the future may flow from local knowledge and a desire to conserve. There is, in other words, the possibility of a meaningful type of territorial cohesion, alert to local conditions, and rooted in community.

5. Conclusions

There is currently little agreement about the quintessence of territorial cohesion. It is instead a multi-faceted term which at its simplest refers to the desirability of introducing a territorial point of view into decision-making and policy review at the EU level. Offering a 'third dimension' to cohesion, it aims at greater competitiveness, and has been understood primarily in economic terms, as the lessening of 'territorial concentrations of GDP in the traditional core of Europe'. Increasingly, though, it is considered to possess more complex and politicized redistributive and compensatory elements, particularly when guided by the principle of solidarity, and latterly, to promote sustainable development, although falling short of advancing an environmentalist agenda. In sum it is an 'umbrella concept',[146] pursuing goals that are not always easy to reconcile,[147] and a 'work

[140] European Environment Agency, 'Territorial Cohesion—Analysis of Environmental Aspects of EU Regional Policy' (EEA, 2008); European Network of Environmental Authorities, 'The Contribution of Structure and Cohesion Funds to a Better Environment' (ENEA, 2008). See also P. Ekins and J. Medhurst, 'The European Structural Funds and Sustainable Development' (2006) 12(4) Evaluation 474.

[141] EEA, 'Territorial Cohesion', 3.

[142] ibid 26.

[143] (2001). See <http://ec.europa.eu/environment/eussd>.

[144] EEA, 'Territorial Cohesion', xvi.

[145] Such indicators make up part of the European Territorial Cohesion Index, being developed under the framework of the ESPON (3.2) project, on which see further Hamez, n 63 above, 401.

[146] Faludi, n 73 above, 568.

[147] ibid.

in progress',[148] the future direction of which seems to be reliant upon a mix of political and academic clarification, interest group advocacy and bureaucratic manoeuvring,[149] and the impact of the Lisbon Treaty.

Perhaps territorial cohesion might best be described in rather muted terms, as a policy concept that currently 'shares in a "policy paradigm" about the development of space in the EU'.[150] As presently configured, that paradigm is focused sharply upon economic growth and competitiveness in a globalized market. There currently seems little chance of a serious redirecting of territorial cohesion towards social and environmental justice, although adherents to a territorial cohesion/European social alliance model argue forcefully that the conceptual apparatus for this is in place and that its realization is just a matter of designing suitable indicators and other measurements. The attempts on the part of the EEA to at least engage with this redirection, by discussing the development of methods for assessing the negative effects of cohesion and structural funding on biodiversity, is a potentially important nod towards this. Seriously engaging solidarity as a principle for guiding thinking about territorial cohesion and its implementation in policy, beyond the 'solidarity' conditions for equality of access to services and equal participation in entrepreneurial activity, would suggest the need for some reframing of the concept to include ideas of interdependence, shared responsibilities and burdens and even redistribution, but most importantly, the possibility of sharing a set of common values—as well as 'concerns'—at the EU level. There also remains the view that, notwithstanding the presence and perception of 'competitive Europe', '... the Europe of solidarity and cooperation already exists, embodied in the economic and social cohesion policy'.[151] From this perspective, territorial cohesion and territorial cooperation—and perhaps territorial solidarity—can still give a new impetus to EU integration, not as an abstract ideal, but as the best way to pursue the common good of all EU citizens. Far less convincing is the assertion that within the current spatial development policy paradigm, the current aim of territorial cohesion is to provide 'some sort of "spatial justice"'.[152]

[148] G.Ross, 'Review of Territorial Cohesion and the European Model of Society' (2007) 27 J of Planning Education and Research 237.
[149] ibid 238. [150] Gualini, n 65 above, 12. [151] Doucet, n 15 above, 1484.
[152] ibid, 1474.

Bibliography

Accetto M., and Zleptnig, S., 'The principle of effectiveness: rethinking its role in Community law' (2005) 11 European Public Law 375.

Adebowale M., *Using the Law: Barriers and Opportunities for Environmental Justice* (London: Capacity Global, 2007).

——*Tackling Social and Environmental Justice* (London: Capacity Global, 2005).

Alexiadou N., 'The Europeanisation of Education Policy: Researching Changing Governance and "New" Modes of Coordination' (2007) 2 (2) Research in Comparative and International Education 102.

Allen D., 'Cohesion and the Structural Funds: Competing Pressures for Reform?' in H. Wallace, W. Wallace and M. A. Pollack (eds) *Policy-Making in the European Union* (5th edn, Oxford: Oxford University Press, 2005) 238.

Alter K., *The European Court's Political Power*. Selected Essays (Oxford: Oxford University Press, 2009) 23.

—— 'Who are the "Masters of the Treaty"? European Governments and the European Court of Justice' (1998) 52 International Organization 121–147.

—— and Vargas J., 'Explaining Variation in the Use of European Litigation Strategies. European Community Law and British Gender Equality Policy' (2000) 33 Comparative Political Studies 452.

Anderson E., 'What is the point of equality?' (1999) 109 Ethics 287–337.

Anderson K. M., 'The Netherlands: Political Competition in a Proportional System' in E. M. Immergut, K. M. Anderson, and I. Schulze (eds) *The Handbook of West European Pension Politics* (Oxford: Oxford University Press, 2007).

—— and Lamping W., 'Europeanization or Persistence of National Differences? Opportunities and Obstacles to European Social Policy Integration' (Paper presented at the 57th Political Studies Annual Conference, April 21–23, 2007, University of Bath).

Annesley C., 'Lisbon and social Europe: towards a European 'adult worker model' welfare system' (2007) 17 (3) Journal of Common Market Studies 195–205.

Baldock J., 'On being a welfare consumer in a consumer society' (2003) 2 Social Policy and Society 65.

Baldwin P., 'Can we define a European Welfare State Model?' in B. Greve (ed) *Comparative Welfare Systems* (London: Macmillan, 1996) 29–44.

—— *The Politics of Social Solidarity: Class Bases of the European Welfare State, 1875–1975* (Cambridge: Cambridge University Press, 1990).

Banting K., 'Canada: nation-building in a federal welfare state' in: H. Obinger, S. Leibfried, and F. G. Castles (eds) *Federalism and the Welfare State. New World and European Experiences* (Cambridge: Cambridge University Press, 2005) 89–137.

Barnard C., '"British Jobs for British Workers": The Lindsey Oil Refinery Dispute and the Future of Contracting in an Integrated EU Market' (2009) ILJ forthcoming.

—— 'The 'Opt-Out' for the UK and Poland from the Charter of Fundamental Rights: Triumph of Rhetoric over Reality?' in S. Griller and J. Ziller (eds) *The Lisbon Treaty: EU Constitutionalism without a Constitutional Treaty* (Wien/NewYork: Springer 2008).

—— 'Social Policy Revisited in the Light of the Constitutional Debate' in C. Barnard (ed) *The Fundamentals of EU Law Revisited* (Oxford: Oxford University Press, 2007).

—— 'Solidarity and New Governance in the Field of Social Policy?' in G. de Búrca and J. Scott (eds) *New Governance and Constitutionalism in Europe and the US* (Oxford: Hart Publishing, 2006).

—— 'Solidarity and New Governance in Social Policy' in G. de Búrca and J. Scott (eds) *Law and New Governance in the EU and the US* (Oxford: Hart Publishing, 2006) 153.

—— *EC Employment Law* (3rd edn, Oxford: Oxford University Press, 2006).

—— 2005 'Case Comment on *Bidar*' (2005) 42 Common Market Law Review 1465.

—— 'EU Citizenship and the Principle of Solidarity' in M. Dougan and E. Spaventa *Social Welfare and EU Law* (Oxford: Hart Publishing, 2003) 157.

—— 'Article 13: Through the Looking Glass of Union Citizenship' in D. O'Keefe and P. Twomey (eds) *Legal Issues of the Amsterdam Treaty* (Oxford: Hart, 1999).

—— and Deakin S., '"Negative" and "Positive" Harmonisation of Labor Law in the European Union', 2002 (8) Columbia Journal of European *Law* 389–413.

Barry J., 'Resistance is Fertile: From Environmental to Sustainability Citizenship' in A. Dobson and D. Bell (eds) *Environmental Citizenship* (London: MIT Press, 2006) 26.

—— 'Green Politics and Intergenerational Justice: Posterity, Progress and the Environment', in B. Fairweather et al (eds) *Environmental Futures* (Aldershot: Avebury, 1999).

—— *Rethinking Green Politics: Nature, Virtue and Progress* (London: Sage, 1999).

—— and Smith K., 'Civic Republicanism and Green Politics' in D. Leighton and S. White (eds) *Building a Citizen Society: The Emerging Politics of Republican Democracy* (London: Lawrence and Wishart, forthcoming).

Barry B., 'Review Article: '"Exit, Voice, and Loyalty"' (1974) 4 British Journal of Political Science 79.

Bartolini S., *Restructuring Europe: Centre Formation, System Building, and Political Structuring Between the Nation-State and the European Union* (Oxford: Oxford University Press, 2005).

Bauman Z., *Consuming Life* (Cambridge: Polity Press, 2007).

Bayertz K. (ed), *Solidarity* (Berlin: Springer, 1999).

—— 'Four Uses of solidarity' in K. Bayertz (ed) *Solidarity* (Berlin: Springer, 1999).

Beck U., *The Cosmopolitan Vision* (Cambridge: Polity Press, 2006).

—— 'Living your own life in a runaway world: individualisation, globalisation and politics' in W. Hutton and A. Giddens (eds) *On the Edge: Living with Global Capitalism* (London: Jonathan Cape, 2000).

—— and Grande E., 'Europe's Way Out of Crisis' (2007) 10 European Journal of Social Theory 67.

Been V., 'Analysing Evidence of Environmental Justice' (1995) 11 Journal of Land Use and Environmental Law 1.

Beland D., and Hansen R., 'Reforming the French Welfare State: Solidarity, Social Exclusion and the Three Crises of Citizenship' (2000) 23 West European Politics 47.

—— and Lecours A., 'The Politics of Territorial Solidarity: Nationalism and Social Policy Reform in Canada, the United Kingdom and Belgium' (2005) 38(6) Comparative Political Studies 676.

Bell D., 'Liberal Environmental Citizenship' (2005) 14 Environmental Politics 179.
—— 'Environmental Justice and Rawls' Difference Principle' (2004) 26 Environmental Ethics 287.
Bell M., 'Civic Citizenship and Migrant Integration' (2007) 13 European Public Law 311.
Bellamy R., and Castiglione D., 'Legitimizing the Euro-"Polity" and its "Regime": The Normative Turn in EU Studies' (2003) 2(1) European Journal of Political Theory 7–34.
Belorgey J.-M., 'La protection sociale dans une union de citoyens', (1998) Droit Social 160.
Bennett C., and Howlett M., 'The Lessons of Learning: Reconciling Theories of Policy Learning and Policy Change' (1992) 25 Policy Sciences 285.
Besson S., and Utzinger A., 'Introduction: Future Challenges of European Citizenship—Facing a Wide-Open Pandora's Box' (2007) 32 European Law Journal 573.
Betten L., and Grief N., *EU Law and Human Rights* (Longman European Law Series: 1998).
Birch A., 'Economic Models in Political Science: The Case of Exit, Voice, and Loyalty' (1975) 5 British Journal of Political Science 69.
Blair T., *The Courage of our Convictions* (London: Fabian Society, 2002).
Bohman J., 'Democracy, solidarity and global exclusion' (2006) 32 (7) Philosophy and Social Criticism 809.
Bohme K., 'Territorial Cohesion: A Policy Phenomenon in Europe or a Global Issue?' (2005) 6(3) Planning Theory and Practice 387.
Bolderson H., and Mabbett D., 'Non-Discriminating Social Policy? Policy scenarios for meeting needs without categorisation' in J. Clasen (ed) *What Future for Social Security? Debates and Reforms in National and Cross-National Perspective* (The Hague: Kluwer, 2001).
Bonoli G., 'Two Worlds of Pension Reform in Western Europe' (2003) 35 Comparative Politics 399–416.
Boon V., and Delanty G., 'Cosmopolitanism and Europe: Historical Considerations and Contemporary Applications' in C. Rumford (ed) *Cosmopolitanism and Europe* (Liverpool: Liverpool University Press, 2007) 19–38.
Borelli S., 'Libertà di circolazione e scelta del sistema di protezione sociale più vantaggioso' (2006) Rivista del Diritto della Sicurezza Sociale 671
Borgmann-Prebil Y., 'The Rule of Reason in European Citizenship' (2008) 14 European Law Journal 328.
Bowman J., '"Challenging Habermas" response to the European democratic deficit' (2007) 33 Philosophy and Social Criticism 736.
Brand M. 'Note on Case C-209/03 *Bidar*' (2005/2006) 12(1) Columbia Journal of European Law 293.
Breton R., 'Identification in Transnational Political Communities' in: K. Knop, S. Ostry, R. Simeon and K. Swinton (eds) *Rethinking Federalism: Citizens, Markets, and Government in a Changing World* (Vancouver: UBC Press, 1995) 40–58.
Brunkhorst H., *Solidarity: From Civic Friendship to a Global Legal Community* (Cambridge MA: MIT Press, 2005).
Büchs M., *New Governance in European Social Policy: The Open Method of Coordination* (Basingstoke: Palgrave Macmillan, 2007).

Calhoun C., 'Constitutional Patriotism and the Public Sphere: Interests, Identity and Solidarity in the Integration of Europe' (2005) 18 International Journal of Politics, Culture and Society 257.

Casas R., 'European Integration and Social Inequalities from an Empirical Perspective' in L. Magnussen and B. Stråth (eds) *European Solidarities. Tensions and Contentions of a Concept* (Brussels/New York: P.I.E. Peter Lang, 2007) 89.

Cholewinski R., *Irregular migrants: access to minimum social rights* (Strasbourg: Council of Europe Publishing, 2005).

Christiansen T., Jørgensen K. E., and Wiener A., 'The Social Construction of Europe' (1999) 6 (4) Journal of European Public Policy 528, 538.

Ciprut J. (ed), *The Future of Citizenship* (Cambridge: MIT Press, 2008).

Citi M., and Rhodes M., 'New Modes of Governance in the EU: Common Objectives vs National Preferences' European Governance Papers (EUROGOV) No N–07–01 (2007), 21 at <http://www.connex-network.org/eurogov/pdf/egp-newgov-N-07-01.pdf>.

Cohen G. A., 'Where the Action Is: On the Side of Distributive Justice' (1997) 26 Philosophy and Public Affairs 3.

Collins H., 'Discrimination, Equality and Social Inclusion' (2003) 66 MLR 16.

—— 'Is there a Third Way in Labour Law?' in J. Conaghan, R. M. Fischl and K. Klare (eds) *Labour Law in an Era of Globalisation: Transformative Practices and Possibilities* (Oxford: Oxford University Press, 2002) 459.

—— *Beyond Employment: Changes in Work and the Future of Labour Law in Europe* (Oxford: Oxford University Press, 2001).

Costello C., and Davies G., 'The Case Law of the Court of Justice in the Field of Sex Equality Since 2000' (2006) 43 Common Market Law Review 1567–1616.

Cotterrell R., 'Images of Europe in Sociolegal Traditions' in V. Gessner, and D. Nelken (eds) *European Ways of Law—Towards a European Sociology of Law* (Oxford and Portland Oregon: Hart Publishing, 2007).

Cousins M., 'Diritti di soggiorno, sicurezza sociale ed il concetto evolutivo di cittadinanza europea' (2008) Rivista del Diritto della Sicurezza Sociale 65.

—— 'Citizenship, Residence and Social Security' (2007) 32 ELR 386.

—— 'Social Security, Social Assistance and the Special Non Contributory Benefits: the Never-ending Story' (2007) 9 European Journal of Social Security 97.

Craig P., 'The legal effect of directives: policy, rules and exceptions' (2009) 34 ELR 349.

Cropper S., and Goodwin M., 'Policy Experiments: Policy Making, Implementation and Learning' in S. Cropper, A. Porter, G. Williams, S. Carlisle, R. Moore, M. O'Neill, C. Roberts and H. Snooks (eds) *Community Health and Wellbeing: Action Research on Health Inequalities* (Bristol: Policy Press, 2007) 46–48.

Daly M., 'Whither EU Social Policy? An Account and Assessment of Developments in the Lisbon Social Inclusion Process' (2007) 37 (1) Journal of Social Policy 1–19.

Danner G., 'Torn Between National Interests and Community Requirements—the Position of European Health Policy' in B.-M. Bellach and H. Stein (eds) *The New Public Health Policy of the European Union. Past Experience, Present Needs, Future Perspectives* (München: Urban und Vogel, 1999) 65–71.

Davies G., 'The Effect of Mrs Watts' Trip to France on the National Health Service' (2007) 18 King's Law Journal 158.

Davies G., 'The Community's Internal Market-Based Competence to Regulate Healthcare: Scope, Strategies and Consequences' (2007) 15 Maastricht Journal of European and Comparative Law 215.

—— 'Abstractness and concreteness in the preliminary reference procedure' in Niamh Nic Shuibhne (ed) *Regulating the Internal Market* (Cheltenham: Edward Elgar, 2006) 210.

—— '"Any Place I Hang My Hat?" or: Residence Is the New Nationality' (2005) 11 European Law Journal 43.

—— 'Health and efficiency: Community law and national health systems in the light of Müller-Fauré' (2004) 67 MLR 94.

Davis P., *Pension Funds. Retirement-Income Security and Capital Markets. An International Perspective* (Oxford: Clarendon Press, 1995).

Davoudi S., 'Understanding Territorial Cohesion' (2005) 20(4) Planning, Practice and Research 433.

Dawson M., 'The ambiguity of social Europe in the open method of co-ordination' (2009) 34 ELR 55.

de Búrca G., (ed) *EU Law and the Welfare State—In Search of Solidarity* (Oxford: Oxford University Press, 2005).

—— and J. Scott, 'Introduction: New Governance, Law and Constitutionalism' in G. de Búrca, and J. Scott (eds) *Law and New Governance in the EU and the US* (Oxford: Hart Publishing, 2006).

de La Porte C., and Nanz P., 'The OMC—a Deliberative-Democratic Mode of Governance? The cases of employment and pensions' (2004) 11 (2) Journal of European Public Policy 267–288.

—— and Pochet P., *Building Social Europe Through the Open Method of Co-Ordination* (Brussels: Peter Lang Publishing, 2002).

—— and Pochet P., 'Supple Coordination at EU Level and the Key Actors' Involvement' in P. Pochet and C. de la Porte (eds) *Building Social Europe through the Open Method of Co-ordination* (Brussels: Peter Lang, 2001).

de Schutter H., 'Nations beyond nationalism' (2007) 50 Inquiry 378.

de Swaan A., 'Perspectives for Transnational Social Policy' (1992) 27 Government and Opposition 33 at 33; 'Perspectives for Transnational Social Policy in Europe: Social Transfers from West to East' in A. de Swaan (ed) *Social Policies Beyond Boarders: The Social Question in International Perspective* (Amsterdam: Amsterdam University Press, 1994) 101–115

de Vries C.E., van Kersbergen K., 'Interests, Identity and Political Allegiance in the European Union' (2007) 42 (2) Acta Politica 307–328.

Deakin S., 'The "Capability" Concept and the Evolution of European Social Policy' in M. Dougan and E. Spaventa (eds) *Social Welfare and EU Law* (Oxford: Hart Publishing, 2005).

—— and Browne J., 'Social Rights and Market Order: Adapting the Capability Approach' in T. Hervey and J. Kenner (eds) *Economic and Social Rights under the EU Charter of Fundamental Rights* (Oxford: Hart Publishing, 2003).

—— and Wilkinson F., *The Law of the Labour Market: Industrialization, Employment, and Legal Evolution* (Oxford: Oxford University Press, 2005).

Dehousse R., 'The Open Method of Coordination: A New Policy Paradigm?' Paper presented at the First Pan-European Conference on European Union Politics: The Politics of European Integration: Academic Acquis and Future Challenges (2002) Bordeaux, 26–28 September 2002, 10 at <http://eucenter.wisc.edu/OMC/Papers/Dehousse.pdf>.

Delanty G., 'Fear of others: insecurity, xenophobia and Europe' (2008) 42 Social Policy and Administration 676.

—— *Community* (London and New York: Routledge, 2003).

Delhey J., 'Does Enlargement Make the European Union Less Cohesive? An Analysis of Trust Between EU Nationalities' (2007) 45 (2) Journal of Common Market Studies 253–279.

—— 'Nationales und transnationales Vertrauen in der Europäischen Union' (2004) 32 (1) Leviathan 15–45.

—— and Newton K.,' Predicting Cross-National Levels of Social Trust: Global Pattern or Nordic Exceptionalism?' (2005) 21 (4) European Sociological Review 311.

Delors J., 'The Social Policy of Europe', Communication to the European Conference of Brussels organized by the European Commission and the Department of European Law of the Catholic University of Louvain, May 1994.

Dembour M., *Who Believes in Human Rights?* (Cambridge: Cambridge University Press, 2006).

Derpmann S., 'Solidarity and Cosmopolitanism' (2009) 12 Ethical Theory and Moral Practice 303.

Díez Medrano J., 'Europeanization and the emergence of a European Society' IBEI working papers 2008/12 (Barcelona, January 2008).

DiMaggio P. J., and Powell W., *The New Institutionalism in Organizational Analysis* (Chicago: University of Chicago Press, 1991).

Dobson A., 'Thick Cosmopolitanism' (2006) 54 Political Studies 165.

—— *Citizenship and the Environment* (Oxford: Oxford University Press, 2003).

Doucet P., 'Territorial Cohesion of Tomorrow: A Path to Cooperation or Competition? (2006) 14 (10) European Planning Studies 1473.

Dougan M., 'When worlds collide! Competing visions of the relationship between direct effect and supremacy' (2007) 44 Common Market Law Review 931.

—— and Spaventa E., 'Wish You Weren't Here...New Models of Social Solidarity in the European Union' in M. Dougan and E. Spaventa (eds) *Social Welfare and EU Law* (Oxford: Hart Publishing, 2005).

—— 'The Constitutional Dimension to the Case Law on Union Citizenship' (2006) 31 ELR 613.

—— 'Fees, Grants, Loans and Dole Cheques: Who Covers the Costs of Migrant Education within the EU?' (2005) 42 Common Market Law Review 943.

—— 'The Court Helps Those Who Help Themselves...The Legal Status of Migrant Work-seekers under Community Law in the Light of the Collins Judgment' (2005) 7 European Journal of Social Security 7.

Dowding K., et al, 'Exit, Voice and Loyalty: Analytical and Empirical Developments' (2000) 37 European Journal of Political Research 469.

Durkheim E., *The Division of Labor in Society* (London: Collier-Macmillan Limited, 1933, translated by Simpson).

Dworkin R., 'What is equality? Part 1: equality of welfare' (1981) 10(3) Philosophy and Public Affairs 185–246

—— 'What is equality? Part 2: equality of resources' (1981) 10(4) Philosophy and Public Affairs 283–345

Ebbinghaus B., Gronwald M., and Wiss T., 'Germany: Departing from Bismarckian Pensions?' in B. Ebbinghaus (ed) *Occupational Pensions in Europe* (Oxford: Oxford University Press, in press)

Eckardt M., 'The open method of coordination on pensions: an economic analysis of its effects on pension reforms' (2005) 15 (3) Journal of European Social Policy 247–267.

Ekins P., and Medhurst J., 'The European Structural Funds and Sustainable Development' (2006) 12 (4) Evaluation 474.

Ellis E., 'Social Advantages: A New Lease of Life' (2003) 40 Common Market Law Review 639.

—— 'The Recent Jurisprudence of the Court of Justice in the Field of Sex Equality' (2000) 37 Common Market Law Review 1403–1426.

Epiney A., 'The Scope of Article 12 EC: Some Remarks on the Influence of European Citizenship' (2007) 13 European Law Journal 611.

Esping-Andersen G., *The Three Worlds of Welfare Capitalism* (Princeton: Princeton University Press, 1990).

—— *Politics Against Markets* (Princeton: Princeton University Press, 1985).

Etzioni A., *New Communitarian Thinking* (University Press of Virginia, 1996).

Evers D., 'Reflections on Territorial Cohesion and European Spatial Planning' (2008) 99(3) Tijdschriftvoor Economische en Sociale Geografie 303.

Everson M., 'The Legacy of the Market Citizen', in J. Shaw and G. More (eds) *New Legal Dynamics of European Integration* (Oxford: Clarendon Press, 1995)

Eylenbosch A., and Verreth K., 'Equal Treatment for Men and Women in Complementary Pensions: Answers or Unresolved Questions?' (1996) (6) Journal of European Social Policy 123–146.

Faist T., 'Social Citizenship in the European Union: Nested Membership' (2001) 39 (1) Journal of Common Market Studies 37–58.

Faludi A., 'Territorial cohesion policy and the European model of society' (2007) 15(4) European Planning Studies 567.

—— 'The Application of the European Spatial Development Perspective' (2003) 74(1) Town Planning Review 1.

Ferrera M., 'National Welfare States and European Integration: In Search of a "Virtuous Nesting"' (2009) 47 (2) Journal of Common Market Studies 219–233.

—— *The Boundaries of Welfare. European Integration and the New Spatial Politics of Social Protection* (Oxford: Oxford University Press, 2005).

—— 'Towards an "Open" Social Citizenship? The New Boundaries of Welfare in the European Union' in G. de Búrca (ed) *EU Law and the Welfare State: In Search of Solidarity* (Oxford: Oxford University Press, 2005) 19–20.

—— 'European Integration and National Social Citizenship. Changing Boundaries, New Structuring?' (2003) 36 (6) Comparative Political Studies 611–652.

—— *European Integration and National Social Sovereignty: Changing Boundaries, New Structuring*? Working Paper C 11 p-3, (University of California at Berkeley, Centre for German and European Studies, 2001) 27–35.

—— and Hemerijck A., 'Recalibrating Europe's Welfare Regimes' in J. Zeitlin, and D. Trubek (eds) *Governing Work and Welfare in a New Economy* (Oxford: Oxford University Press, 2003).

—— Hemerijck A., and Rhodes M., *The Future of Social Europe. Recasting Work and Welfare in the New Economy* (Oeiras: Celta Editora, 2000).

—— and Sacchi S., 'A More Social EU? In What Areas? In What Forms?' URGE Issue Paper, No 1/2007, 5, available on <http://www.urge.it>.

Fiegle T., *Solidarité and Solidarität: the concept of solidarity in France and Germany in the nineteenth century*', in N. Karagiannis (ed) *European Solidarity* (Liverpool: Liverpool University Press, 2007) 48.

Findlay M., *Governing Through Globalised Crime* (Devon, UK: Willan Publishing, 2008).

Fischer J., 'From Confederacy to Federation: Thoughts on the Finality of European Integration', speech delivered at the Humboldt University Berlin, 12 May 2000, available at <www.auswaertigesamt.de/diplo/en/Infoservice/Presse/Reden/Archiv/2000/000512-FromConfederacyto.html>.

Fletcher G., *Loyalty. An Essay on the Morality of Relationships* (Oxford: Oxford University Press, 1993).

Foucault M., 'Power/Knowledge: Selected Interviews and other Writings' in C. Gordon (ed) *Power/Knowledge: Selected Interviews and other Writings* (Harlow: Longman and Pearson Education, 1980) 156.

Fredman S., 'The Ideology of New labour' in C. Barnard, S. Deakin and G. Morris (eds) The Future of Labour Law: Liber Amicorum Sir Bob Hepple QC (Oxford: Hart Publishing, 2004) 10.

Freedland M., *The Personal Employment Contract* (Oxford: Oxford University Press, 2003).

Hatzopoulos V. G., 'Killing National Health and Insurance Systems but healing Patients? The European Market for Health Care Services After the Judgments of the ECJ in Vanbraekel and Peerbooms' (2002) 39 Common Market Law Review 683.

Galtung J., 'Twenty-Five Years of Peace Research: Ten Challenges and Some Responses' (1985) 22 Journal of Peace Research 141.

Geddes A., and Guiraudon V., 'Britain, France, and EU Anti-Discrimination Policy: The Emergence of an EU Policy Paradigm' (2004) 27(2) West European Politics 334–353.

Gerstenberg O., and Sabel C. F., 'Directly Deliberative Polyarchy: An Institutional Ideal for Europe?' in C. Joerges and R. Dehousse (eds) *Good Governance in Europe's Integrated Market* (Oxford: Oxford University Press, 2002) 289.

Giannakourou G., 'Towards a European Spatial Planning Policy: Theoretical Dilemmas and Institutional Implications (1996) 4(5) European Planning Studies 595.

Giddens A., *Europe in the Global Age* (Cambridge: Polity Press, 2007).

—— *The Third Way and its Critics* (Cambridge: Polity Press, 2000).

—— 'A Social Model for Europe?' in A. Giddens, P. Diamond, and R. Liddle (eds) *Global Europe, Social Europe* (Cambridge: Polity Press, 2006) 25.

Gilbar R., and Bar-Mor H., 'Justice, Equality and Solidarity: The Limits of the Right to Health Care in Israel' (2008) 16 Med L Rev 225.

Giubboni S., 'Libertà di mercato e cittadinanza sociale europea' (2007) 4 Diritto Immigrazione Cittadinanza 13.

—— 'Free movement of persons and European solidarity' (2007) 13 European Law Journal 360.

—— and G. Orlandini, *La libera circolazione dei lavoratori. Principi e tendenze* (Bologna: Il Mulino, 2007) 166.

—— 'Libertà di circolazione e protezione sociale nell'Unione europea' (1998) Giornale di Diritto del Lavoro e di Relazioni Industriali 81.

Glazer N., *Affirmative Discrimination: Ethnic Inequality and Public Policy* (Cambridge: Harvard University Press, 1987).

Golynker O., 'Student loans: The European concept of social justice according to *Bidar*' (2006) 31 ELR 390.

—— *Ubiquitous Citizens of Europe. The Paradigm of Partial Migration* (Antwerp: Intersentia, 2006).

—— 'Jobseekers' Rights in the European Union: Challenges of Changing the Paradigm of Social Solidarity' (2005) 30 ELR 111.

Goodin R. E., *Reasons for Welfare. The Political Theory of the Welfare State* (Princeton: Princeton University Press, 1988).

Gornitzka A., The Open Method of Co-Ordination as Practice: A Watershed in European Education Policy? (2006) Working Paper No 16, Oslo: Arena Centre for European Studies, University of Oslo, at <http://www.arena.uio.no/publications/working-papers2005>.

—— 'Coordinating Policies for a 'Europe of knowledge': Emerging Practices of the "Open Method of Coordination" in education and research' (2005) Working Paper No 16. Oslo: Arena Centre for European Studies, University of Oslo, at <http://www.arena.uio.no/publications/working-papers2005>.

Gualini E., '"Territorial Cohesion" as a Category of Agency: the Missing Dimension in the EU Spatial Policy Debate' (2008) 28 European Journal of Spatial Development 7.

Guéhenno J., 'From Territorial Communities to Communities of Choice: Implications for Democracy' in W. Streeck (ed) *Internationale Wirtschaft, Nationale Demokratie. Herausforderungen für die Demokratietheorie* (Frankfurt/Main: Campus, 1998) 137.

Habermas J., 'Europa: Vision und Votum' (2007) 5 Blätter für deutsche und internationale Politik 517–520.

—— 'Das illusionäre "Nein der Linken"', Blätter für deutsche und internationale Politik (2005) 755–757.

—— 'Why Europe needs a Constitution' (2001) Sept–Oct New Left Review 5.

—— *The Post-National Constellation* (Cambridge: Polity Press, 2000).

—— 'The European Nation-State and the Pressures of Globalisation' (1999) 235 Left Review 46–59.

—— *The Inclusion of the Other: Studies in Political Theory* (Cambridge: MIT Press, 1998.

Hajer J., 'Transnational Networks as Transnational Policy Discourse: Some Observations on the Politics of Spatial Development in Europe', in A. Faludi and W. Salet (eds) *The Revival of Strategic Planning* (Dordrecht: Kluwer, 2000).

Hall S., referring to Foucault, 'Foucault: Power, Knowledge and Discourse', in M. Wetherell et al (eds) *Discourse Theory and Practice: A Reader* (London: Sage Publications, Reprint 2002, Original edition 2001) 72.

Halleskov L., 'The Long-Term Residents Directive: a fulfillment of the Tampere objective of near-equality?' (2005) 7 European Journal of Migration and Law 181.

Haltern U., 'Integration Through Law' in A. Wiener, and T. Diez (eds) *European Integration Theory* (Oxford: Oxford University Press, 2004) 177–196.

—— 'Pathos and Patina: The Failure and Promise of Constitutionalism in the European Imagination' (2003) 9 European Law Journal 14–44.

Halvorsen K., 'Legitimacy of Welfare States in Transitions from Homogeneity to Multiculturality: A Matter of Trust' in S. Mau, and B. Veghte (eds) *Social Justice, Legitimacy and the Welfare State* (Aldershot: Ashgate, 2007) 239–259.

Hamann A., and Ruiz Fabri H., 'Transnational networks and constitutionalism' (2009) 6 International Journal of Constitutional Law 481.

Hamez G., 'Territorial Cohesion: How to Operationalize and Measure the Concept?' (2005) 6 Planning Theory and Practice 400.

Hannah L., *Inventing retirement: the development of occupational pensions in Britain* (Cambridge: Cambridge University Press, 1986).

Harvey D., *A Brief History of Neoliberalism* (Oxford: Oxford University Press, 2007).

Hassler J., Mora J. V. R., Storesletten, K., and Zilibotti F., 'The Survival of the Welfare State' (August 2001) CEPR Discussion Paper No 2905. Available on <http://www.ssrn.com>.

Hatzopoulos V., 'A (More) Social Europe: Apolitical Crossroad or a Legal One Way? Dialogues between Luxembourg and Lisbon' (2005) 42 Common Market Law Review 1599.

—— 'Killing National Health and Insurance Systems but Healing Patients? The European Market for Health Care Services after the Judgments of the ECJ in Vanbraekel and Peerbooms' (2002) 39 Common Market Law Review 683.

Haverland M., 'When the Welfare State Meets the Regulatory State: EU Occupational Pension Policy' (2007) 14 (6) Journal of European Public Policy 886–904.

Hayward T., 'Ecological Citizenship: Justice, Rights and the Virtue of Resourcefulness' (2006) 15 Environmental Politics 435.

Healey P., 'The Place of "Europe" in Contemporary Spatial Strategy Making' (1998) 5 European Urban and Regional Studies 139.

Heidenreich M., 'Regional Inequalities in the Enlarged Europe' (2003) 13 (4) Journal of European Social Policy 313–333.

—— 'Territoriale Ungleichheiten in der erweiterten EU' (2003) 55 (1) Kölner Zeitschrift für Soziologie und Sozialpsychologie 1–28.

—— and Wunder C., 'Patterns of Regional Inequality in the Enlarged Union' (2007) 24 (1) European Sociological Review 19–36.

Héritier A., 'Containing Negative Integration' in R. Mayntz and W. Streeck (eds) *Die Reformierbarkeit der Demokratie. Innovationen und Blockaden. Festschrift für Fritz W. Scharpf* (Frankfurt a.M./New York: Campus, 2003) 101.

Hervey T., 'The Current Legal Framework on the Right to Seek Health Care Abroad in the European Union' (2006/2007) 9 The Cambridge Yearbook of European Legal Studies 261.

—— and McHale J., 'Law, Health and the European Union' (2005) 25 Legal Studies 228.

—— 'Social Solidarity: a Buttress against Internal Market law?', in J. Shaw (ed) *Social Law and Policy in an Evolving European Union* (Oxford: Hart Publishing, 2000).

—— 'Sex equality in social protection: New institutionalist perspectives on the allocation of competence' (1998) 4 European Law Journal 196–219.

—— and Trubek L., 'Freedom to Provide Health Care Services Within the EU: An Opportunity for a Transformative Directive' (2006–2007) 13 Columbia Journal of European Law 623.

Heyd D., 'Justice and Solidarity: The Contractarian Case against Global Justice' (2007) 38 (1) Journal of Social Philosophy 112.

Hilson C., 'Legitimacy and Rights in the EU: Questions of Identity' (2007) 14 Journal of European Public Policy 527.

—— 'New Social Movements: The Role of Legal Opportunity' (2002) 9 Journal of European Public Policy 238, 242.

Hingel A. J., Education Policies and European Governance: contribution to the Interservice Groups on European Governance (2001) Development of Educational Policies, March, DG EAC/A/1. Brussels: European Commission Directorate-General for Education and Culture. <http://europe.eu.int/governance/areas/group12/contribution_education_eu.pdf>.

Hirschman A., *Exit, Voice and Loyalty—Responses to Decline in Firms, Organisations and States* (Cambridge, MA: Harvard University Press, 1970).

Hohfeld W., *Fundamental Legal Conceptions* (London: Yale University Press, 1964).

Holder J., 'Building Spatial Europe'. 'Building Spatial Europe: An Environmental Justice Perspective' in J. Scott (ed) *Environmental Protection: EU Law and Governance* (Oxford: Oxford University Press, 2009).

Hollinger D., 'From Identity to Solidarity' (2006) 135 (Fall) Daedalus 4.

Honneth A., *The Struggle for Recognition: The Moral Grammar of Social Conflicts* (Cambridge: Polity Press, 1996).

Hooghe L., 'Europe Divided? Elite vs Public Opinion on European Integration' (2003) 4 (3) European Union Politics 281–304.

—— and Marks G., *Multi-Level Governance and European Integration* (Lanham: Rowman and Littlefield, 2001).

—— T. Reeskens, Stolle D., and Trappers A., 'Ethnic Diversity and Generalised Trust in Europe. A Cross-National Multilevel Study' (2009) 42 (2) Comparative Political Study 198–223.

Höreth M., 'No Way Out For the Beast? The Unsolved Legitimacy Problem of European Governance' (1999) 6 (2) Journal of European Public Policy 249–268.

Horowitz D., *The Courts and Social Policy* (Washington: The Brookings Institution, 1977).

Hoskyns K., *Integrating Gender. Women, Law and Politics in the European Union* (London: Verso, 1996).

Hutton W., *The World We Are In* (London: Abacus, 2002) 91.

Immergut E. M., Anderson K. M., and Schulze I. (eds) *The Handbook of West European Pension Politics* (Oxford: Oxford University Press, 2007).

Jacobs F., 'Citizenship of the European Union—A Legal Analysis' (2007) European Law Journal 591.

Jans J. H., 'The effect in national legal systems of the prohibition of discrimination on grounds of age as a general principle of Community law' (2007) 34 (1) Legal Issues of European Integration 53–66.

Jensen O., and Richardson T., *Making European Space: Mobility, Power and Territorial Identity* (Routledge, 2004).

Jepsen M., and Pascual, A. S. 'The European Social Model: an Exercise in deconstruction' (2005) 15 Journal of European Social Policy 231.

Joerges C., 'Democracy and European Integration: A legacy of Tensions, a Re-conceptualisation and Recent True Conflicts', EUI Working Papers Law No 2007/25.

—— 'Integration through de-legalisation? An irritated heckler' European Governance Papers (EUROGOV) No N–07–03, <http://www.connex-network.org/eurogov/pdf/egp-newgov-N-07-03.pdf>.

—— and Rödl, F. '"Social Market Economy" as Europe's Social Model?' EUI Working Papers Law No 2004/8.

Kääriäinen J., and Lehtoninen H. 'The variety of social capital in welfare state regimes—a comparison of 21 countries' (2006) 8 European Societies 27.

Karagiannis N. (ed), *European Solidarity* (Liverpool: Liverpool University Press, 2007).

—— 'European Solidarity with "the Rest of the World"' in N. Karagiannis (ed) *European Solidarity* (Liverpool: Liverpool University Press, 2007) ch 12.

Keat R., 'Citizens, Consumers and the Environment: Reflections on the Economy of the Earth' (1994) 3 Environmental Values 333.

Kenner J., 'New Frontiers in EU Labour Law: From Flexicurity to Flex-security' in S. Currie and M. Dougan (eds) *Fifty Years of the Treaty of Rome* (Oxford: Hart Publishing, 2009).

Keune M., and Jepsen M. (eds) 'Not balanced and hardly New: The European Commission's Quest for Flexicurity', European Trade Union Institute for Research, Education, Health and Safety, Working Paper 2007.01, 11, at <http://www.etui.org/research/activities/Employment-and-social-policies/Reports-and-working-papers/2007/WP-2007.01>.

Kleinman M., *A European Welfare State? European Union Social Policy in Context* (Houndsmill Basingstoke: Palgrave, 2002).

Kohler-Koch B., 'European Governance and System Integration' in E. Oddvar, C. Jörges and F. Rödl (eds) *Law and Democracy in the Post-National Union* (ARENA, Centre for European Studies, Oslo, 2008) 93.

Komter A., *Social Solidarity and the Gift* (New York: Cambridge University Press, 2005).

Korpi W., and Palme J., 'Inequality, and Poverty in the Western Countries' (1998) 63(5) American Sociological Review 661–687.

Kostakopoulou D., 'European Citizenship: Writing the Future' (2007) 13 European Law Journal 623.

—— 'Ideas, Norms and European Citizenship. Explaining Institutional Change' (2005) MLR 233.

Krajewski M., Neergaard U., and van de Gronden J. (eds), *The Changing Legal Framework for Services of General Interest in Europe: Between Competition and Solidarity* (The Hague: T M C Asser Press, 2009).

Kumar K., 'The Question of European Identity: Europe in the American Mirror' (2008) 11 European Journal of Social Theory 87.

Kunoy B., 'A Union of National Citizens: The Origins of the Court's Lack of Avant-gardisme in the Chen Case' (2006) 43 Common Market Law Review 179.

Kvesko I., 'Is There Anything Left Outside the Reach of the European Court of Justice?' (2006) 33 Legal Issues of Economic Integration 405.

Kymlicka W., *Contemporary Political Philosophy: An Introduction* (2nd edn, Oxford: Oxford University Press, 2002).

Ladeur K.-H., 'We, the European People . . . —Relâche?' (2008) 14 European Law Journal 147.

Lamping W., 'European Union Social Policy: Towards a Post-National Welfare State?' in K. Schubert, S. Hegelich, and U. Bazant (eds) *The Handbook of European Welfare Systems* (London/New York: Routledge, 2009) 495–510.

—— 'European Integration and Health Policy—a Peculiar Relationship' in M. Steffen (ed) *Health Governance in Europe. Issues, Challenges, Theories* (London: Routledge, 2005) 18–48.

Lamping W., 'Grenzverschiebungen. Das Verhältnis von Sozialpolitik und Wirtschaftspolitik auf EU-Ebene und die Neubestimmungen des "Sozialen"' in A. Evers, and R. G. Heinze (eds) *Sozialpolitik. Ökonomisierung und Entgrenzung* (Wiesbaden: VS-Verlag, 2008) 115–135.

Lang N., 'L'attuazione in Italia della direttiva 2004/38/CE sulla libera circolazione dei cittadini dell'Unione europea', (2007) 2 Diritto Immigrazione Cittadinanza 43.

Lange B., and Alexiadou N., 'New Forms of European Union Governance in the Education Sector? A Preliminary Analysis of the Open Method of Co-Ordination' (2007) 6 (4) European Educational Research Journal 321.

Lasser M. 'Anticipating Three Models of Judicial Control, Debate and Legitimacy: The European Court of Justice, the Cour de cassation and the United States Supreme Court' Jean Monnet Working Paper 1/03. Available at <http://www.jeanmonnetprogram.org>.

Laver M., 'Exit, Voice, and Loyalty Revisited: The Strategic Production and Consumption of Public and Private Goods' (1976) 6 British Journal of Political Science 463.

Le Grand J., *The Other Invisible Hand: Delivering Public Services through Choice and Competition* (Princeton: Princeton University Press, 2007).

Leibfried S., 'Social Policy' in H. Wallace, W. Wallace and M. A. Pollack (eds) *Policy-Making in the European Union* (5th edn, Oxford: Oxford University Press, 2005).

—— 'Towards a European Welfare State? On Integrating Poverty Regimes into the European Community', in C. Jones (ed) *New Perspectives on the Welfare State in Europe* (London/New York, Routledge 1993) 145.

—— and P. Pierson, 'Social Policy. Left to Courts and Markets?' in H. Wallace, and W. Wallace (eds) *Policy-Making in the European Union* (4th edn, Oxford: Oxford University Press, 2000) 267–292.

—— and —— (eds) *European Social Policy. Between Fragmentation and Integration* (Washington DC: The Brookings Institution Press, 1995).

—— and —— 'Semi-Sovereign Welfare States: Social Policy in a Multi-Tiered Europe' in S. Leibfried, and P. Pierson (eds) European Social Policy. *Between Fragmentation and Integration* (Washington, DC: Brooking Institution Press, 1995) 43–77.

—— and M. Zürn, 'Von der nationalen zur postnationalen Konstellation' in S. Leibfried, and M. Zürn (eds) *Transformationen des Staates?* (Frankfurt a.M.: Suhrkamp, 2006) 19–68.

Lenaerts K., Arts D., and Maselis I., *Procedural Law of the EU* (2nd edn, London: Sweet & Maxwell, 2006) 187–193.

Levinson D.J., 'Rights Essentialism and Remedial Equilibration' (June 1999) University of Virginia Law School, Legal Studies Working Paper No 99–5. Available on <http://www.ssrn.com>.

Lhernould J.-P., 'L'accès aux prestations sociales des citoyens de l'Union Européenne' (2001) Droit Social 1103.

Lippolis V., *La cittadinanza europea* (Bologna: Il Mulino, 1994).

Lister R., Citizenship: *Feminist Perspectives* (Basingstoke: Macmillan, 1997).

Loader I., and Walker N., *Civilizing Security* (Cambridge: Cambridge University Press, 2007).

Lyon-Caen A., 'Lessons from the European Experience' in B. Hepple (ed) *Social and Labour Rights in a Global Context: International and Comparative Perspectives* (Cambridge: Cambridge University Press, 2002), 186–189.

Maas W., 'The Genesis of European Rights' (2005) 43 Journal of Common Market Studies 1009.

Mabbett D., 'Aspirational legalism and the role of the Equality and Human Rights Commission in equality policy' (2008) 79 (1) Political Quarterly 45–52.

—— 'Learning by Numbers? The Use of Indicators in the Co-Ordination of Social Inclusion Policies in Europe' (2007) 14 (1) Journal of European Public Policy 78.

—— 'The development of rights-based social policy in the European Union: The example of disability rights' (2005) 43 Journal of Common Market Studies 95–118.

—— 'Why Have Disability Categories in Social Security?' (2003) Vol 11, No 3, Benefits 163–168.

MacDonald E., and Cholewinski R., 'The Migrant Workers Convention in Europe—obstacles to the ratification of the international convention on the protection of the rights of all migrant workers and members of their families: EU/EEA perspectives' (Paris: UNESCO, 2007) 68–69.

MacGregor S., 'No Sustainability Without Justice' in A. Dobson and D. Bell (eds) *Environmental Citizenship* (London: MIT Press, 2006) 116.

Maduro M., 'Reforming the Market or the State? Article 30 and the European Constitution: Economic Freedom and Political Rights' (1997) 3 ELR 5.

Magnette P., and Papadopoulos Y., 'On the politicization of the European consociation: A middle way between Hix and Bartolini', European Governance Papers (EUROGOV) No C–08–01 <http://www.connex-network.org/eurogov/pdf/egp-connex-C-08-01.pdf>. (last visited 5 July 2008).

Magnusson L., and Strath B. (eds), *European Solidarities—Tensions and Contentions of a Concept* (Brussels/New York: Peter Lang, 2007).

—— and —— *A European Social Citizenship? Preconditions for Future Policies from a Historical Perspective* (Bruxelles: Peter Lang, 2004).

Manganaris E., 'The principle of supremacy of Community law in Greece—from direct challenge to non-application' (1999) 24 ELR 426.

Mantouvalou V., 'Servitude and forced labour in the 21st century: the human rights of domestic workers' (2006) 35 ILJ 395.

Marquand D., *The New Reckoning: Capitalism, States, and Citizens* (Oxford: Polity, 1997).

Marshall T. H., *Citizenship and Social Class* (Cambridge, Cambridge University Press, 1950).

Martin D., 'Case Comments on *Ritter-Coulais* Case C-152/03, and *Ioannidis* Case C-258/04' (2006) 8 European Journal of Migration and Law 231.

Martinsen D., 'Towards an Internal Health Market with the European Court' (2005) 28 (5) West European Politics 1035–1056.

Mau S., 'Europäische Solidaritäten' (2008) 21 Aus Politik und Zeitgeschichte 9–14.

—— 'Soziale Ungleichheit in der Europäischen Union' (2004) B 38 Aus Politik und Zeitgeschichte 38–46.

McCrudden C., 'Theorising European equality law' in C. Costello and E. Barry (eds) *Equality in Diversity: The New Equality Directives* (Dublin: Irish Centre for European Law, 2003) 1–31.

McEwen N., and Moreno L. (eds), *The Territorial Politics of Welfare* (London: Routledge, 2005).

McHale J., 'Rights to Medical Treatment in EU Law' (2007) 15 Med L Rev 99.

McHale J. V., 'Framing a right to treatment in English law? Watts in retrospective' (2007) 14 Maastricht Journal of European and Comparative Law 263.

Meier Jaeger M., 'Welfare regimes and attitudes towards redistribution: the regime hypothesis revisited' (2006) 22 European Sociological Review 157.

Melucci A., *Challenging Codes: Collective Action in the Information Age* (Cambridge: Cambridge University Press, 1996).

Menendez A., 'The Sinews of Peace: Rights to Solidarity in the Charter of Fundamental Rights of the Union' in E. Eriksen et al, *The Chartering of Europe* (Oslo: Arena, 2001) 201.

Mény Y., 'De La Démocratie en Europe: Old Concepts and New Challenges' (2003) 41 (1) Journal of Common Market Studies 1–13.

Michal D., 'Perspectives and Next Steps Towards Territorial Cohesion', ESPON Seminar, Portoroz, 2 June 2008.

Micheletti M., 'Why More Women? Issues of Gender and Political Consumerism' in M. Micheletti, A. Follesdal and D. Stolle (eds) *Politics, Products and Markets: Exploring Political Consumerism Past and Present* (London: Transaction Publishers, 2004) 251.

—— et al, 'Introduction' in M. Micheletti, A. Follesdal and D. Stolle (eds) *Politics, Products and Markets: Exploring Political Consumerism Past and Present* (London: Transaction Publishers, 2004).

Miller D., *Citizenship and National Identity* (Cambridge: Polity, 2000).

—— 'Social Justice and Environmental Goods' in A. Dobson (ed) *Fairness and Futurity* (Oxford: Oxford University Press, 1999).

—— *On Nationality* (Oxford: Clarendon, 1995).

Minckler H., 'Enzyklopädie der Ideen der Zukunft: Solidarität' in J. Beckert et al (ed) *Transnationale Solidarität-Chancen und Grenzen* (Frankfurt a.M.: Campus, 2004).

Mitsilegas V., 'Measuring irregular migration: implications for law, policy and human rights' in B. Bogusz, R. Cholewinski, A. Cygan and E. Szyszczak (eds) *Irregular migrants: theoretical, European and international perspectives* (Leiden: Martinus Nijhoff Publishers, 2004) 29

Müller J.-W., 'A general theory of constitutional patriotism' (2008) International Journal of Constitutional Law 72.

Münch I., 'Constructing a European Society by Jurisdiction' (2008) 14 European Law Journal 519.

Murphy M., 'Between Facts, Norms and a Post-National Constellation: Habermas, Law and European Social Policy' (2005) 12 (1) Journal of European Public Policy 143–156.

Nebbia P., 'Article 16 EC and unfair terms in the provision of public services to consumers' in M. Maresca (ed) *Diritto e Politiche Dell'Unione Europea* (Torino: G. Giappichelli Editore, 2007) 32.

Neocleous M., *Critique of Security* (Edinburgh: Edinburgh University Press, 2008).

Newdick C., 'Preserving Social Citizenship in Health Care Markets: There May Be Trouble Ahead' (2008) 2 McGill Journal of Law and Health 93, 104.

—— 'Citizenship, Free Movement and Health Care: Cementing Individual Rights by Corroding Social Solidarity' (2006) 43 Common Market Law Review 1645.

Nutley S., and Webb J., 'Evidence in the Policy Process', in H. Davies, S. Nutley and P. Smith (eds) *What Works? Evidence Based Policy and Practice in Public Services* (Bristol: The Policy Press, 2000) 20.

O'Brien C., 'Case Comment on Case C-212/05, *Gertraud Hartmann v. Freistaat Bayern*; Case C-213/05, *Wendy Geven v. Land Nordrhein–Westfalen*; Case C-287/05, *D.P.W. Hendrix v. Raad van Bestuur van het Uitvoeringsinstituut Werknemersverzekeringen*' (2008) 45 Common Market Law Review 499.

—— 'Reframing Deliberative Cosmopolitanism: Perspectives on Transnationalisation and Post-national Democracy from Labour Law' (2008) 9 German Law Journal 1035–1037.

O'Leary S., 'Solidarity and Citizenship Rights in the Charter of Fundamental Rights of the European Union' in G. de Búrca (ed) *EU Law and the Welfare State: In Search of Solidarity* (Oxford: Oxford University Press, 2005) 39

Obermaier A., 'The National Judiciary—Sword of the European Court of Justice Rulings: The Example of Kohll/Decker Jurisprudence' (2008) 14 European Law Journal 735.
Offe C., 'Obligations versus costs: Types and Contexts of Solidarity Action' in N. Karagiannis (ed) *European Solidarity* (Liverpool: Liverpool University Press, 2007) 113.
—— 'Is There, or Can There be, a European Society?' in Katenhusen and Lamping (eds) *Demokratien in Europa. Der Einfluss der europäischen Integration auf Wandel, Leistungsfähigkeit und neue Konturen des demokratischen Verfassungsstaates* (Opladen: Leske & Budrich, 2003) 71–89.
—— 'Politische Legitimation durch Mehrheitsentscheidung?' in B. Guggenberger, and C. Offe (eds) *An den Grenzen der Mehrheitsdemokratie. Politik und Soziologie der Mehrheitsregel* (Opladen: Leske & Budrich, 1984) 150–183.
Orlandini G., 'Libera prestazione e servizi sociali. Il caso dell'accesso cross-border alle prestazioni di cura', in S. Sciarra (ed) *Solidarietà, mercato e concorrenza nel welfare italiano. Profili di diritto interno e comunitario* (Bologna: Il Mulino, 2007) 171.
Paci M., 'Welfare, solidarietà sociale e coesione della società nazionale' (2008) Stato e Mercato 1.
Palier B., and Pochet P., 'Toward a European Social Policy—At Last?' in N. Jabko, and C. Parsons (eds) *The State of the European Union. With US or Against US? European Trends in American Perspective* (Oxford: Oxford University Press, 2005).
Paulucci F., Den Exter A., and Van de Ven W., 'Solidarity in competitive health insurance markets: analysing the relevant EC legal framework' (2006) 1 Health Economics, Policy and Law 107.
Peers S., *EU Justice and Home Affairs Law* (2nd edn, Oxford: Oxford University Press, 2006) 297.
—— 'Immigration, asylum and the European Union Charter of Fundamental Rights' (2001) 3 European Journal of Migration and Law 141.
Pensky M., 'Solidarity as fact or norm?: Social integration between system and lifeworld' (2006) 32 (7) Philosophy and Social Criticism 819.
Pettit P., *Republicanism: A Theory of Freedom and Government* (Oxford: Oxford University Press, 1999).
Philippopulous-Mihalopoulos A., 'When "No" means "Yes": A Constitution for Europe and the Limits of Ignorance' in, H. Petersen, A. Kjaer, H. Krunke and M. Madsen (eds) *Paradoxes of European Legal Integration* (Aldershot: Ashgate, 2008) 29.
Pierson P., 'Irresistible Forces, Immovable Objects: Post-industrial Welfare States Confront Permanent Austerity' (1998) 4 Journal of European Public Policy 539–560.
—— 'The Path to European Integration. A Historical Institutionalist Analysis' (1996) 29 (2) Comparative Political Studies 123–163.
—— *Dismantling the Welfare State. Reagan, Thatcher, and the Politics of Retrenchment* (Cambridge: Cambridge University Press, 1994).
Pogge T., 'On the Site of Distributive Justice: Reflections on Cohen and Murphy' (2000) 29 Philosophy and Public Affairs 137.
Prechal S., and de Vries S., 'Seamless web of judicial protection in the internal market?' (2009) 34 ELR 5.
Prosser T., 'Regulation and Social Solidarity' (2006) 33 Journal of Law and Society 364.
Quassoli F., 'Migrants in the Italian underground economy' (1999) 23 International Journal of Urban and Regional Research 212.

Radaelli C., 'Who Learns What? Policy Learning and the Open Method of Coordination', Paper prepared for the ESRC seminar series: 'Implementing the Lisbon Strategy: Policy Learning Inside and Outside the Open Method', European Research Institute, University of Birmingham (2004), 26 November 2004, at <http://eric.ex.ac.uk/exeter/bitstream/10036/23652/1/RadaelliPolicyLearning.pdf> (last visited 31 July 2009).

Rawls J., *A Theory of Justice*. (6th edn, Cambridge, MA: Harvard University Press, Revised 2003).

Reale A., 'Representation of Interests, Participatory Democracy and Lawmaking in the European Union: Which Role and Which Rules for the Social Partners?' Jean Monnet Working Paper 15/03.

Rehg W., 'Solidarity and the Common Good: An analytic framework' (2007) 38 (1) Journal of Social Philosophy 7.

Rieder C., 'The EC Commission's New Adopted Baby: Health Care' (2007/08) 14 The Columbia Journal of European Law 145.

Rokkan S., 'Dimensions of State Formation and Nation-building: a Possible Paradigm for Research on Variations within Europe' in C. Tilly (ed) *The Formation of National States in Western Europe* (Princeton: Princeton University Press, 1975) 562–600.

Roller E., *Einstellungen der Bürger zum Wohlfahrtsstaat der Bundesrepublik Deutschland* (Opladen: Leske & Budrich, 1992).

Rorty R., *Contingency, Irony, and Solidarity* (Cambridge: Cambridge University Press 1989).

Rose N., 'Government, Authority and Expertise in Advanced Liberalism' (1993) 22 (3) Economy and Society 283.

Ross M., 'A healthy approach to services of general economic interest? The BUPA judgment of the Court of First Instance' (2009) 34 ELR 127.

—— 'Promoting solidarity: From public services to a European model of competition?' (2007) 44 Common Market Law Review 1057.

—— 'Effectiveness in the European legal order(s): beyond supremacy to constitutional proportionality?' (2006) 31 ELR 476.

Rothstein B., 'Social capital in the social democratic welfare state' (2001) 29 Politics and Society 207.

—— *Just Institutions Matter: The Moral and Political Logic of the Universal Welfare State* (Cambridge: Cambridge University Press, 1998).

Rott P., 'Consumers and services of general interest: Is EC consumer law the future?' (2007) 30 Journal of Consumer Policy 49.

Rowe M., and Taylor M., 'Community-Led Regeneration: Learning Loops or Reinvented Wheels?' in D. Taylor and S. Balloch (eds) *The Politics of Evaluation: Participation and Policy Implementation* (Bristol: The Policy Press, 2005).

Rumford C. (ed), *Cosmopolitanism and Europe* (Liverpool: Liverpool University Press, 2007).

Sabel C.F., and Zeitlin J., 'Learning from Difference: The New Architecture of Experimentalist Governance in the EU' (2008) 14 (3) European Law Journal, 271–327.

Sagoff M., *The Economy of the Earth: Philosophy, Law and the Environment* (Cambridge: Cambridge University Press, 1988).

Sargeant M., 'The Employment Equality (Age) Regulations 2006: A Legitimisation of Age Discrimination in Employment' (2006) 35 (3) ILJ 209–227.

Sauter W., 'Services of general economic interest and universal services in EU law' (2008) 33 ELR 167.

Scharpf F.W., in 'Legitimate Diversity: The New Challenge of European Integration', in T. A. Börzel and R. A. Cichowski (eds) *The State of the European Union. Law, Politics, and Society* (Oxford: Oxford University Press, 2003) 79–104.

—— 'Problem-Solving Effectiveness and Democratic accountability in the EU', Working Paper 03/1 of the Max Planck Institute for the Study of Societies, Cologne. 2003.

—— 'The European Social Model. Coping with the Challenges of Diversity' (2002) 40(4) Journal of Common Market Studies, 645–670.

—— 'Notes Toward a Theory of Multilevel Governing in Europe', Discussion Paper 00/5 of the Max Planck Institute for the Study of Societies, Cologne, 2000.

—— *Governing in Europe: Effective and Democratic*? (Oxford: Oxford University Press, 1999).

—— 'Demokratieprobleme in der europäischen Mehrebenenpolitik' in W. Merkel, and A. Busch (eds) *Demokratie in Ost und West* (Frankfurt a.M.: Suhrkamp, 1999) 672.

—— 'Negative and Positive Integration in the Political Economy of European Welfare States' in Y. Mény/ M. Rhodes (eds) *The Future of European Welfare— A New Social Contrac*t (London: Macmillan, 1998) 155–177.

—— 'Economic Integration, Democracy and the Welfare State' (1997) 4 Journal of European Public Policy 18–36.

—— and Schmidt V. A., (eds) Welfare and Work in the Open Economy. Vol 2. *Diverse Responses to Common Challenges* (Oxford: Oxford University Press, 2000).

Schiek D., 'The ECJ decision in Mangold: A further twist on effects of directives and constitutional relevance of Community equality legislation' (2006) 35(3) ILJ 329–341.

Schmähl W., 'EU Enlargement and Social Security. Some Dimensions of a Complex Topic' (2004) January/February Intereconomics 21–28.

Schmidt C., 'The Principle of Non-discrimination in Respect of Age: Dimensions of the ECJ's *Mangold* Judgment' (2005) 7 (5) German Law Journal 505–524.

Schmidt M. G., 'Zur Leistungsfähigkeit von Demokratien' in Katenhusen/Lamping (eds) *Demokratien in Europa. Der Einfluss der europäischen Integration auf Wandel, Leistungsfähigkeit und neue Konturen des demokratischen Verfassungsstaates* (Opladen: Leske & Budrich, 2003) 269–283.

Schmitter P.C., 'What is there to legitimise in the European Union and how must this be accomplished?' Jean Monnet Working Paper No 6/01, Harvard Law School, 2001.

Schon P., 'Territorial Cohesion in Europe' (2005) 6(3) Planning Theory and Practice 389.

Schulze I., and Jochem S., 'Germany: Beyond Policy Gridlock.' in E. M. Immergut, K. M. Anderson and I. Schulze (eds) *The Handbook of West European Pension Politics* (Oxford: Oxford University Press, 2007) 660–710.

Schwarte C., and Adebowale M., *Environmental Justice and Race Equality in the European Union* (London: Capacity Global, 2007) available at <http://www.capacity.org.uk/downloads/CC-EJ%20in%20EU.pdf>.

Schwartz J., 'From Domestic to Global Solidarity: the Dialectic of the Particular and Universal in the Building of Social Solidarity' (2007) 38 Journal of Social Philosophy 131.

Scott J. (ed), *Environmental Protection: EU Law and Governance* (Oxford: Oxford University Press, 2009).

Sen A., 'Equality of what?' in R. Goodin and P. Pettit (eds) *Contemporary Political Philosophy: An Anthology* (Oxford: Blackwell, 2005).

—— *Capability as Freedom* (Oxford: Oxford University Press, 1999).

Serrano A., 'Recent Developments. Improvements in Cross-Border Access to Health Care Within the European Union' (2002) 43 Harvard International Law Journal 553.

Seyfang G., 'Shopping for Sustainability: Can Sustainable Consumption Promote Ecological Citizenship?' (2005) 14 Environmental Politics 290.

Shaw J., *The Transformation of Citizenship in the European Union* (Cambridge: Cambridge University Press, 2007).

Simon J., *Governing Through Crime, How the War on Crime Transformed American Democracy and Created a Culture of Fear* (Oxford: Oxford University Press, 2007).

Sint M., (2004) 8 Shared Spaces Newsletter of VROM, the Netherlands Ministry of Spatial Planning and Environment, 4, cited by S. Davoudi, 'Understanding Territorial Cohesion' (2005) 20(4) Planning, Practice and Research 433.

Slaughter S., 'The Republican State: An Alternative Foundation for Global Environmental Governance' in J. Barry and R. Eckersley (eds) *The State and the Global Ecological Crisis* (Cambridge, Massachusetts: MIT Press, 2005).

Sohrab J. A., 'An Overview of the Equality Directive On Social Security and Its Implementation in Four Social Security Systems' (1994) 4(4) Journal of European Social Policy 263–276.

Sole C., and Parella S., 'The labour market and racial discrimination in Spain' (2003) 29 Journal of Ethnic and Migration Studies 121.

Somek A., 'Solidarity decomposed: being and time in European citizenship' (2007) 32 ELR 787.

—— 'Solidarity Decomposed. Being and Time in European Citizenship' University of Iowa Legal Studies Research Paper (No 07/13, 2007) 55.

Souto-Otero M., Fleckenstein T., and Dacombe R., 'Filling in the Gaps: European Governance, the Open Method of Co-Ordination and the European Commission' (2008) 23(3) Journal of Education Policy 231–249.

Spaventa E., 'From Gebhard to Carpenter: Towards a (Non-) Economic European Constitution' (2004) 41 Common Market Law Review 743.

Spinner-Halev J., 'Democracy, Solidarity and Post-nationalism' (2008) 56 (3) Political Studies 604.

Stevenson N., 'European Cosmopolitan Solidarity: Questions of Citizenship, Difference and Post-materialism' (2006) 9(4) European Journal of Social Theory 485.

Stjernø S., *Solidarity in Europe. The History of an Idea* (Cambridge: Cambridge University Press, 2005).

Stöger K., 'The freedom of establishment and the market access of hospital operators' (2006) 17 European Business Law Review 1545.

Stolle D., and Hooghe M., 'Consumers as Political Participants? Shifts in Political Action Repertoires in Western Societies', M. Micheletti, A. Follesdal and D. Stolle (eds) *Politics, Products and Markets: Exploring Political Consumerism Past and Present* (London: Transaction Publishers, 2004) 284.

Stone Sweet A., *The Judicial Construction of Europe* (Oxford: Oxford University Press, 2004).

—— and T. Brunell, 'Constructing a Supranational Constitution: Dispute Resolution and Governance in the European Community' (1998) 92 American Political Science Review 63–81.

—— and R. Cichowski, 'Sex Equality' in A. Stone Sweet (ed) *The Judicial Construction of Europe* (Oxford: Oxford University Press, 2004) 156.

Streeck W., 'From Market Making to State Building? Reflections on the Political Economy of European Social Policy', in S. Leibfried, and P. Pierson (eds) *European Social Policy. Between Fragmentation and Integration* (Washington DC: The Brookings Institution Press, 1995).

—— 'Neo-Voluntarism: A New European Social Policy Regime?' in G. Marks, F. Scharpf, P. Schmitter, and W. Streeck (eds) *Governance in the European Union* (London: Sage, 1996) 64–94.

Sunstein C., 'Beyond the Republican Revival' (1988) 97 Yale Law Journal 1539.

—— 'On the expressive function of law' (1996) 144 University of Pennsylvania Law Review 2021.

Supiot A., *Beyond Employment: Changes in Work and the Future of Labour Law in Europe* (Oxford: Oxford University Press, 2001).

Sykes O., 'Strength From Diversity' (2008) Town and Country Planning 430.

Sykes R., 'The Future for Social Policy in Europe?' in R. Sykes, and P. Alcock (eds) *Developments in European Social Policy. Convergence and Diversity* (Bristol: Policy Press, 1998) 251–264.

Szyszczak E., *The Regulation of the State in Competitive Markets in the EU* (Oxford: Hart, 2007).

—— 'The New paradigm for Social Policy: A Virtuous Circle' (2001) 38 Common Market Law Review 1125.

Telo M., 'Governance and Government in the European Union: The Open Method of Coordination' in M. J. Rodrigues (ed) *The New Knowledge Economy in Europe* (Cheltenham: Edward Elgar, 2002) 249.

Temple Lang J., 'Privatisation of Social Welfare: European Union Competition Law Rules' in M. Dougan and E. Spaventa (eds) *Social Welfare and EU Law* (Oxford: Hart, 2005) 45.

Thome H., 'Solidarity: Theoretical Perspectives for Empirical Research', K. Bayertz (ed) *Solidarity* (Dordrecht: Kluwer, 1999) 126.

Threlfall M., 'European Social Integration: Harmonization, Convergence and Single Social Areas' (2003) 13 (2) Journal of European Social Policy 121–139.

Thym D., 'Respect for private and family life under Article 8 ECHR in immigration cases: a human right to regularize illegal stay?' (2008) 57 International and Comparative Law Quarterly 87.

Titmuss R. M., *Commitment to Welfare* (London: Unwin University Books, 1968).

Tomuschat C., 'Case Comment on *Martínez Sala*' (2000) 449 Common Market Law Review 455.

Toner H., 'Non-discriminatory Obstacles to the Exercise of Treaty Rights—Articles 39, 43, and 18 EC' (2004) 23 Yearbook of European Law 275.

Trenz H.-J., 'Elements of a sociology of European integration' ARENA Working Paper 11/2008 at <http://www.arena.uio.no>.

—— 'In search of the European Public Sphere: between normative overstretch and empirical disenchantment' ARENA Working Paper 12/2008 at <http://www.arena.uio>.

Trüdinger E.-V., 'Have They Gone too Far? Attitudes Towards the Transfer of Policies on the EU level', in D. Fuchs, R. Magni-Berton, and A. Roger (eds) *Euroscepticism. Images of Europe among mass publics and political elites* (Opladen: Barbara Budrich, 2009) 135–155.

Turner B. S., 'The Erosion of Citizenship' (2001) 52 The British Journal of Sociology 189.

Urlesberger F., 'Ein gemeinsamer Markt für Kranke—Zweiter Anlauf' (2003) 38 Zeitschrift für Arbeitsrecht und Sozialrecht 265.

Vakulenko A., 'Islamic dress in human rights jurisprudence: a critique of current trends' (2007) 7 Human Rights Law Review 717.

van Kersbergen K., 'The Politics of Solidarity and the Changing Boundaries of the Welfare State' (2006) 5 (4) European Political Science 377–394.

van Nuffel P., 'Patient's Free Movement Rights and Cross-Border Access to Healthcare' (2005) 12 Maastricht Journal of European and Comparative Law 253.

van der Mei A.P., 'EU Law and Education: Promotion of Student Mobility versus Protection of the Education Systems', in M. Dougan and E. Spaventa (eds) *Social Welfare and EU Law* (Oxford and Portland, Oregon: Hart Publishing, 2005) 219.

—— 'Union Citizenship and the "De-nationalisation" of the Territorial Welfare State' (2005) European Journal of Migration and Law 203.

—— *Free Movement of Persons within the European Community. Cross-Border Access to Public Benefits* (Oxford/Portland, Oregon: 2003).

van Parijs P., *Cultural Diversity Versus Economic Solidarity* (De Broeck University, 2003).

Varga C., Kiss I., and Ember I., 'The Lack of Environmental Justice in Central and Eastern Europe' (2002) 11 Environmental Health Perspectives 110.

Vaughan-Whitehead D., *EU Enlargement versus Social Europe? The Uncertain Future of the European Social Model* (Cheltenham: Edward Elgar, 2003).

Verschueren H., 'European (Internal) Migration Law as an Instrument for Defining the Boundaries of National Solidarity Systems' (2007) European Journal of Migration and Law 307.

Vischer R., 'Solidarity, Subsidiarity, and the Consumerist Impetus of American Law' University of St Thomas School of Law, Legal Studies Research Paper No 07–08 at <http://www.ssrn.com/link/st-thomas-legal-studies.html>.

Vobruba G., 'The Enlargement Crisis of the European Union: Limits on the Dialectics of Integration and Expansion' (2003) 13 (1) Journal of European Social Policy 35–62.

Vollaard H., 'Solidarity, Territoriality, and Healthcare: Cross-National Policy Learning in Europe' in D. Levi-Four, and E. Vigoda-Gadot (eds) *International Public Policy and Management* (New York: Marcel Dekker, 2004) 267.

Wagner J., 'German firms plan "pan-European pensions"' (2006) <http://www.ipe.com>, 23 March 2006.

—— 'Germany implements pension fund directive' (2005) <http://www.ipe.com>, 12 July 2005.

—— D. Brooksbank and B. Evans-Pritchard, 'New pensions portability plan facing criticism' (2005) <http://www.ipe.com>, 21 October 2005.

Ward I., *A Critical Introduction to European Law* (Cambridge: Cambridge University Press, 2009).

Weber M., 'The concept of solidarity in the study of world politics: towards a critical theoretic understanding' (2007) 33 (4) Review of International Studies 693.

Wedderburn Lord, 'Labour Law 2008: 40 Years On' (2007) 36 ILJ 397.

Weiler J. H. H., 'A Constitution for Europe? Some Hard Choices' (2002) 40 Journal of Common Market Studies 563.

—— 'European Citizenship and Human Rights', in A. Winter (ed) *Reforming the Treaty on the European Union—The Legal Debate* (The Hague, London, Boston: Kluwer, 1997) 57.

—— 'After Maastricht: Community Legitimacy in Post-1992 Europe' in W. J. Adams, (ed) *Singular Europe. Economy and Polity of the European Community After 1992* (Ann Arbor: University of Michigan Press, 1993) 11–41.

—— 'Community, Member-States and European Integration' (1982) 21 (1) Journal of Common Market Studies 39–56.

Weissbrodt D., 'The protection of non-citizens in international human rights law' in R. Cholewinski, R. Perruchoud and E. MacDonald (eds) *International migration law—developing paradigms and key challenges* (The Hague: TMC Asser Press, 2007) 221

Wernicke S., 'Au nom de qui? The European Court of Justice between Member States, civil society and Union citizens' (2007) 13 European Law Journal 380.

Wetherell M., 'Themes in Discourse Research: The Case of Diana' in M. Wetherell et al (eds) *Discourse Theory and Practices: A Reader* (London: Sage Publications, reprint 2002, original edition 2001) 15.

Widdershoven C., 'Dutch Government critical of portability directive' (2006) <http://www.ipe.com>, 24 March 2006.

Wieland J., 'Germany in the European Union—The Maastricht Decision of the Bundesverfassungsgericht' (1994) 5 European Journal of International Law 259–266.

Wilde L., 'Book Review of Stjernø, *Solidarity in Europe: The History of an Idea* (Cambridge: Cambridge University Press, 2005)' (2007) 6 Contemporary Political Theory 117.

——'The concept of solidarity: emerging from the theoretical shadows?' (2007) 9 British Journal of Politics and International Relations 171.

Wildt A., 'Solidarity: Its History and Contemporary Definition', in K. Bayertz (ed) *Solidarity* (Dordrecht: Kluwer, 1999) 217.

Williams C., 'A critical evaluation of public policy towards undeclared work in the European Union' (2008) 30 Journal of European Integration 273, 274.

Xuereb P., 'The Future of Europe: Solidarity and Constitutionalism: Towards a Solidarity Model' (2002) 27 ELR 643.

Zeitlin J., 'The Open Method of Coordination in Action. Theoretical Promise, Empirical Realities, Reform Strategy' in J. Zeitlin and P. Pochet (eds) *The Open Method of Coordination in Action. The European Employment and Social Inclusion Strategies* (Brussels: Peter Lang, 2005) 447–503.

—— 'Social Europe and Experimentalist Governance: Towards a New Constitutional Compromise?' in de Búrca (ed) *EU Law and the Welfare State* (Oxford: Oxford University Press, 2005) 225.

Zoll R., *La solidarietà. Eguaglianza e differenza* (Bologna: 2003).

Index